FINDER™

[redacted]

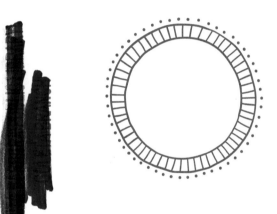

FINDER ™

VOICE

CARLA SPEED McNEIL

DARK HORSE BOOKS®

Publisher
MIKE RICHARDSON

Editors
RACHEL EDIDIN and **KATIE MOODY**

Assistant Editors
JEMIAH JEFFERSON and **JOHN SCHORK**

Designer
JUSTIN COUCH

Special thanks to **CARY GRAZZINI** and **SUSAN TARDIF**.

DARK HORSE BOOKS
A division of Dark Horse Comics, Inc.
10956 SE Main Street
Milwaukie, OR 97222

DarkHorse.com

To find a comic shop in your area,
call the Comic Shop Locator Service:
(888) 266-4226

First Edition: February 2011
ISBN 978-1-59582-651-0

1 3 5 7 9 10 8 6 4 2

Printed by Transcontinental Gagné, Louiseville, QC, Canada.

one:

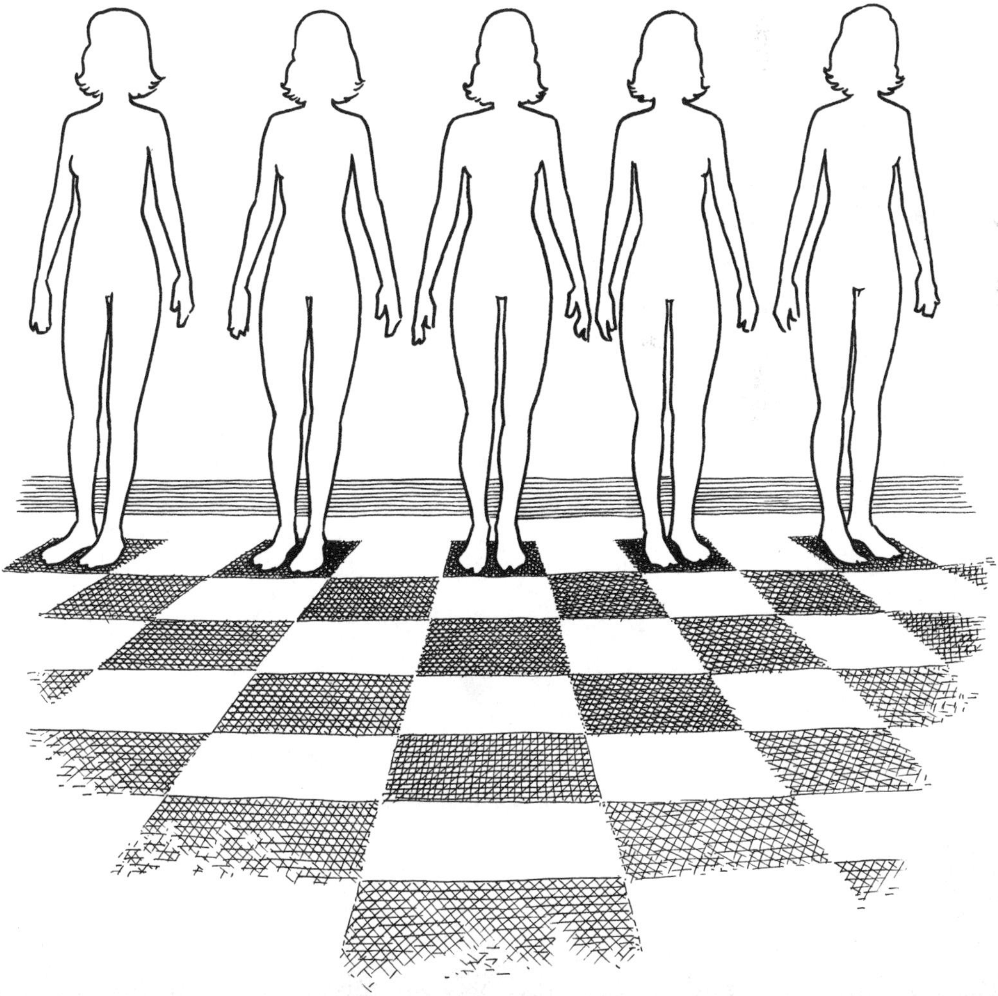

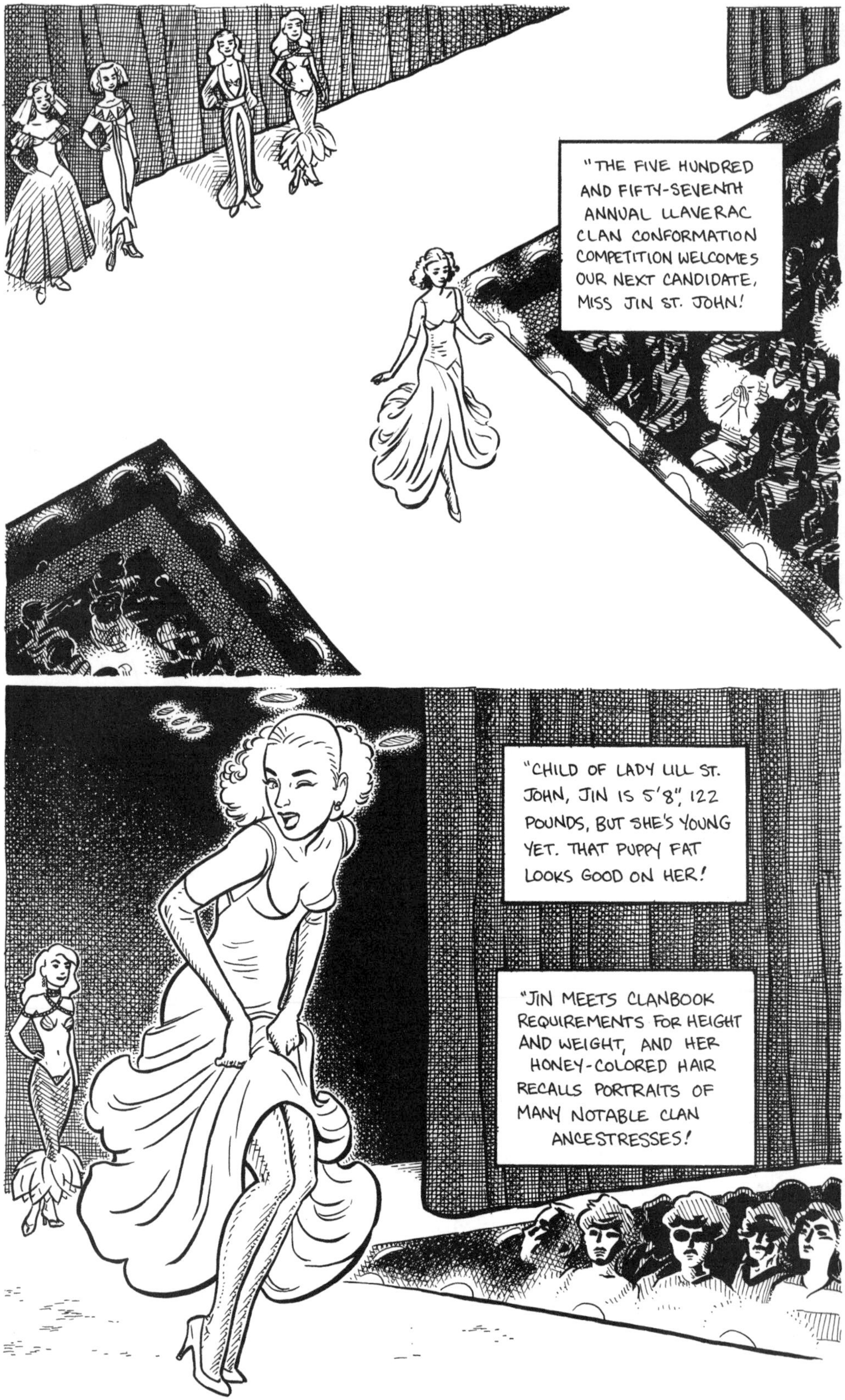
"THE FIVE HUNDRED AND FIFTY-SEVENTH ANNUAL LLAVERAC CLAN CONFORMATION COMPETITION WELCOMES OUR NEXT CANDIDATE, MISS JIN ST. JOHN!
"CHILD OF LADY LILL ST. JOHN, JIN IS 5'8", 122 POUNDS, BUT SHE'S YOUNG YET. THAT PUPPY FAT LOOKS GOOD ON HER!
"JIN MEETS CLANBOOK REQUIREMENTS FOR HEIGHT AND WEIGHT, AND HER HONEY-COLORED HAIR RECALLS PORTRAITS OF MANY NOTABLE CLAN ANCESTRESSES!

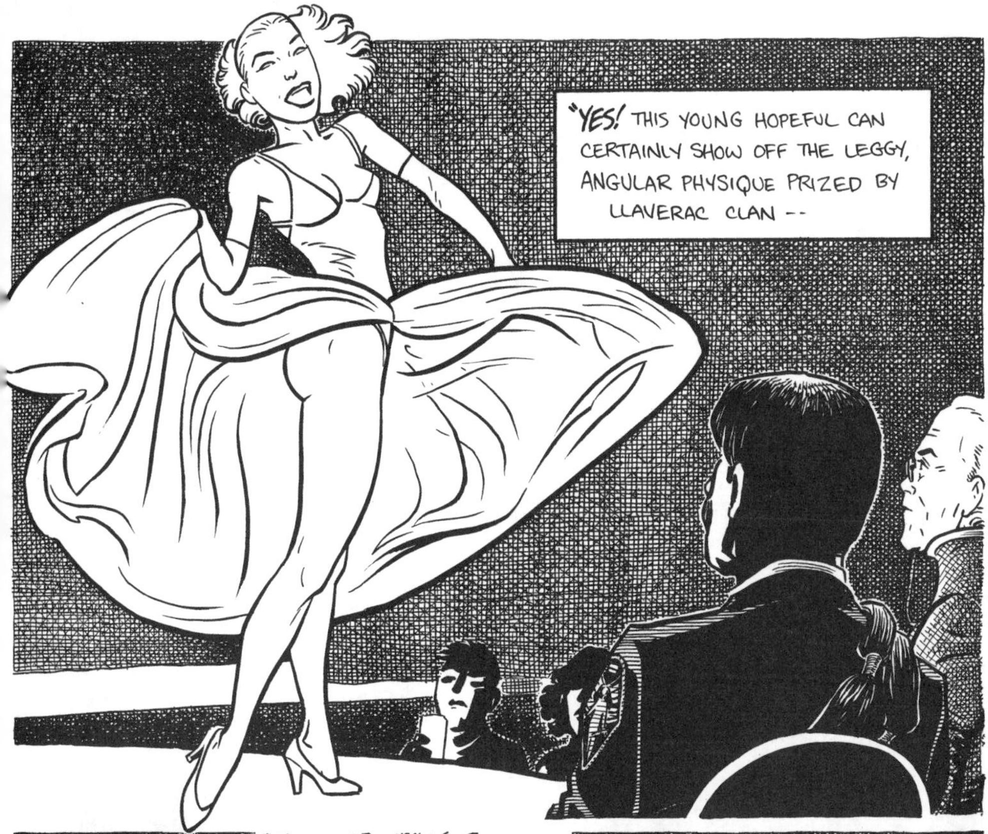
"YES! THIS YOUNG HOPEFUL CAN CERTAINLY SHOW OFF THE LEGGY, ANGULAR PHYSIQUE PRIZED BY LLAVERAC CLAN --

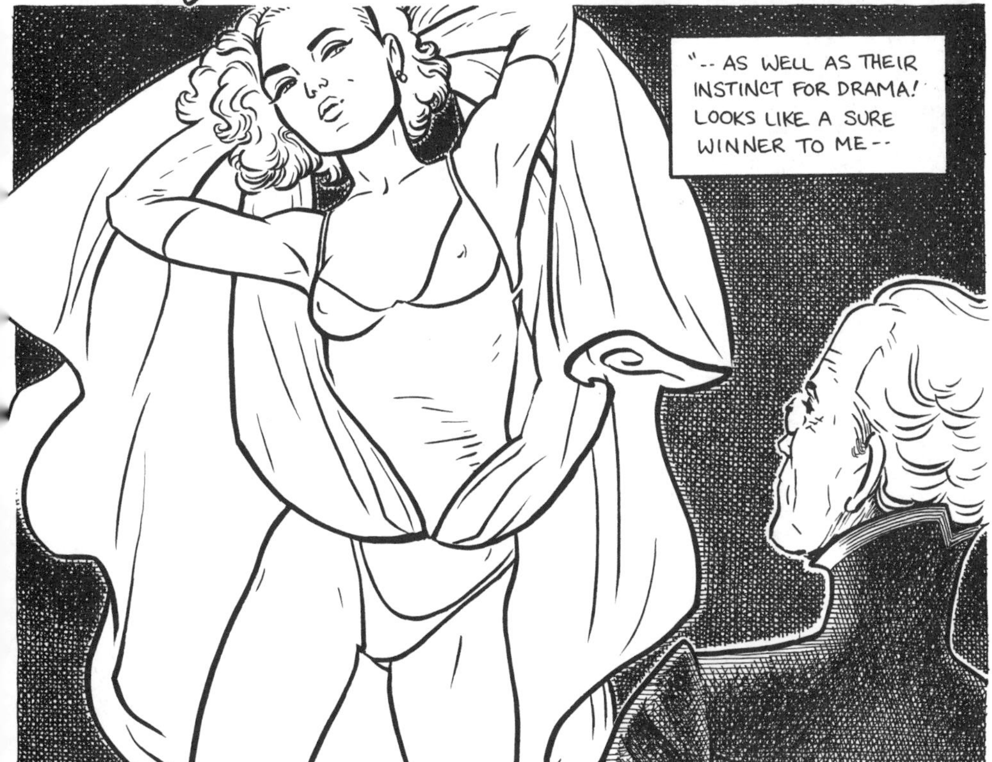
"-- AS WELL AS THEIR INSTINCT FOR DRAMA! LOOKS LIKE A SURE WINNER TO ME --

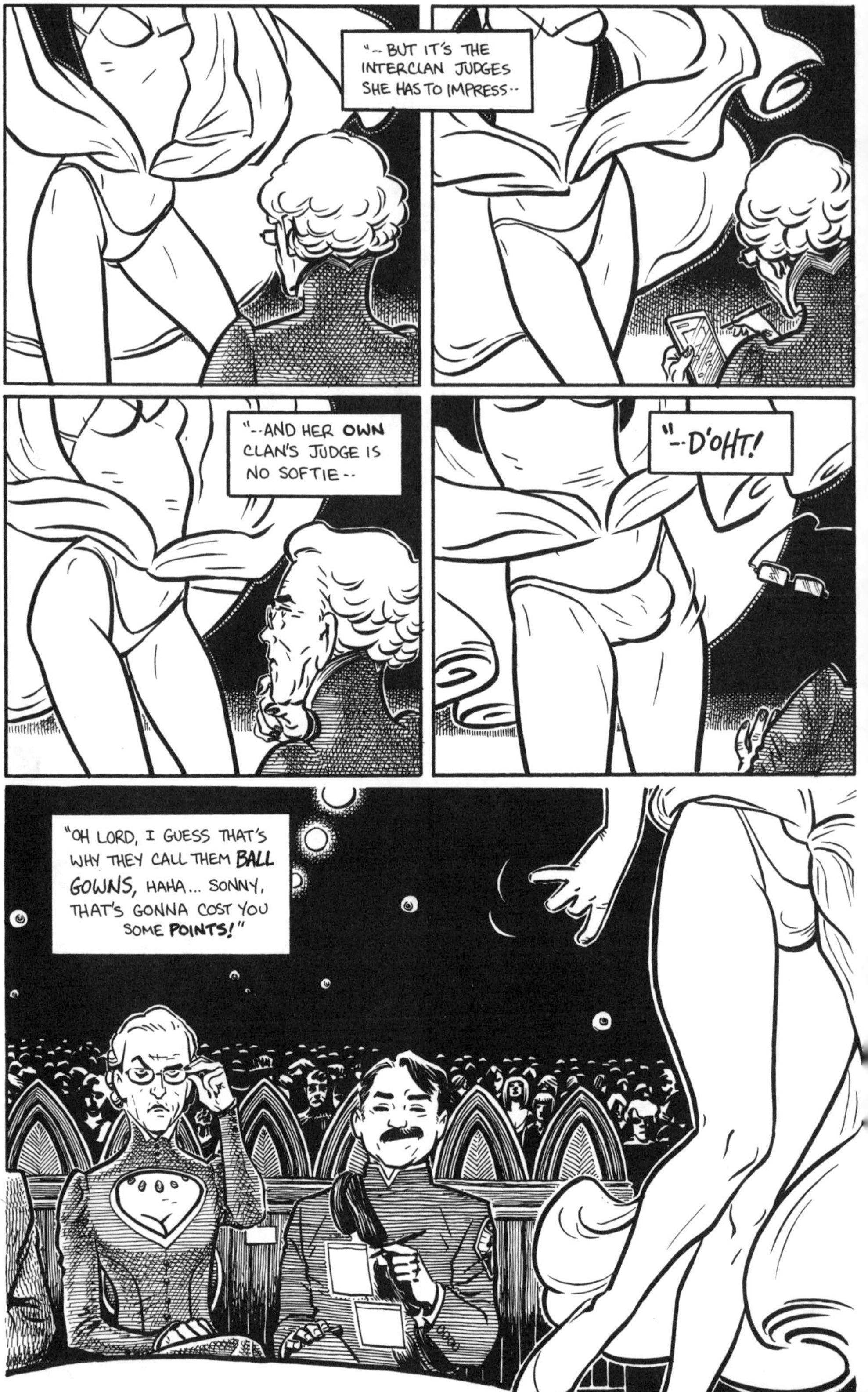
"--BUT IT'S THE INTERCLAN JUDGES SHE HAS TO IMPRESS--
"--AND HER **OWN** CLAN'S JUDGE IS NO SOFTIE--
"--D'OHT!
"OH LORD, I GUESS THAT'S WHY THEY CALL THEM **BALL GOWNS**, HAHA... SONNY, THAT'S GONNA COST YOU SOME **POINTS!**"

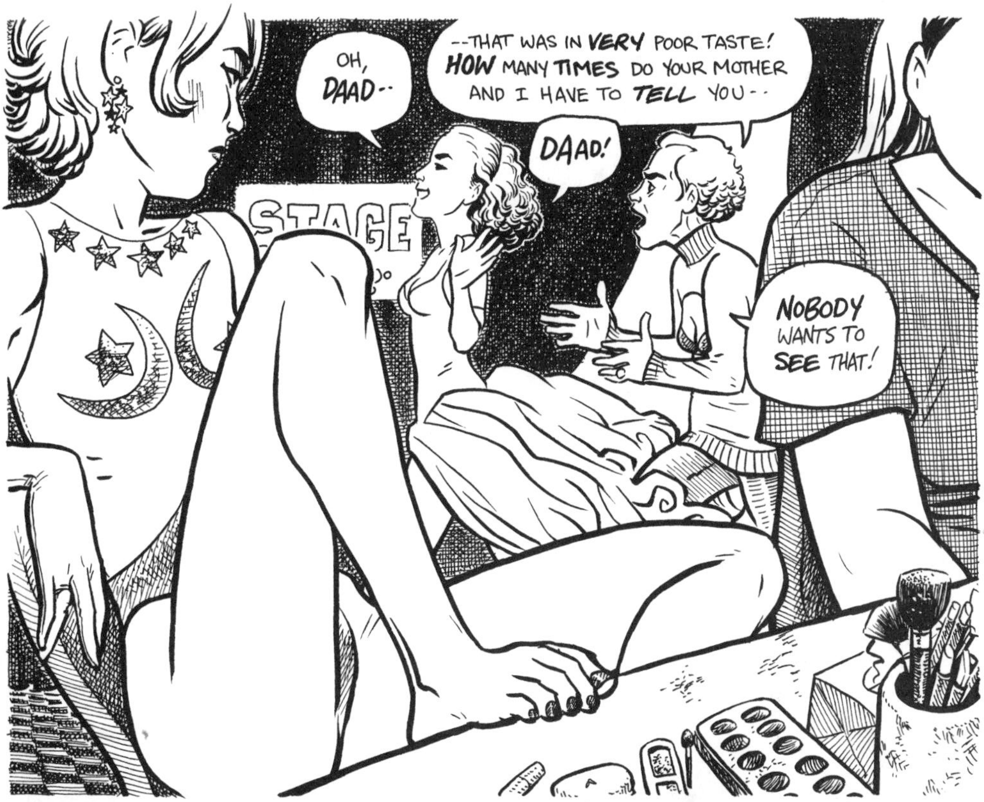
OH, DAAD--
--THAT WAS IN VERY POOR TASTE! HOW MANY TIMES DO YOUR MOTHER AND I HAVE TO TELL YOU--
DAAD!
NOBODY WANTS TO SEE THAT!
STAGE

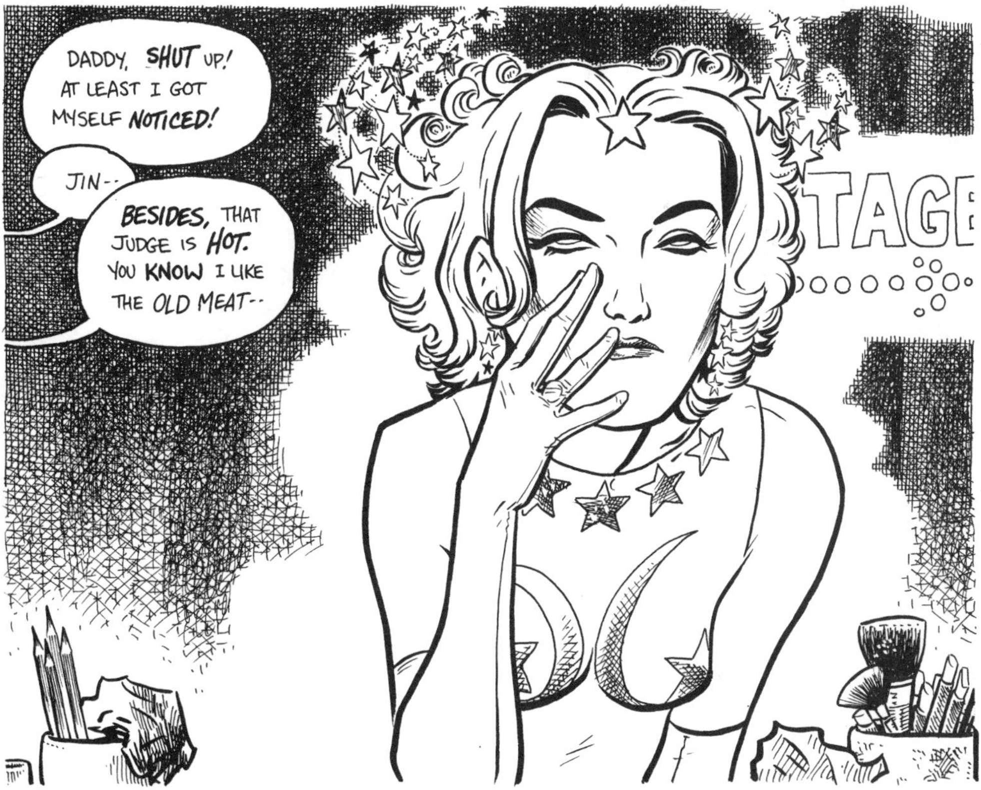
DADDY, SHUT UP! AT LEAST I GOT MYSELF NOTICED!
JIN--
BESIDES, THAT JUDGE IS HOT. YOU KNOW I LIKE THE OLD MEAT--
TAGE

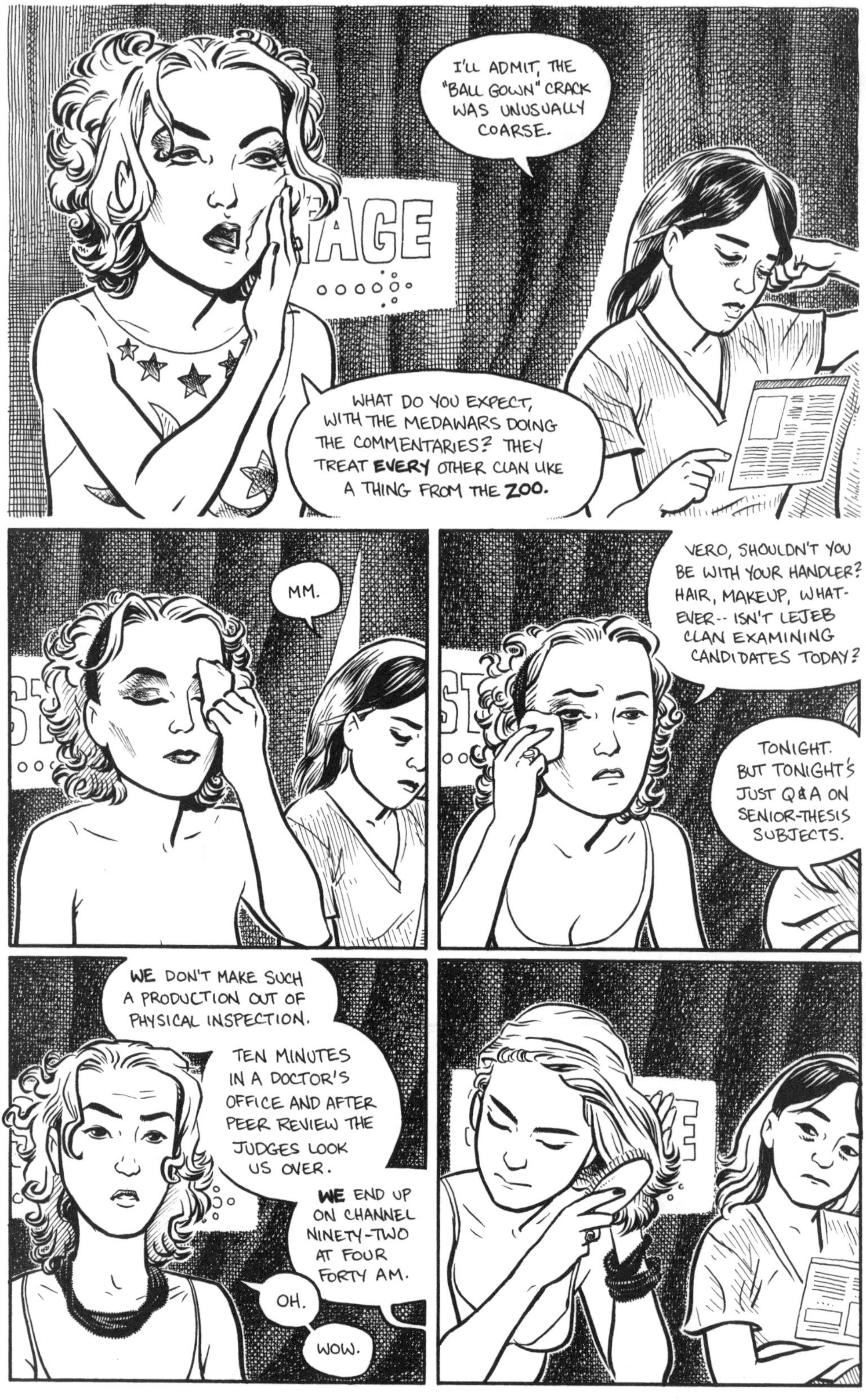
I'LL ADMIT, THE "BALL GOWN" CRACK WAS UNUSUALLY COARSE.
WHAT DO YOU EXPECT, WITH THE MEDAWARS DOING THE COMMENTARIES? THEY TREAT **EVERY** OTHER CLAN LIKE A THING FROM THE **ZOO.**
MM.
VERO, SHOULDN'T YOU BE WITH YOUR HANDLER? HAIR, MAKEUP, WHAT-EVER-- ISN'T LEJEB CLAN EXAMINING CANDIDATES TODAY?
TONIGHT. BUT TONIGHT'S JUST Q&A ON SENIOR-THESIS SUBJECTS.
WE DON'T MAKE SUCH A PRODUCTION OUT OF PHYSICAL INSPECTION.
TEN MINUTES IN A DOCTOR'S OFFICE AND AFTER PEER REVIEW THE JUDGES LOOK US OVER.
WE END UP ON CHANNEL NINETY-TWO AT FOUR FORTY AM.
OH.
WOW.

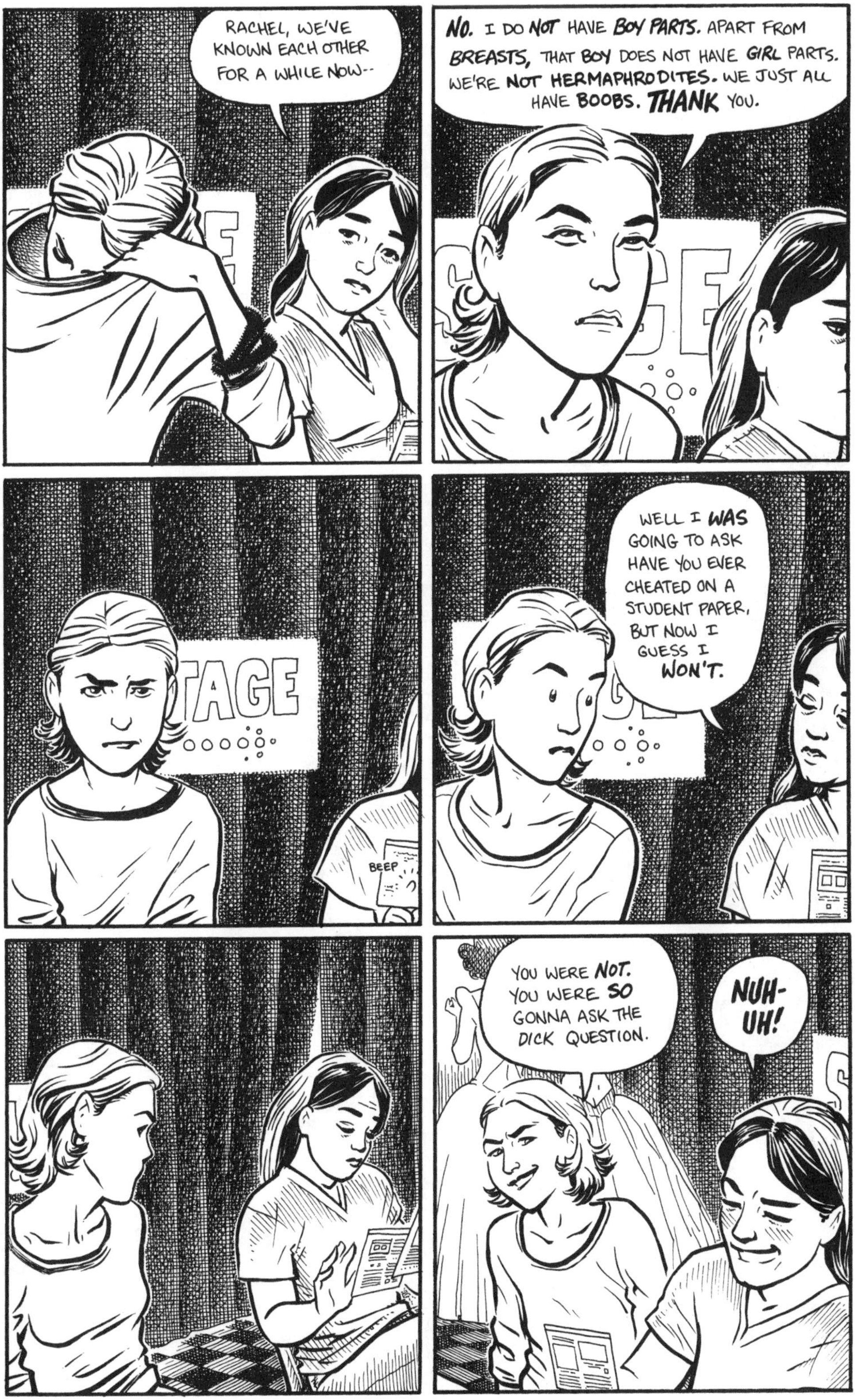

RACHEL, WE'VE KNOWN EACH OTHER FOR A WHILE NOW--
NO. I DO NOT HAVE BOY PARTS. APART FROM BREASTS, THAT BOY DOES NOT HAVE GIRL PARTS. WE'RE NOT HERMAPHRODITES. WE JUST ALL HAVE BOOBS. THANK YOU.
TAGE
BEEP
WELL I WAS GOING TO ASK HAVE YOU EVER CHEATED ON A STUDENT PAPER, BUT NOW I GUESS I WON'T.
YOU WERE NOT. YOU WERE SO GONNA ASK THE DICK QUESTION.
NUH-UH!

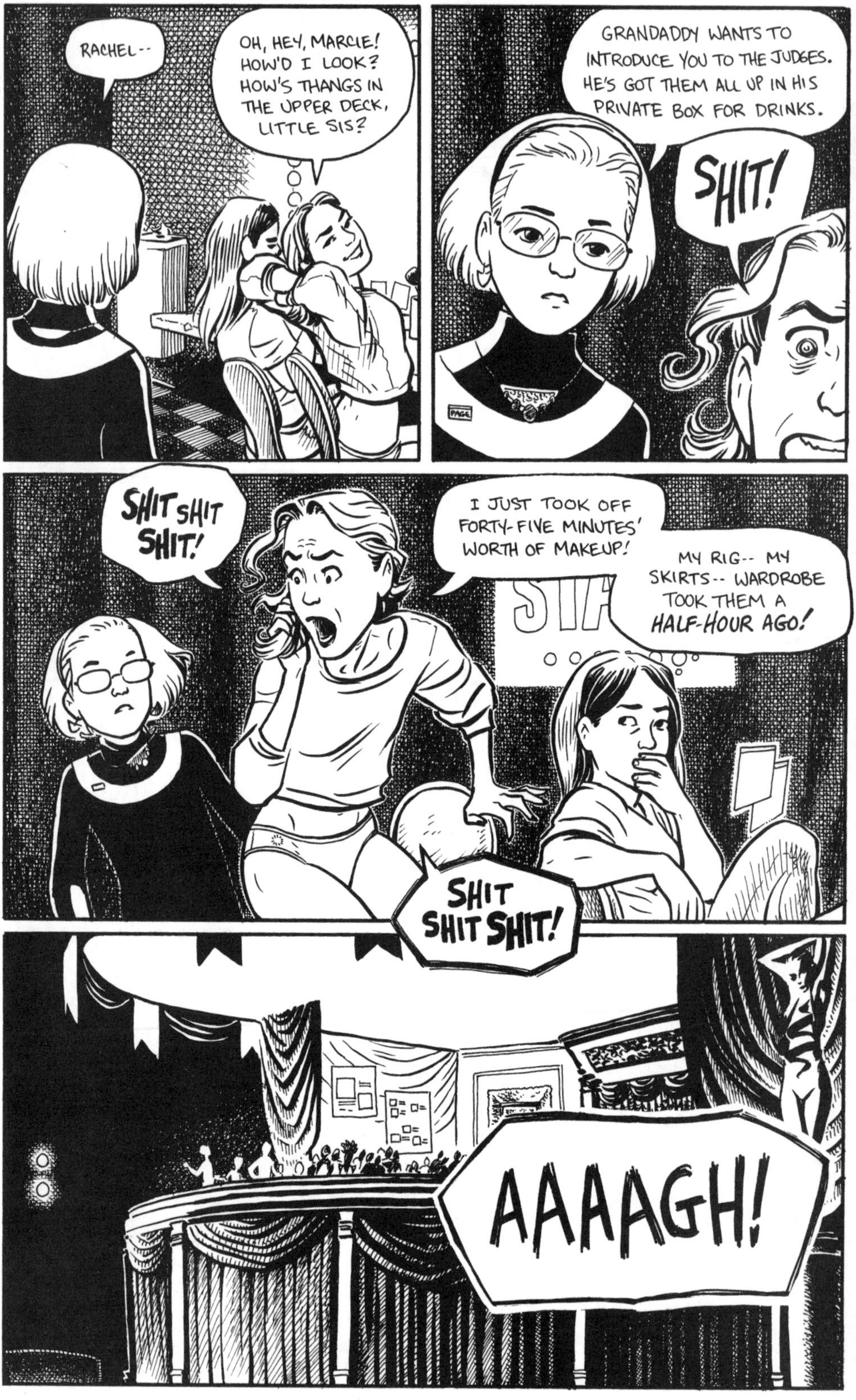
RACHEL--
OH, HEY, MARCIE! HOW'D I LOOK? HOW'S THANGS IN THE UPPER DECK, LITTLE SIS?
GRANDADDY WANTS TO INTRODUCE YOU TO THE JUDGES. HE'S GOT THEM ALL UP IN HIS PRIVATE BOX FOR DRINKS.
PAGE
SHIT!
SHIT SHIT SHIT!
I JUST TOOK OFF FORTY-FIVE MINUTES' WORTH OF MAKEUP!
MY RIG-- MY SKIRTS-- WARDROBE TOOK THEM A HALF-HOUR AGO!
SHIT SHIT SHIT!
AAAAGH!

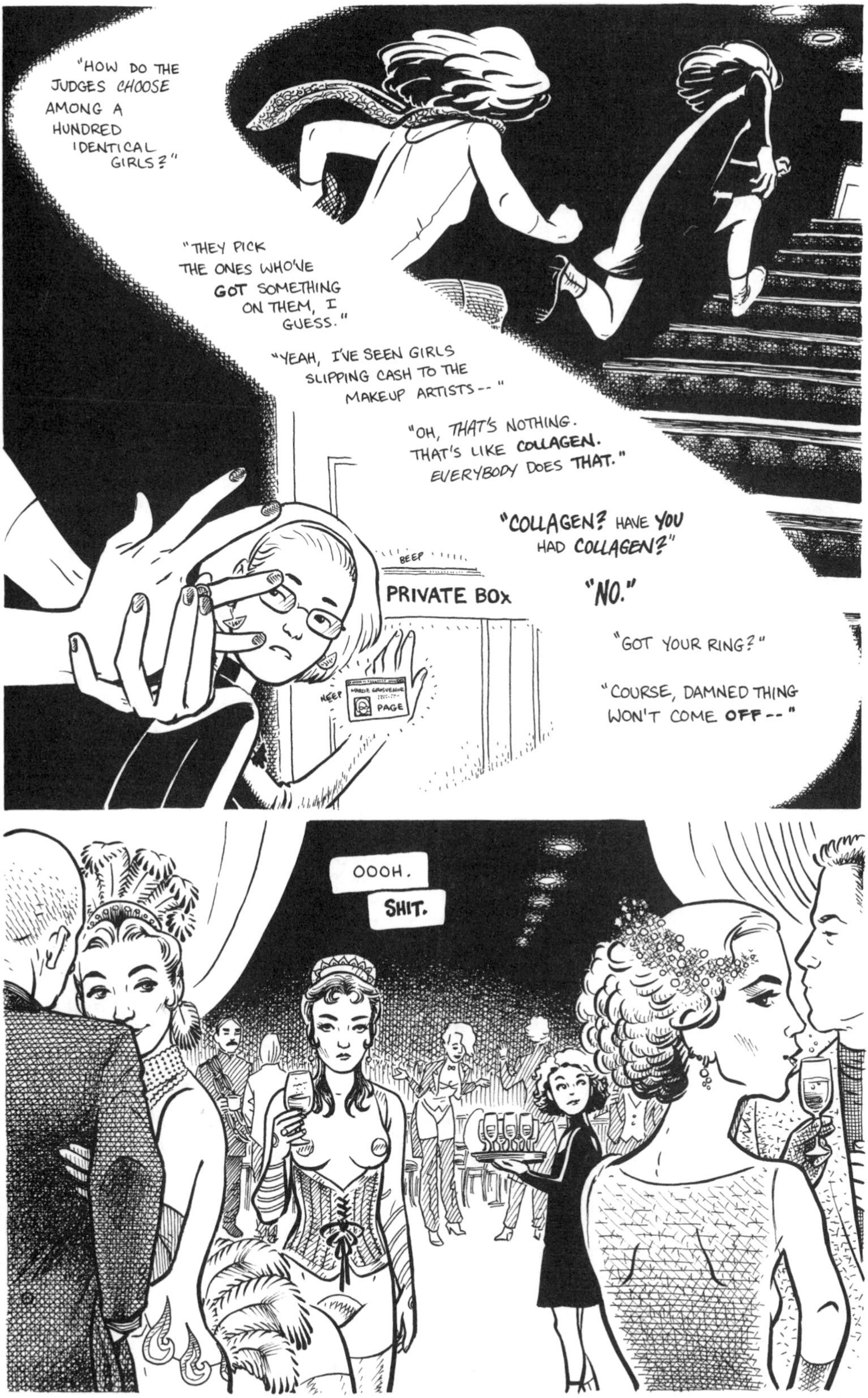
"HOW DO THE JUDGES *CHOOSE* AMONG A HUNDRED IDENTICAL GIRLS?"
"THEY PICK THE ONES WHO'VE **GOT** SOMETHING ON THEM, I GUESS."
"YEAH, I'VE SEEN GIRLS SLIPPING CASH TO THE MAKEUP ARTISTS--"
"OH, *THAT'S* NOTHING. THAT'S LIKE **COLLAGEN.** *EVERYBODY* DOES **THAT.**"
"COLLAGEN? HAVE **YOU** HAD **COLLAGEN?"**
BEEP
PRIVATE BOX
NEEP
MARCIE GROSVENOR
PAGE
"NO."
"GOT YOUR RING?"
"COURSE, DAMNED THING WON'T COME **OFF**--"
OOOH.
SHIT.

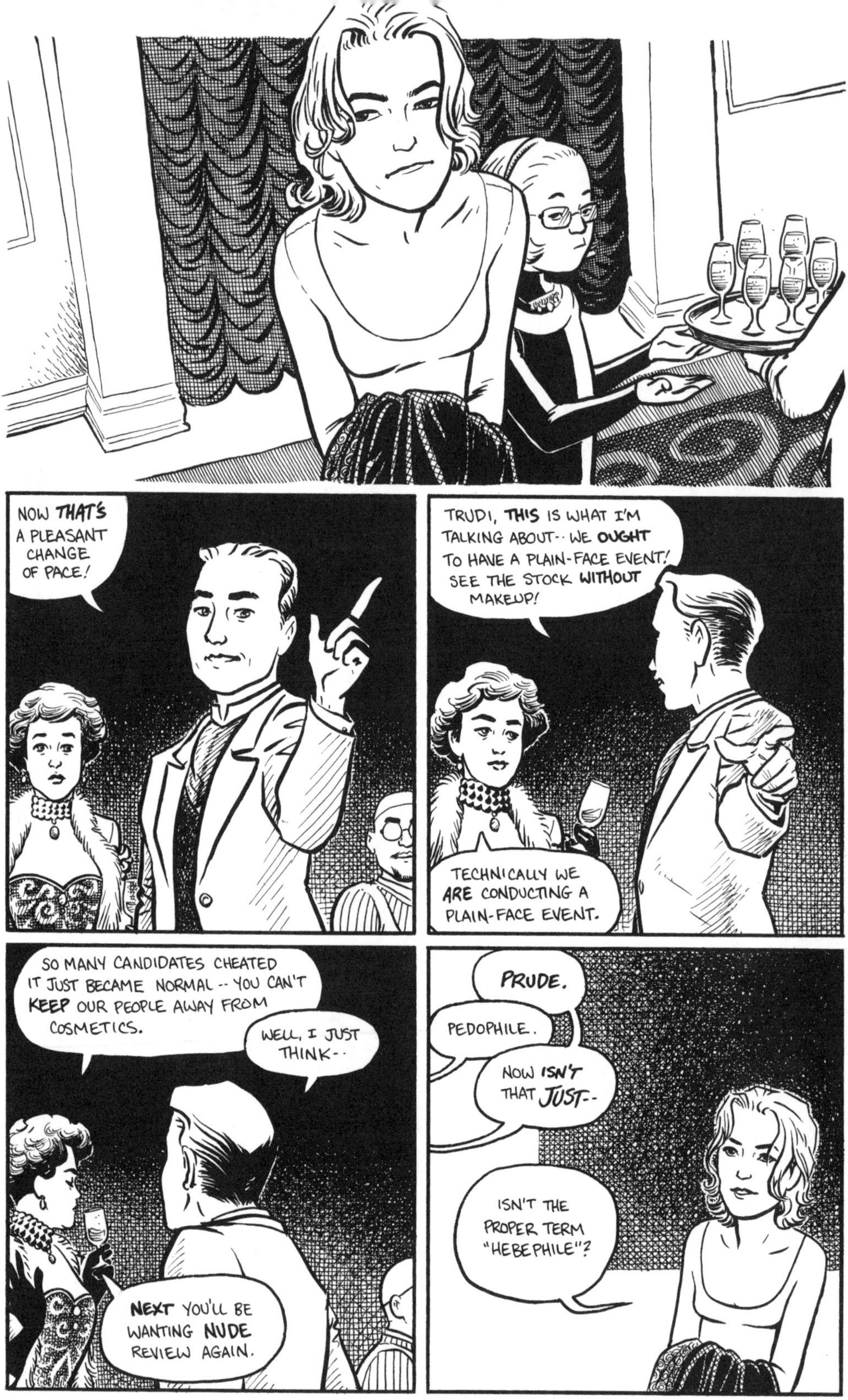
NOW THAT'S A PLEASANT CHANGE OF PACE!
TRUDI, THIS IS WHAT I'M TALKING ABOUT-- WE OUGHT TO HAVE A PLAIN-FACE EVENT! SEE THE STOCK WITHOUT MAKEUP!
TECHNICALLY WE ARE CONDUCTING A PLAIN-FACE EVENT.
SO MANY CANDIDATES CHEATED IT JUST BECAME NORMAL -- YOU CAN'T KEEP OUR PEOPLE AWAY FROM COSMETICS.
WELL, I JUST THINK--
NEXT YOU'LL BE WANTING NUDE REVIEW AGAIN.
PRUDE.
PEDOPHILE.
NOW ISN'T THAT JUST--
ISN'T THE PROPER TERM "HEBEPHILE"?

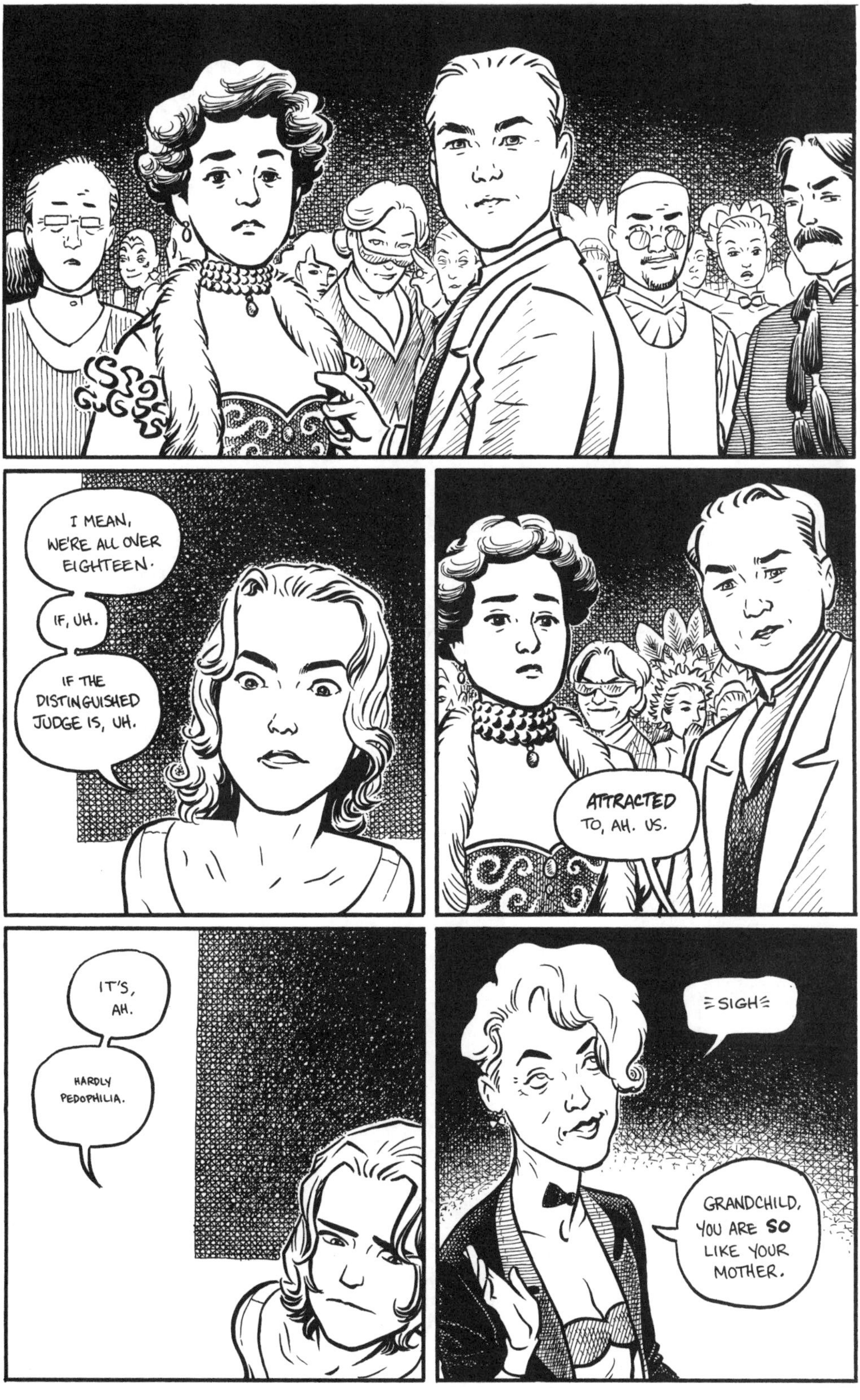
I MEAN, WE'RE ALL OVER EIGHTEEN.
IF, UH.
IF THE DISTINGUISHED JUDGE IS, UH.
ATTRACTED TO, AH. US.
IT'S, AH.
HARDLY PEDOPHILIA.
SIGH
GRANDCHILD, YOU ARE SO LIKE YOUR MOTHER.

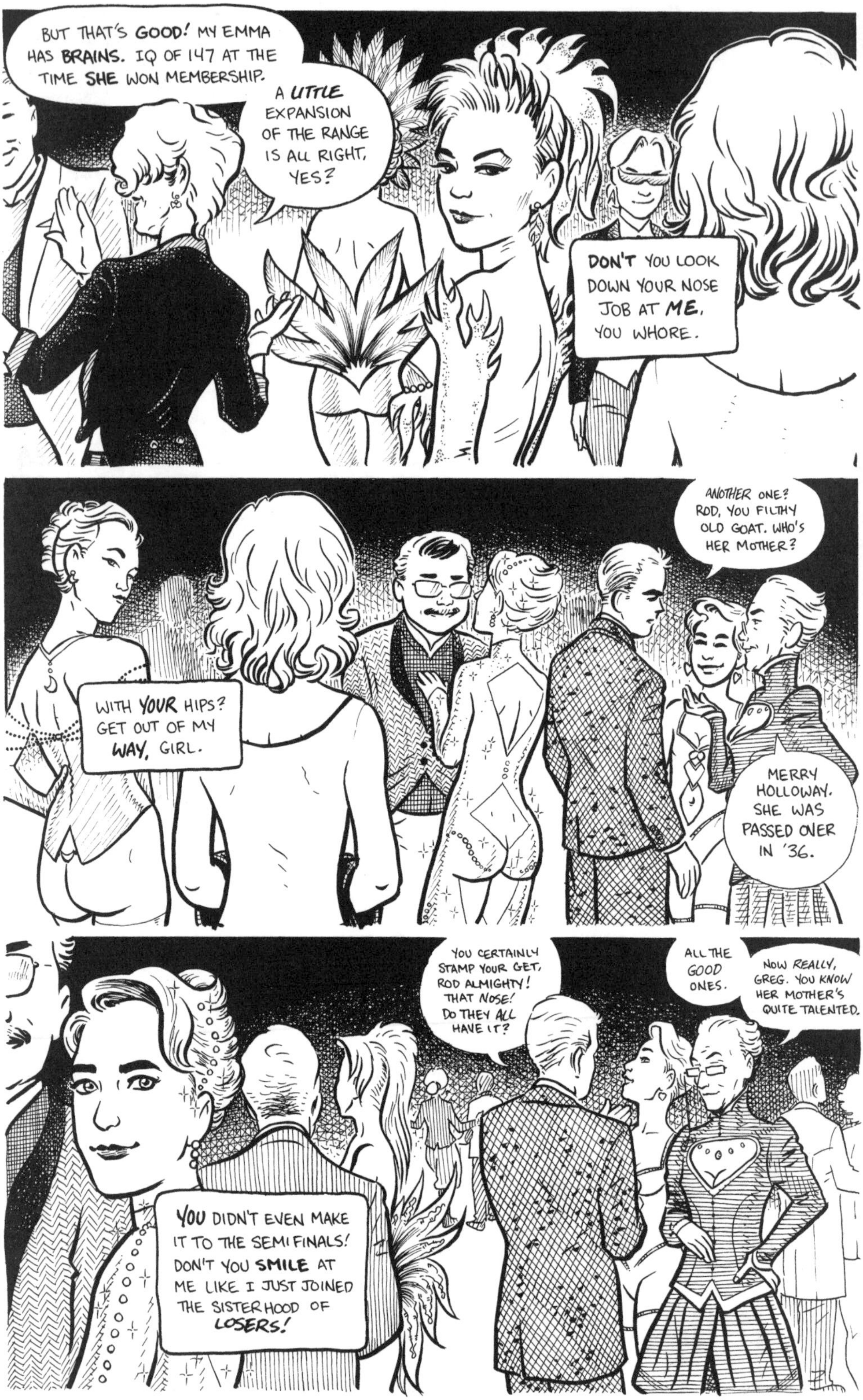
BUT THAT'S GOOD! MY EMMA HAS BRAINS. IQ OF 147 AT THE TIME SHE WON MEMBERSHIP.
A LITTLE EXPANSION OF THE RANGE IS ALL RIGHT, YES?
DON'T YOU LOOK DOWN YOUR NOSE JOB AT ME, YOU WHORE.
WITH YOUR HIPS? GET OUT OF MY WAY, GIRL.
ANOTHER ONE? ROD, YOU FILTHY OLD GOAT. WHO'S HER MOTHER?
MERRY HOLLOWAY. SHE WAS PASSED OVER IN '36.
YOU DIDN'T EVEN MAKE IT TO THE SEMIFINALS! DON'T YOU SMILE AT ME LIKE I JUST JOINED THE SISTERHOOD OF LOSERS!
YOU CERTAINLY STAMP YOUR GET, ROD ALMIGHTY! THAT NOSE! DO THEY ALL HAVE IT?
ALL THE GOOD ONES.
NOW REALLY, GREG. YOU KNOW HER MOTHER'S QUITE TALENTED.

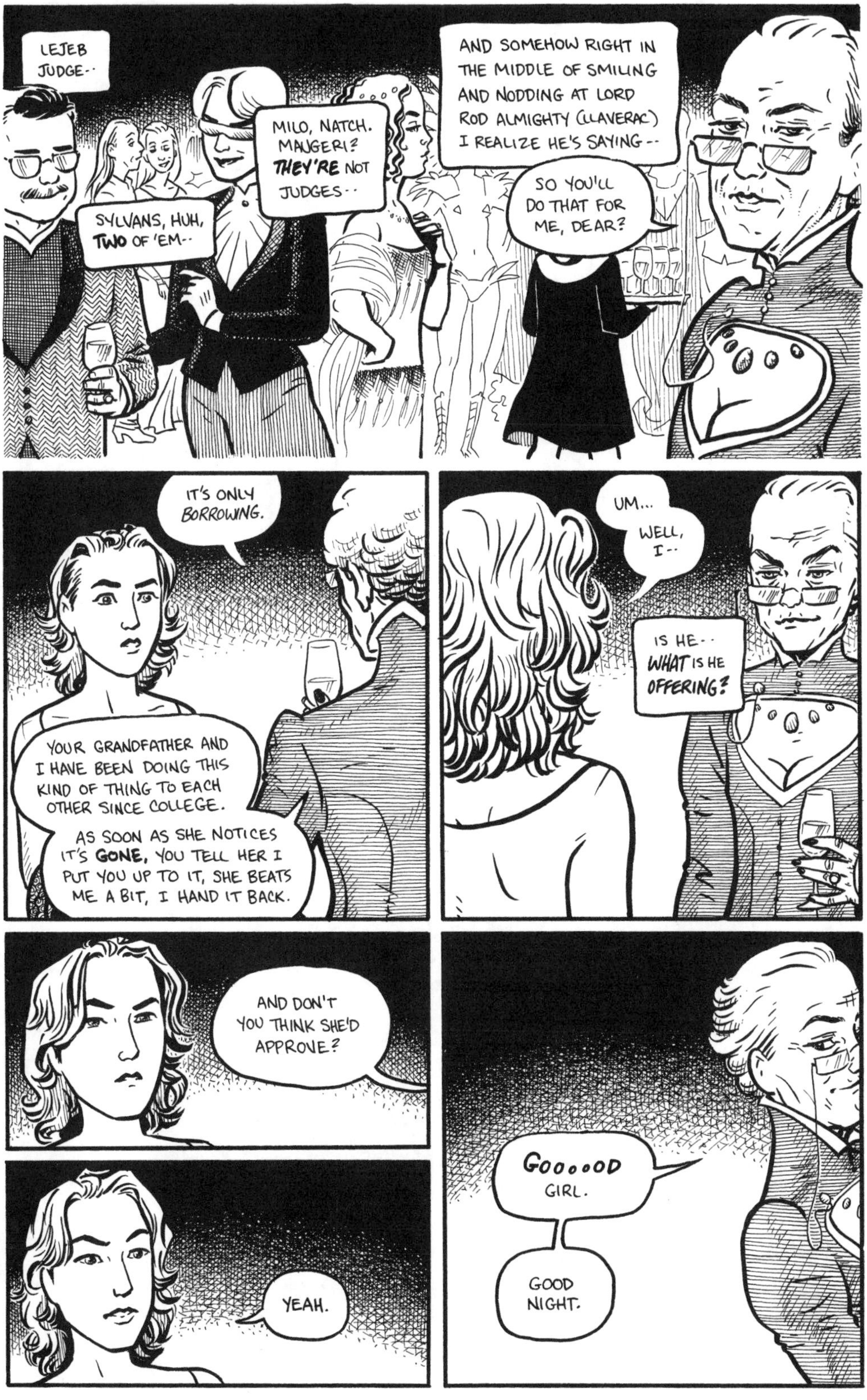
LEJEB JUDGE--
SYLVANS, HUH, TWO OF 'EM--
MILO, NATCH. MAUGERI? THEY'RE NOT JUDGES--
AND SOMEHOW RIGHT IN THE MIDDLE OF SMILING AND NODDING AT LORD ROD ALMIGHTY (LLAVERAC) I REALIZE HE'S SAYING--
SO YOU'LL DO THAT FOR ME, DEAR?
IT'S ONLY BORROWING.
YOUR GRANDFATHER AND I HAVE BEEN DOING THIS KIND OF THING TO EACH OTHER SINCE COLLEGE.
AS SOON AS SHE NOTICES IT'S GONE, YOU TELL HER I PUT YOU UP TO IT, SHE BEATS ME A BIT, I HAND IT BACK.
UM...
WELL, I--
IS HE-- WHAT IS HE OFFERING?
AND DON'T YOU THINK SHE'D APPROVE?
YEAH.
GOOOOOD GIRL.
GOOD NIGHT.

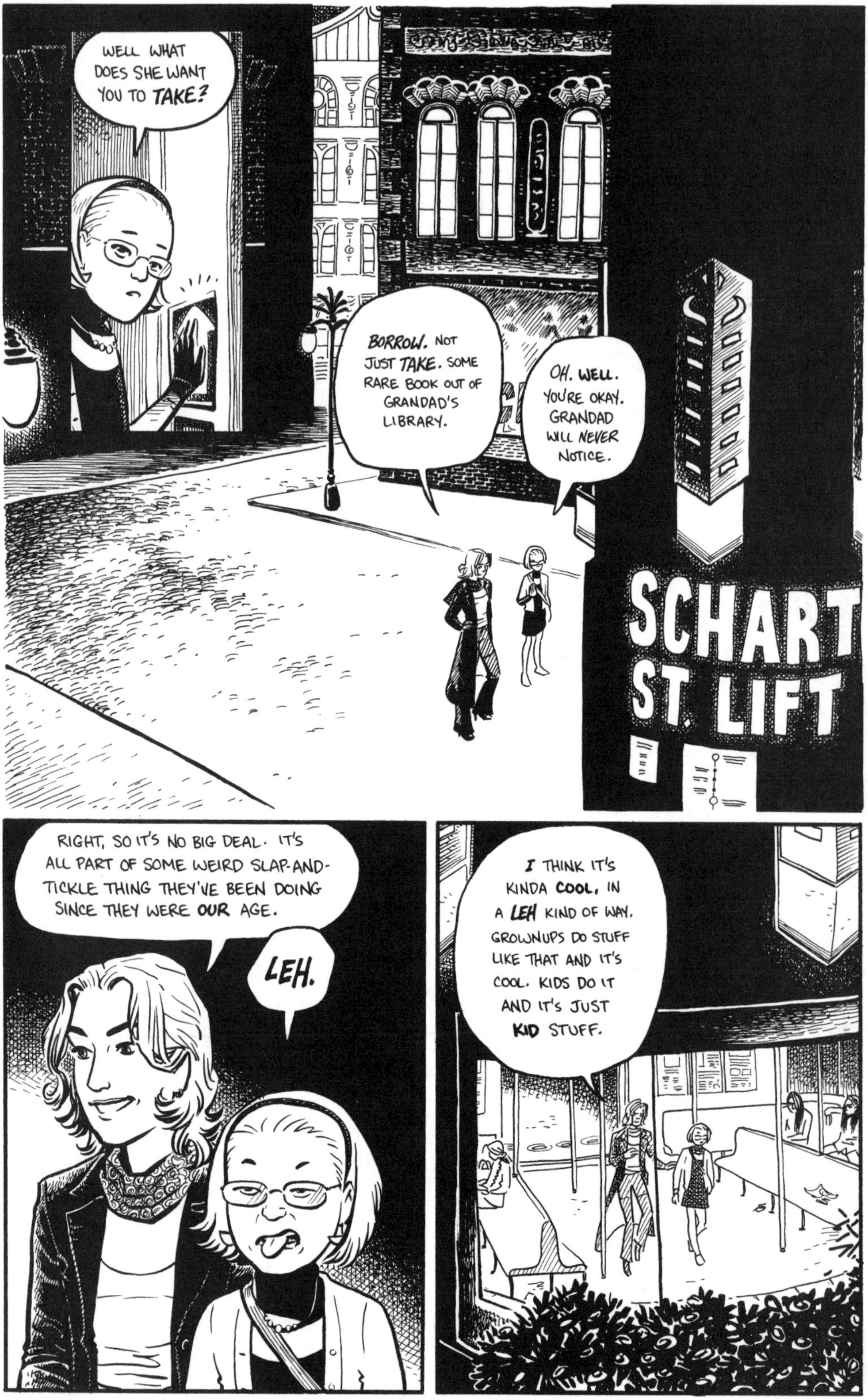
WELL WHAT DOES SHE WANT YOU TO TAKE?
BORROW. NOT JUST TAKE. SOME RARE BOOK OUT OF GRANDAD'S LIBRARY.
OH. WELL. YOU'RE OKAY. GRANDAD WILL NEVER NOTICE.
SCHART ST. LIFT
RIGHT, SO IT'S NO BIG DEAL. IT'S ALL PART OF SOME WEIRD SLAP-AND-TICKLE THING THEY'VE BEEN DOING SINCE THEY WERE OUR AGE.
LEH.
I THINK IT'S KINDA COOL, IN A LEH KIND OF WAY. GROWNUPS DO STUFF LIKE THAT AND IT'S COOL. KIDS DO IT AND IT'S JUST KID STUFF.

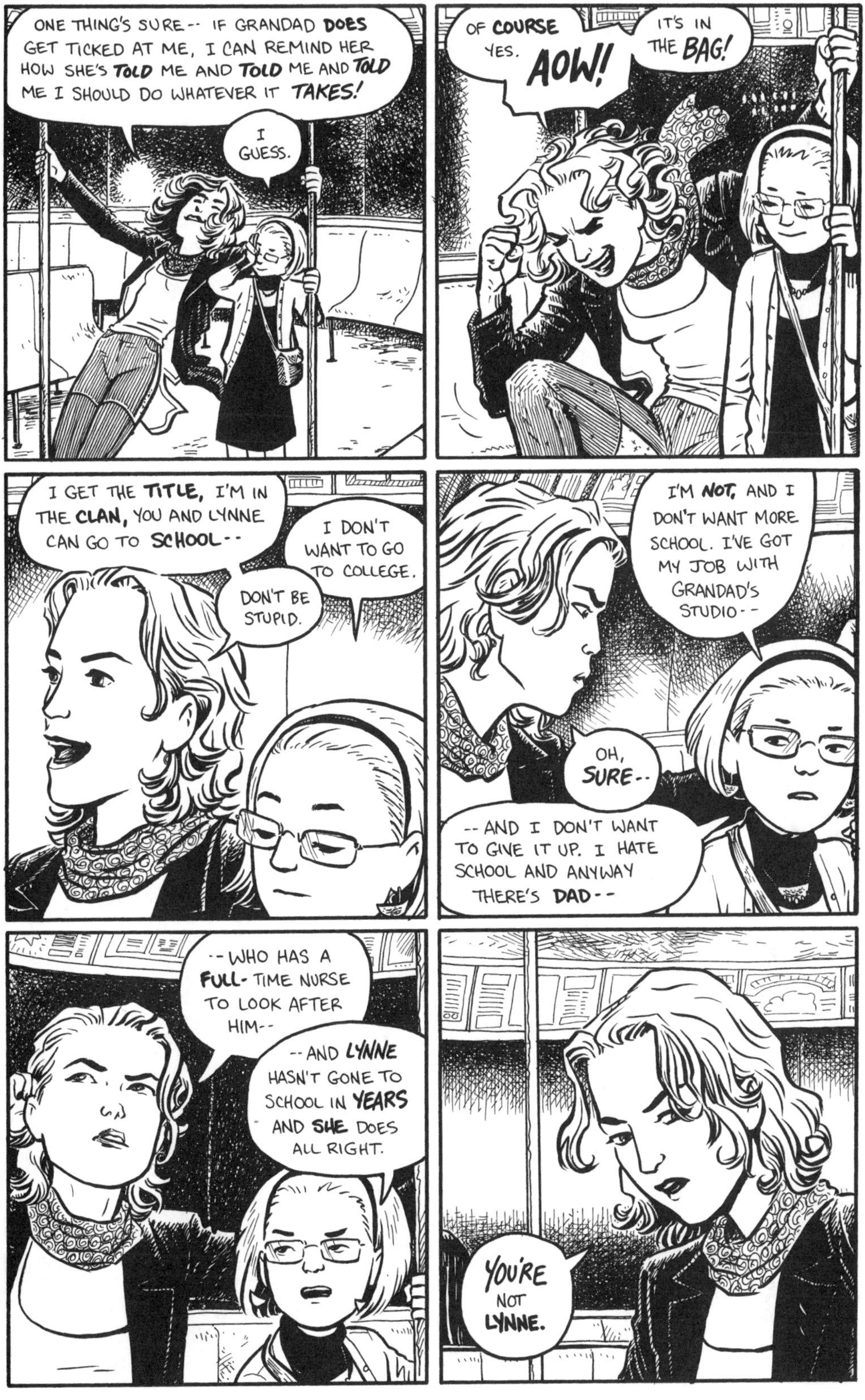
ONE THING'S SURE-- IF GRANDAD DOES GET TICKED AT ME, I CAN REMIND HER HOW SHE'S TOLD ME AND TOLD ME AND TOLD ME I SHOULD DO WHATEVER IT TAKES!
I GUESS.
OF COURSE YES.
AOW!
IT'S IN THE BAG!
I GET THE TITLE, I'M IN THE CLAN, YOU AND LYNNE CAN GO TO SCHOOL--
I DON'T WANT TO GO TO COLLEGE.
DON'T BE STUPID.
I'M NOT, AND I DON'T WANT MORE SCHOOL. I'VE GOT MY JOB WITH GRANDAD'S STUDIO--
OH, SURE--
--AND I DON'T WANT TO GIVE IT UP. I HATE SCHOOL AND ANYWAY THERE'S DAD--
--WHO HAS A FULL-TIME NURSE TO LOOK AFTER HIM--
--AND LYNNE HASN'T GONE TO SCHOOL IN YEARS AND SHE DOES ALL RIGHT.
YOU'RE NOT LYNNE.

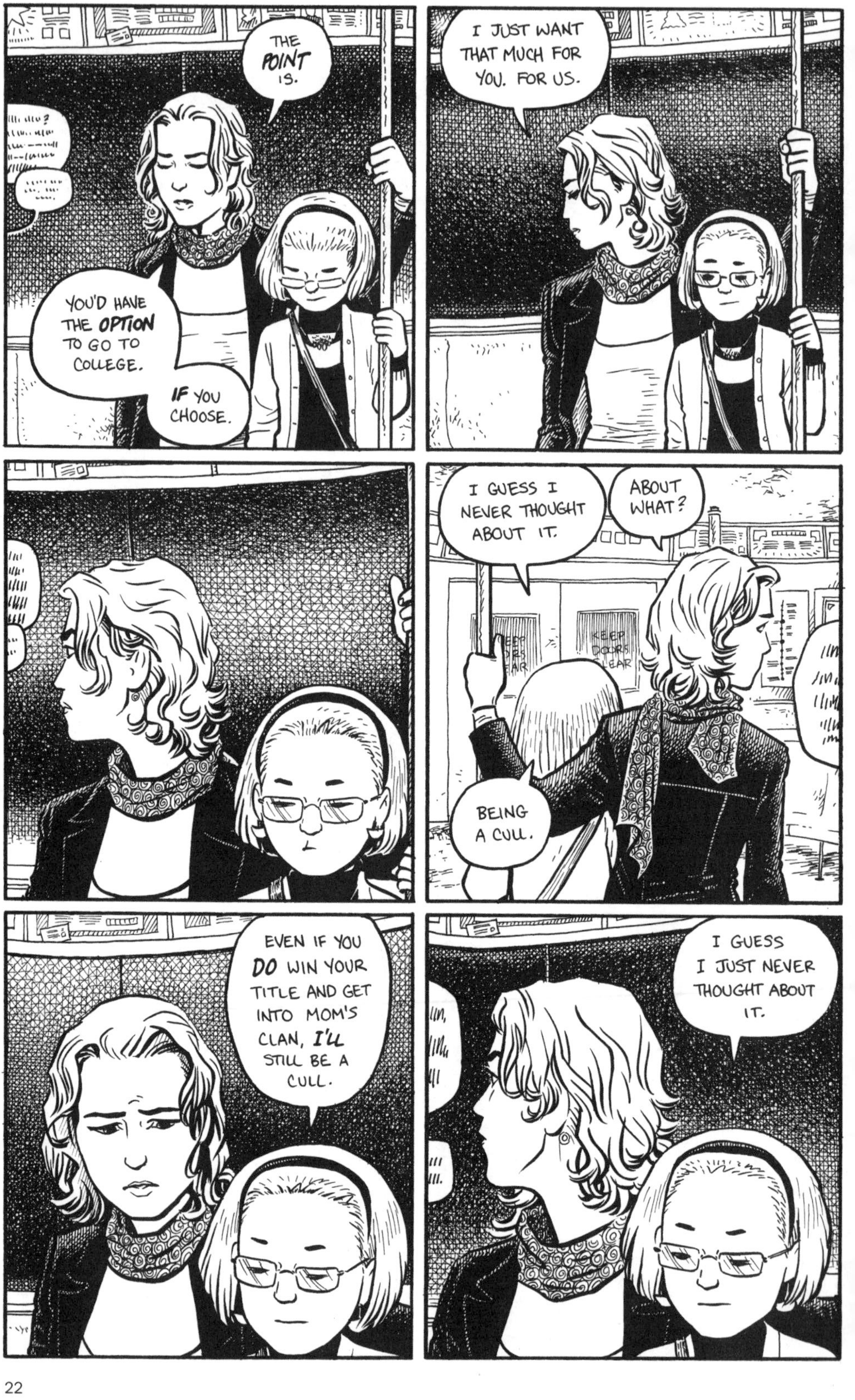
THE POINT IS.
YOU'D HAVE THE OPTION TO GO TO COLLEGE.
IF YOU CHOOSE.
I JUST WANT THAT MUCH FOR YOU. FOR US.
I GUESS I NEVER THOUGHT ABOUT IT.
ABOUT WHAT?
BEING A CULL.
KEEP DOORS CLEAR
EVEN IF YOU DO WIN YOUR TITLE AND GET INTO MOM'S CLAN, I'LL STILL BE A CULL.
I GUESS I JUST NEVER THOUGHT ABOUT IT.

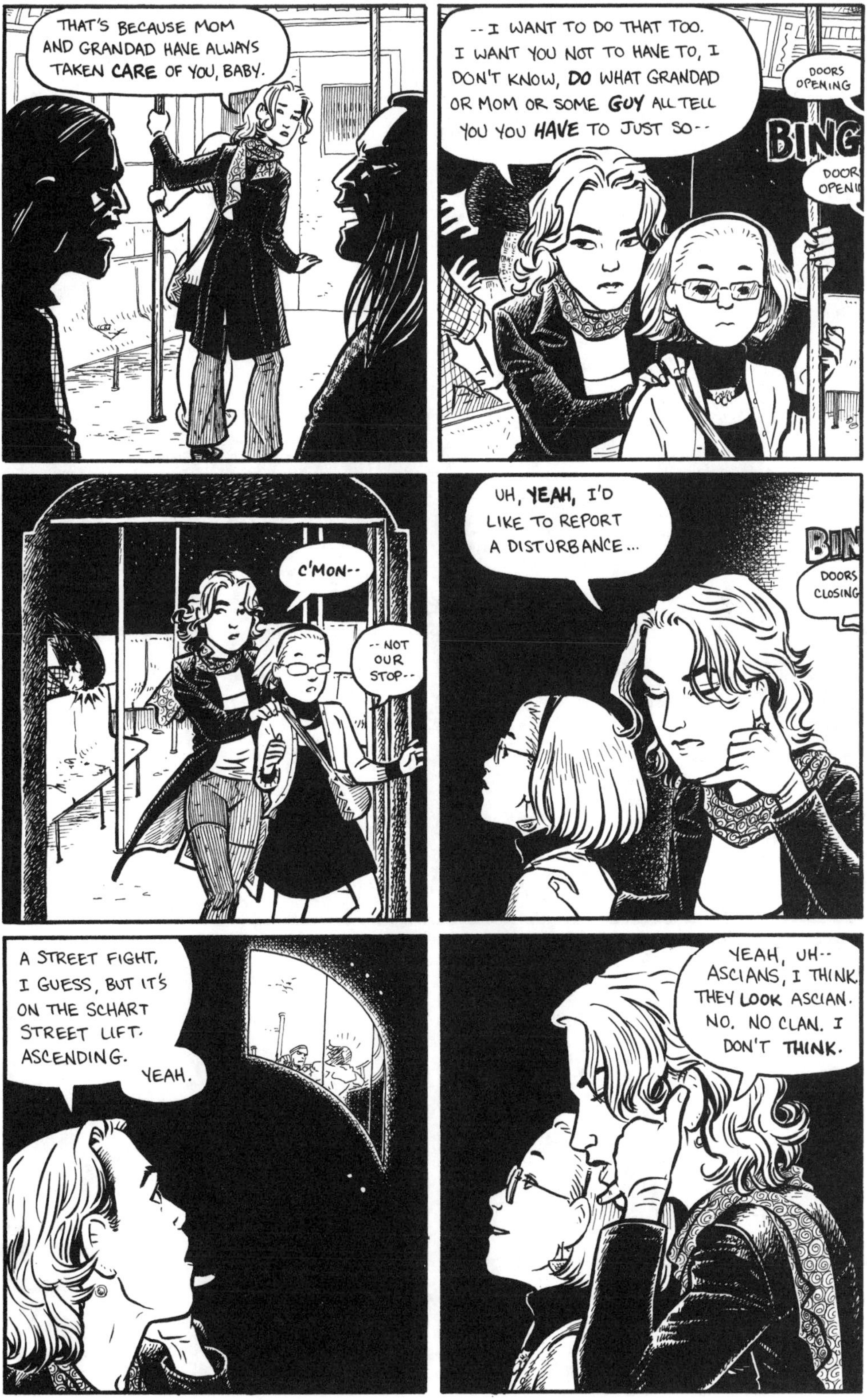
THAT'S BECAUSE MOM AND GRANDAD HAVE ALWAYS TAKEN CARE OF YOU, BABY.
--I WANT TO DO THAT TOO. I WANT YOU NOT TO HAVE TO, I DON'T KNOW, DO WHAT GRANDAD OR MOM OR SOME GUY ALL TELL YOU YOU HAVE TO JUST SO--
DOORS OPENING
BING
C'MON--
--NOT OUR STOP--
UH, YEAH, I'D LIKE TO REPORT A DISTURBANCE...
DOORS CLOSING
A STREET FIGHT, I GUESS, BUT IT'S ON THE SCHART STREET LIFT. ASCENDING.
YEAH.
YEAH, UH-- ASCIANS, I THINK. THEY LOOK ASCIAN. NO. NO CLAN. I DON'T THINK.

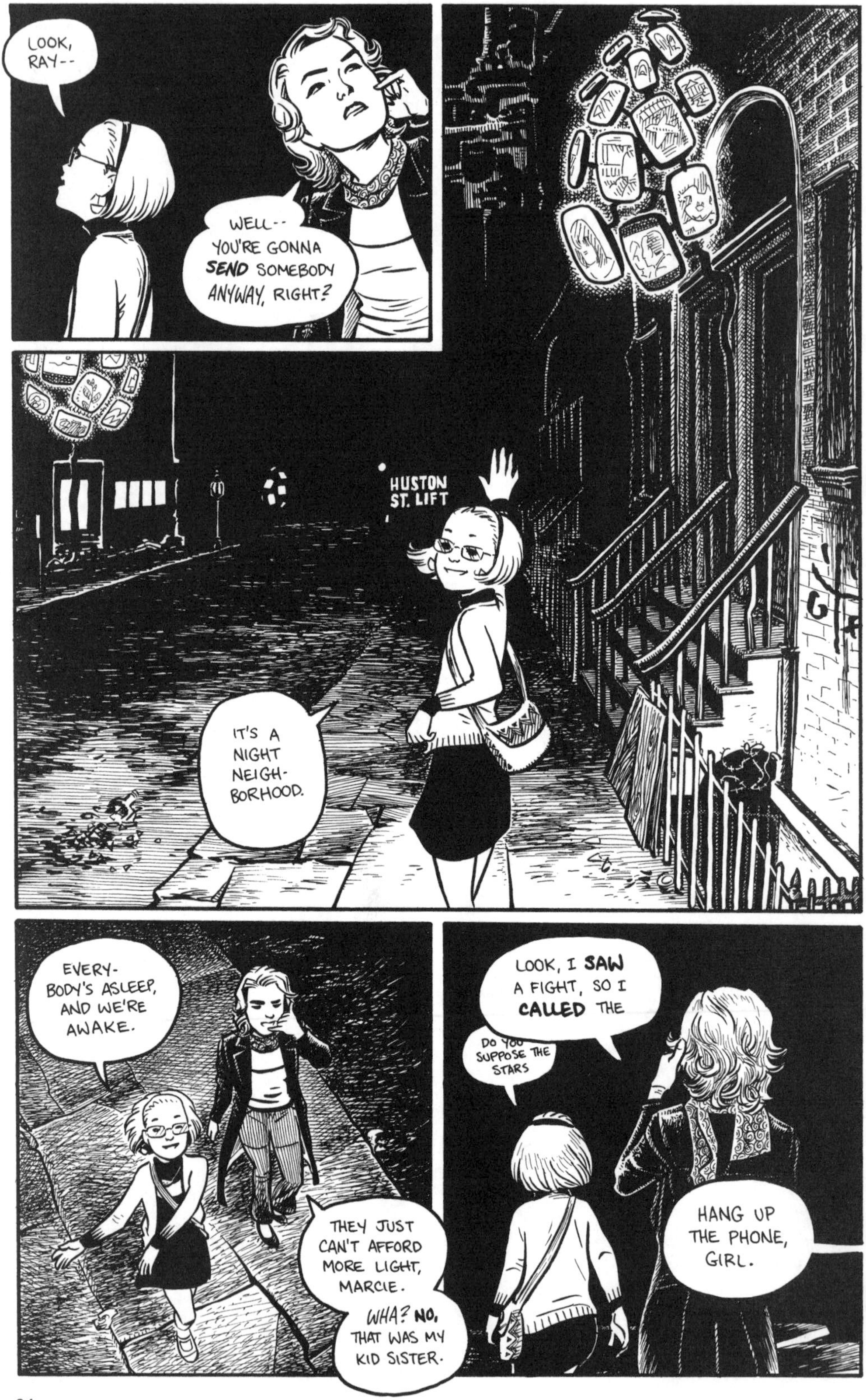
LOOK, RAY--
WELL-- YOU'RE GONNA SEND SOMEBODY ANYWAY, RIGHT?
HUSTON ST. LIFT
IT'S A NIGHT NEIGH-BORHOOD.
EVERY-BODY'S ASLEEP, AND WE'RE AWAKE.
THEY JUST CAN'T AFFORD MORE LIGHT, MARCIE.
WHA? NO, THAT WAS MY KID SISTER.
LOOK, I SAW A FIGHT, SO I CALLED THE
DO YOU SUPPOSE THE STARS
HANG UP THE PHONE, GIRL.

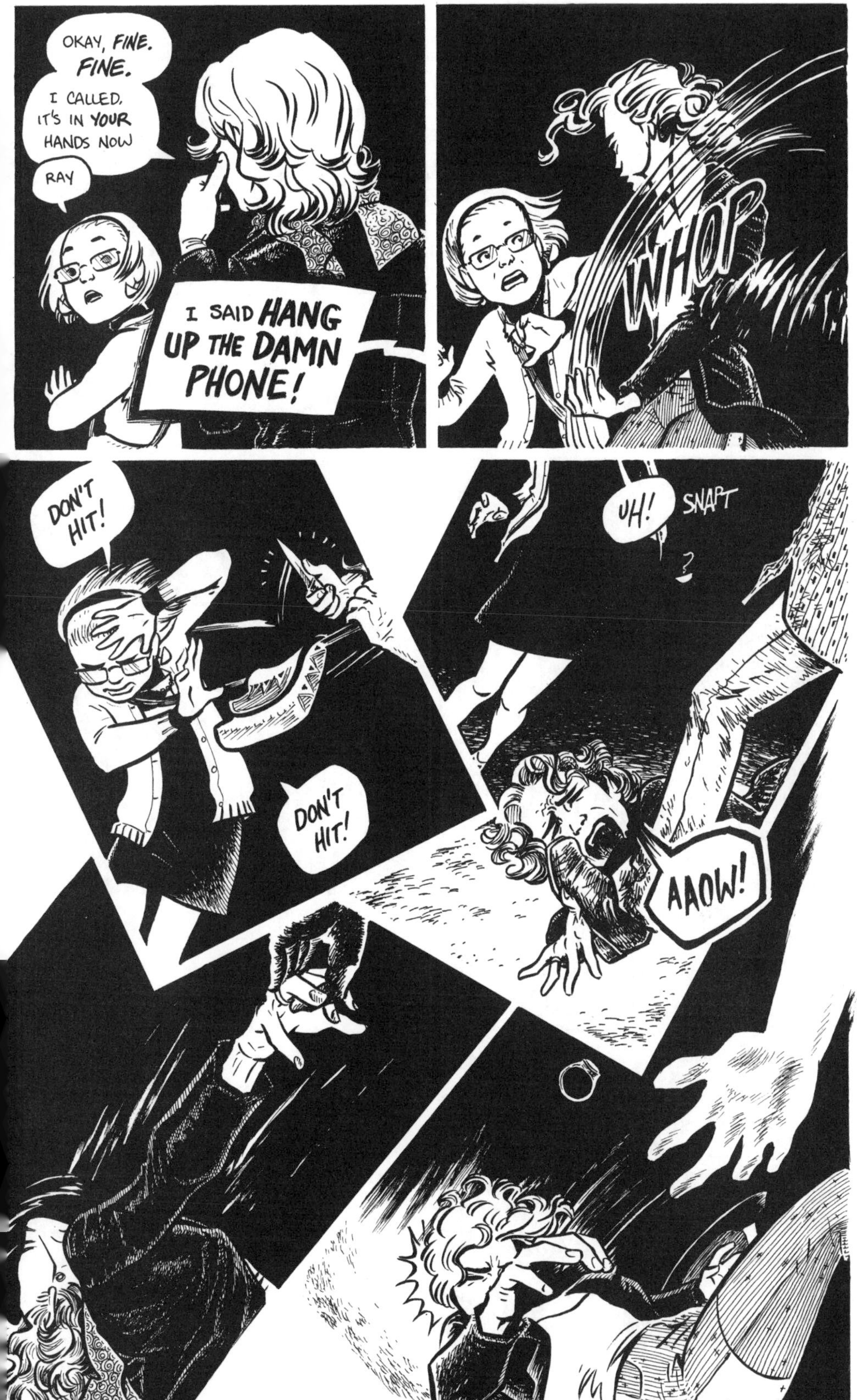
OKAY, FINE. FINE.
I CALLED. IT'S IN YOUR HANDS NOW
RAY
I SAID HANG UP THE DAMN PHONE!
WHOP
DON'T HIT!
DON'T HIT!
UH!
SNAP
?
AAOW!

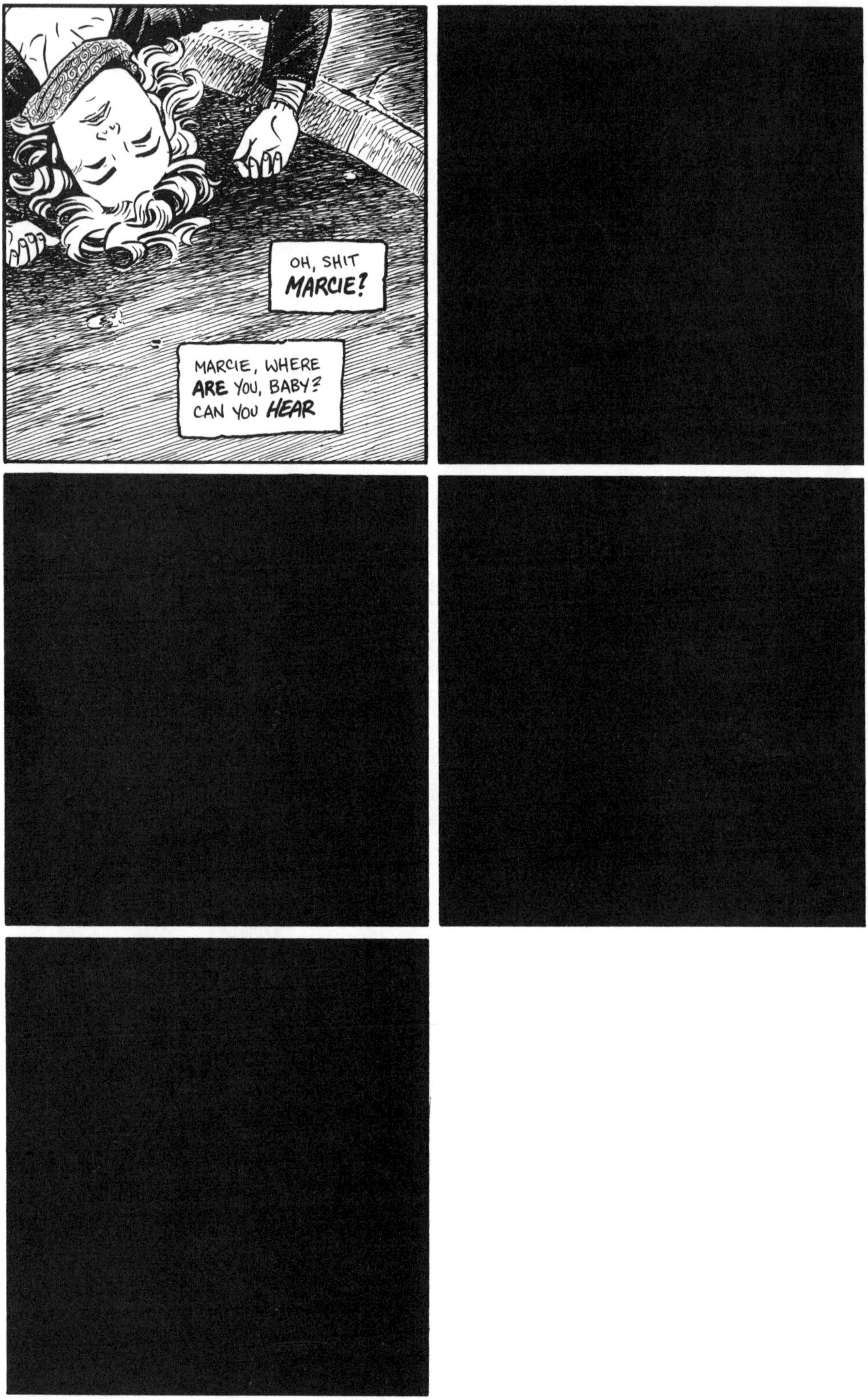
OH, SHIT
MARCIE?
MARCIE, WHERE ARE YOU, BABY? CAN YOU HEAR

two:

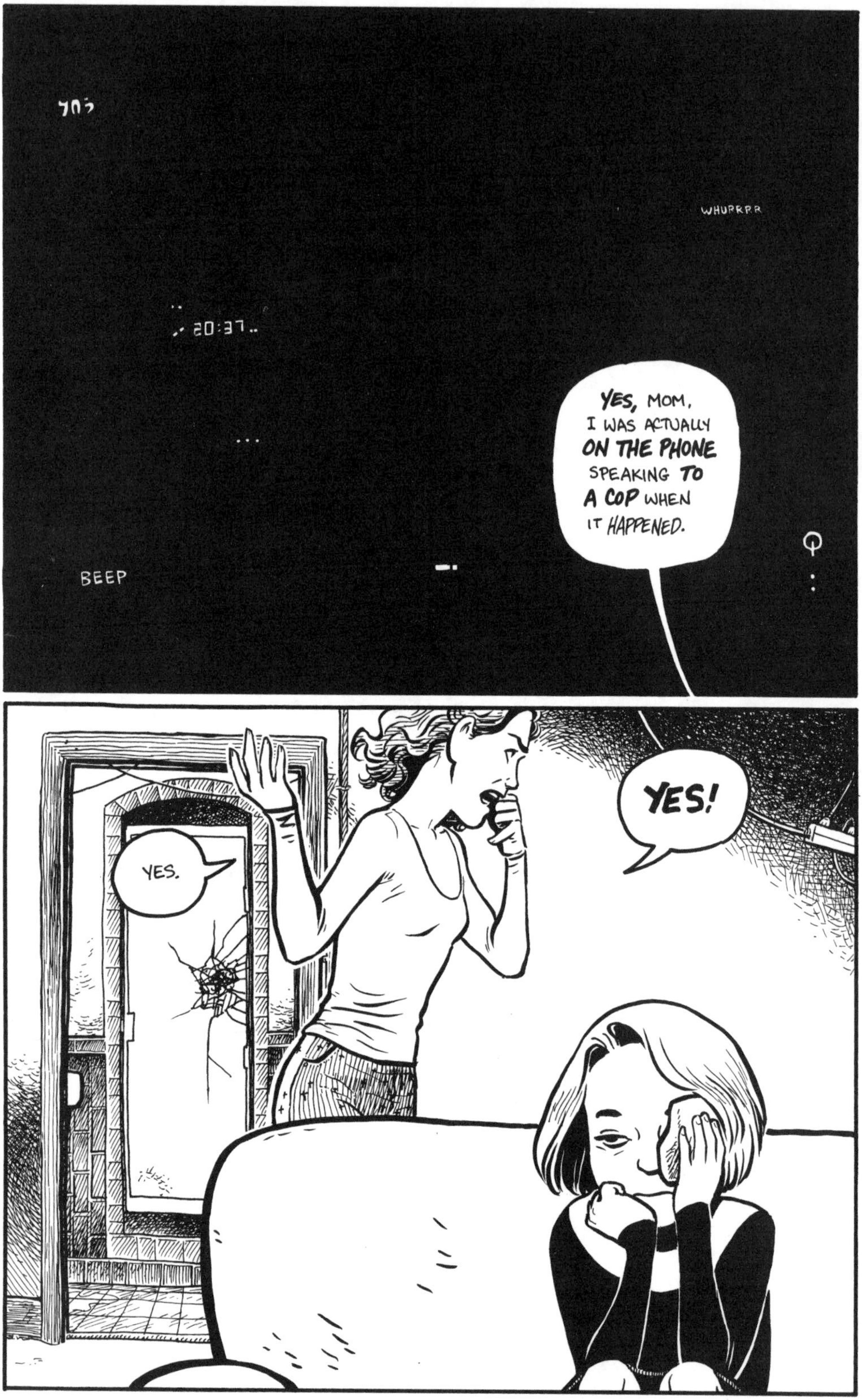
WHURRRR
20:37
BEEP
YES, MOM, I WAS ACTUALLY ON THE PHONE SPEAKING TO A COP WHEN IT HAPPENED.
YES!
YES.

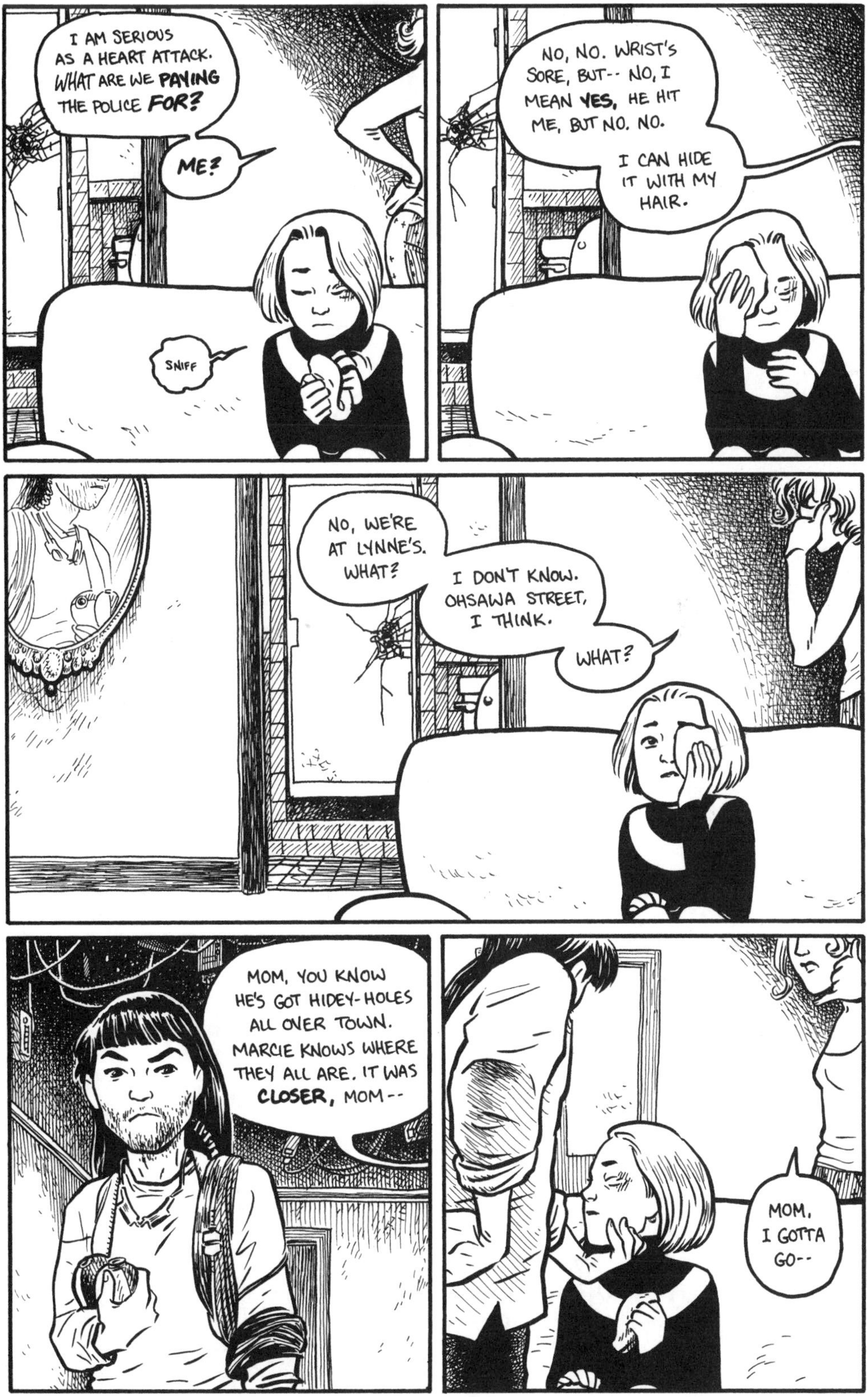
I AM SERIOUS AS A HEART ATTACK. WHAT ARE WE PAYING THE POLICE FOR?
ME?
SNIFF
NO, NO. WRIST'S SORE, BUT-- NO, I MEAN YES, HE HIT ME, BUT NO. NO.
I CAN HIDE IT WITH MY HAIR.
NO, WE'RE AT LYNNE'S. WHAT?
I DON'T KNOW. OHSAWA STREET, I THINK.
WHAT?
MOM, YOU KNOW HE'S GOT HIDEY-HOLES ALL OVER TOWN. MARCIE KNOWS WHERE THEY ALL ARE. IT WAS CLOSER, MOM--
MOM, I GOTTA GO--

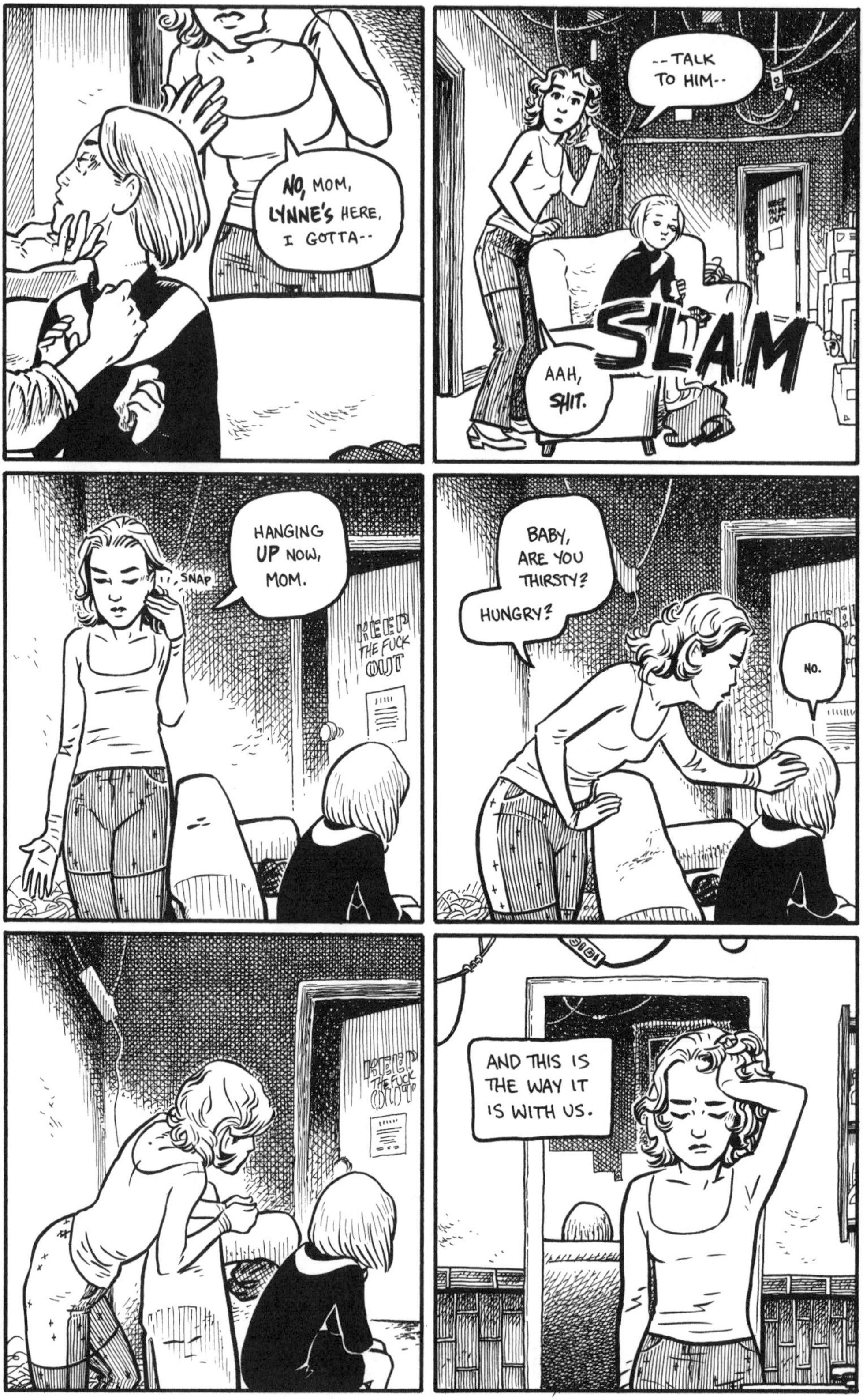
NO, MOM, LYNNE'S HERE, I GOTTA--
--TALK TO HIM--
AAH, SHIT.
SLAM
SNAP
HANGING UP NOW, MOM.
KEEP THE FUCK OUT
BABY, ARE YOU THIRSTY?
HUNGRY?
NO.
KEEP THE FUCK OUT
AND THIS IS THE WAY IT IS WITH US.

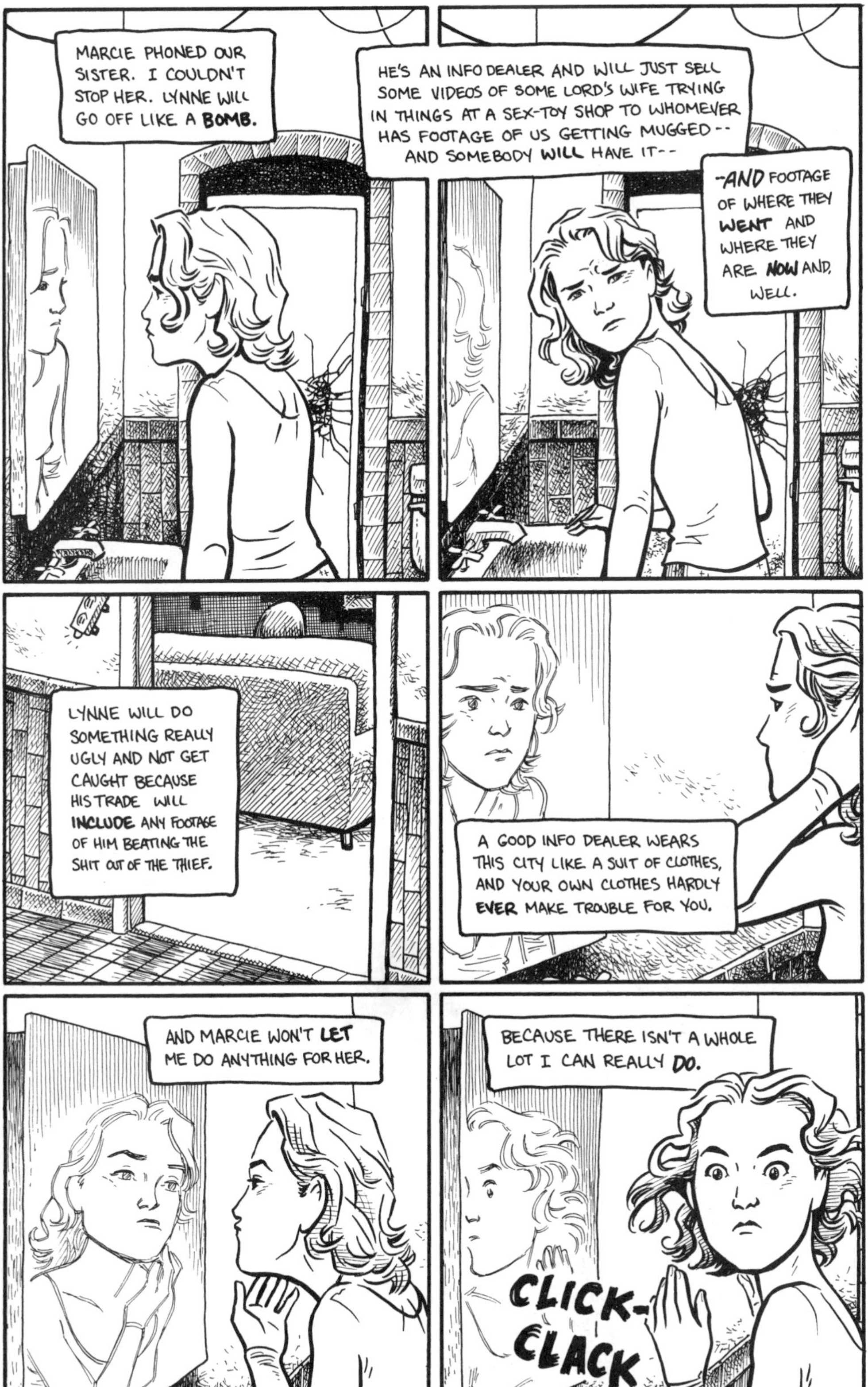
MARCIE PHONED OUR SISTER. I COULDN'T STOP HER. LYNNE WILL GO OFF LIKE A **BOMB.**
HE'S AN INFO DEALER AND WILL JUST SELL SOME VIDEOS OF SOME LORD'S WIFE TRYING IN THINGS AT A SEX-TOY SHOP TO WHOMEVER HAS FOOTAGE OF US GETTING MUGGED-- AND SOMEBODY **WILL** HAVE IT--
-**AND** FOOTAGE OF WHERE THEY **WENT** AND WHERE THEY ARE **NOW** AND, WELL.
LYNNE WILL DO SOMETHING REALLY UGLY AND NOT GET CAUGHT BECAUSE HIS TRADE WILL **INCLUDE** ANY FOOTAGE OF HIM BEATING THE SHIT OUT OF THE THIEF.
A GOOD INFO DEALER WEARS THIS CITY LIKE A SUIT OF CLOTHES, AND YOUR OWN CLOTHES HARDLY **EVER** MAKE TROUBLE FOR YOU.
AND MARCIE WON'T **LET** ME DO ANYTHING FOR HER.
BECAUSE THERE ISN'T A WHOLE LOT I CAN REALLY **DO.**
CLICK-CLACK

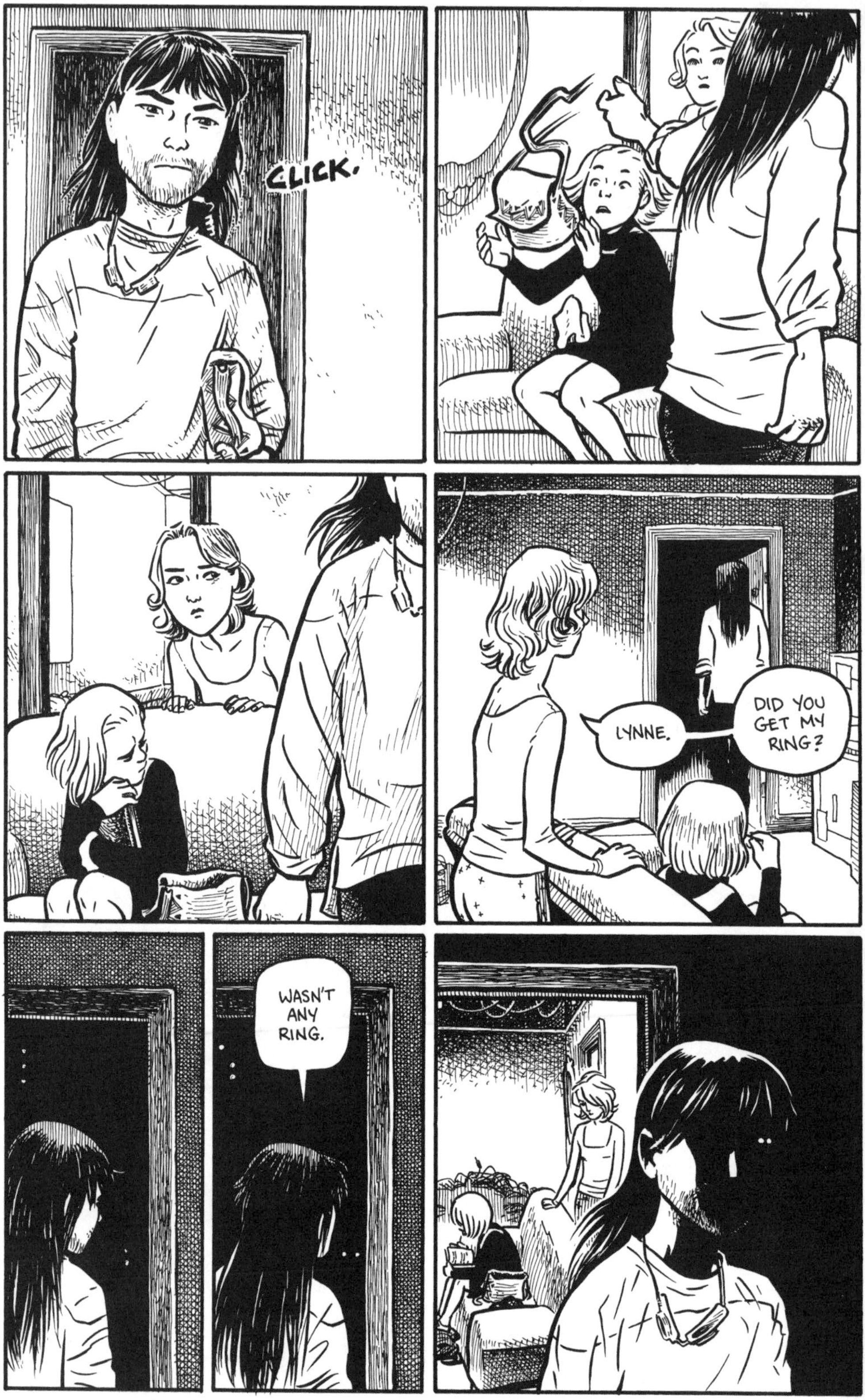
CLICK.
LYNNE.
DID YOU GET MY RING?
WASN'T ANY RING.

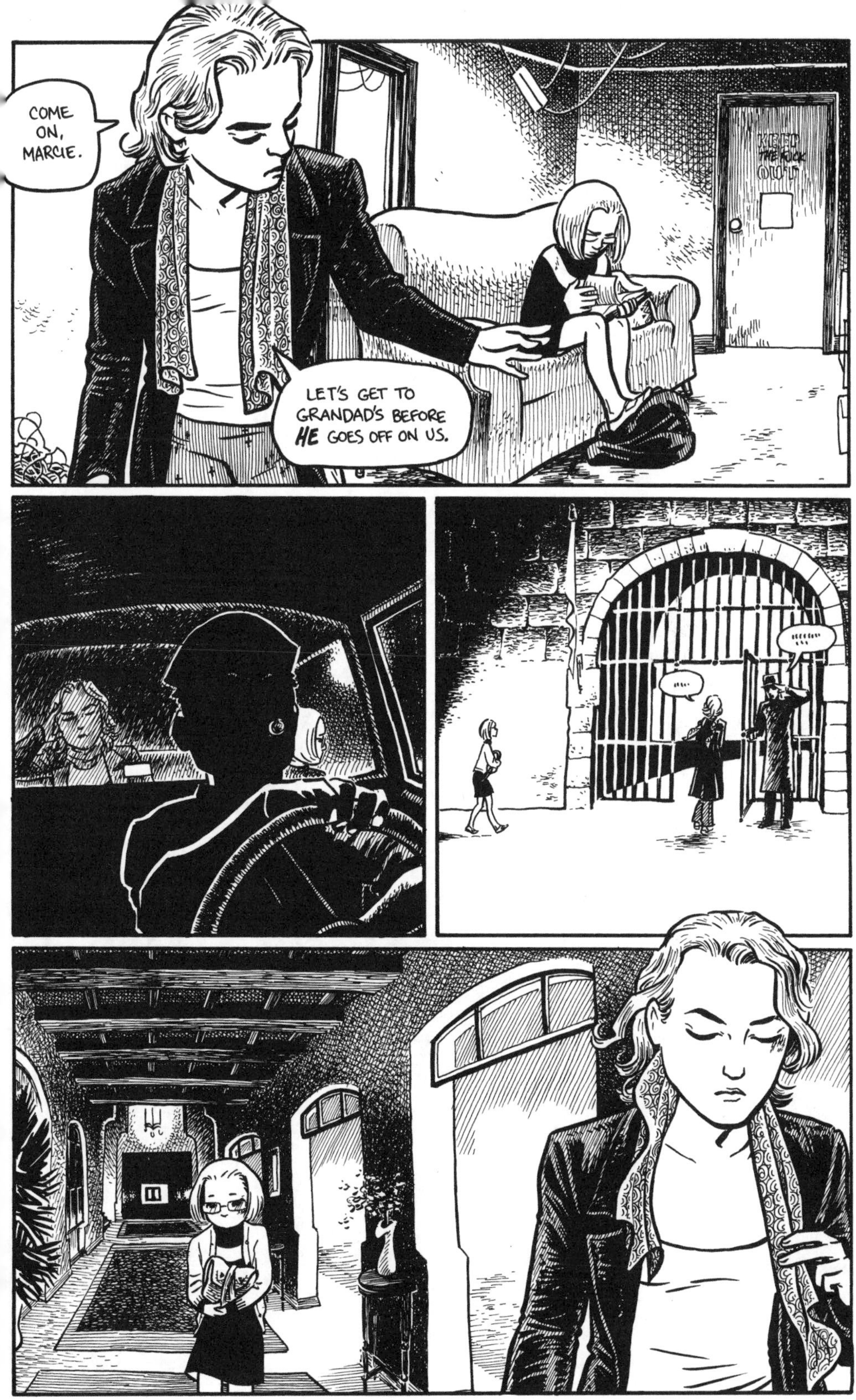
COME ON, MARCIE.
LET'S GET TO GRANDAD'S BEFORE HE GOES OFF ON US.
KEEP THE FUCK OUT
"....."
"...."

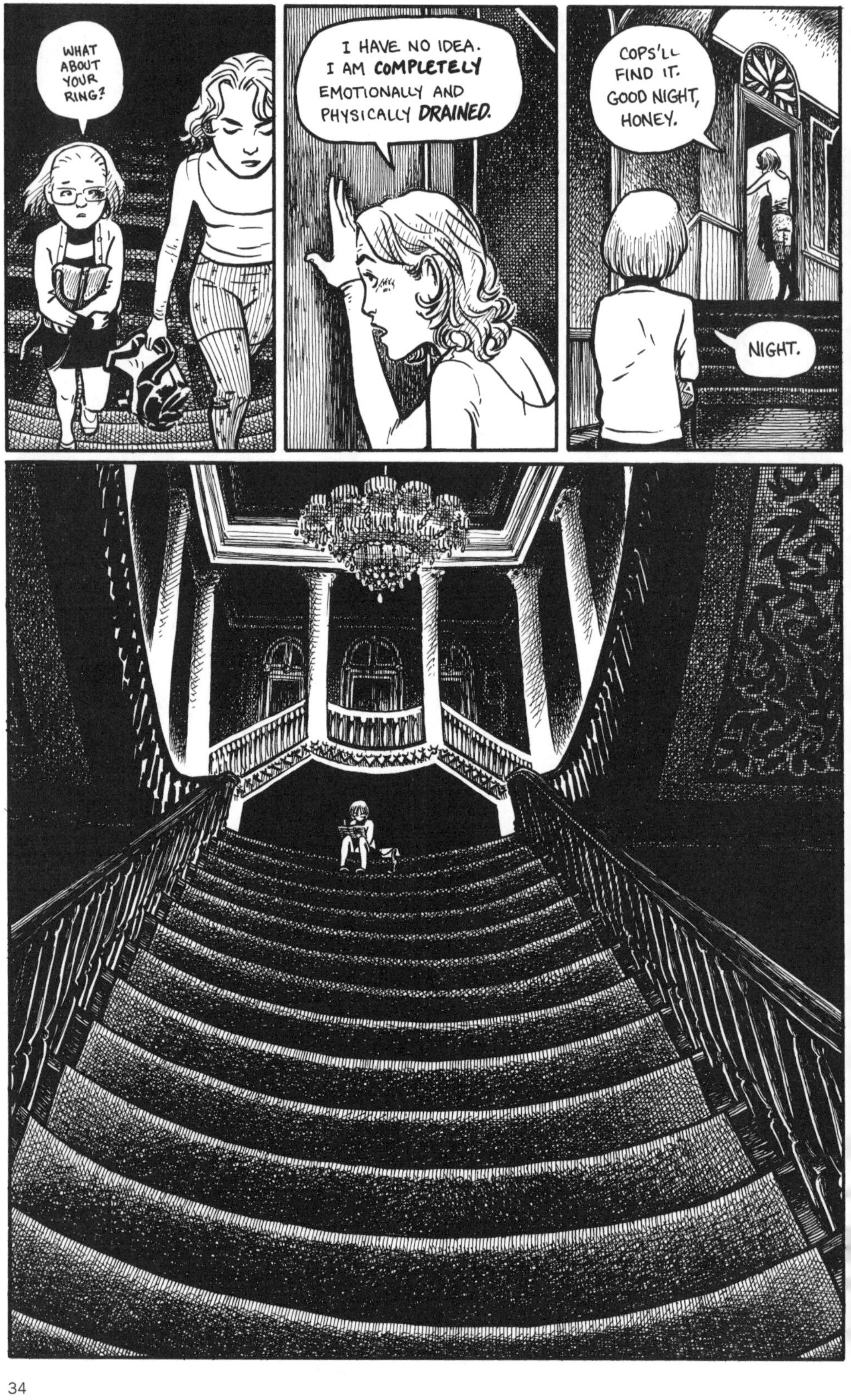
WHAT ABOUT YOUR RING?
I HAVE NO IDEA. I AM **COMPLETELY** EMOTIONALLY AND PHYSICALLY **DRAINED.**
COPS'LL FIND IT. GOOD NIGHT, HONEY.
NIGHT.

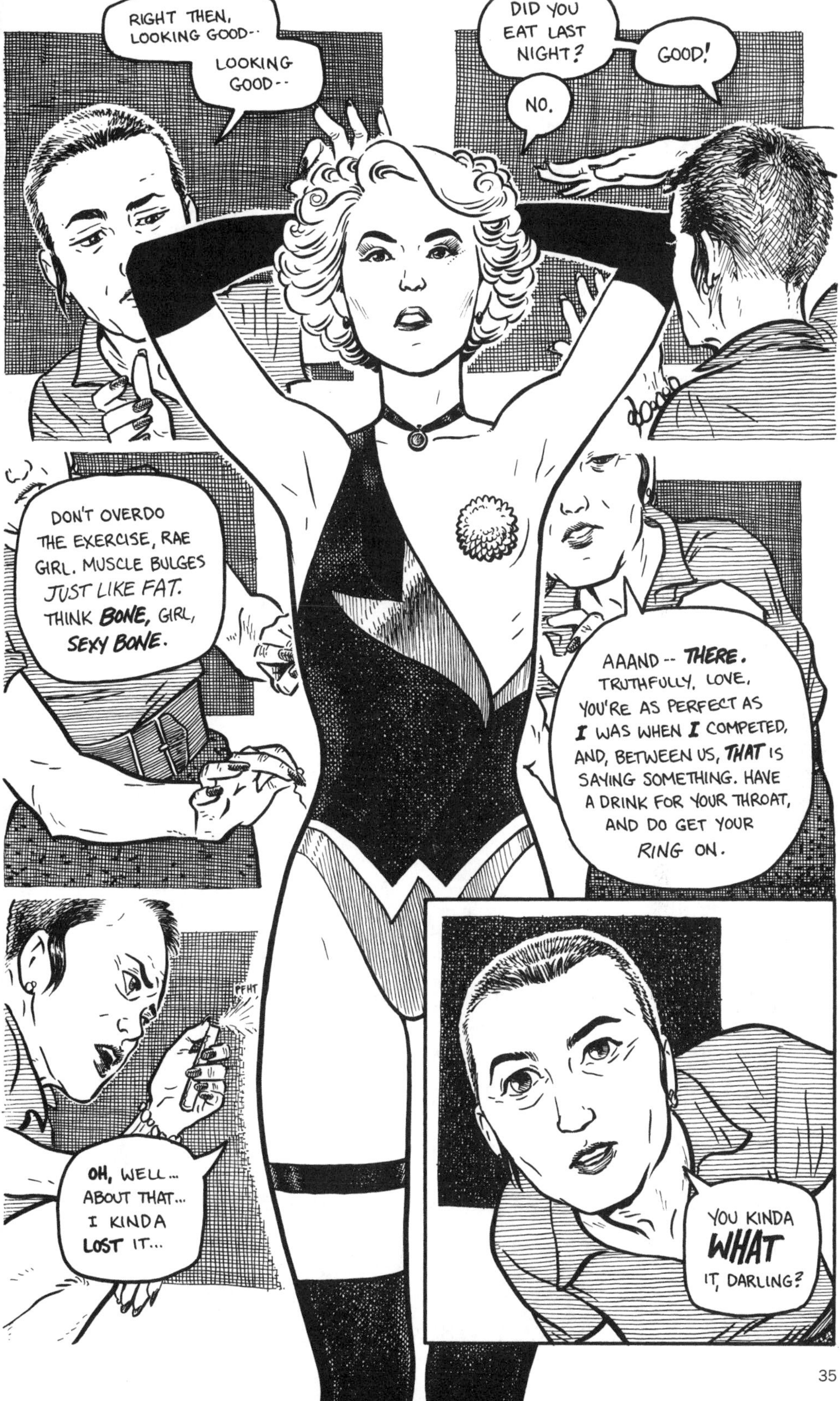
RIGHT THEN, LOOKING GOOD--
LOOKING GOOD--
DID YOU EAT LAST NIGHT?
NO.
GOOD!
DON'T OVERDO THE EXERCISE, RAE GIRL. MUSCLE BULGES JUST LIKE FAT. THINK BONE, GIRL, SEXY BONE.
AAAND -- THERE. TRUTHFULLY, LOVE, YOU'RE AS PERFECT AS I WAS WHEN I COMPETED, AND, BETWEEN US, THAT IS SAYING SOMETHING. HAVE A DRINK FOR YOUR THROAT, AND DO GET YOUR RING ON.
PFHT
OH, WELL... ABOUT THAT... I KINDA LOST IT...
YOU KINDA WHAT IT, DARLING?

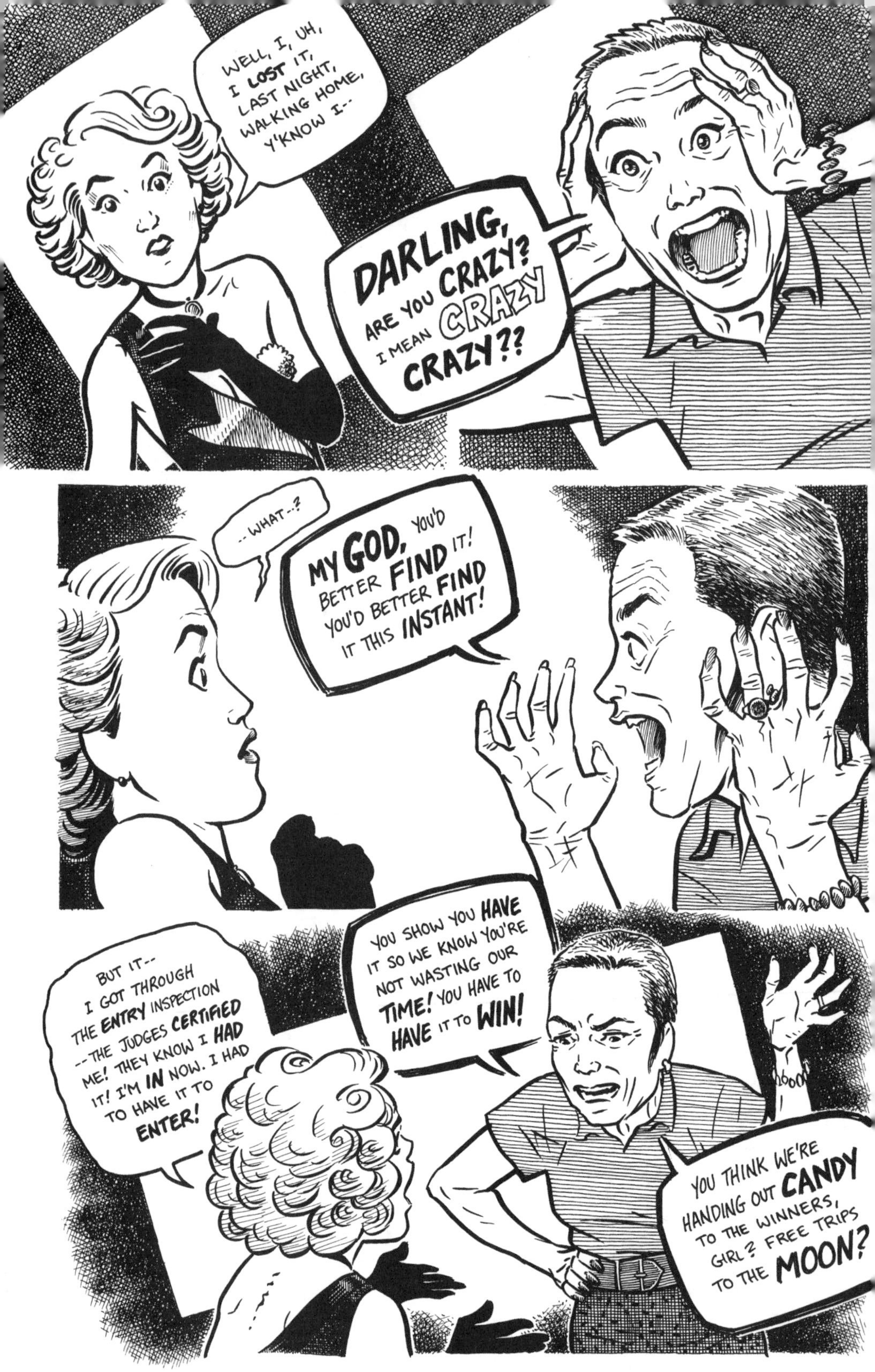
WELL, I, UH, I LOST IT, LAST NIGHT, WALKING HOME, Y'KNOW I--
DARLING, ARE YOU CRAZY? I MEAN CRAZY CRAZY??
--WHAT--?
MY GOD, YOU'D BETTER FIND IT! YOU'D BETTER FIND IT THIS INSTANT!
BUT IT-- I GOT THROUGH THE ENTRY INSPECTION --THE JUDGES CERTIFIED ME! THEY KNOW I HAD IT! I'M IN NOW. I HAD TO HAVE IT TO ENTER!
YOU SHOW YOU HAVE IT SO WE KNOW YOU'RE NOT WASTING OUR TIME! YOU HAVE TO HAVE IT TO WIN!
YOU THINK WE'RE HANDING OUT CANDY TO THE WINNERS, GIRL? FREE TRIPS TO THE MOON?

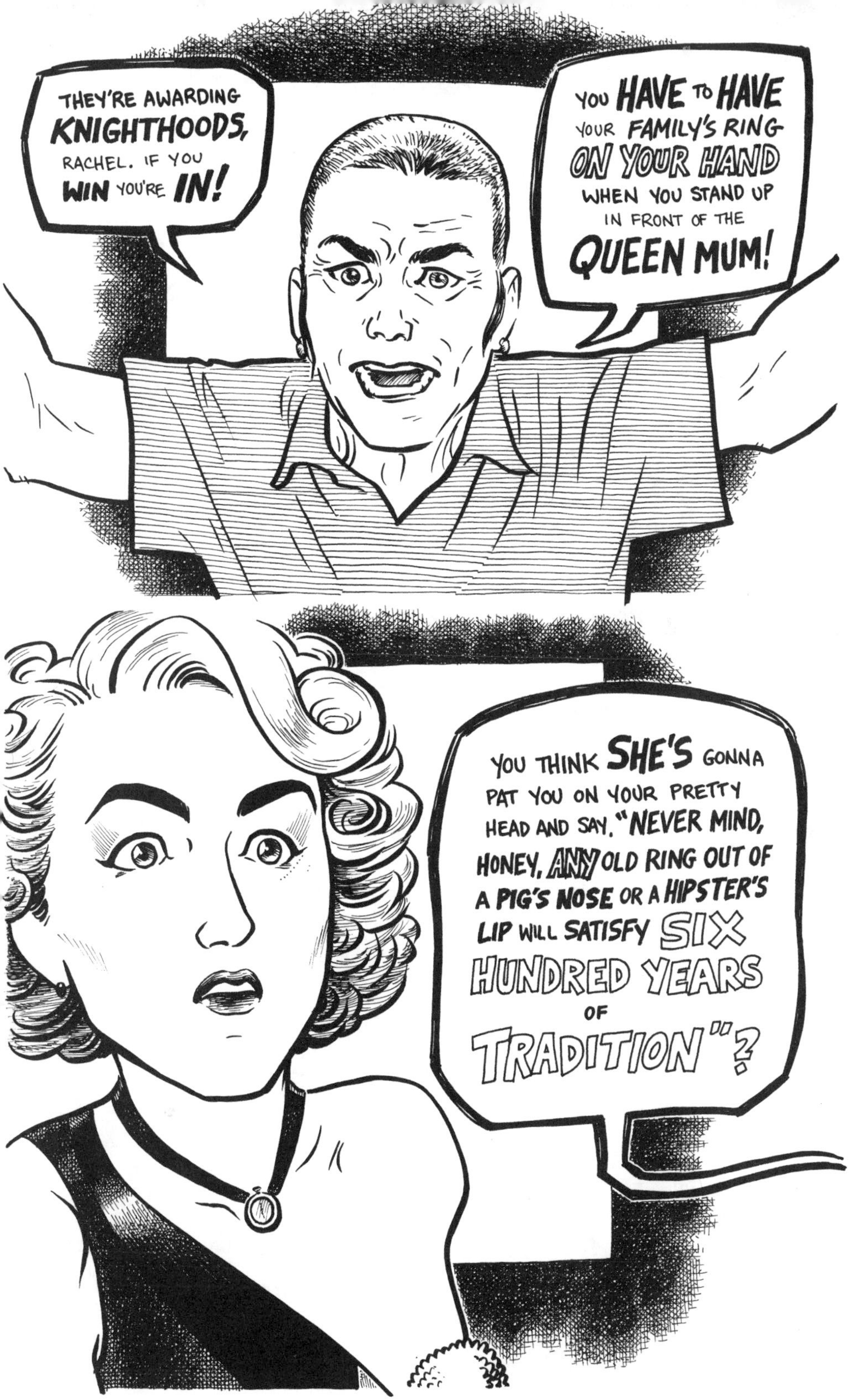
THEY'RE AWARDING KNIGHTHOODS, RACHEL. IF YOU WIN YOU'RE IN!
YOU HAVE TO HAVE YOUR FAMILY'S RING ON YOUR HAND WHEN YOU STAND UP IN FRONT OF THE QUEEN MUM!
YOU THINK SHE'S GONNA PAT YOU ON YOUR PRETTY HEAD AND SAY, "NEVER MIND, HONEY, ANY OLD RING OUT OF A PIG'S NOSE OR A HIPSTER'S LIP WILL SATISFY SIX HUNDRED YEARS OF TRADITION"?

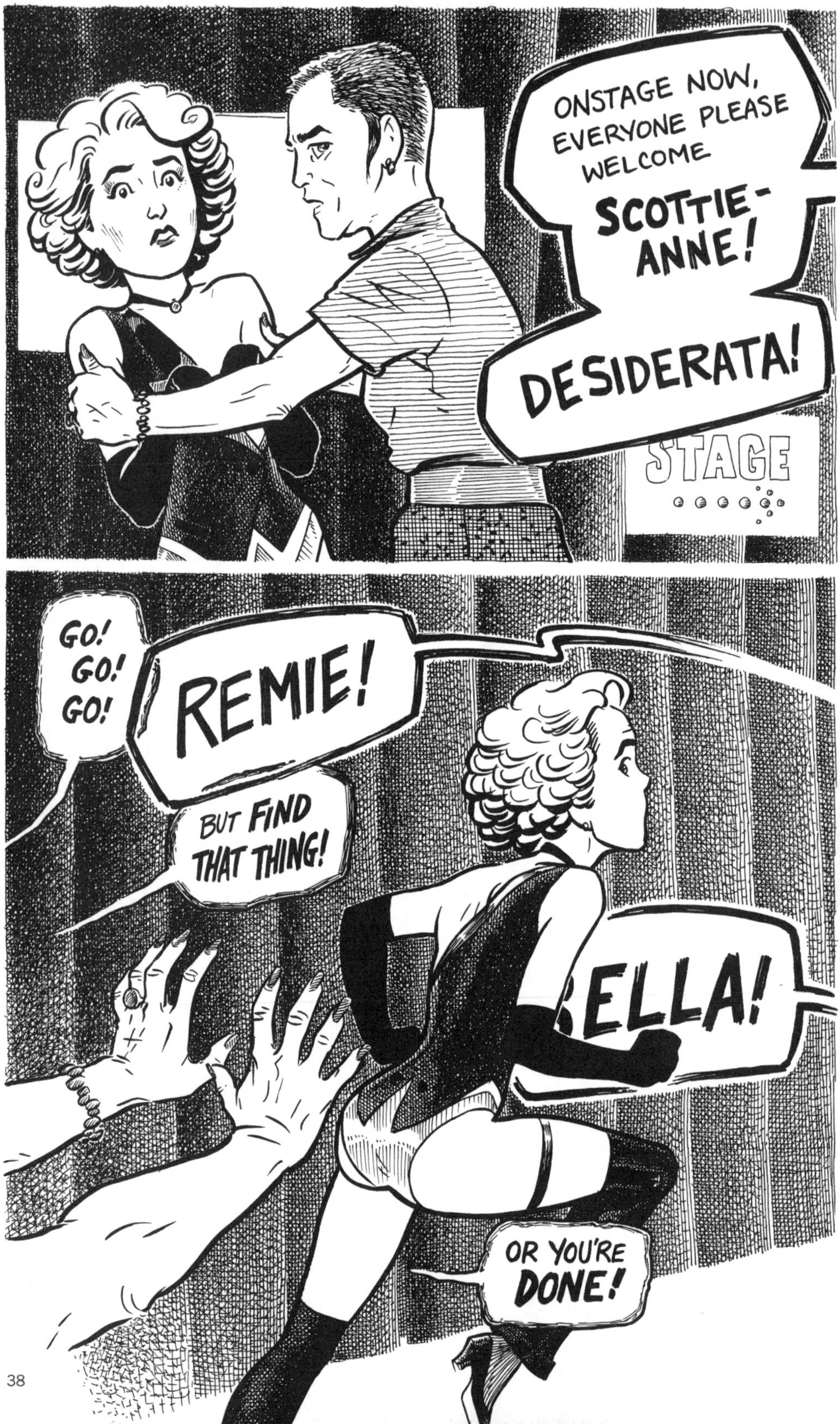
ONSTAGE NOW, EVERYONE PLEASE WELCOME SCOTTIE-ANNE!
DESIDERATA!
STAGE
GO! GO! GO!
REMIE!
BUT FIND THAT THING!
ELLA!
OR YOU'RE DONE!

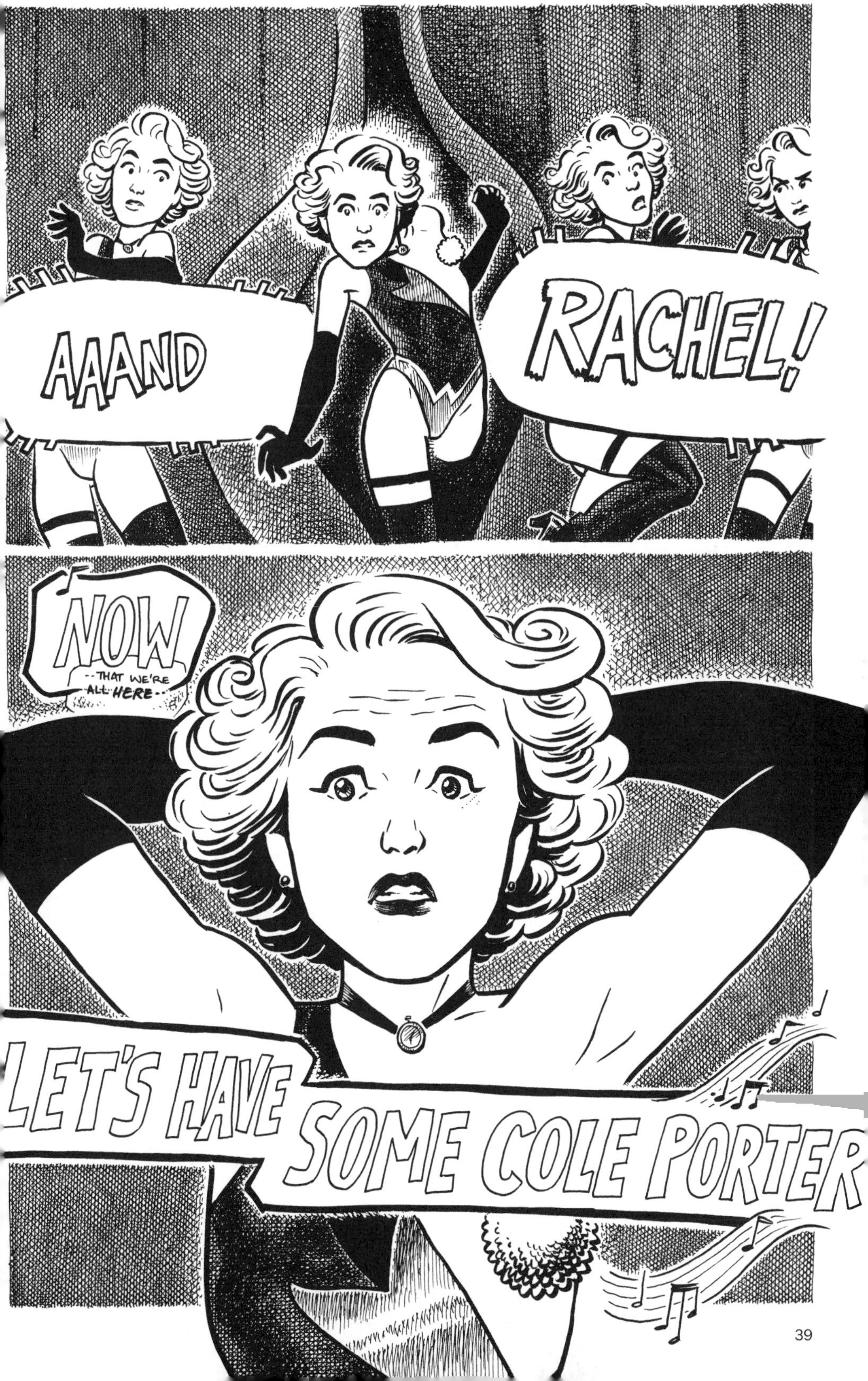
AAAND
RACHEL!
NOW
--THAT WE'RE ALL HERE--
LET'S HAVE SOME COLE PORTER

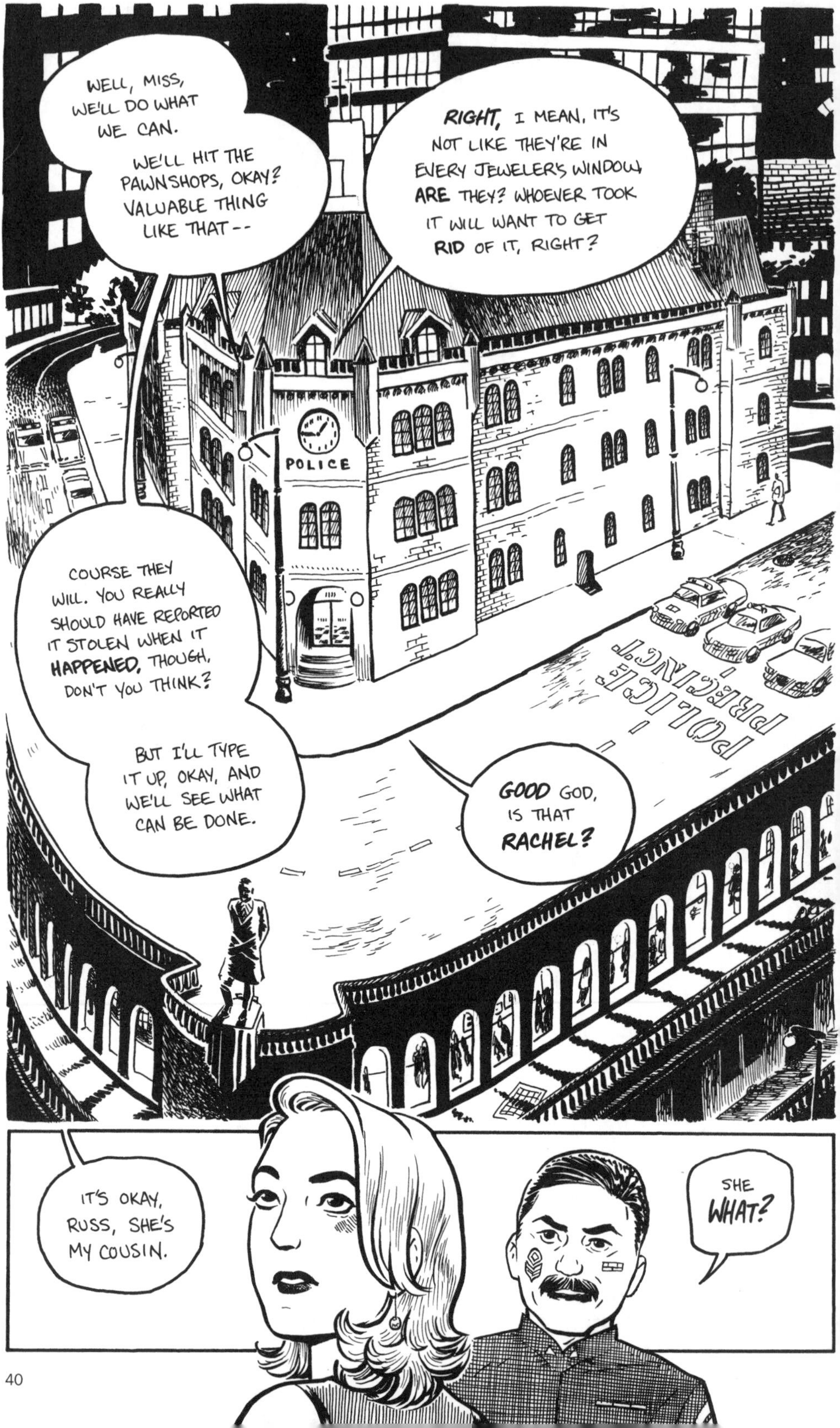
WELL, MISS, WE'LL DO WHAT WE CAN.
WE'LL HIT THE PAWNSHOPS, OKAY? VALUABLE THING LIKE THAT--
RIGHT, I MEAN, IT'S NOT LIKE THEY'RE IN EVERY JEWELER'S WINDOW, ARE THEY? WHOEVER TOOK IT WILL WANT TO GET RID OF IT, RIGHT?
POLICE
POLICE PRECINCT
COURSE THEY WILL. YOU REALLY SHOULD HAVE REPORTED IT STOLEN WHEN IT HAPPENED, THOUGH, DON'T YOU THINK?
BUT I'LL TYPE IT UP, OKAY, AND WE'LL SEE WHAT CAN BE DONE.
GOOD GOD, IS THAT RACHEL?
IT'S OKAY, RUSS, SHE'S MY COUSIN.
SHE WHAT?

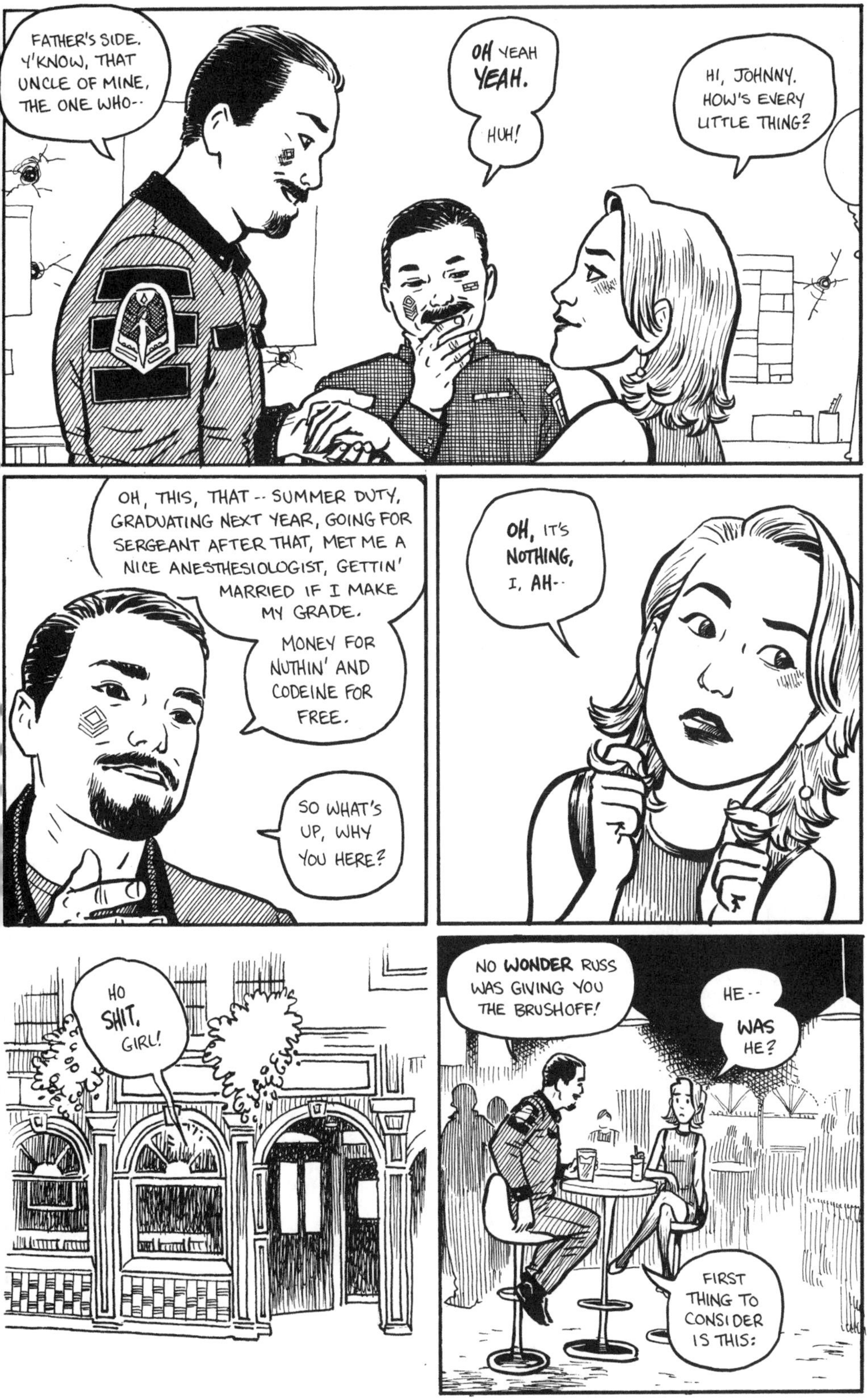
FATHER'S SIDE. Y'KNOW, THAT UNCLE OF MINE, THE ONE WHO--
OH YEAH YEAH.
HUH!
HI, JOHNNY. HOW'S EVERY LITTLE THING?
OH, THIS, THAT -- SUMMER DUTY, GRADUATING NEXT YEAR, GOING FOR SERGEANT AFTER THAT, MET ME A NICE ANESTHESIOLOGIST, GETTIN' MARRIED IF I MAKE MY GRADE.
MONEY FOR NUTHIN' AND CODEINE FOR FREE.
SO WHAT'S UP, WHY YOU HERE?
OH, IT'S NOTHING, I, AH--
HO SHIT, GIRL!
NO WONDER RUSS WAS GIVING YOU THE BRUSHOFF!
HE-- WAS HE?
FIRST THING TO CONSIDER IS THIS:

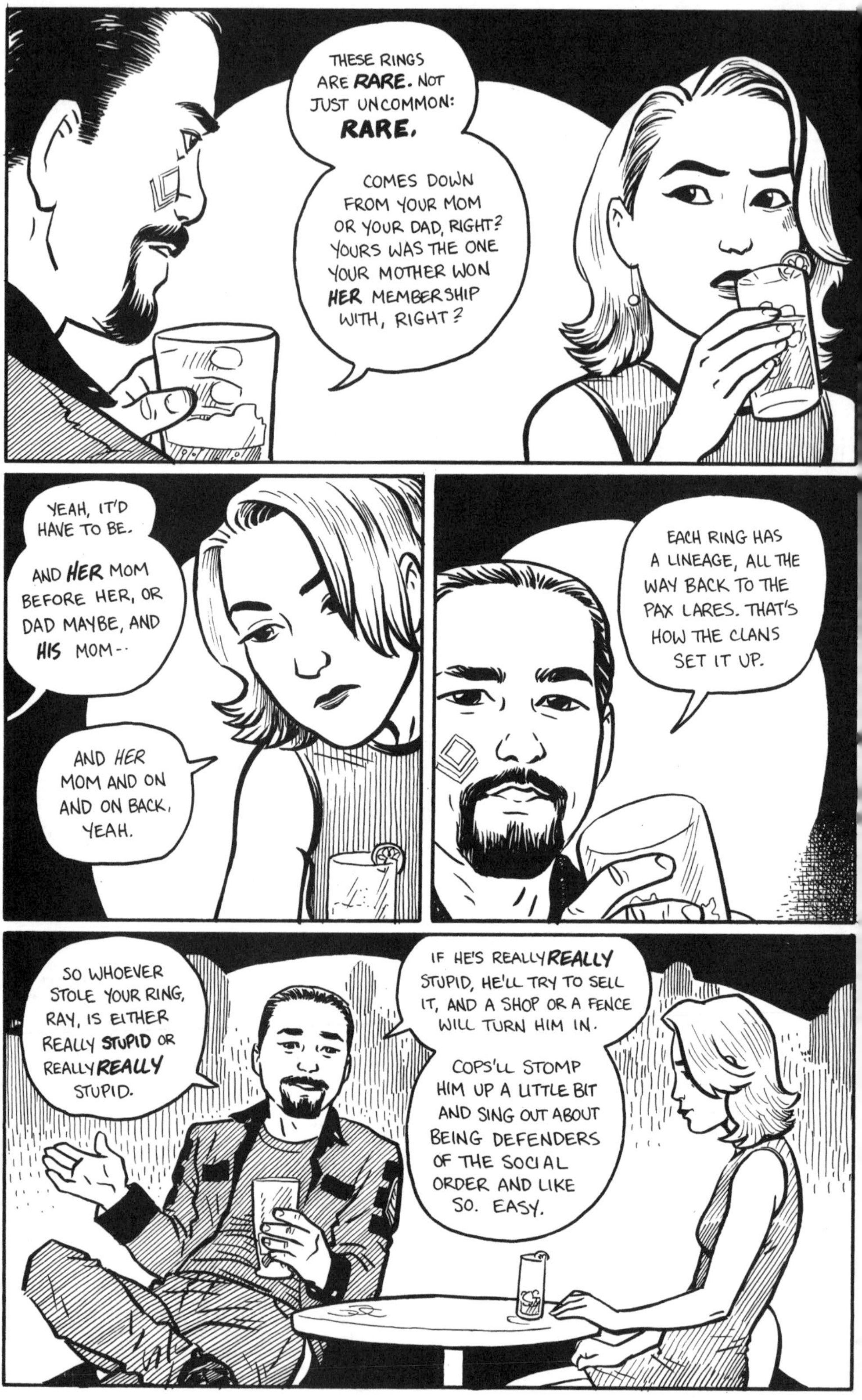
THESE RINGS ARE **RARE.** NOT JUST UNCOMMON: **RARE.**
COMES DOWN FROM YOUR MOM OR YOUR DAD, RIGHT? YOURS WAS THE ONE YOUR MOTHER WON **HER** MEMBERSHIP WITH, RIGHT?
YEAH, IT'D HAVE TO BE.
AND **HER** MOM BEFORE HER, OR DAD MAYBE, AND **HIS** MOM--
AND *HER* MOM AND ON AND ON BACK, YEAH.
EACH RING HAS A LINEAGE, ALL THE WAY BACK TO THE PAX LARES. THAT'S HOW THE CLANS SET IT UP.
SO WHOEVER STOLE YOUR RING, RAY, IS EITHER REALLY **STUPID** OR REALLY **REALLY** STUPID.
IF HE'S REALLY **REALLY** STUPID, HE'LL TRY TO SELL IT, AND A SHOP OR A FENCE WILL TURN HIM IN.
COPS'LL STOMP HIM UP A LITTLE BIT AND SING OUT ABOUT BEING DEFENDERS OF THE SOCIAL ORDER AND LIKE SO. EASY.

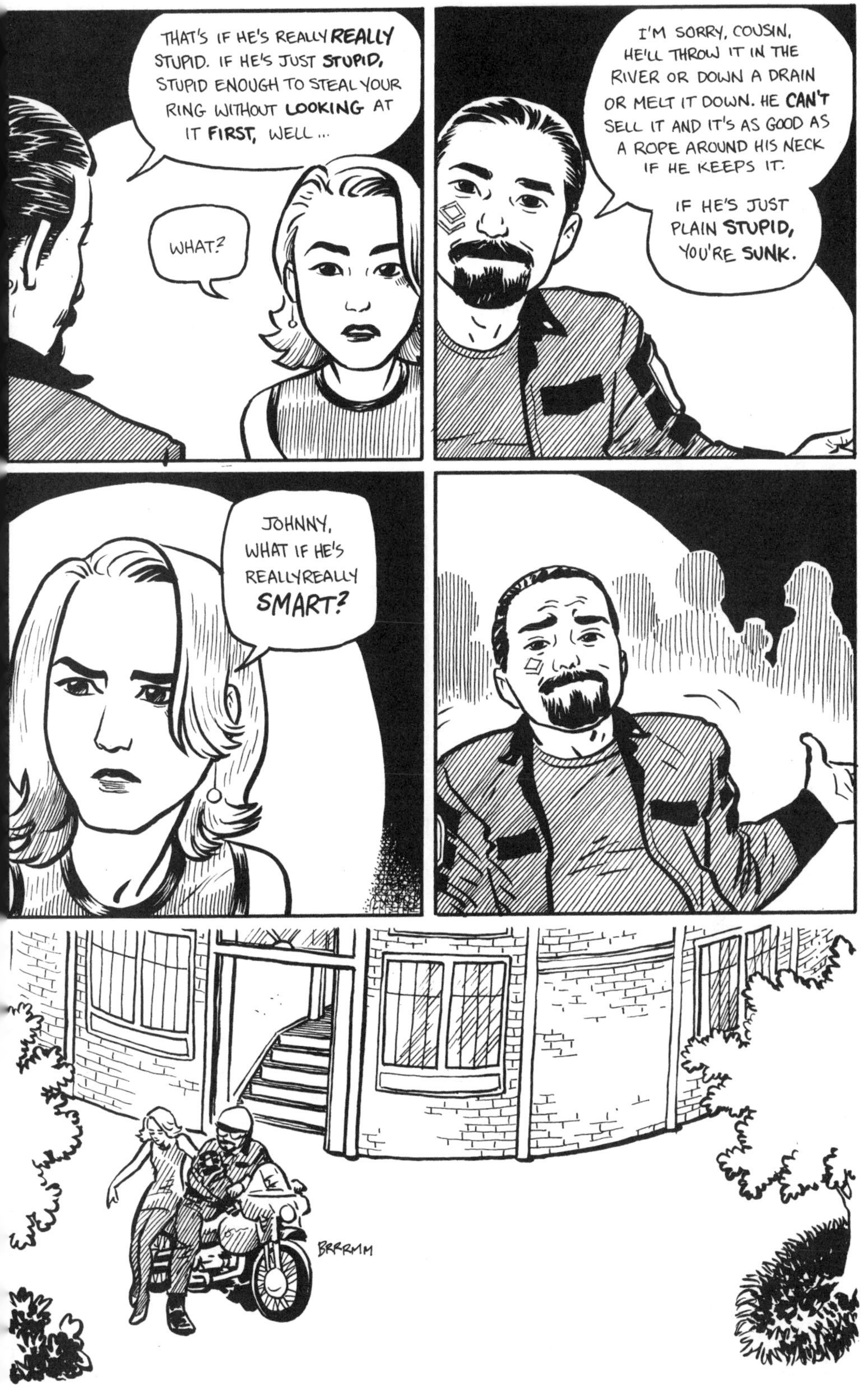
THAT'S IF HE'S REALLY REALLY STUPID. IF HE'S JUST STUPID, STUPID ENOUGH TO STEAL YOUR RING WITHOUT LOOKING AT IT FIRST, WELL...
WHAT?
I'M SORRY, COUSIN. HE'LL THROW IT IN THE RIVER OR DOWN A DRAIN OR MELT IT DOWN. HE CAN'T SELL IT AND IT'S AS GOOD AS A ROPE AROUND HIS NECK IF HE KEEPS IT.
IF HE'S JUST PLAIN STUPID, YOU'RE SUNK.
JOHNNY, WHAT IF HE'S REALLYREALLY SMART?
BRRRMM

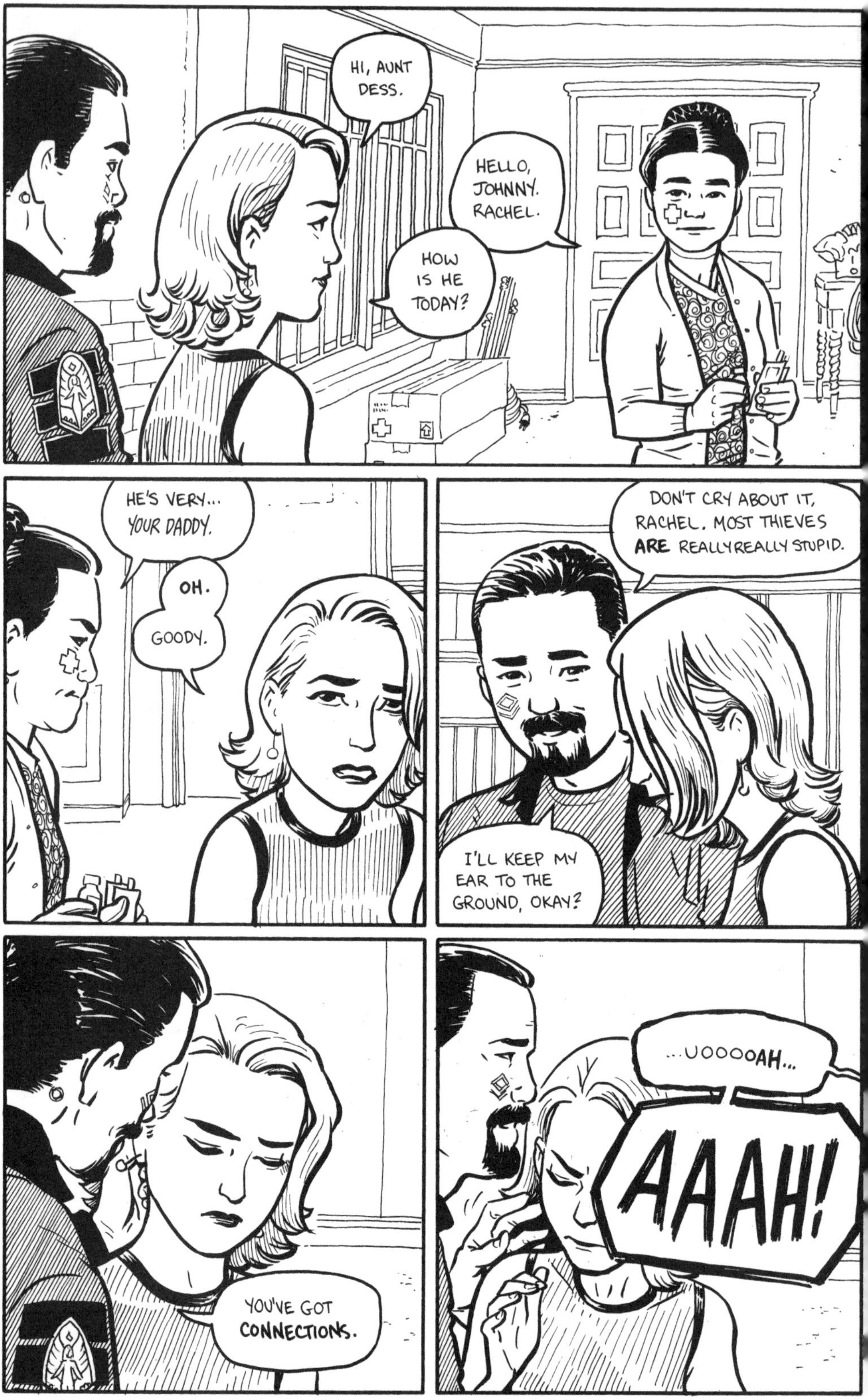
HI, AUNT DESS.
HELLO, JOHNNY. RACHEL.
HOW IS HE TODAY?
HE'S VERY... YOUR DADDY.
OH.
GOODY.
DON'T CRY ABOUT IT, RACHEL. MOST THIEVES ARE REALLYREALLY STUPID.
I'LL KEEP MY EAR TO THE GROUND, OKAY?
YOU'VE GOT CONNECTIONS.
...UOOOOAH...
AAAH!

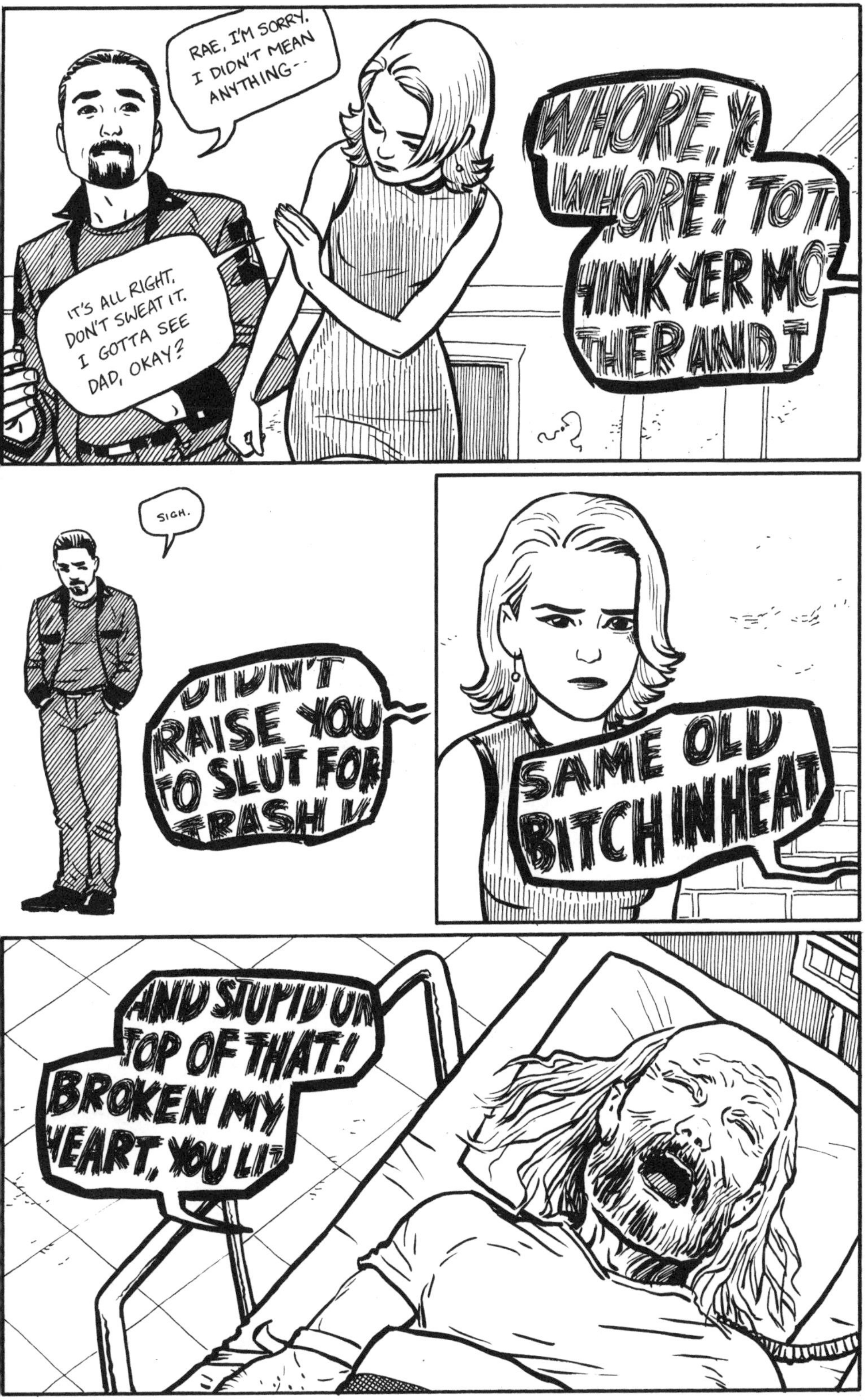
RAE, I'M SORRY. I DIDN'T MEAN ANYTHING--
IT'S ALL RIGHT. DON'T SWEAT IT. I GOTTA SEE DAD, OKAY?
WHORE, YO WHORE! TO THINK YER MOTHER AND I
SIGH.
DIDN'T RAISE YOU TO SLUT FOR TRASH
SAME OLD BITCH IN HEAT
AND STUPID ON TOP OF THAT! BROKEN MY HEART, YOU LIT

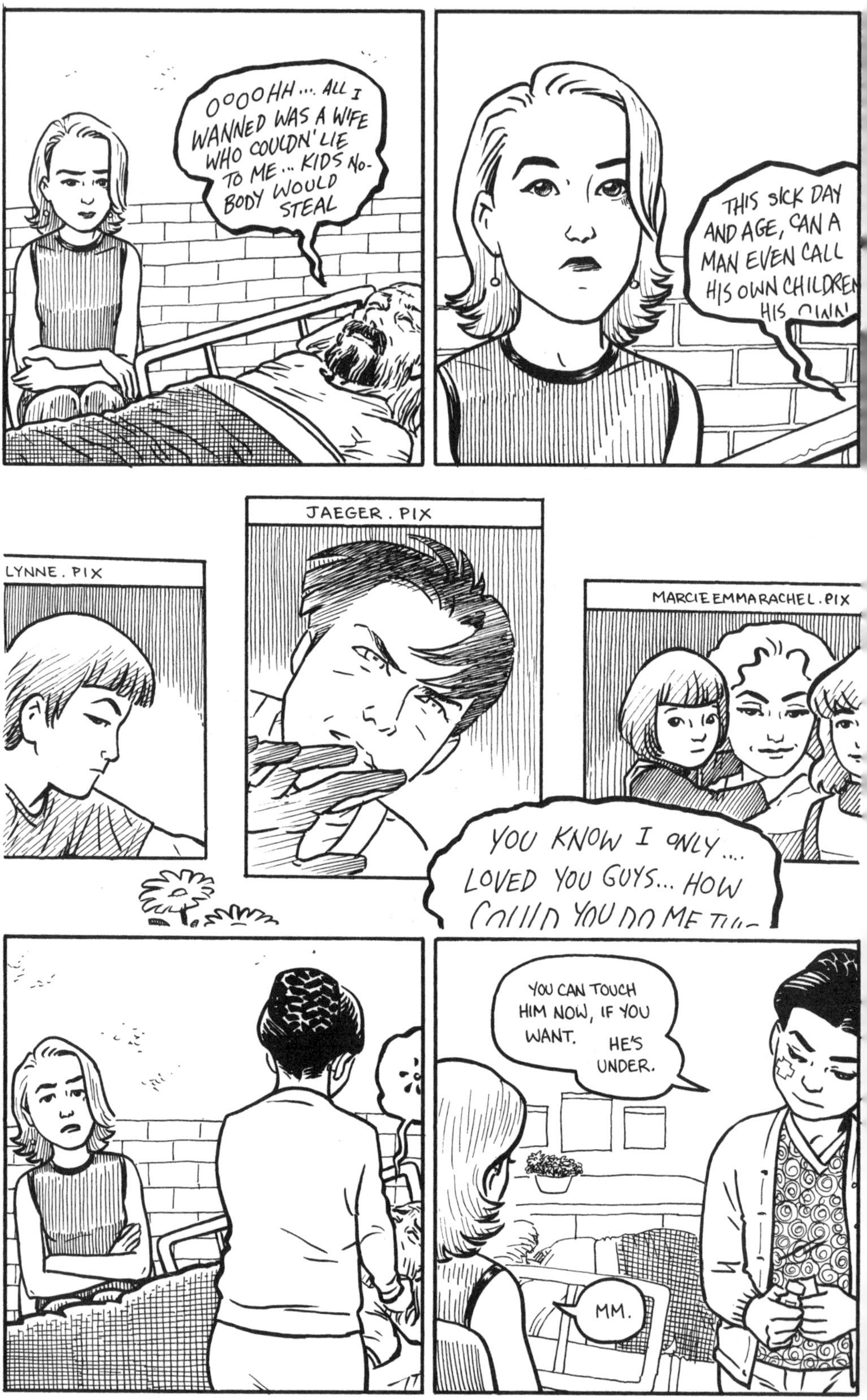

OOOOHH... ALL I WANNED WAS A WIFE WHO COULDN' LIE TO ME... KIDS NO-BODY WOULD STEAL
THIS SICK DAY AND AGE, CAN A MAN EVEN CALL HIS OWN CHILDREN
LYNNE. PIX
JAEGER. PIX
MARCIEEMMARACHEL.PIX
YOU KNOW I ONLY.... LOVED YOU GUYS... HOW
YOU CAN TOUCH HIM NOW, IF YOU WANT. HE'S UNDER.
MM.

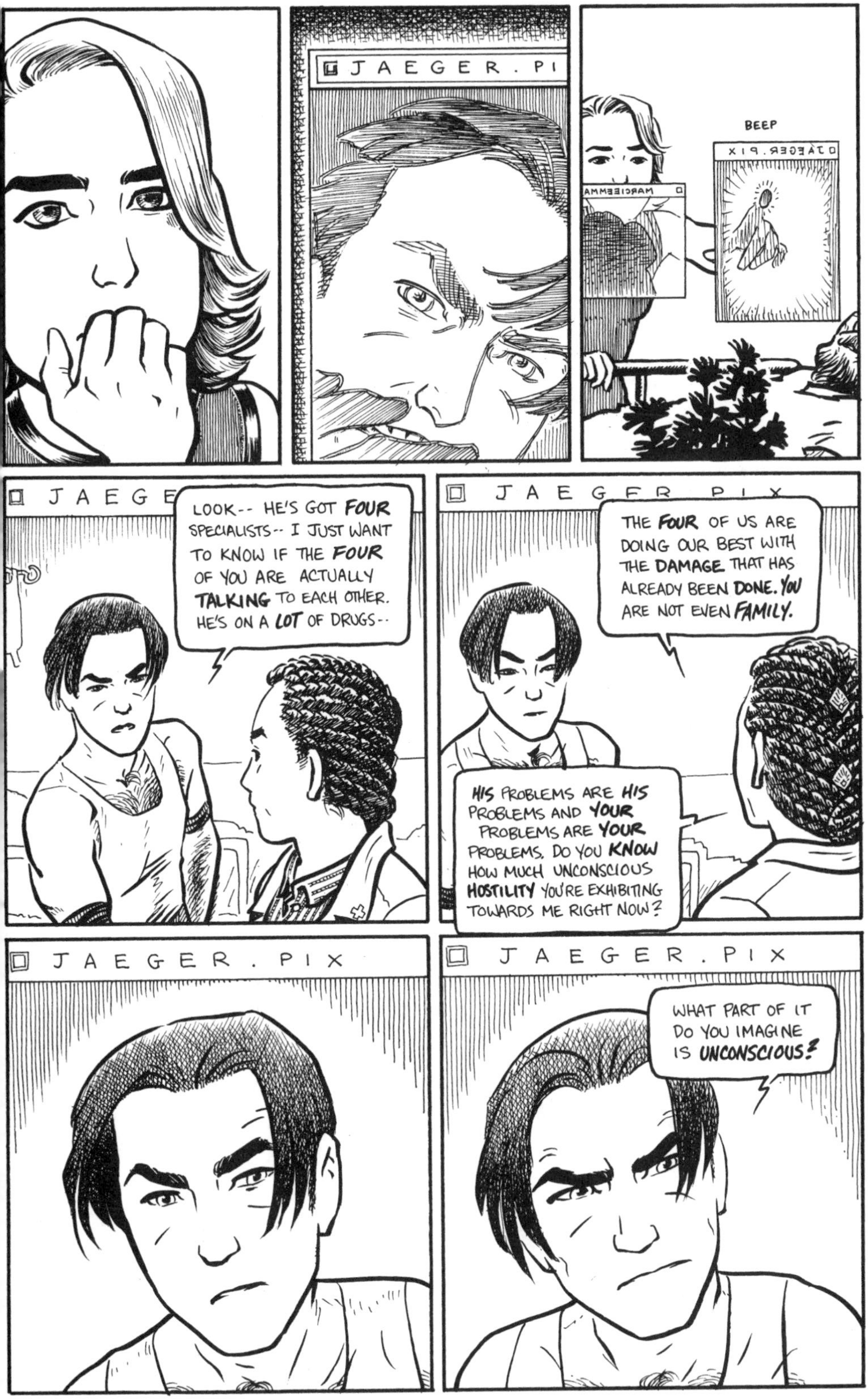
JAEGER.PI
BEEP
JAEGER.PIX
MARCIEMMA
JAEGE
LOOK-- HE'S GOT FOUR SPECIALISTS-- I JUST WANT TO KNOW IF THE FOUR OF YOU ARE ACTUALLY TALKING TO EACH OTHER. HE'S ON A LOT OF DRUGS--
JAEGER.PIX
THE FOUR OF US ARE DOING OUR BEST WITH THE DAMAGE THAT HAS ALREADY BEEN DONE. YOU ARE NOT EVEN FAMILY.
HIS PROBLEMS ARE HIS PROBLEMS AND YOUR PROBLEMS ARE YOUR PROBLEMS. DO YOU KNOW HOW MUCH UNCONSCIOUS HOSTILITY YOU'RE EXHIBITING TOWARDS ME RIGHT NOW?
JAEGER.PIX
JAEGER.PIX
WHAT PART OF IT DO YOU IMAGINE IS UNCONSCIOUS?

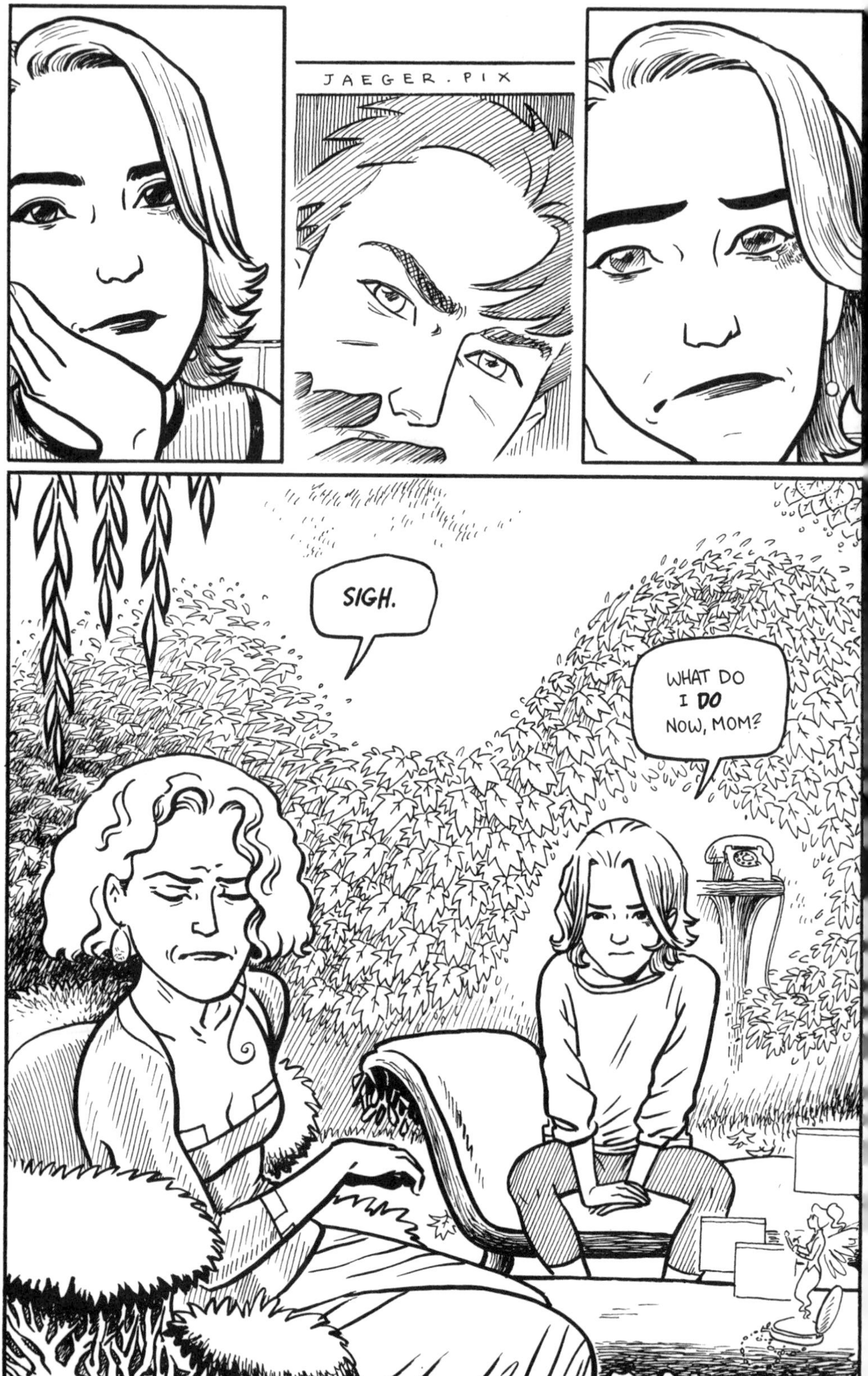
JAEGER.PIX
SIGH.
WHAT DO I DO NOW, MOM?

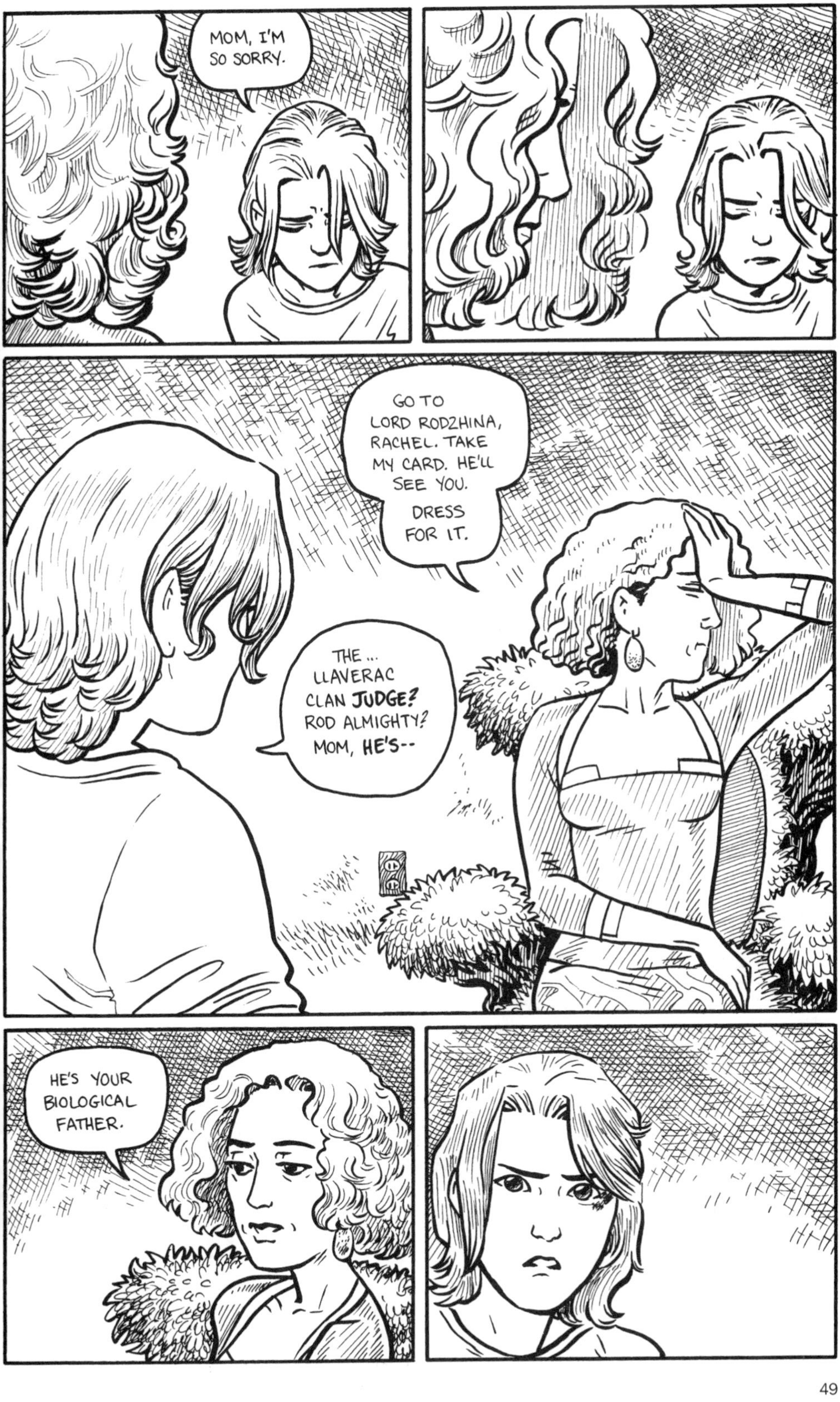
MOM, I'M SO SORRY.
GO TO LORD RODZHINA, RACHEL. TAKE MY CARD. HE'LL SEE YOU.
DRESS FOR IT.
THE... LLAVERAC CLAN JUDGE? ROD ALMIGHTY? MOM, HE'S--
HE'S YOUR BIOLOGICAL FATHER.

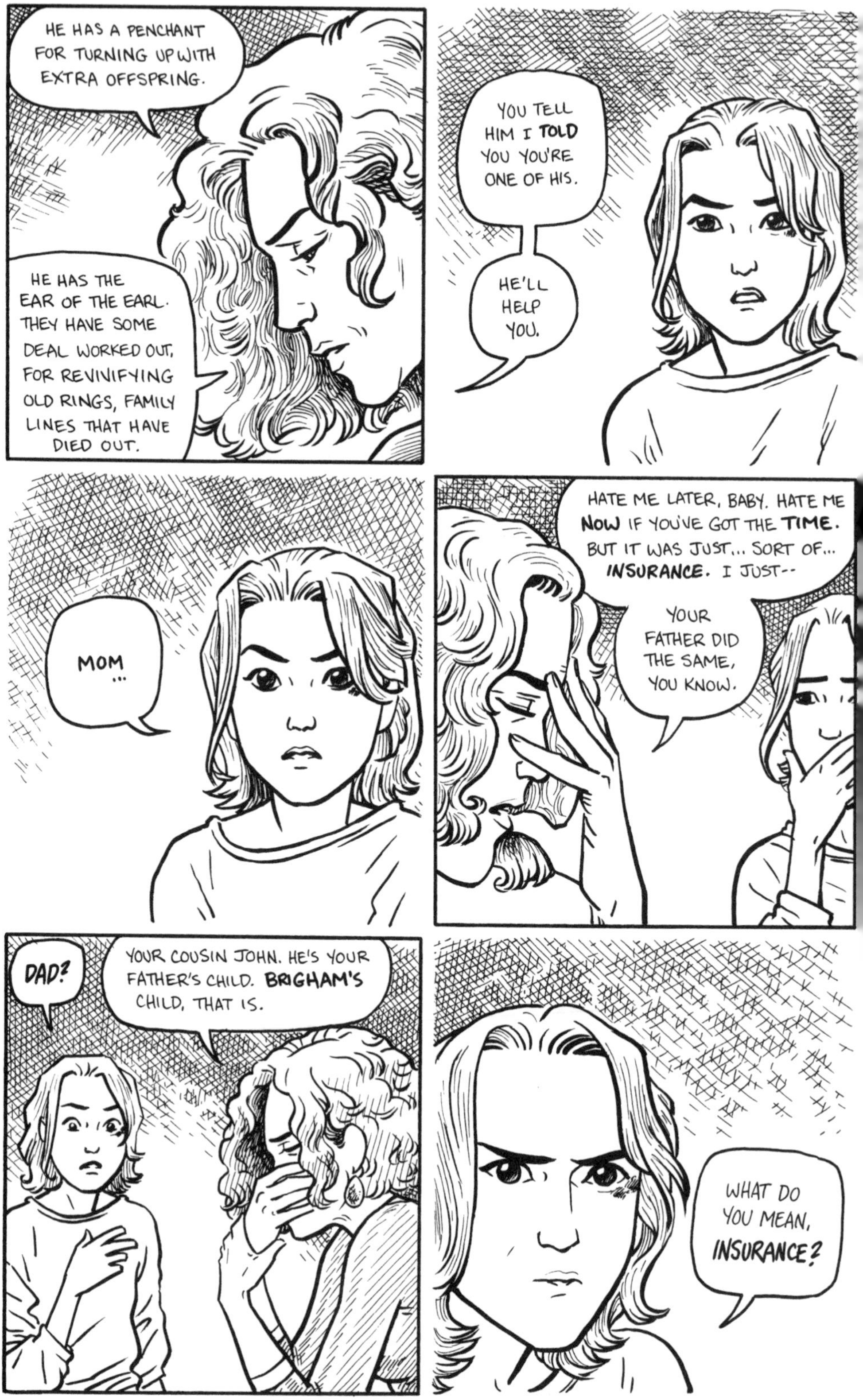
HE HAS A PENCHANT FOR TURNING UP WITH EXTRA OFFSPRING.
HE HAS THE EAR OF THE EARL. THEY HAVE SOME DEAL WORKED OUT, FOR REVIVIFYING OLD RINGS, FAMILY LINES THAT HAVE DIED OUT.
YOU TELL HIM I **TOLD** YOU YOU'RE ONE OF HIS.
HE'LL HELP YOU.
MOM...
HATE ME LATER, BABY. HATE ME **NOW** IF YOU'VE GOT THE **TIME**. BUT IT WAS JUST... SORT OF... ***INSURANCE***. I JUST--
YOUR FATHER DID THE SAME, YOU KNOW.
DAD?
YOUR COUSIN JOHN. HE'S YOUR FATHER'S CHILD. **BRIGHAM'S** CHILD, THAT IS.
WHAT DO YOU MEAN, **INSURANCE?**

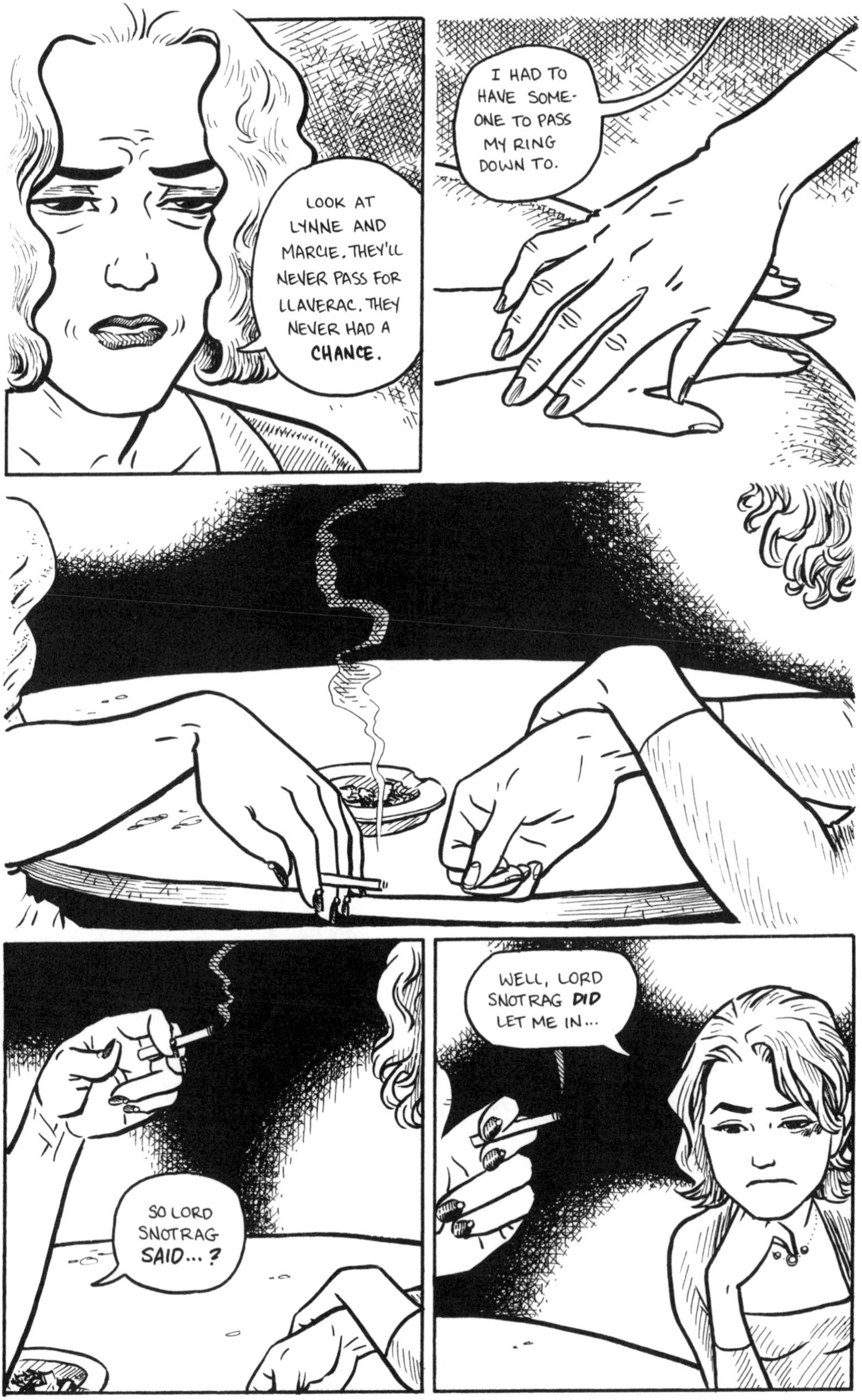
LOOK AT LYNNE AND MARCIE. THEY'LL NEVER PASS FOR LLAVERAC. THEY NEVER HAD A **CHANCE.**
I HAD TO HAVE SOME-ONE TO PASS MY RING DOWN TO.
SO LORD SNOTRAG **SAID...?**
WELL, LORD SNOTRAG **DID** LET ME IN...

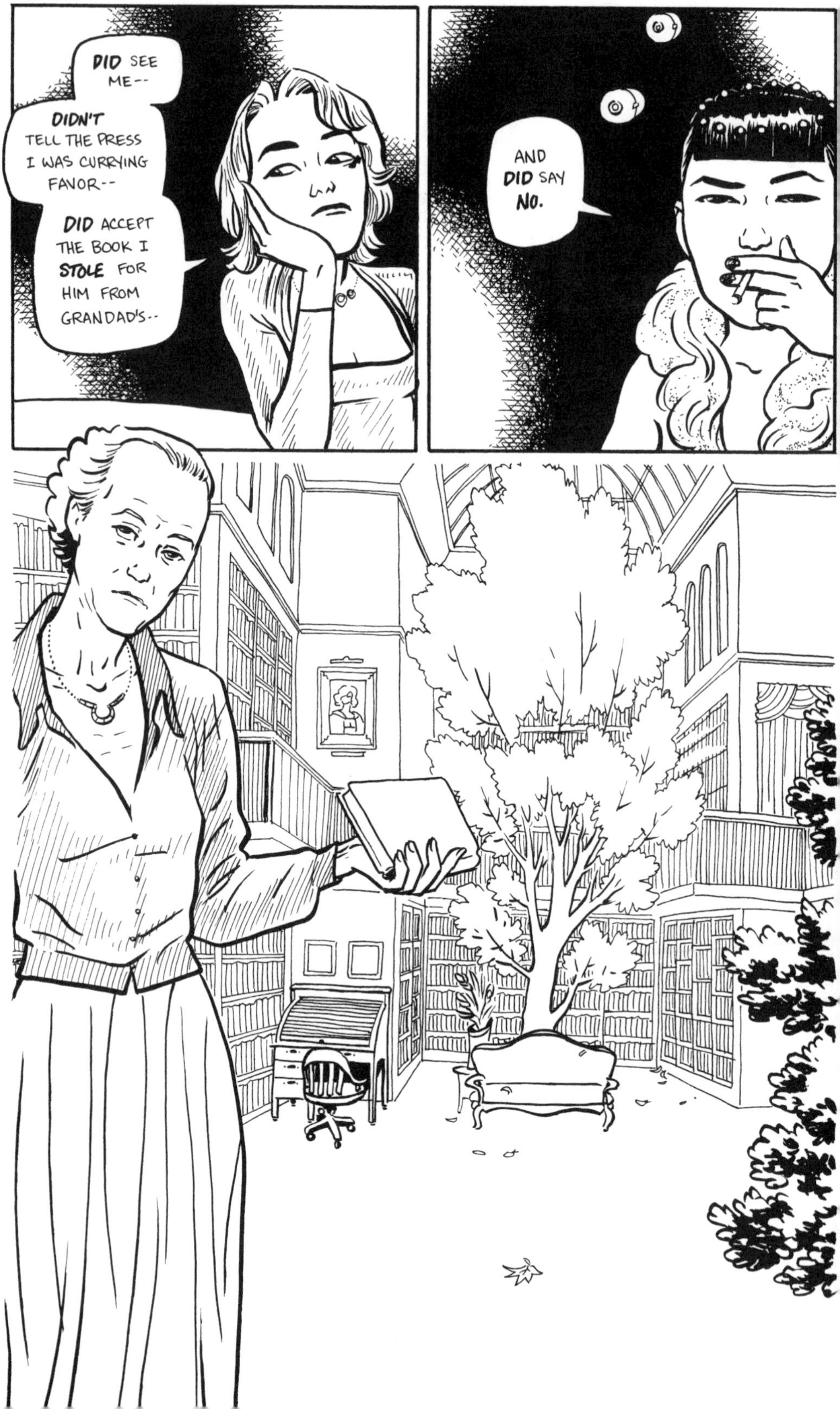
DID SEE ME--
DIDN'T TELL THE PRESS I WAS CURRYING FAVOR--
DID ACCEPT THE BOOK I STOLE FOR HIM FROM GRANDAD'S--
AND DID SAY NO.

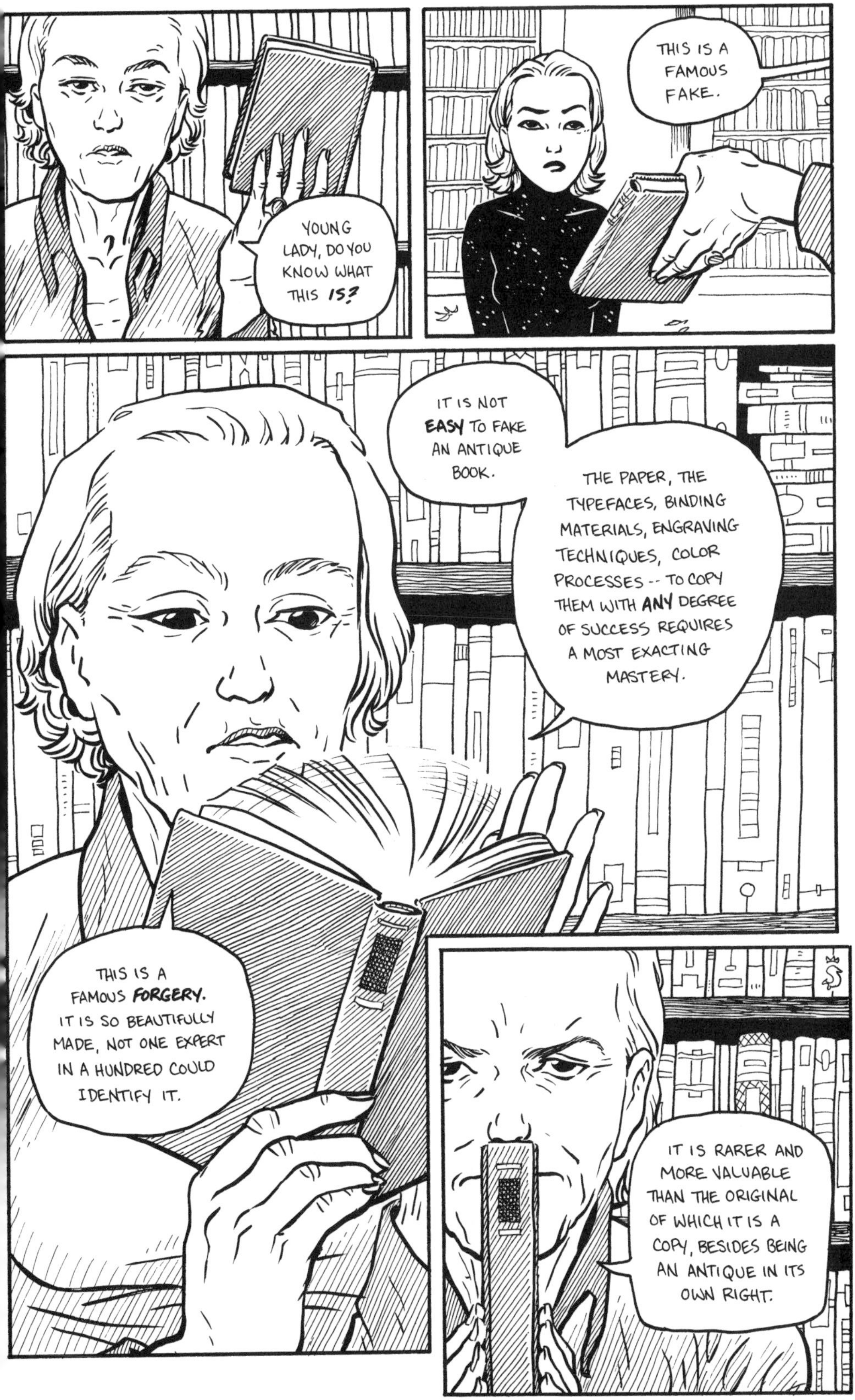
YOUNG LADY, DO YOU KNOW WHAT THIS IS?
THIS IS A FAMOUS FAKE.
IT IS NOT EASY TO FAKE AN ANTIQUE BOOK.
THE PAPER, THE TYPEFACES, BINDING MATERIALS, ENGRAVING TECHNIQUES, COLOR PROCESSES -- TO COPY THEM WITH ANY DEGREE OF SUCCESS REQUIRES A MOST EXACTING MASTERY.
THIS IS A FAMOUS FORGERY. IT IS SO BEAUTIFULLY MADE, NOT ONE EXPERT IN A HUNDRED COULD IDENTIFY IT.
IT IS RARER AND MORE VALUABLE THAN THE ORIGINAL OF WHICH IT IS A COPY, BESIDES BEING AN ANTIQUE IN ITS OWN RIGHT.

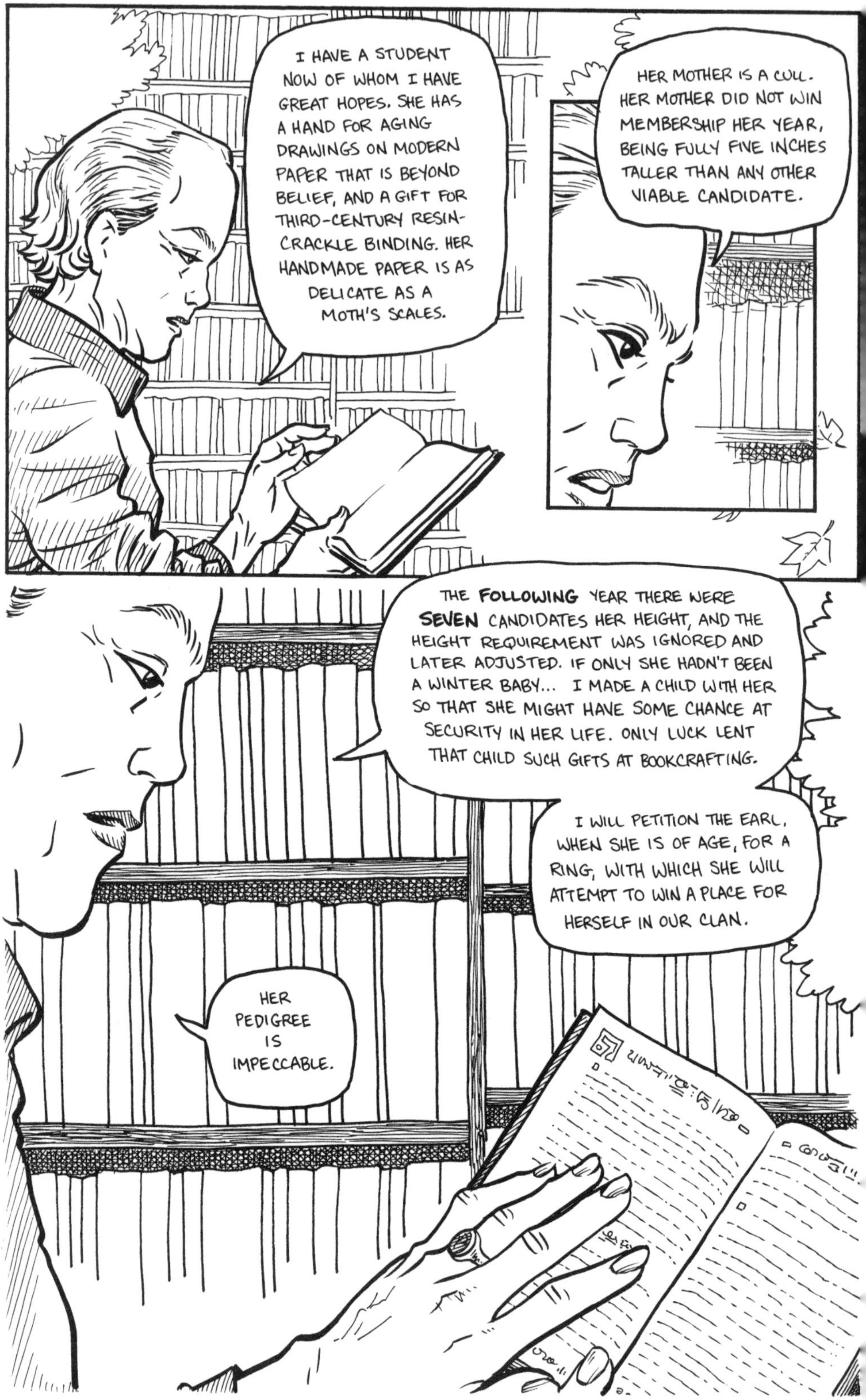
I HAVE A STUDENT NOW OF WHOM I HAVE GREAT HOPES. SHE HAS A HAND FOR AGING DRAWINGS ON MODERN PAPER THAT IS BEYOND BELIEF, AND A GIFT FOR THIRD-CENTURY RESIN-CRACKLE BINDING. HER HANDMADE PAPER IS AS DELICATE AS A MOTH'S SCALES.
HER MOTHER IS A CULL. HER MOTHER DID NOT WIN MEMBERSHIP HER YEAR, BEING FULLY FIVE INCHES TALLER THAN ANY OTHER VIABLE CANDIDATE.
THE **FOLLOWING** YEAR THERE WERE **SEVEN** CANDIDATES HER HEIGHT, AND THE HEIGHT REQUIREMENT WAS IGNORED AND LATER ADJUSTED. IF ONLY SHE HADN'T BEEN A WINTER BABY... I MADE A CHILD WITH HER SO THAT SHE MIGHT HAVE SOME CHANCE AT SECURITY IN HER LIFE. ONLY LUCK LENT THAT CHILD SUCH GIFTS AT BOOKCRAFTING.
I WILL PETITION THE EARL, WHEN SHE IS OF AGE, FOR A RING, WITH WHICH SHE WILL ATTEMPT TO WIN A PLACE FOR HERSELF IN OUR CLAN.
HER PEDIGREE IS IMPECCABLE.

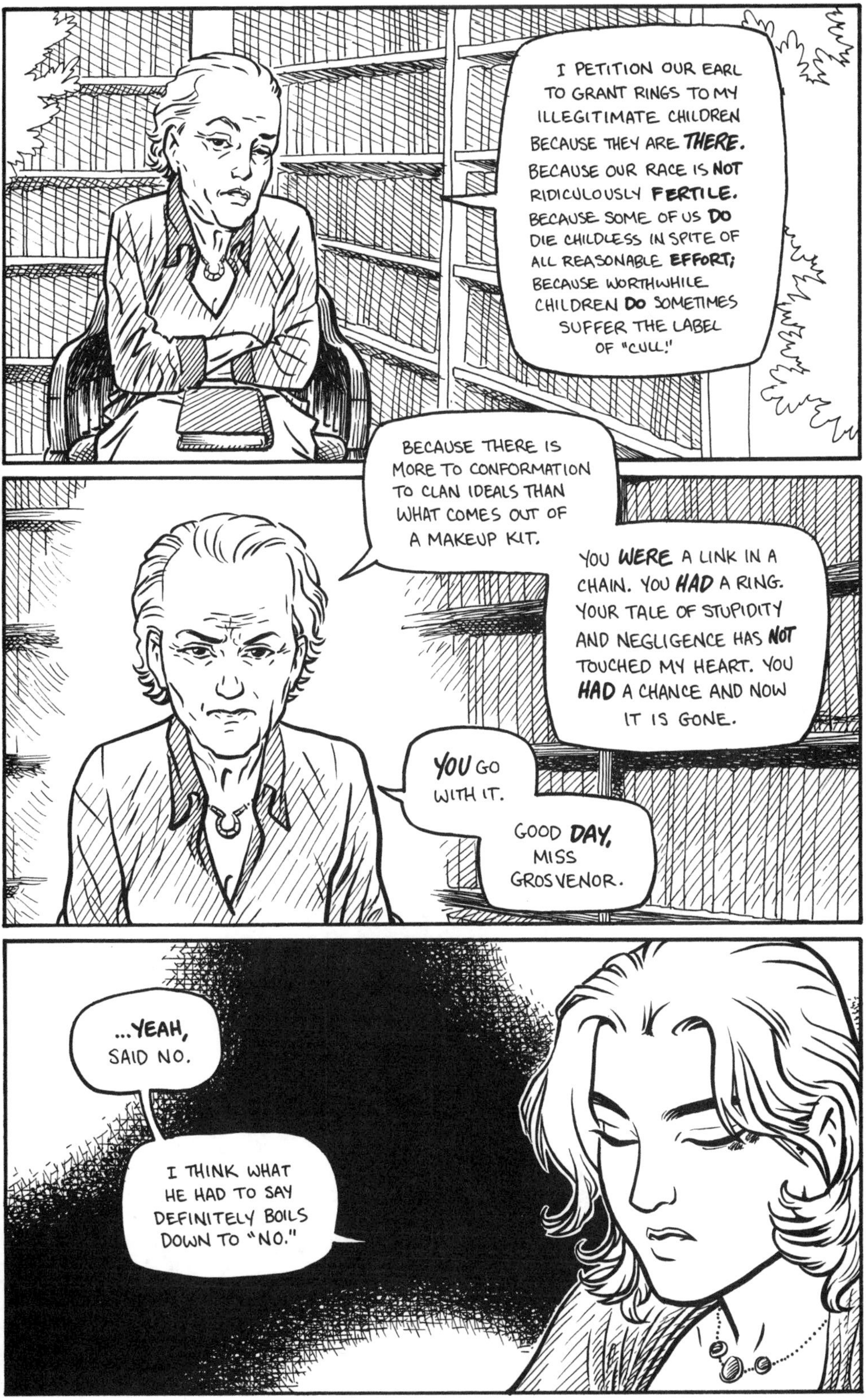
I PETITION OUR EARL TO GRANT RINGS TO MY ILLEGITIMATE CHILDREN BECAUSE THEY ARE THERE. BECAUSE OUR RACE IS NOT RIDICULOUSLY FERTILE. BECAUSE SOME OF US DO DIE CHILDLESS IN SPITE OF ALL REASONABLE EFFORT; BECAUSE WORTHWHILE CHILDREN DO SOMETIMES SUFFER THE LABEL OF "CULL."
BECAUSE THERE IS MORE TO CONFORMATION TO CLAN IDEALS THAN WHAT COMES OUT OF A MAKEUP KIT.
YOU WERE A LINK IN A CHAIN. YOU HAD A RING. YOUR TALE OF STUPIDITY AND NEGLIGENCE HAS NOT TOUCHED MY HEART. YOU HAD A CHANCE AND NOW IT IS GONE.
YOU GO WITH IT.
GOOD DAY, MISS GROSVENOR.
...YEAH, SAID NO.
I THINK WHAT HE HAD TO SAY DEFINITELY BOILS DOWN TO "NO."

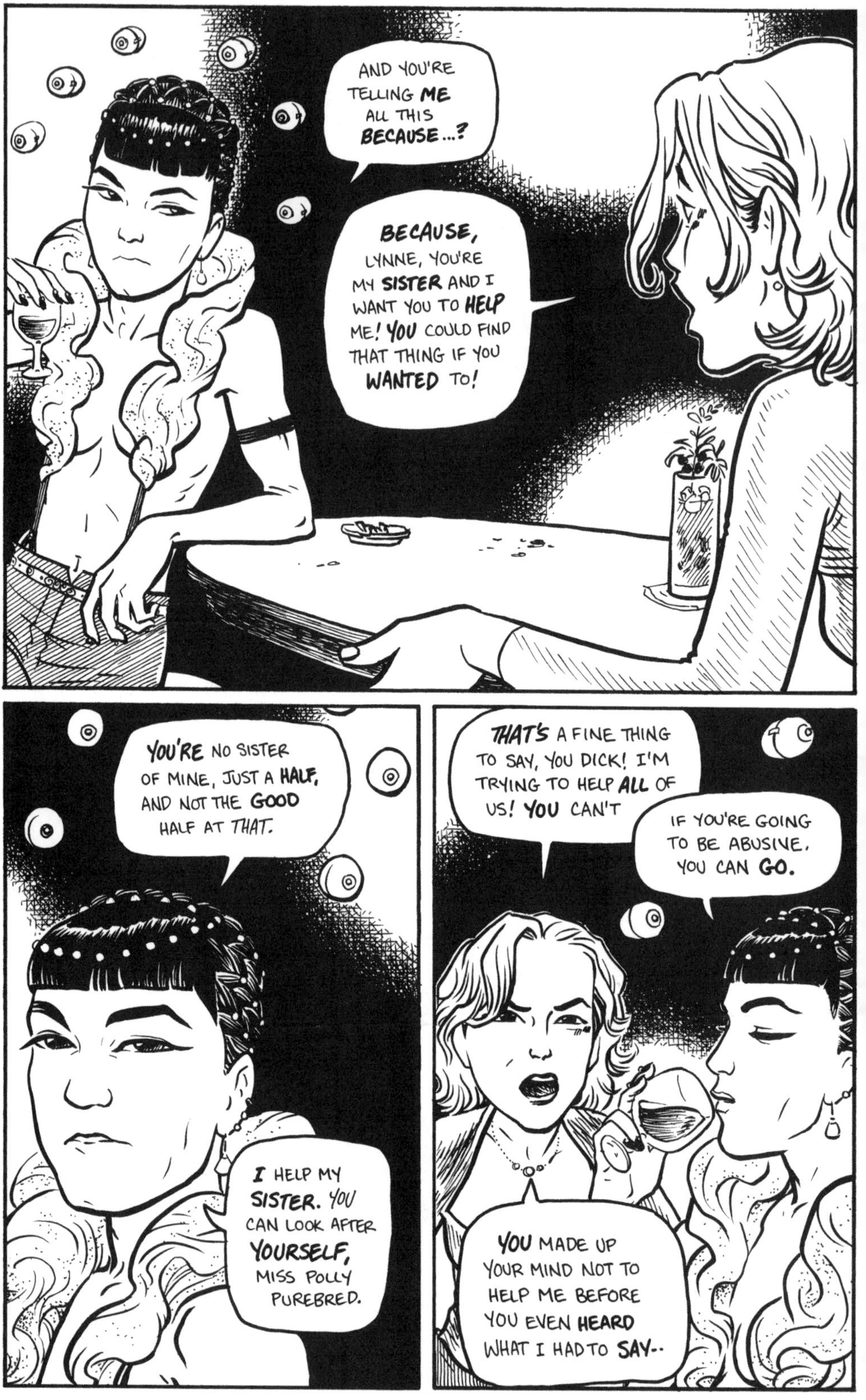
AND YOU'RE TELLING ME ALL THIS BECAUSE...?
BECAUSE, LYNNE, YOU'RE MY SISTER AND I WANT YOU TO HELP ME! YOU COULD FIND THAT THING IF YOU WANTED TO!
YOU'RE NO SISTER OF MINE, JUST A HALF, AND NOT THE GOOD HALF AT THAT.
I HELP MY SISTER. YOU CAN LOOK AFTER YOURSELF, MISS POLLY PUREBRED.
THAT'S A FINE THING TO SAY, YOU DICK! I'M TRYING TO HELP ALL OF US! YOU CAN'T
IF YOU'RE GOING TO BE ABUSIVE, YOU CAN GO.
YOU MADE UP YOUR MIND NOT TO HELP ME BEFORE YOU EVEN HEARD WHAT I HAD TO SAY..

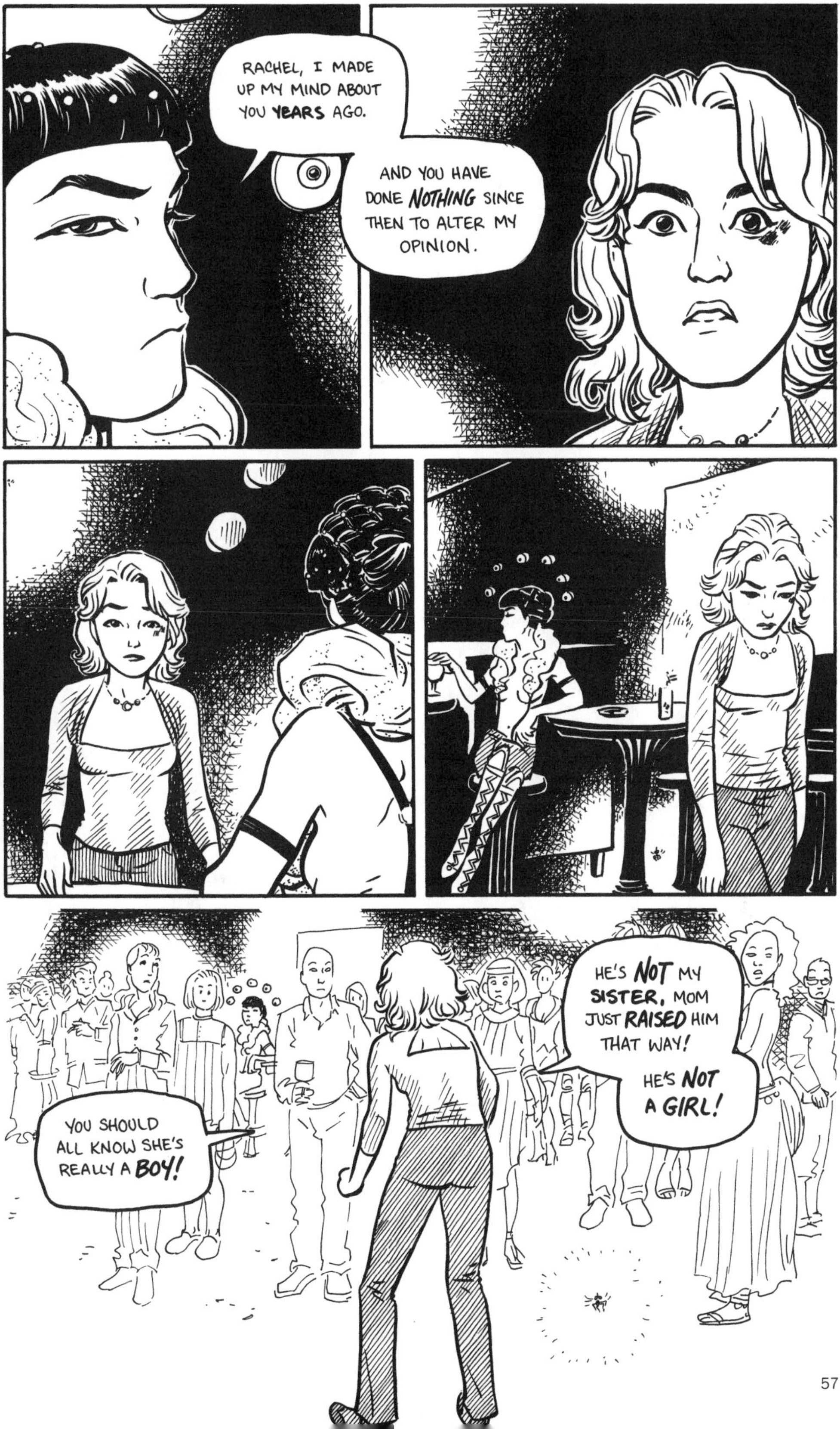
RACHEL, I MADE UP MY MIND ABOUT YOU YEARS AGO.
AND YOU HAVE DONE NOTHING SINCE THEN TO ALTER MY OPINION.
YOU SHOULD ALL KNOW SHE'S REALLY A BOY!
HE'S NOT MY SISTER, MOM JUST RAISED HIM THAT WAY!
HE'S NOT A GIRL!

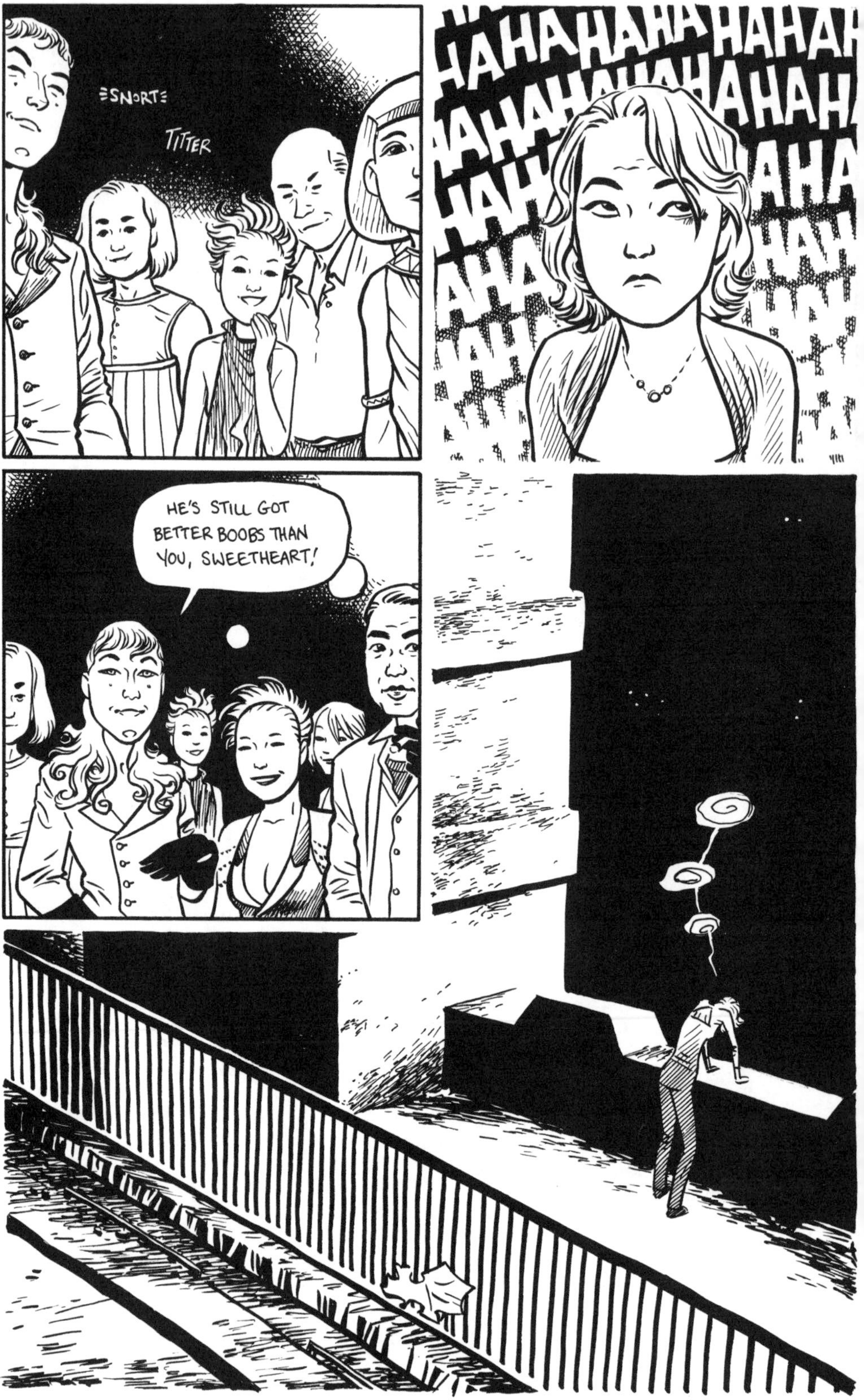
SNORT
TITTER
HAHAHAHAHAHAHAH
HE'S STILL GOT BETTER BOOBS THAN YOU, SWEETHEART!

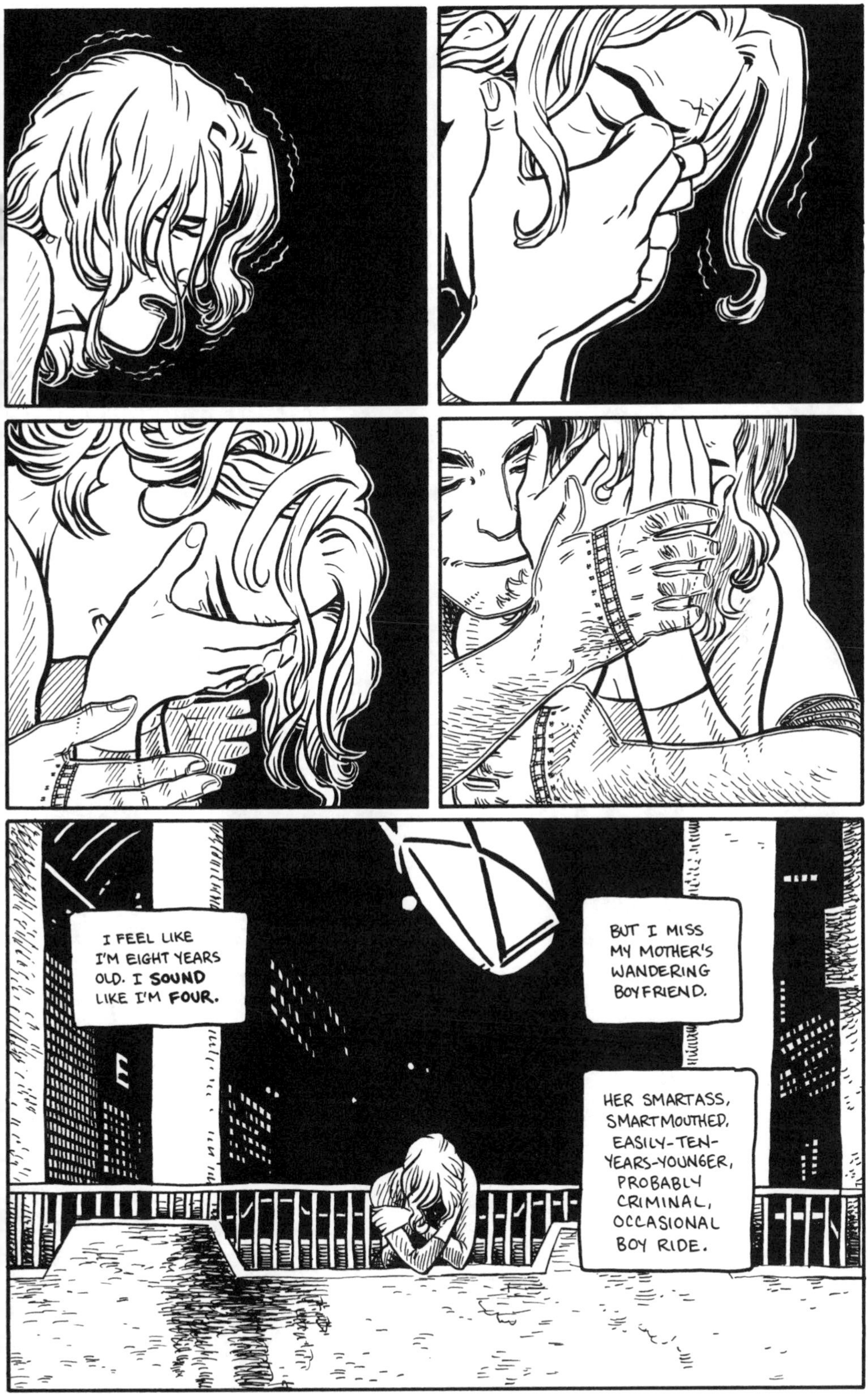
I FEEL LIKE I'M EIGHT YEARS OLD. I **SOUND** LIKE I'M **FOUR**.
BUT I MISS MY MOTHER'S WANDERING BOYFRIEND.
HER SMARTASS, SMARTMOUTHED, EASILY-TEN-YEARS-YOUNGER, PROBABLY CRIMINAL, OCCASIONAL BOY RIDE.

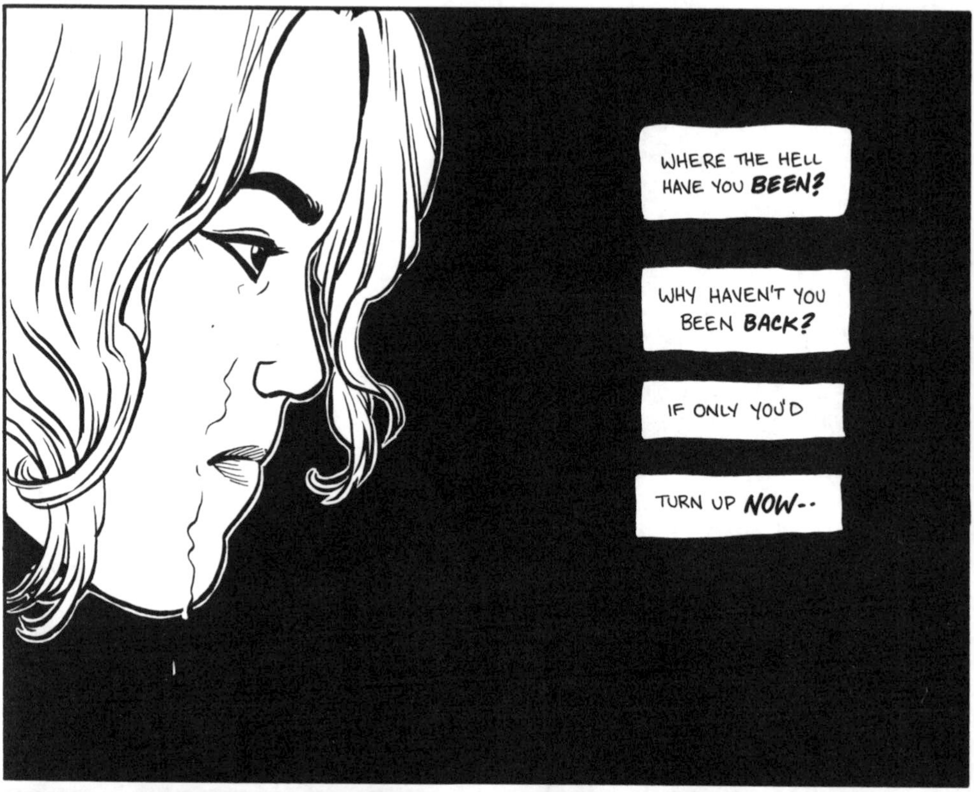
WHERE THE HELL HAVE YOU **BEEN?**
WHY HAVEN'T YOU BEEN **BACK?**
IF ONLY YOU'D
TURN UP **NOW**--

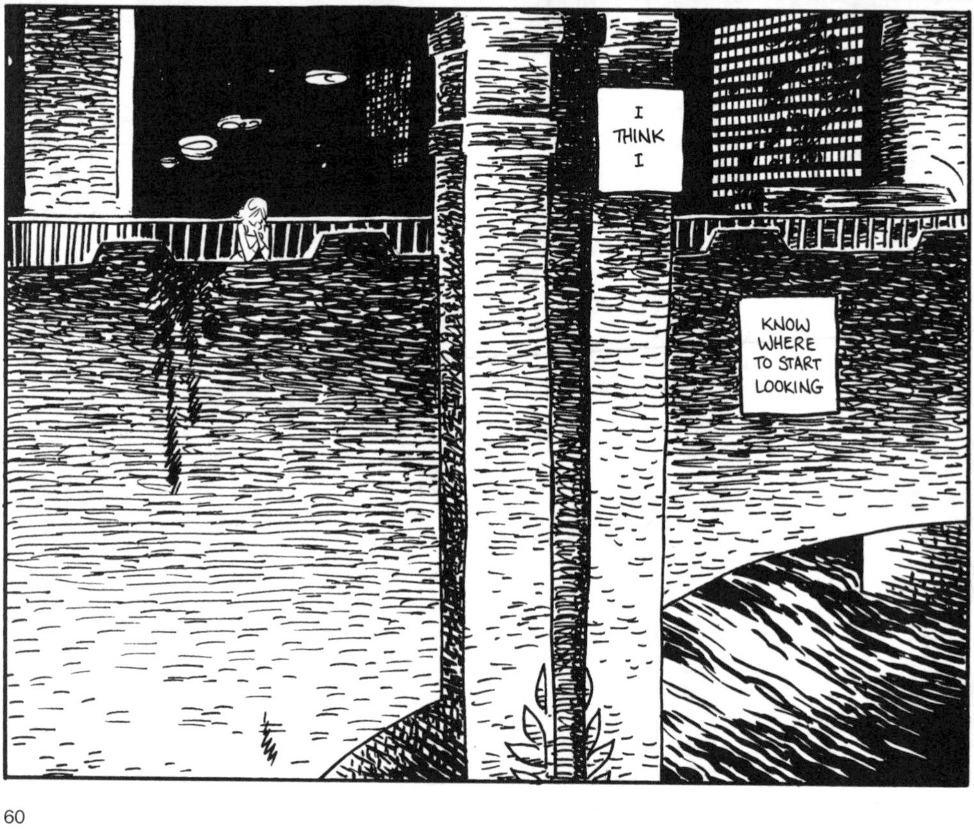
I THINK I
KNOW WHERE TO START LOOKING

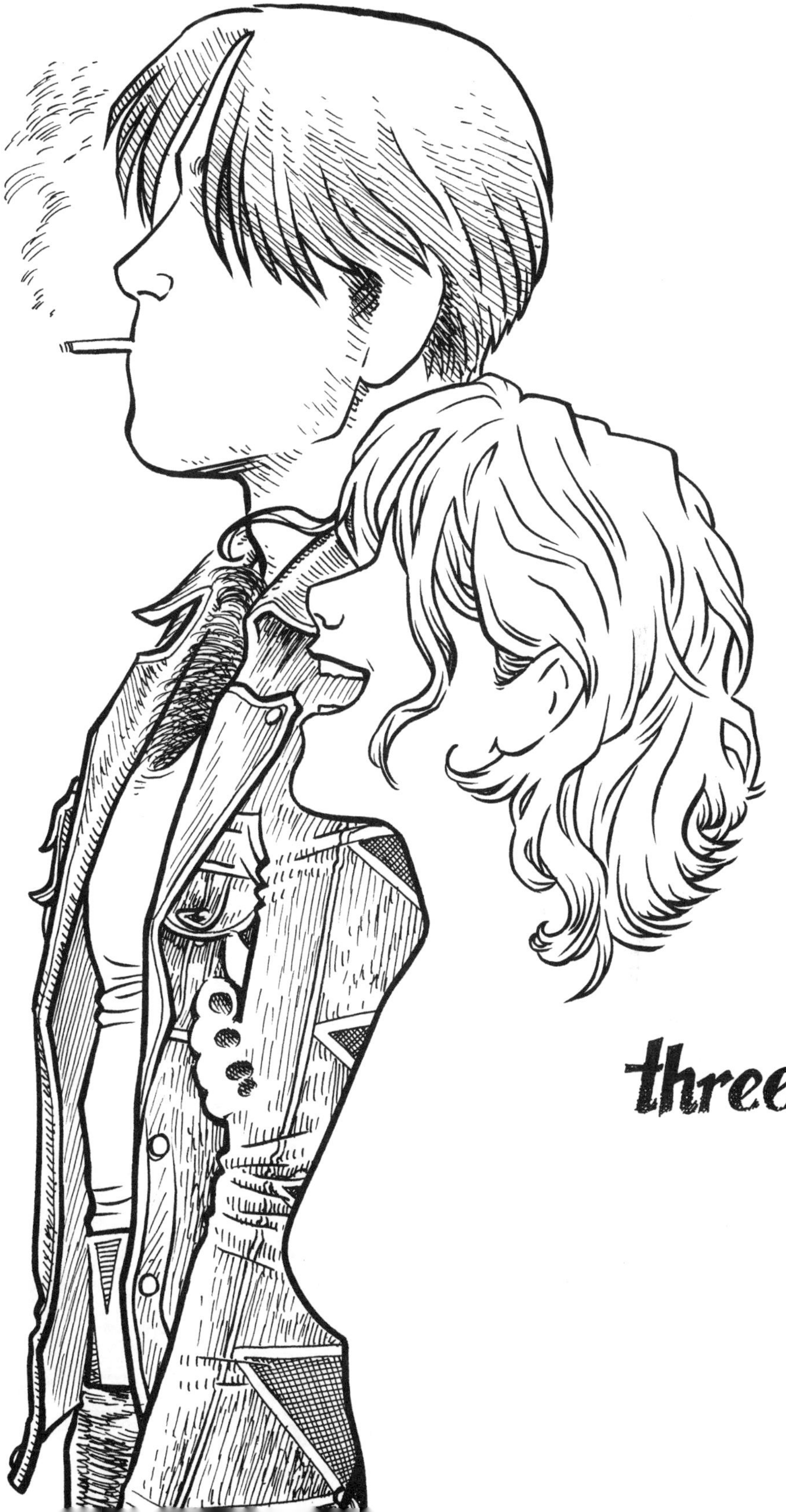

three:

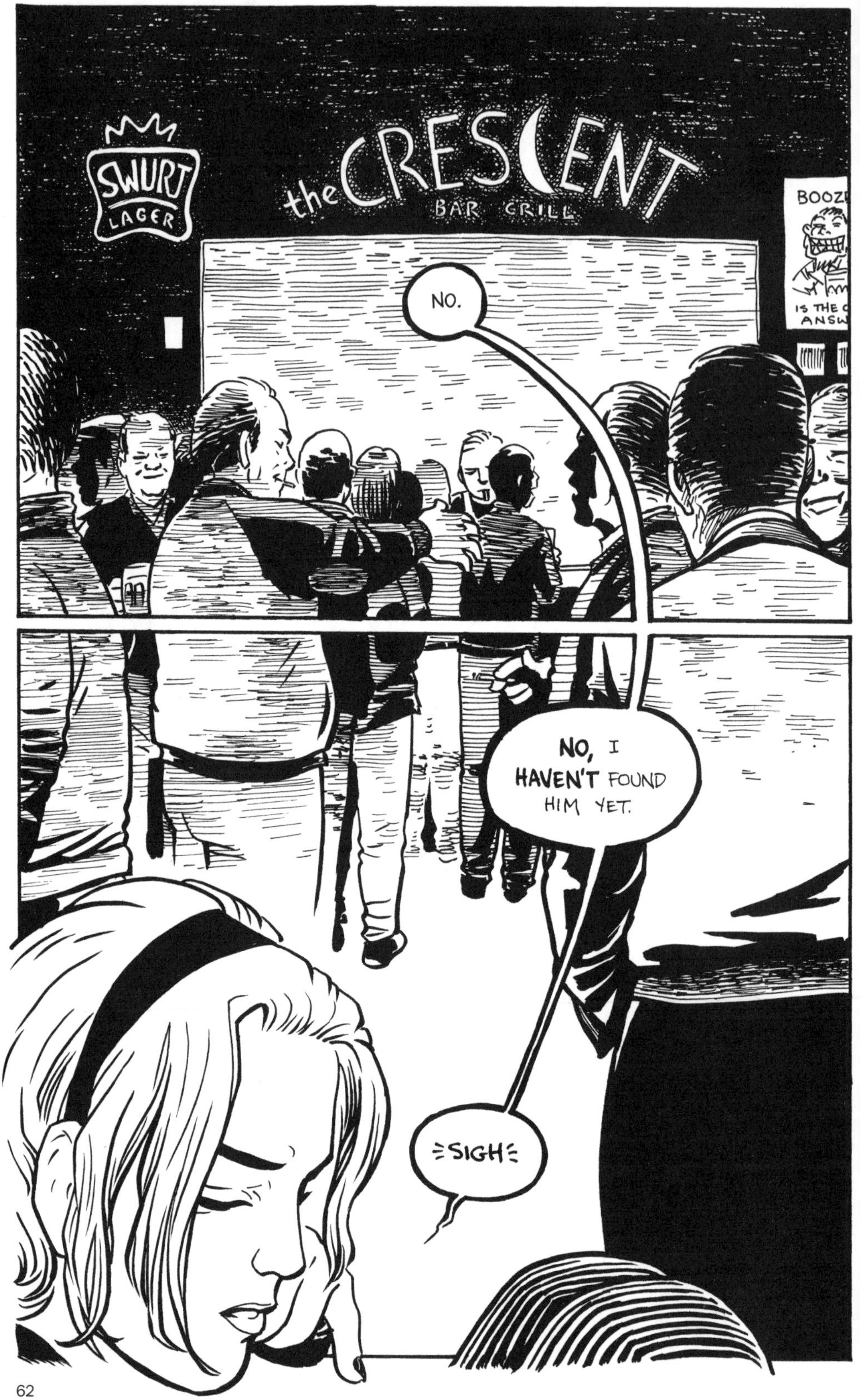
SWURT
LAGER
the CRESCENT
BAR GRILL
BOOZE
IS THE
ANSW
NO.
NO, I HAVEN'T FOUND HIM YET.
SIGH

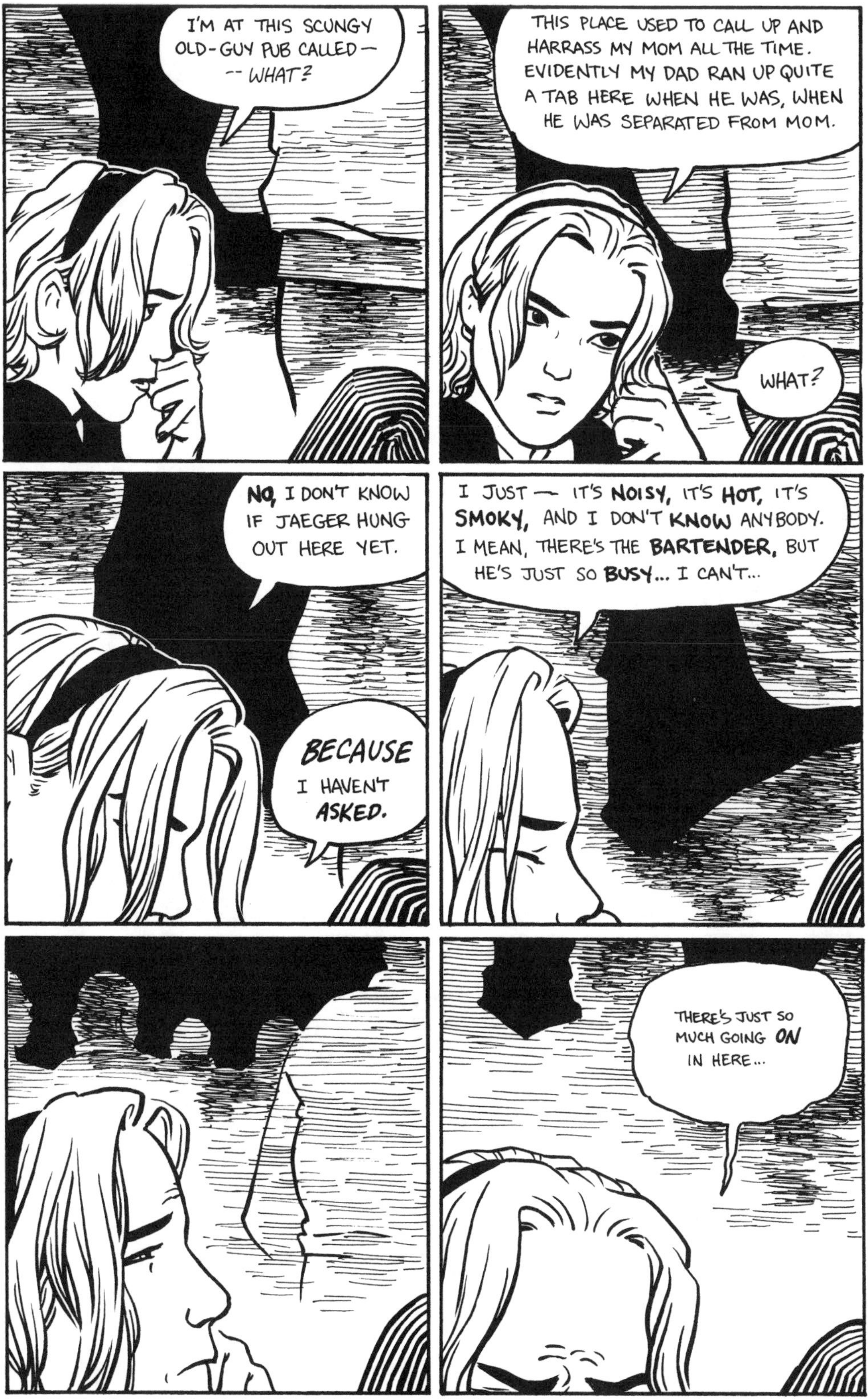
I'M AT THIS SCUNGY OLD-GUY PUB CALLED—
-- WHAT?
THIS PLACE USED TO CALL UP AND HARRASS MY MOM ALL THE TIME. EVIDENTLY MY DAD RAN UP QUITE A TAB HERE WHEN HE WAS, WHEN HE WAS SEPARATED FROM MOM.
WHAT?
NO, I DON'T KNOW IF JAEGER HUNG OUT HERE YET.
BECAUSE I HAVEN'T ASKED.
I JUST — IT'S NOISY, IT'S HOT, IT'S SMOKY, AND I DON'T KNOW ANYBODY. I MEAN, THERE'S THE BARTENDER, BUT HE'S JUST SO BUSY... I CAN'T...
THERE'S JUST SO MUCH GOING ON IN HERE...

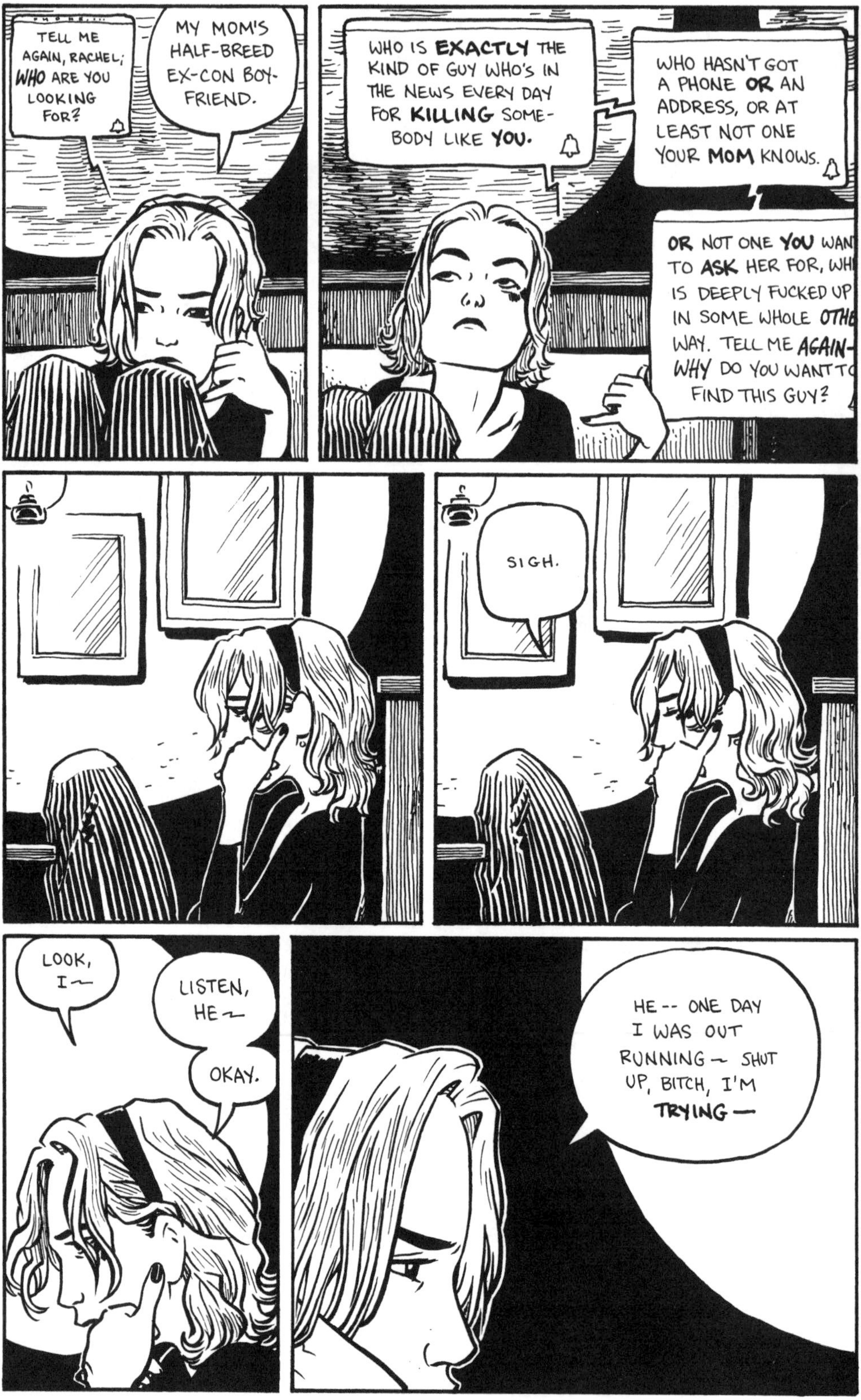
TELL ME AGAIN, RACHEL; WHO ARE YOU LOOKING FOR?
MY MOM'S HALF-BREED EX-CON BOY-FRIEND.
WHO IS EXACTLY THE KIND OF GUY WHO'S IN THE NEWS EVERY DAY FOR KILLING SOME-BODY LIKE YOU.
WHO HASN'T GOT A PHONE OR AN ADDRESS, OR AT LEAST NOT ONE YOUR MOM KNOWS.
SIGH.
LOOK, I—
LISTEN, HE—
OKAY.
HE -- ONE DAY I WAS OUT RUNNING— SHUT UP, BITCH, I'M TRYING—

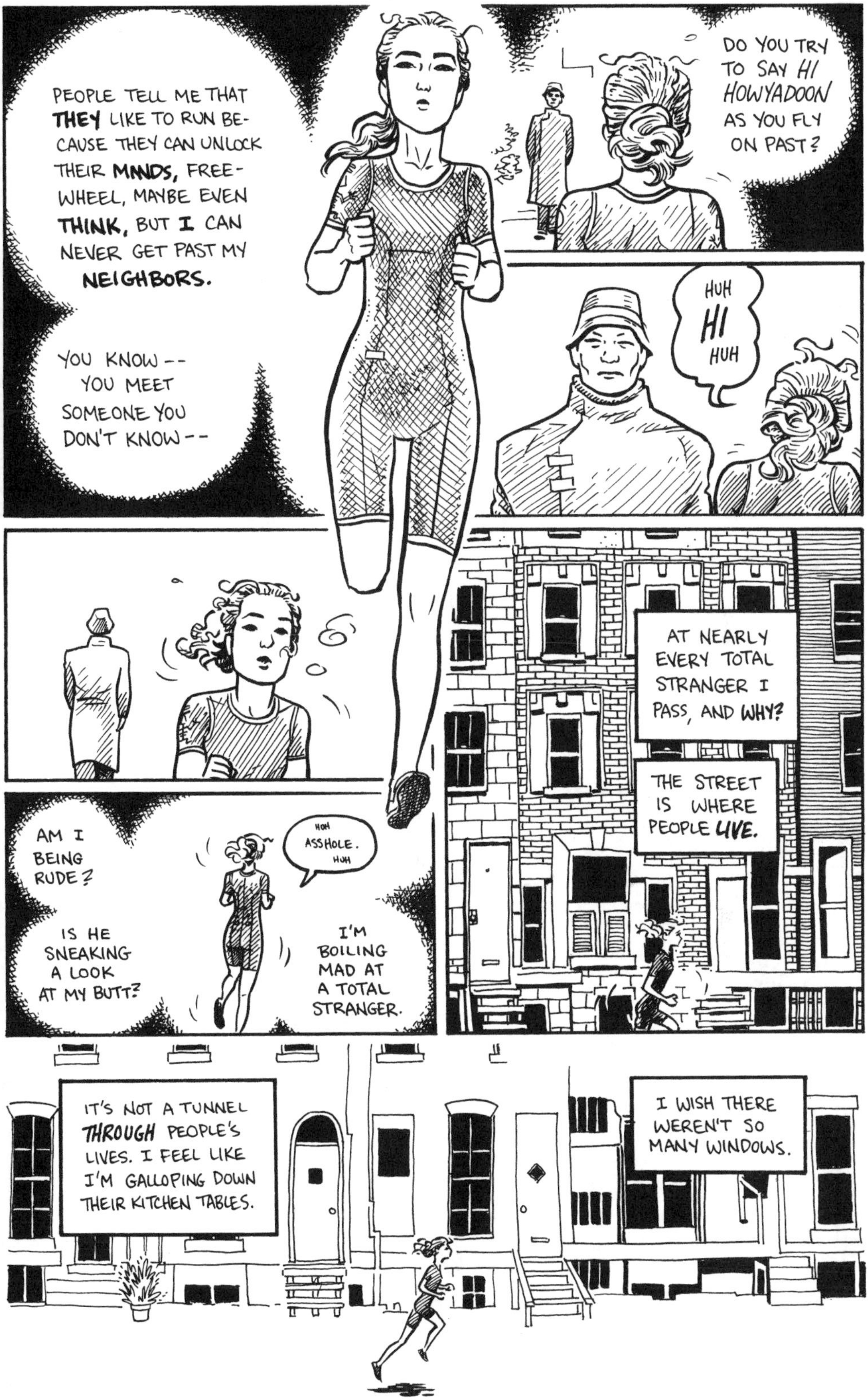
PEOPLE TELL ME THAT THEY LIKE TO RUN BECAUSE THEY CAN UNLOCK THEIR MINDS, FREE-WHEEL, MAYBE EVEN THINK, BUT I CAN NEVER GET PAST MY NEIGHBORS.
YOU KNOW -- YOU MEET SOMEONE YOU DON'T KNOW --
DO YOU TRY TO SAY HI HOWYADOON AS YOU FLY ON PAST?
HUH HI HUH
AT NEARLY EVERY TOTAL STRANGER I PASS, AND WHY?
THE STREET IS WHERE PEOPLE LIVE.
AM I BEING RUDE?
IS HE SNEAKING A LOOK AT MY BUTT?
HUH ASSHOLE. HUH
I'M BOILING MAD AT A TOTAL STRANGER.
IT'S NOT A TUNNEL THROUGH PEOPLE'S LIVES. I FEEL LIKE I'M GALLOPING DOWN THEIR KITCHEN TABLES.
I WISH THERE WEREN'T SO MANY WINDOWS.

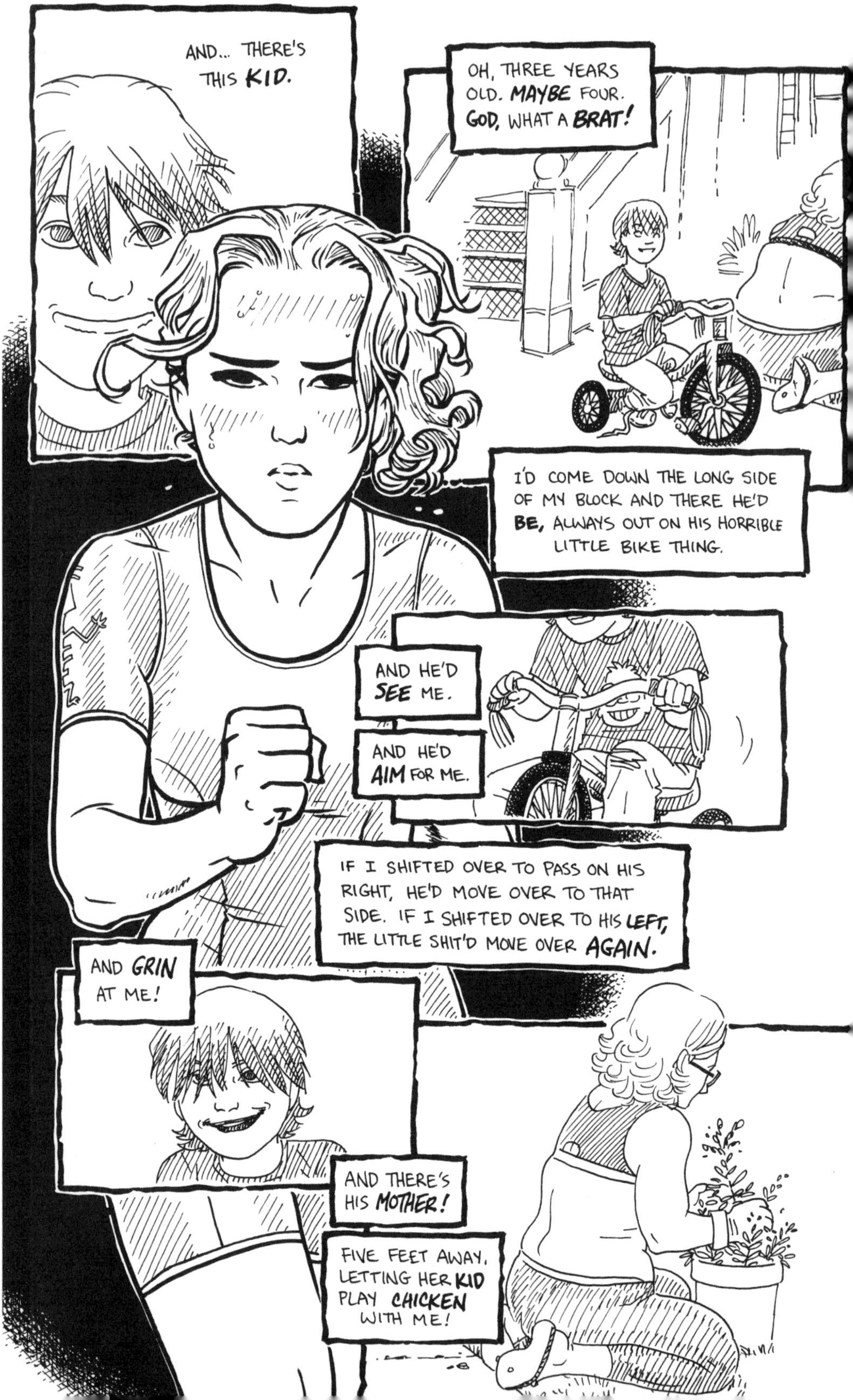
AND... THERE'S THIS **KID**.
OH, THREE YEARS OLD. **MAYBE** FOUR. **GOD**, WHAT A **BRAT**!
I'D COME DOWN THE LONG SIDE OF MY BLOCK AND THERE HE'D **BE**, ALWAYS OUT ON HIS HORRIBLE LITTLE BIKE THING.
AND HE'D **SEE** ME.
AND HE'D **AIM** FOR ME.
IF I SHIFTED OVER TO PASS ON HIS RIGHT, HE'D MOVE OVER TO THAT SIDE. IF I SHIFTED OVER TO HIS **LEFT**, THE LITTLE SHIT'D MOVE OVER **AGAIN**.
AND **GRIN** AT ME!
AND THERE'S HIS **MOTHER**!
FIVE FEET AWAY, LETTING HER **KID** PLAY **CHICKEN** WITH ME!

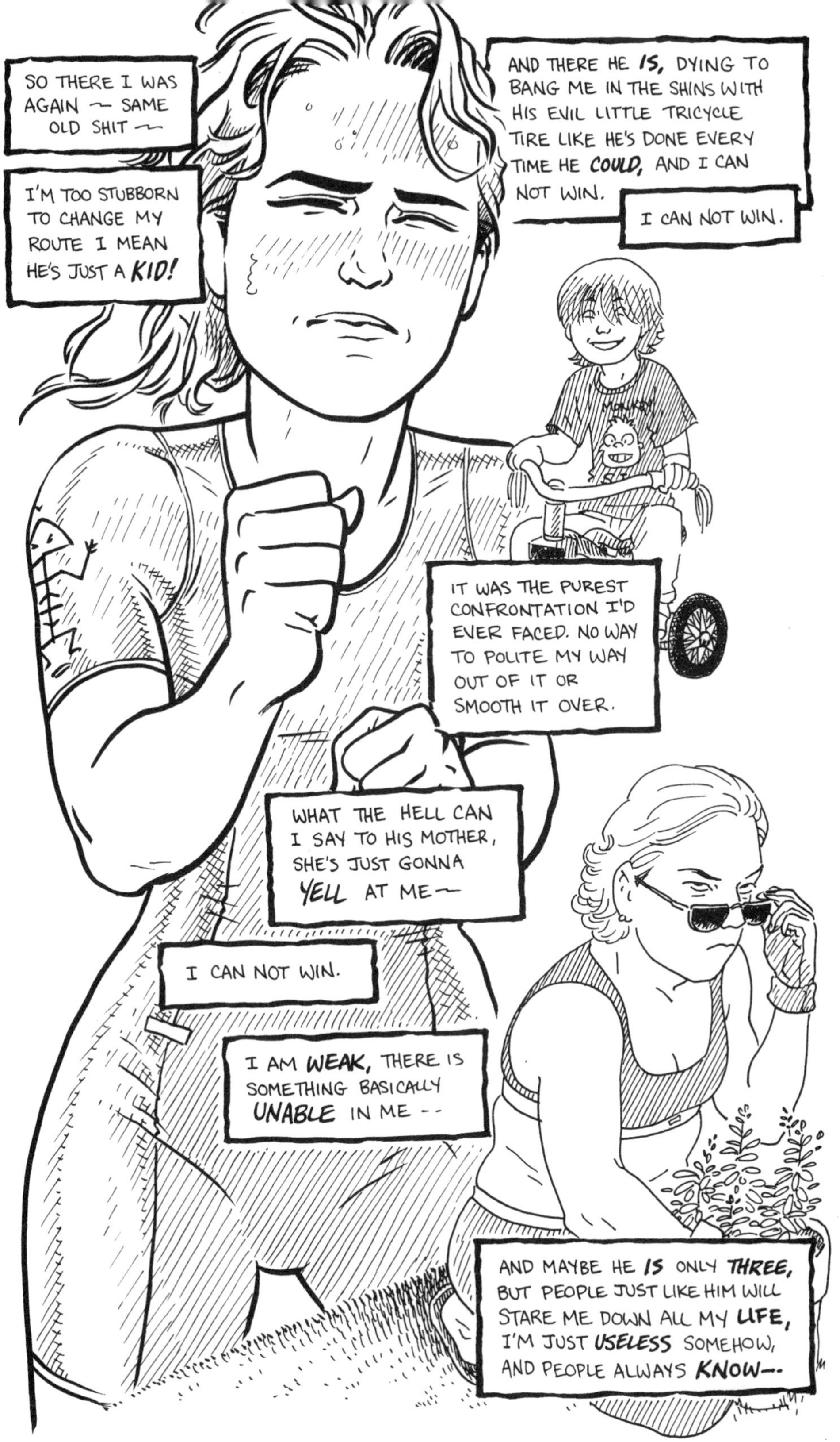

SO THERE I WAS AGAIN ~ SAME OLD SHIT ~
I'M TOO STUBBORN TO CHANGE MY ROUTE I MEAN HE'S JUST A KID!
AND THERE HE IS, DYING TO BANG ME IN THE SHINS WITH HIS EVIL LITTLE TRICYCLE TIRE LIKE HE'S DONE EVERY TIME HE COULD, AND I CAN NOT WIN.
I CAN NOT WIN.
IT WAS THE PUREST CONFRONTATION I'D EVER FACED. NO WAY TO POLITE MY WAY OUT OF IT OR SMOOTH IT OVER.
WHAT THE HELL CAN I SAY TO HIS MOTHER, SHE'S JUST GONNA YELL AT ME ~
I CAN NOT WIN.
I AM WEAK, THERE IS SOMETHING BASICALLY UNABLE IN ME --
AND MAYBE HE IS ONLY THREE, BUT PEOPLE JUST LIKE HIM WILL STARE ME DOWN ALL MY LIFE, I'M JUST USELESS SOMEHOW, AND PEOPLE ALWAYS KNOW--.

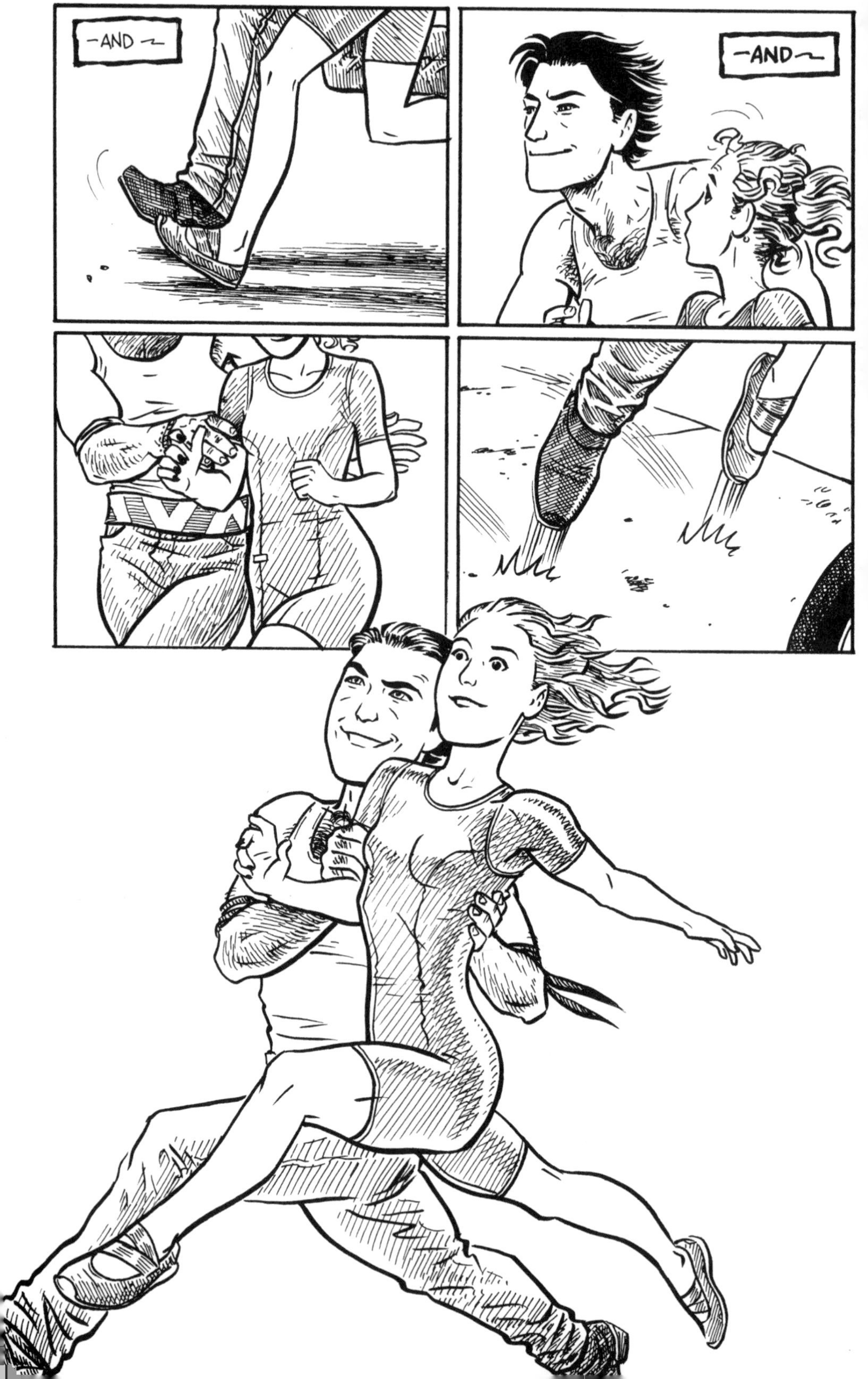

—AND—
—AND—

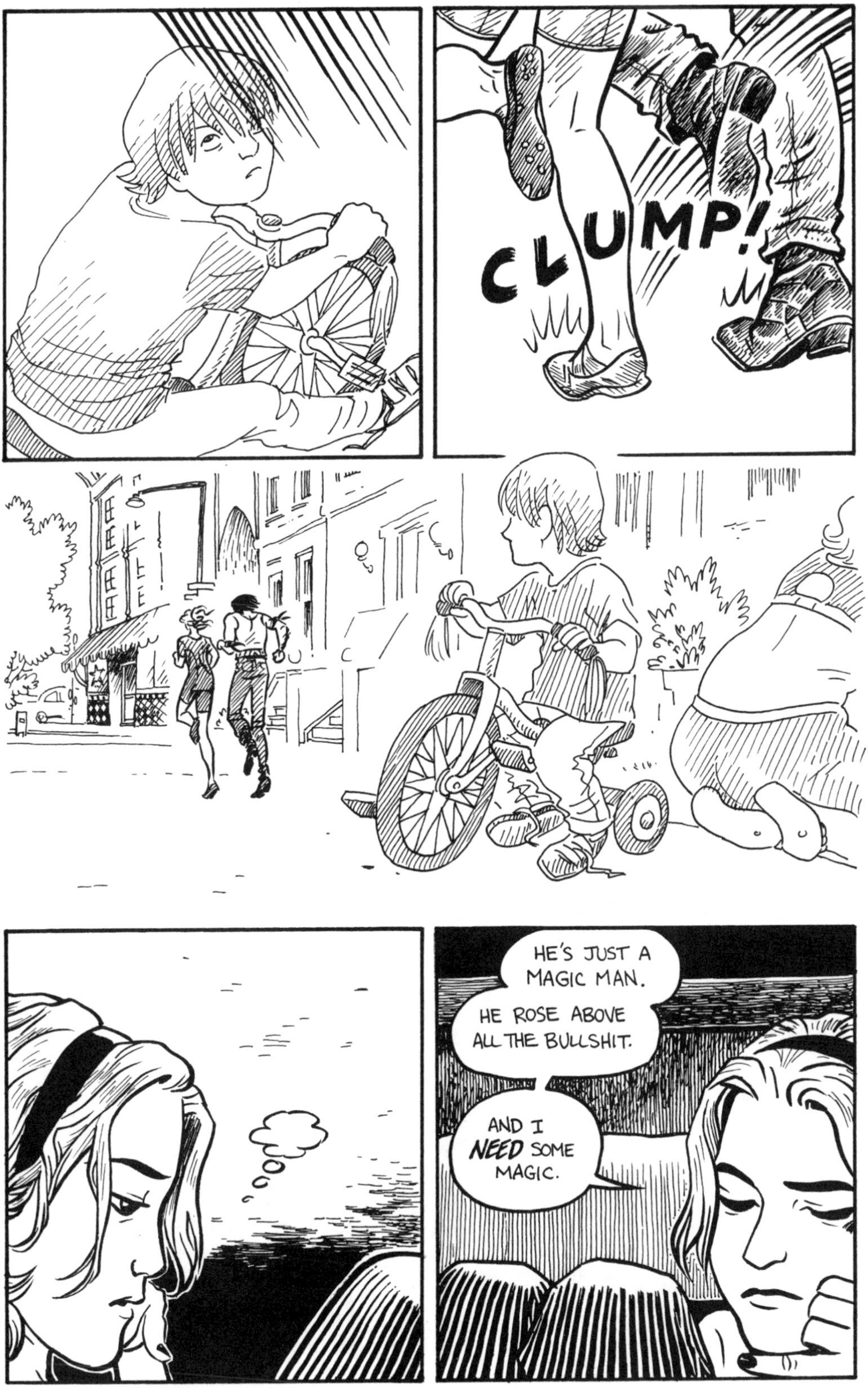
CLUMP!
HE'S JUST A MAGIC MAN.
HE ROSE ABOVE ALL THE BULLSHIT.
AND I *NEED* SOME MAGIC.

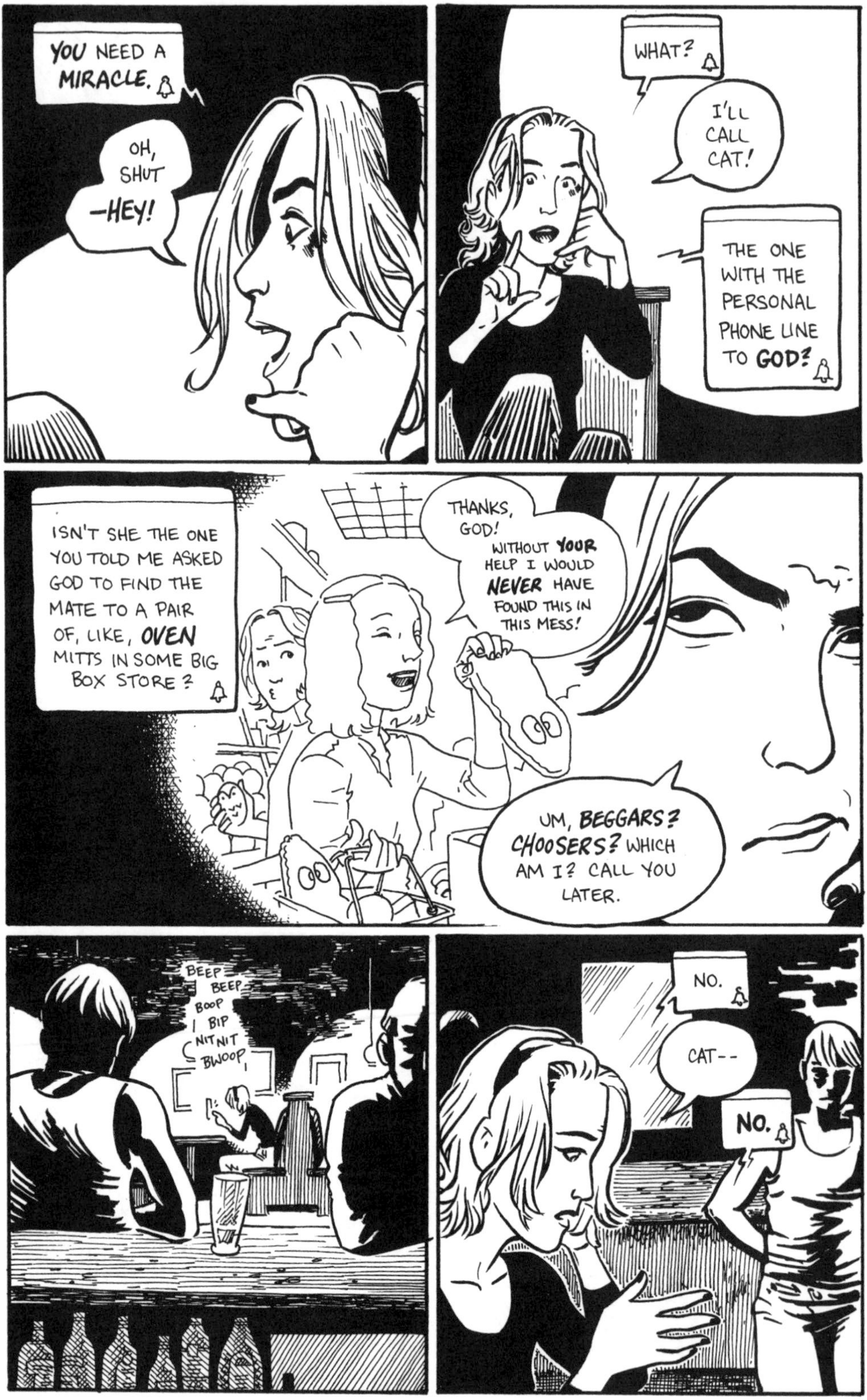
YOU NEED A MIRACLE.
OH, SHUT —HEY!
WHAT?
I'LL CALL CAT!
THE ONE WITH THE PERSONAL PHONE LINE TO GOD?
ISN'T SHE THE ONE YOU TOLD ME ASKED GOD TO FIND THE MATE TO A PAIR OF, LIKE, OVEN MITTS IN SOME BIG BOX STORE?
THANKS, GOD! WITHOUT YOUR HELP I WOULD NEVER HAVE FOUND THIS IN THIS MESS!
UM, BEGGARS? CHOOSERS? WHICH AM I? CALL YOU LATER.
BEEP BEEP BOOP BIP NITNIT BWOOP
NO.
CAT--
NO.

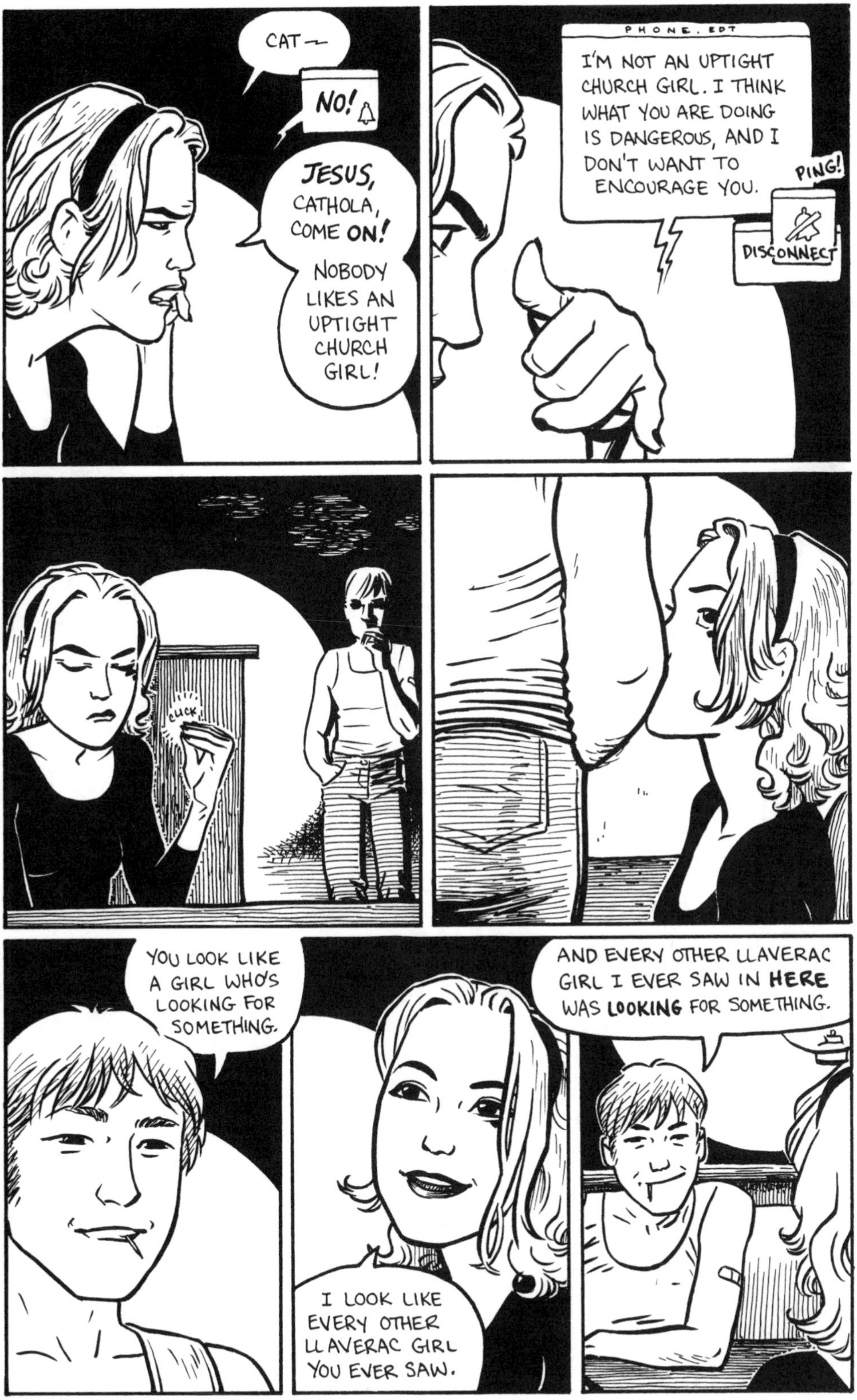
CAT—
NO!
JESUS, CATHOLA, COME ON!
NOBODY LIKES AN UPTIGHT CHURCH GIRL!
PHONE.EDT
I'M NOT AN UPTIGHT CHURCH GIRL. I THINK WHAT YOU ARE DOING IS DANGEROUS, AND I DON'T WANT TO ENCOURAGE YOU.
PING!
DISCONNECT
CLICK
YOU LOOK LIKE A GIRL WHO'S LOOKING FOR SOMETHING.
I LOOK LIKE EVERY OTHER LLAVERAC GIRL YOU EVER SAW.
AND EVERY OTHER LLAVERAC GIRL I EVER SAW IN HERE WAS LOOKING FOR SOMETHING.

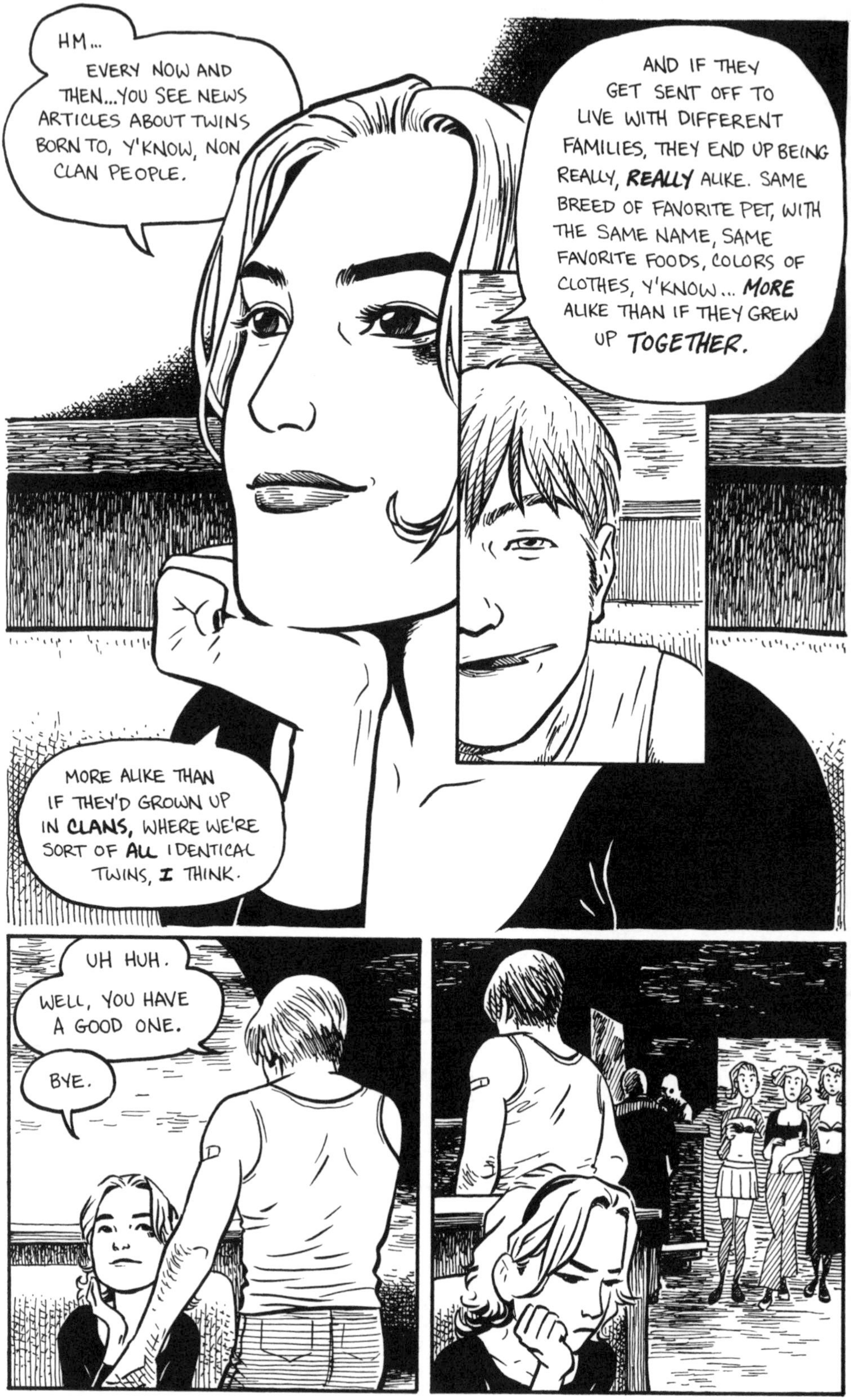
HM... EVERY NOW AND THEN... YOU SEE NEWS ARTICLES ABOUT TWINS BORN TO, Y'KNOW, NON CLAN PEOPLE.
AND IF THEY GET SENT OFF TO LIVE WITH DIFFERENT FAMILIES, THEY END UP BEING REALLY, **REALLY** ALIKE. SAME BREED OF FAVORITE PET, WITH THE SAME NAME, SAME FAVORITE FOODS, COLORS OF CLOTHES, Y'KNOW... **MORE** ALIKE THAN IF THEY GREW UP **TOGETHER.**
MORE ALIKE THAN IF THEY'D GROWN UP IN **CLANS,** WHERE WE'RE SORT OF **ALL** IDENTICAL TWINS, **I** THINK.
UH HUH.
WELL, YOU HAVE A GOOD ONE.
BYE.

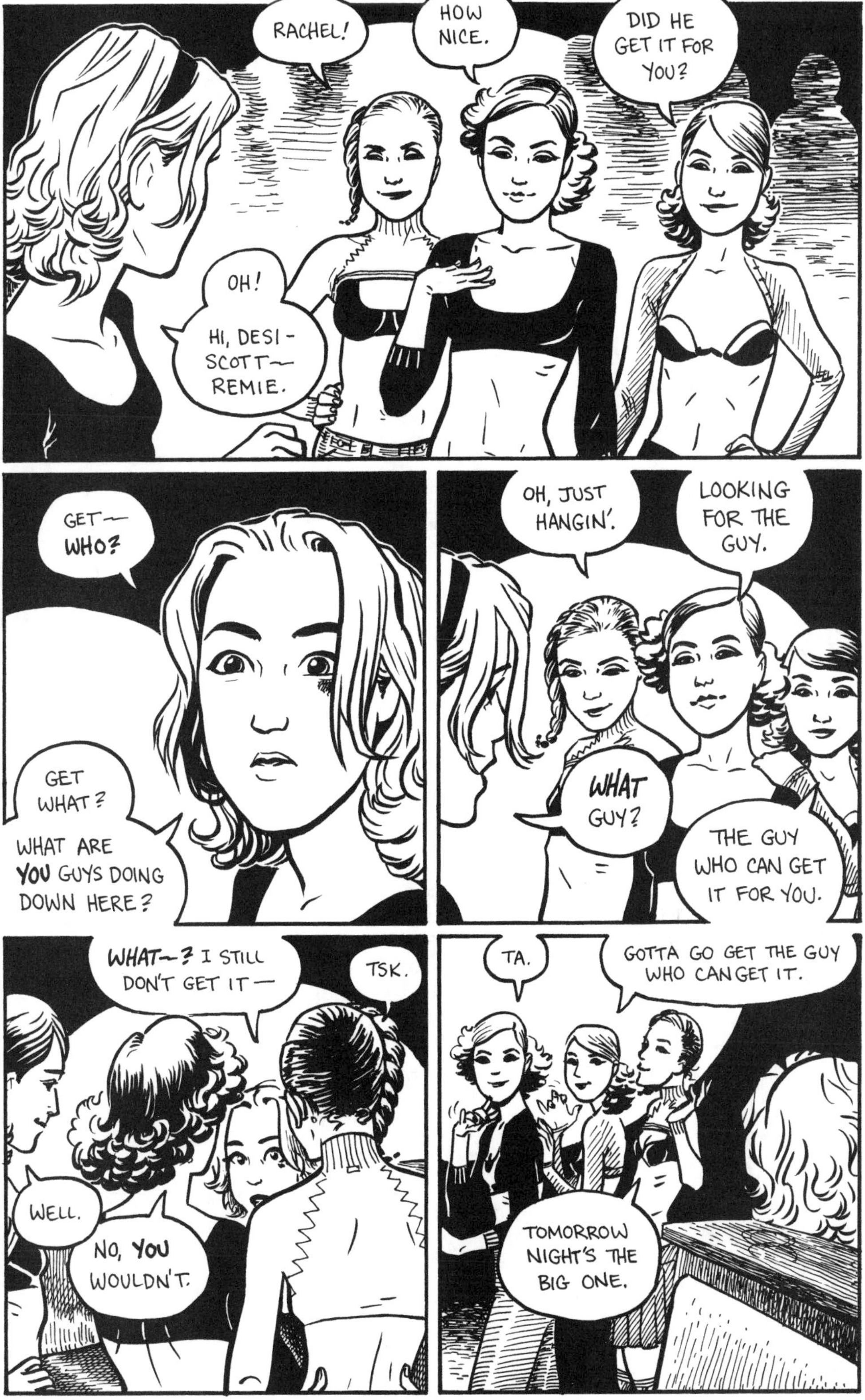
RACHEL!
HOW NICE.
DID HE GET IT FOR YOU?
OH!
HI, DESI- SCOTT- REMIE.
GET- WHO?
GET WHAT?
WHAT ARE YOU GUYS DOING DOWN HERE?
OH, JUST HANGIN'.
LOOKING FOR THE GUY.
WHAT GUY?
THE GUY WHO CAN GET IT FOR YOU.
WHAT-? I STILL DON'T GET IT-
TSK.
WELL.
NO, YOU WOULDN'T.
TA.
GOTTA GO GET THE GUY WHO CAN GET IT.
TOMORROW NIGHT'S THE BIG ONE.

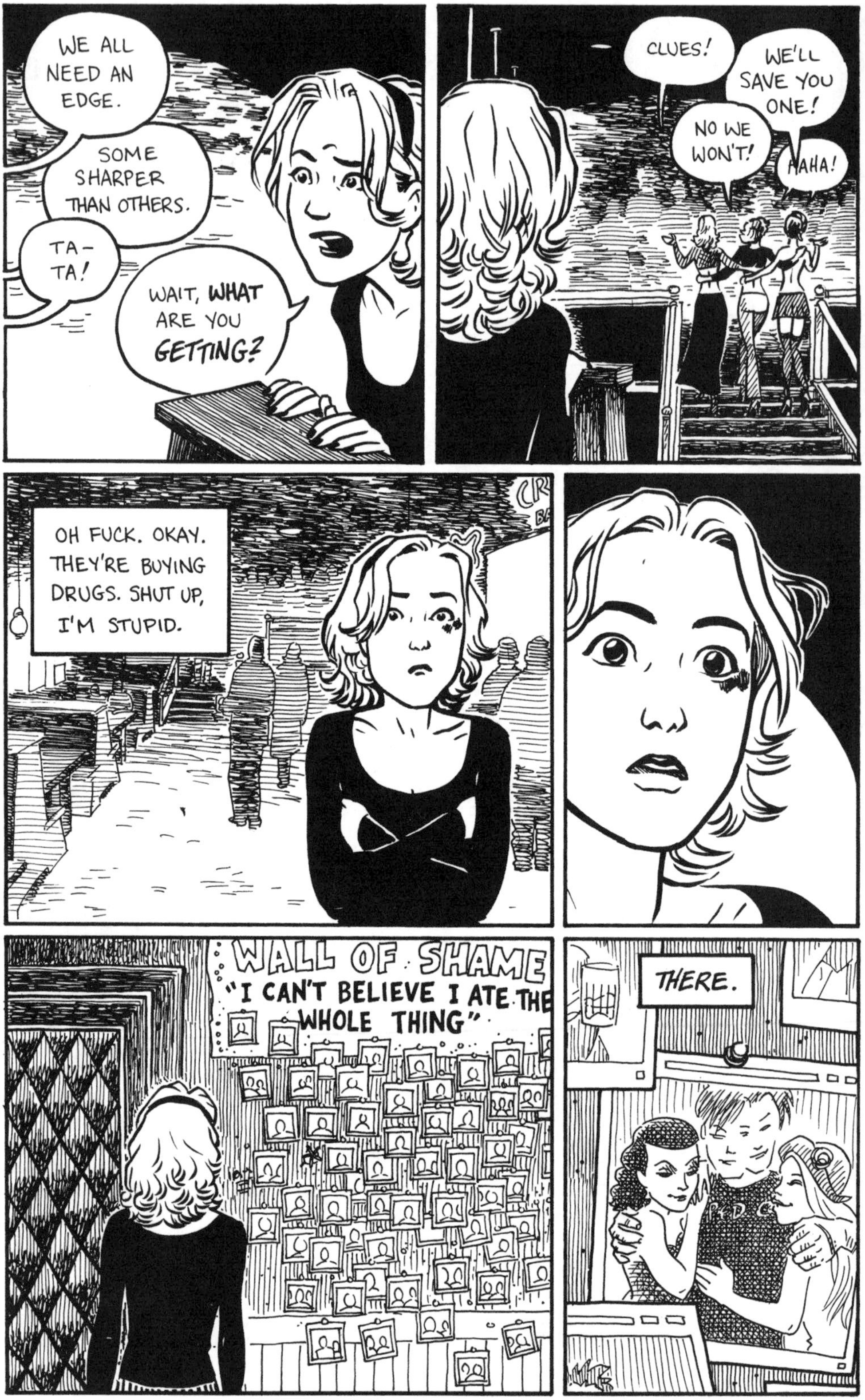
WE ALL NEED AN EDGE.
SOME SHARPER THAN OTHERS.
TA-TA!
WAIT, WHAT ARE YOU GETTING?
CLUES!
WE'LL SAVE YOU ONE!
NO WE WON'T!
HAHA!
OH FUCK. OKAY. THEY'RE BUYING DRUGS. SHUT UP, I'M STUPID.
WALL OF SHAME
"I CAN'T BELIEVE I ATE THE WHOLE THING"
THERE.

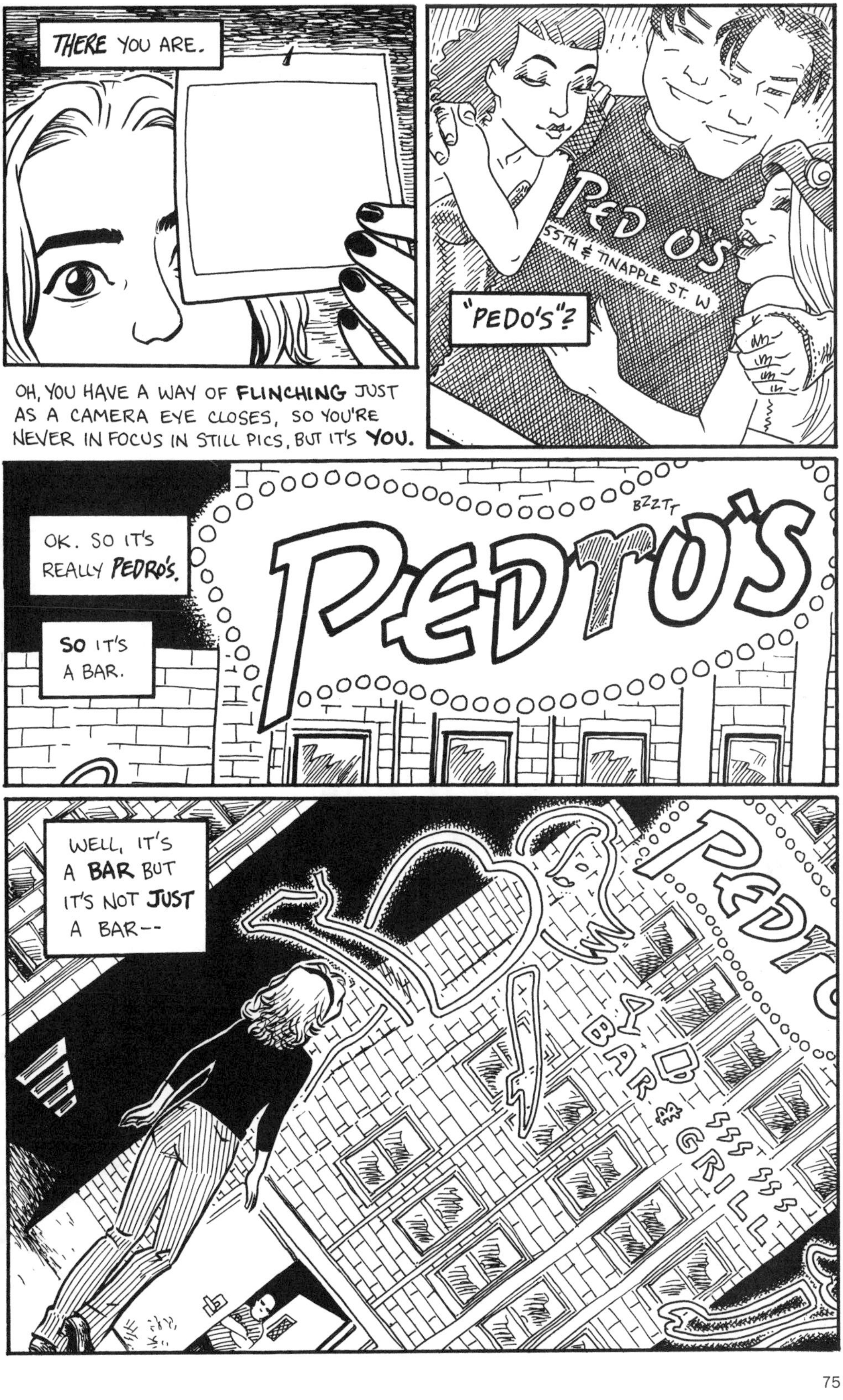
THERE YOU ARE.
OH, YOU HAVE A WAY OF FLINCHING JUST AS A CAMERA EYE CLOSES, SO YOU'RE NEVER IN FOCUS IN STILL PICS, BUT IT'S YOU.
PEDO'S
55TH & TINAPPLE ST. W
"PEDO'S"?
OK. SO IT'S REALLY PEDRO'S.
SO IT'S A BAR.
BZZTT
PEDRO'S
WELL, IT'S A BAR BUT IT'S NOT JUST A BAR--
PEDRO'S
BAR & GRILL

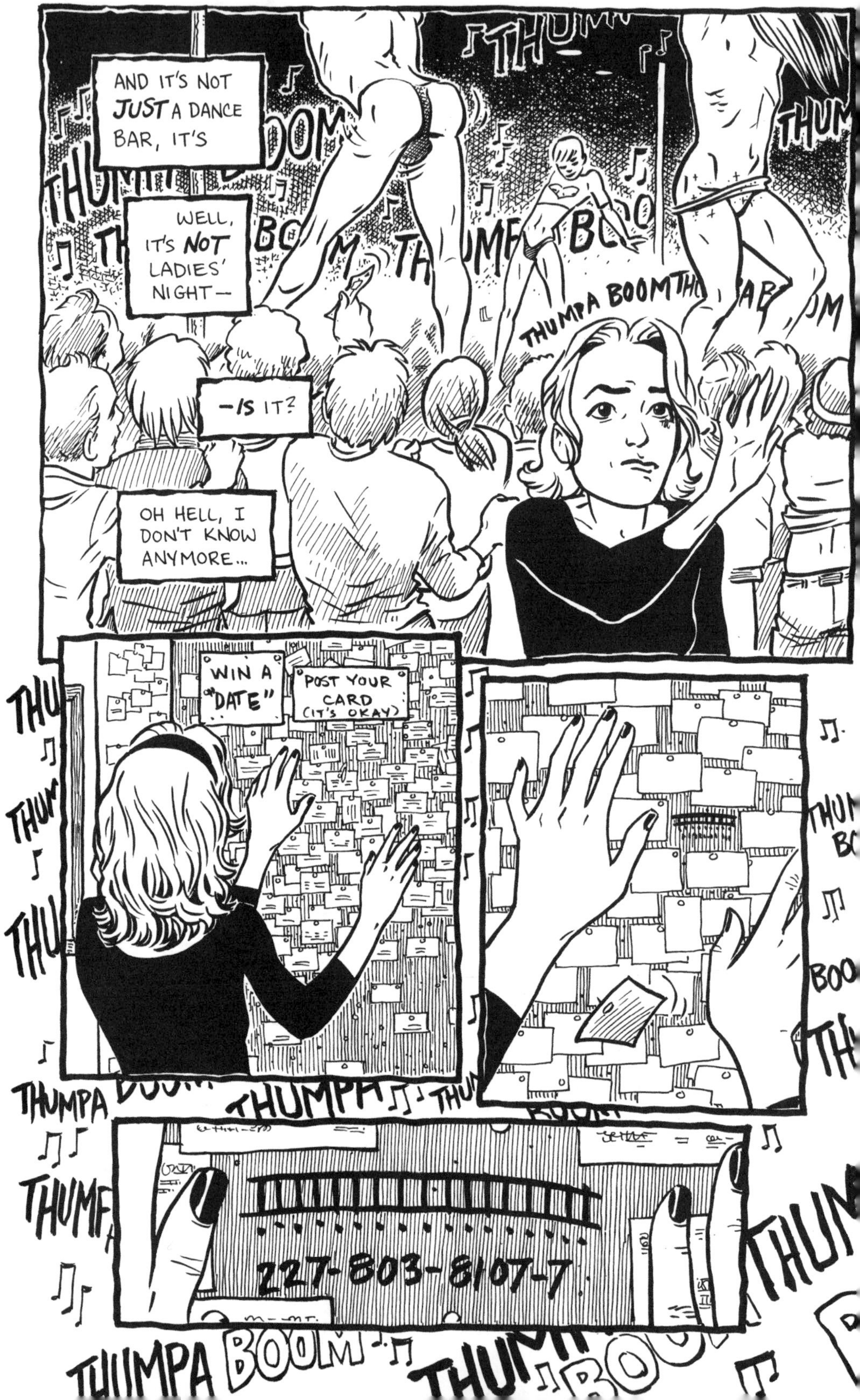
AND IT'S NOT JUST A DANCE BAR, IT'S
WELL, IT'S NOT LADIES' NIGHT--
--IS IT?
OH HELL, I DON'T KNOW ANYMORE...
THUMPA BOOMTHU
WIN A "DATE"
POST YOUR CARD (IT'S OKAY)
THUMPA
THUMPA BOOM
227-803-8107-7

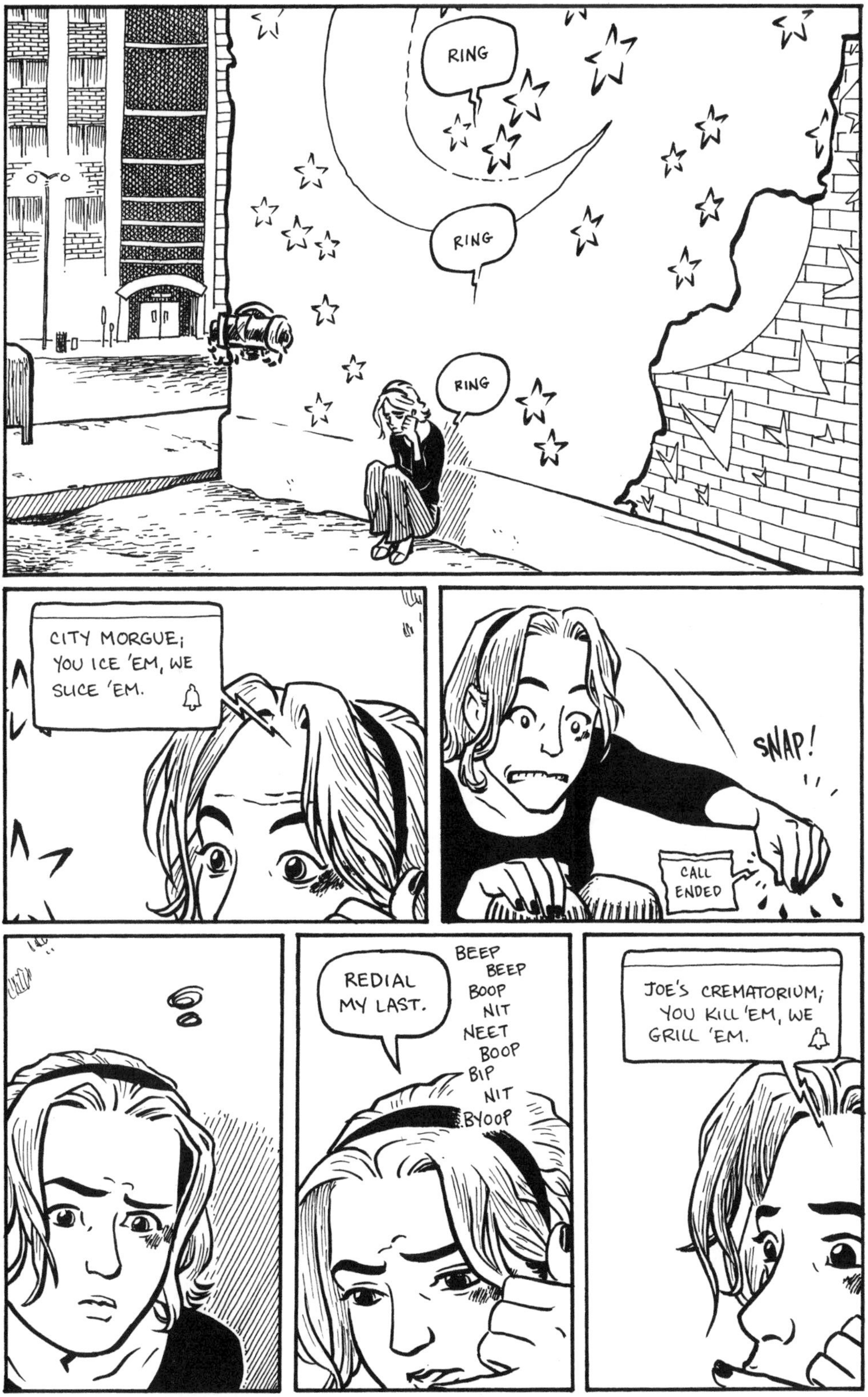
RING
RING
RING
CITY MORGUE; YOU ICE 'EM, WE SLICE 'EM.
SNAP!
CALL ENDED
REDIAL MY LAST.
BEEP BEEP BOOP NIT NEET BOOP BIP NIT BYOOP
JOE'S CREMATORIUM; YOU KILL 'EM, WE GRILL 'EM.

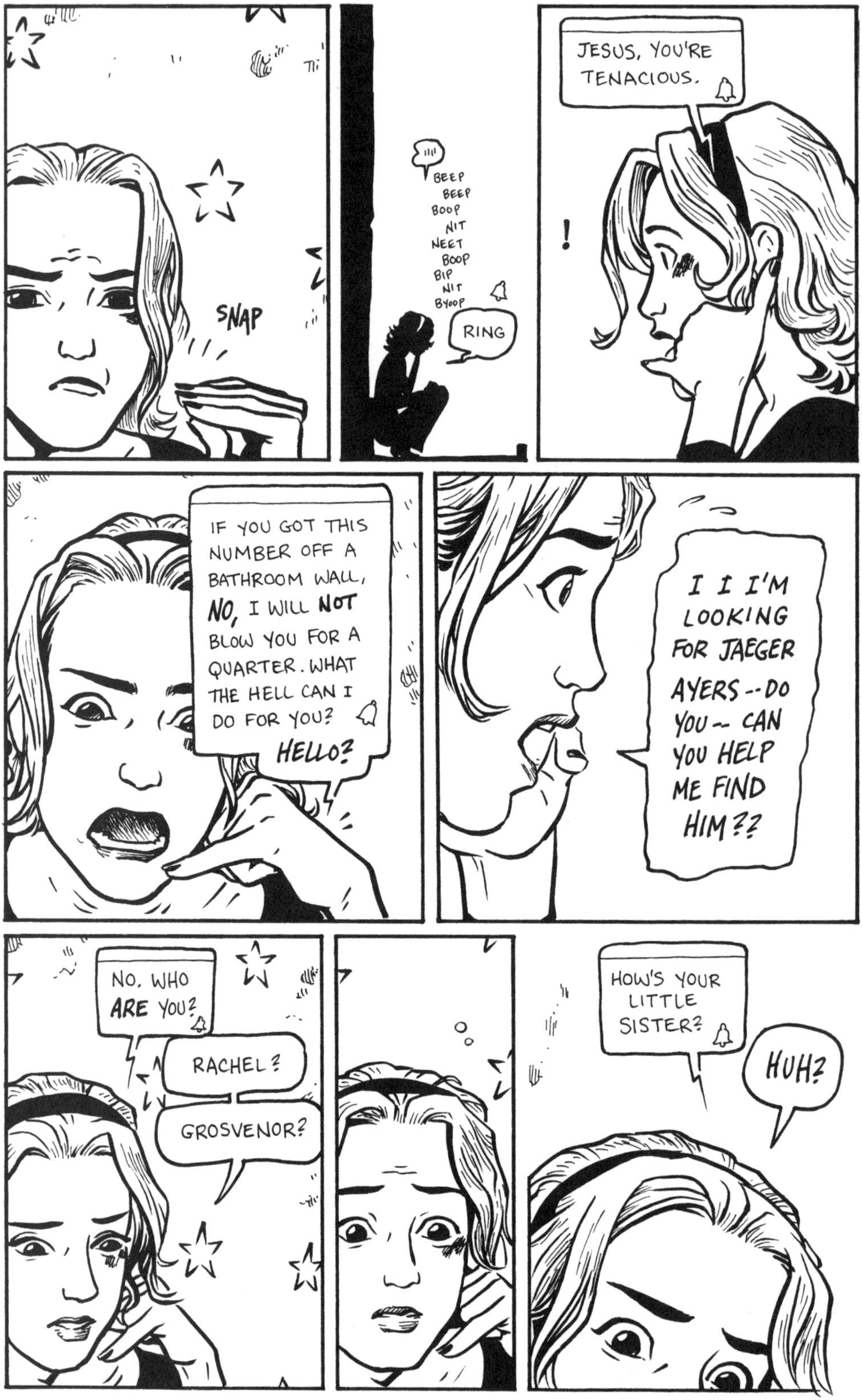
SNAP
BEEP BEEP BOOP NIT NEET BOOP BIP NIT BYOOP
RING
!
JESUS, YOU'RE TENACIOUS.
IF YOU GOT THIS NUMBER OFF A BATHROOM WALL, NO, I WILL NOT BLOW YOU FOR A QUARTER. WHAT THE HELL CAN I DO FOR YOU?
HELLO?
I I I'M LOOKING FOR JAEGER AYERS --DO YOU-- CAN YOU HELP ME FIND HIM??
NO. WHO ARE YOU?
RACHEL?
GROSVENOR?
HOW'S YOUR LITTLE SISTER?
HUH?

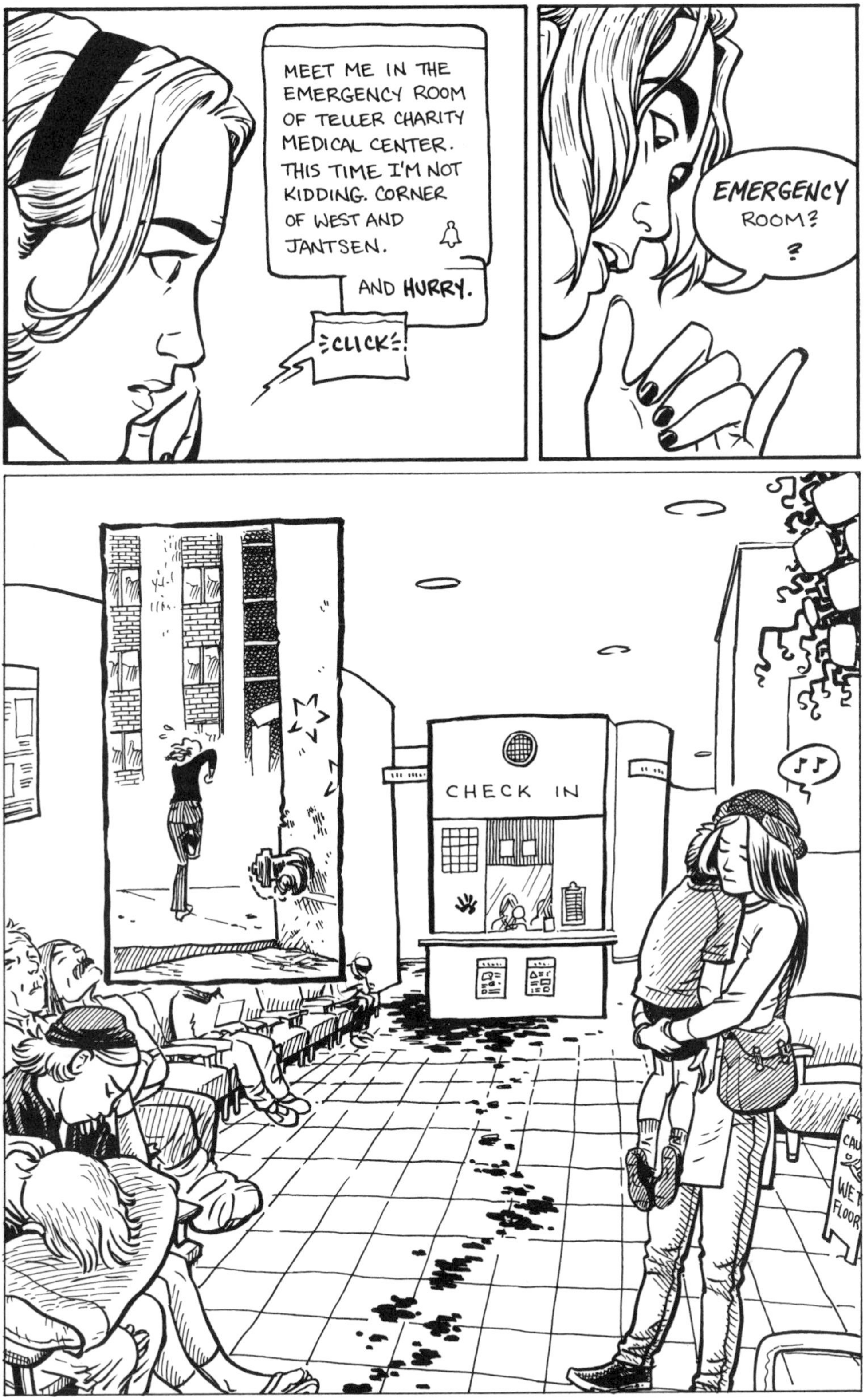
MEET ME IN THE EMERGENCY ROOM OF TELLER CHARITY MEDICAL CENTER. THIS TIME I'M NOT KIDDING. CORNER OF WEST AND JANTSEN.
AND HURRY.
CLICK
EMERGENCY ROOM? ?
CHECK IN

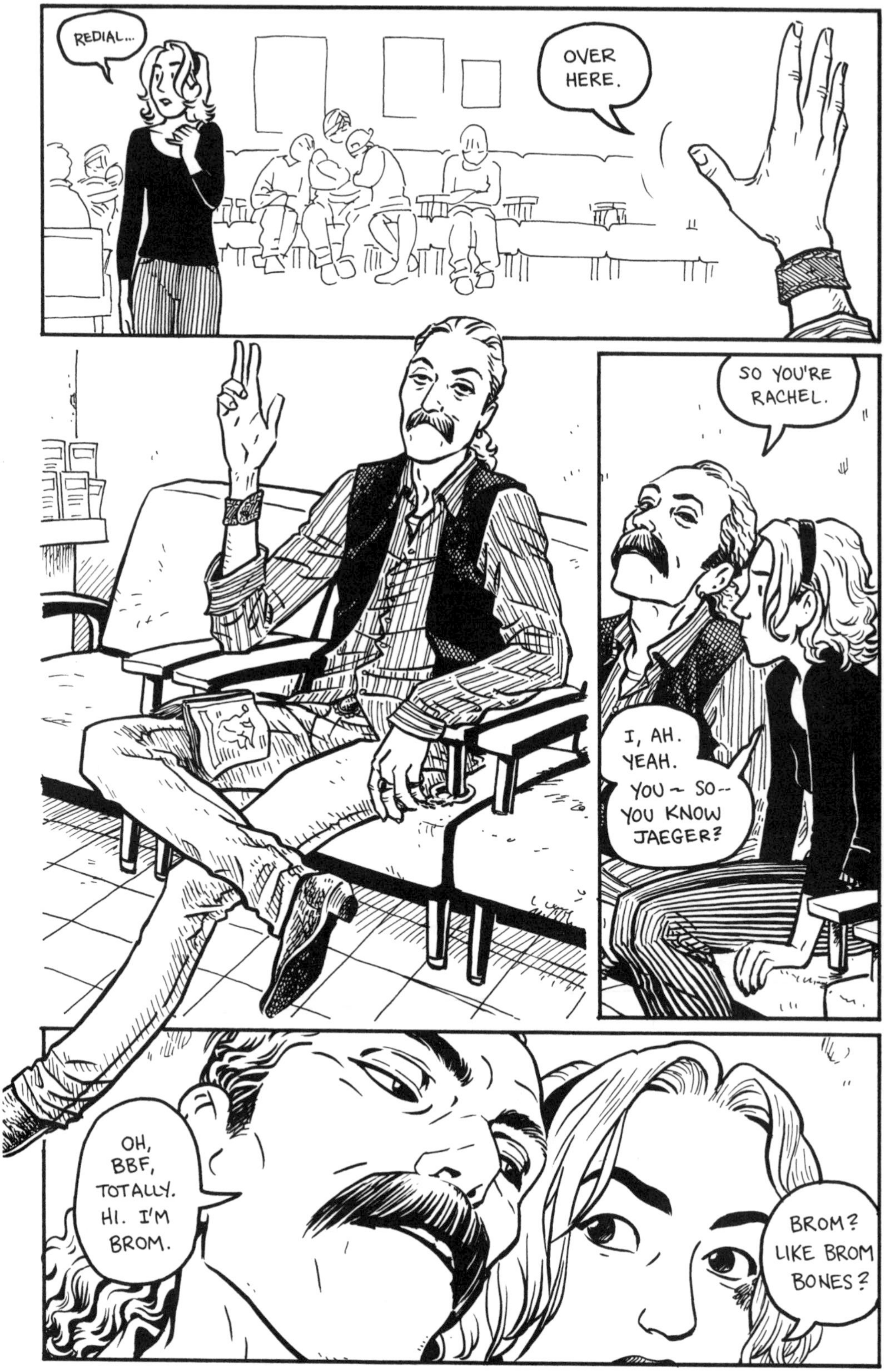
REDIAL...
OVER HERE.
SO YOU'RE RACHEL.
I, AH. YEAH. YOU~ SO-- YOU KNOW JAEGER?
OH, BBF, TOTALLY. HI. I'M BROM.
BROM? LIKE BROM BONES?

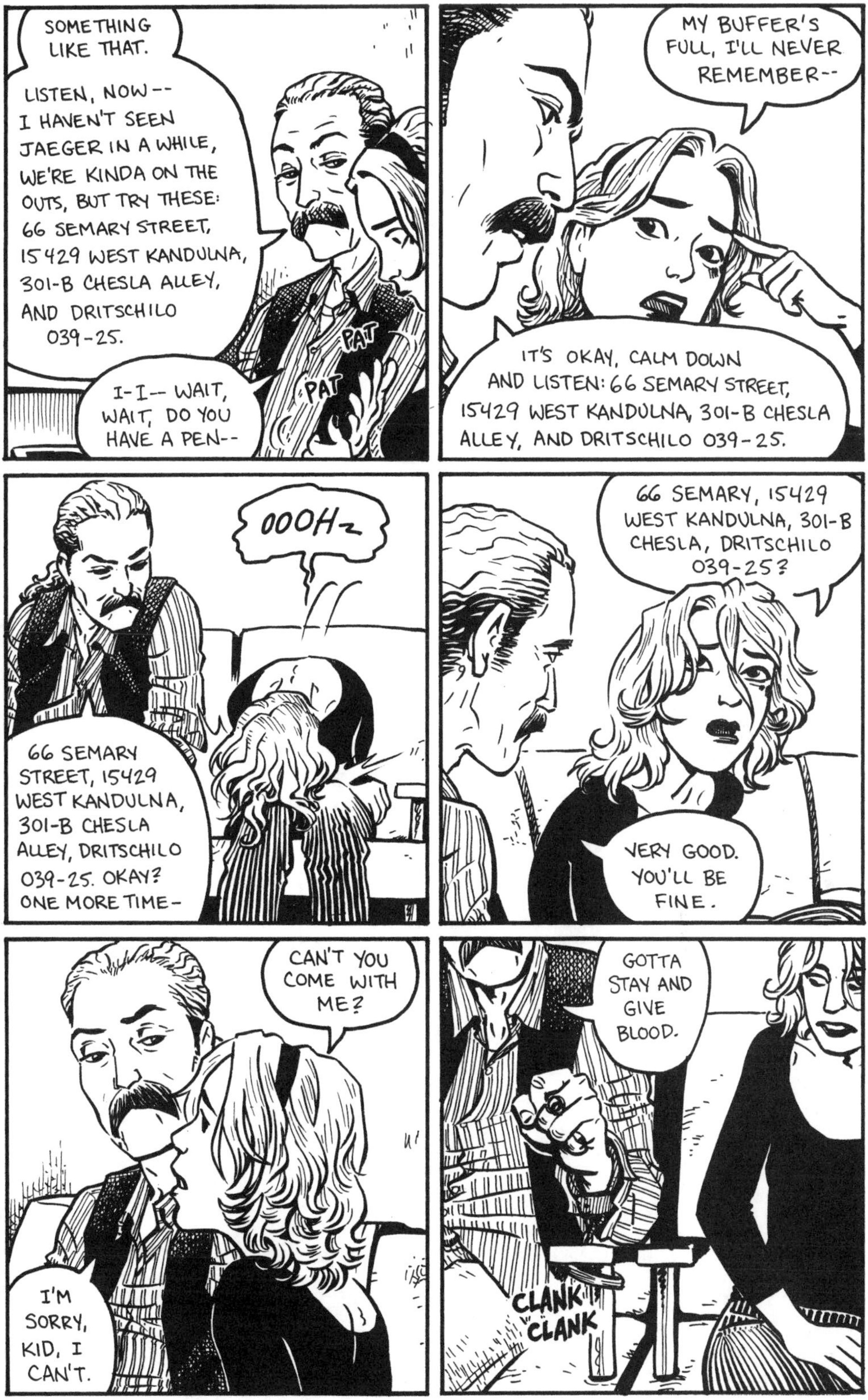
SOMETHING LIKE THAT.
LISTEN, NOW-- I HAVEN'T SEEN JAEGER IN A WHILE, WE'RE KINDA ON THE OUTS, BUT TRY THESE: 66 SEMARY STREET, 15429 WEST KANDULNA, 301-B CHESLA ALLEY, AND DRITSCHILO 039-25.
I-I-- WAIT, WAIT, DO YOU HAVE A PEN--
PAT
PAT
MY BUFFER'S FULL, I'LL NEVER REMEMBER--
IT'S OKAY, CALM DOWN AND LISTEN: 66 SEMARY STREET, 15429 WEST KANDULNA, 301-B CHESLA ALLEY, AND DRITSCHILO 039-25.
OOOH-
66 SEMARY STREET, 15429 WEST KANDULNA, 301-B CHESLA ALLEY, DRITSCHILO 039-25. OKAY? ONE MORE TIME-
66 SEMARY, 15429 WEST KANDULNA, 301-B CHESLA, DRITSCHILO 039-25?
VERY GOOD. YOU'LL BE FINE.
CAN'T YOU COME WITH ME?
I'M SORRY, KID, I CAN'T.
GOTTA STAY AND GIVE BLOOD.
CLANK
CLANK

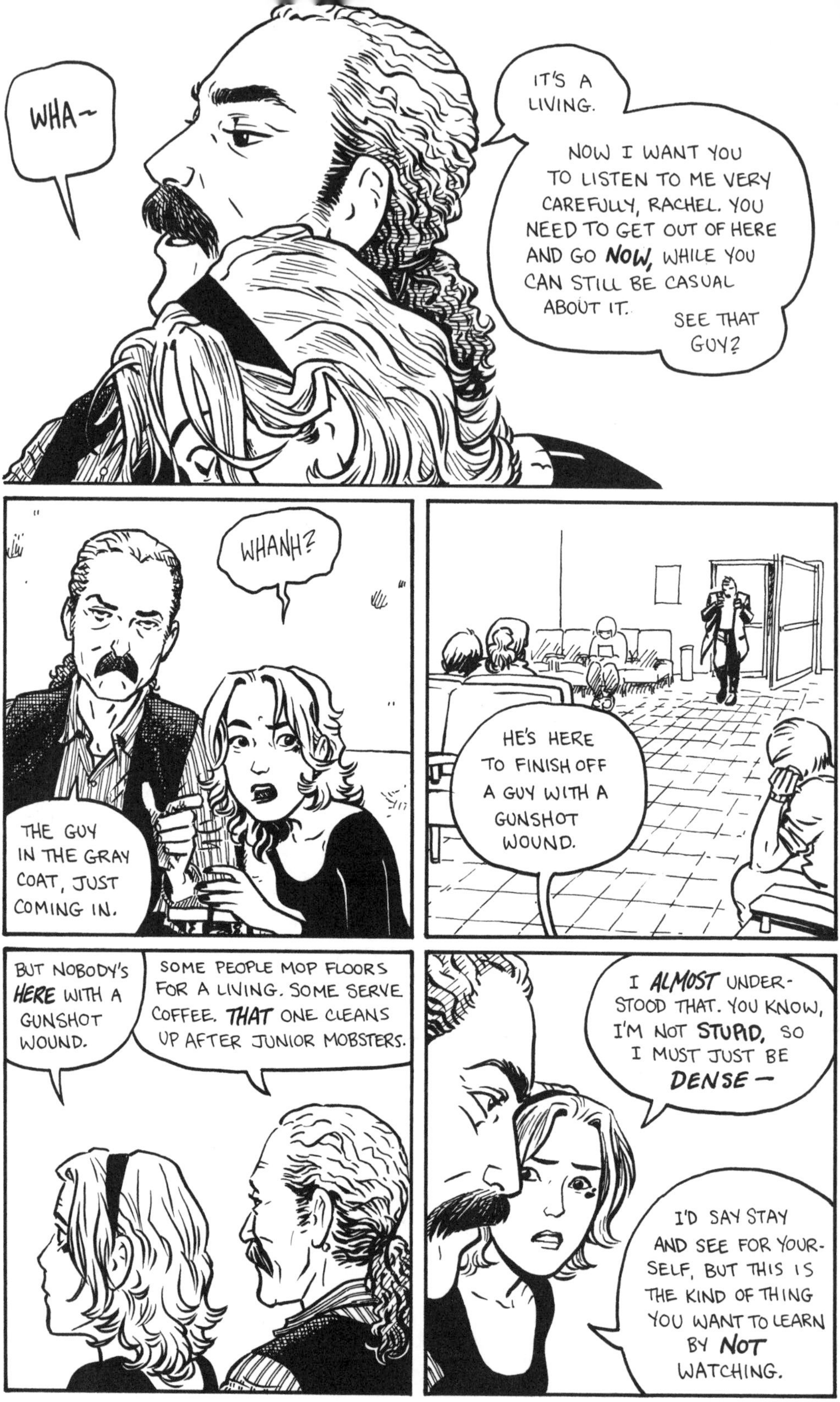
WHA–
IT'S A LIVING.
NOW I WANT YOU TO LISTEN TO ME VERY CAREFULLY, RACHEL. YOU NEED TO GET OUT OF HERE AND GO NOW, WHILE YOU CAN STILL BE CASUAL ABOUT IT.
SEE THAT GUY?
WHANH?
THE GUY IN THE GRAY COAT, JUST COMING IN.
HE'S HERE TO FINISH OFF A GUY WITH A GUNSHOT WOUND.
BUT NOBODY'S HERE WITH A GUNSHOT WOUND.
SOME PEOPLE MOP FLOORS FOR A LIVING. SOME SERVE COFFEE. THAT ONE CLEANS UP AFTER JUNIOR MOBSTERS.
I ALMOST UNDERSTOOD THAT. YOU KNOW, I'M NOT STUPID, SO I MUST JUST BE DENSE–
I'D SAY STAY AND SEE FOR YOURSELF, BUT THIS IS THE KIND OF THING YOU WANT TO LEARN BY NOT WATCHING.

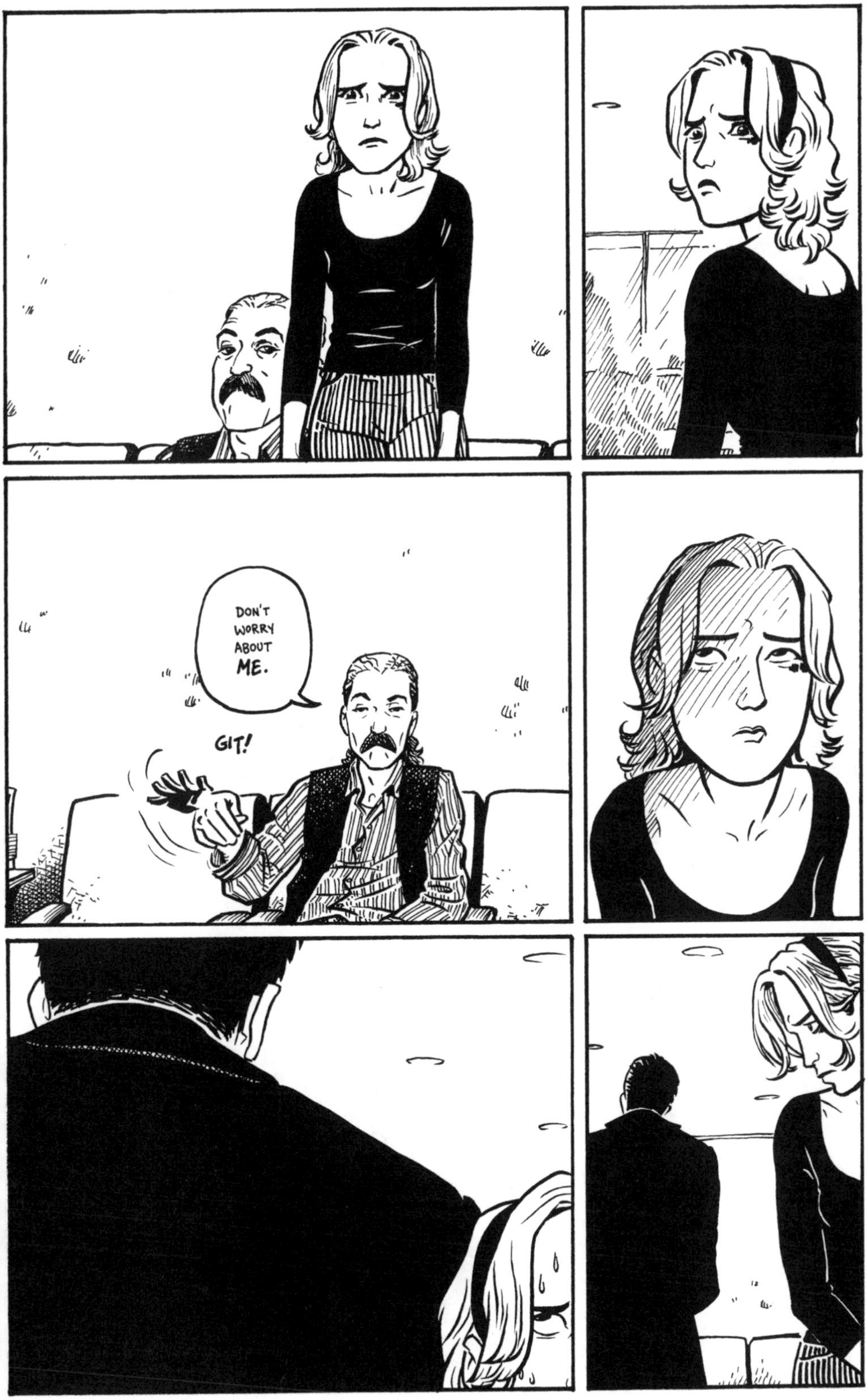
DON'T WORRY ABOUT ME.
GIT!

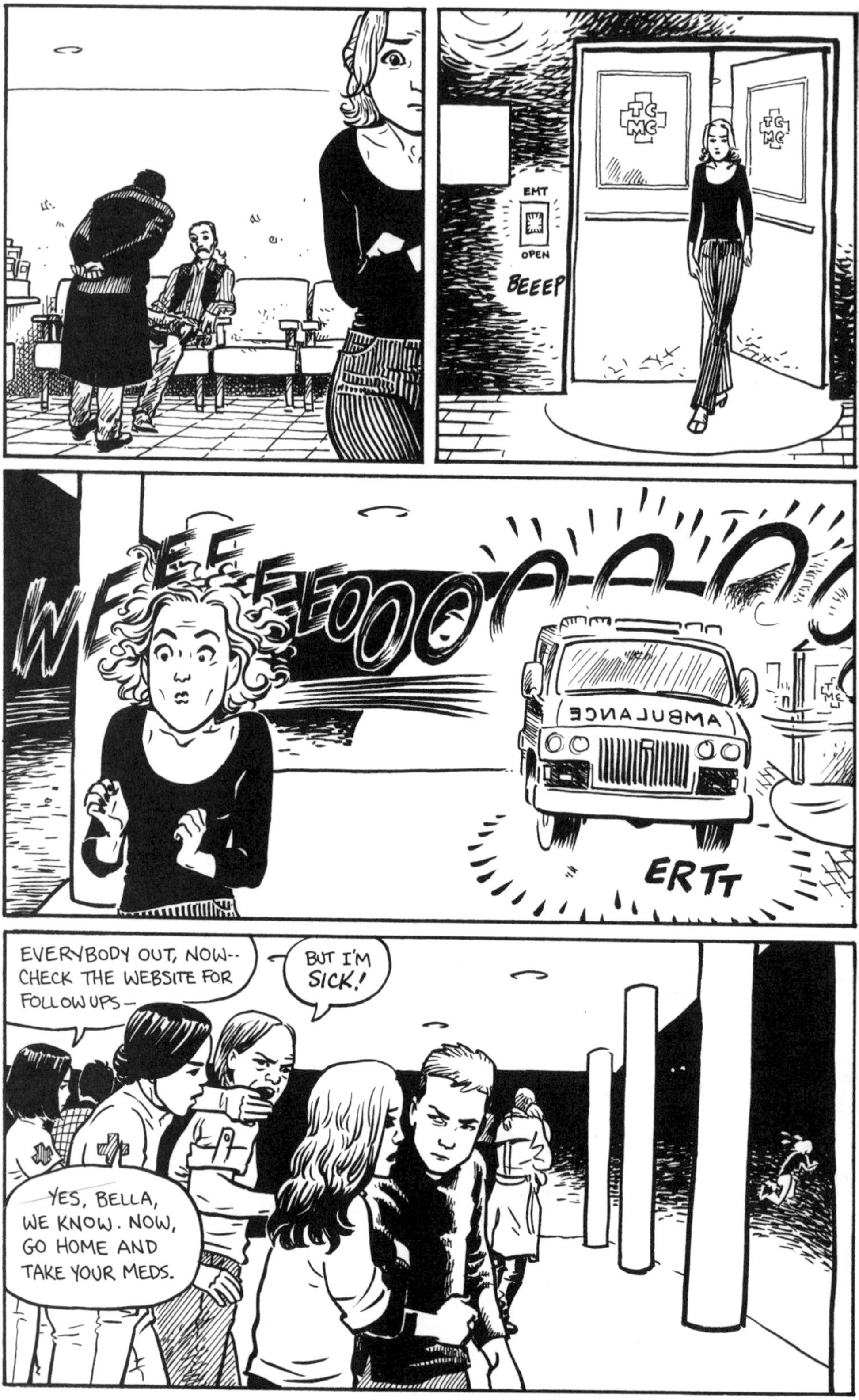
TCMC
EMT
OPEN
BEEEP
WEEEEOOOO
AMBULANCE
ERTT
EVERYBODY OUT, NOW--
CHECK THE WEBSITE FOR
FOLLOW UPS—
BUT I'M
SICK!
YES, BELLA,
WE KNOW. NOW,
GO HOME AND
TAKE YOUR MEDS.

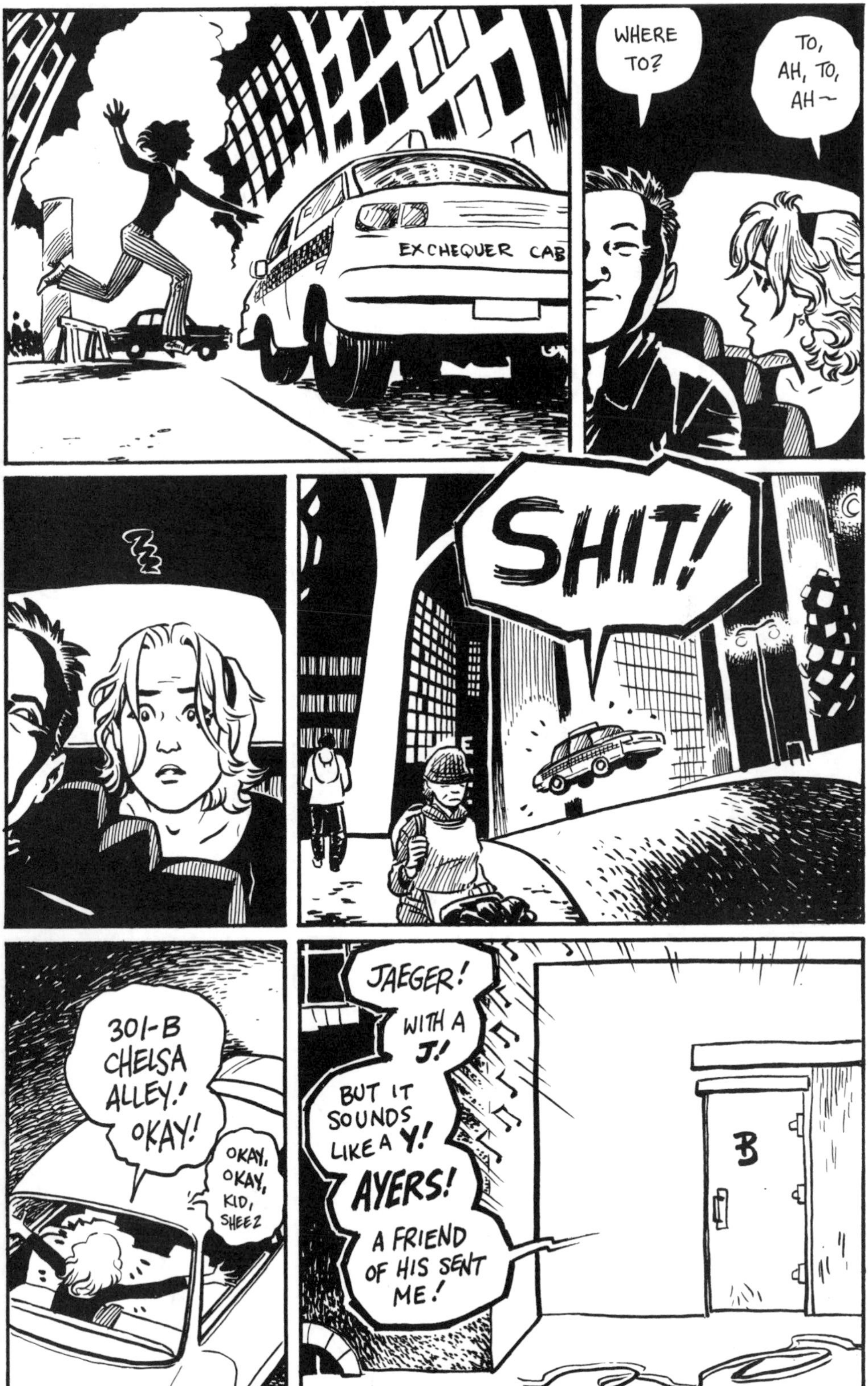
EXCHEQUER CAB
WHERE TO?
TO, AH, TO, AH~
SHIT!
301-B CHELSA ALLEY! OKAY!
OKAY, OKAY, KID, SHEEZ
JAEGER! WITH A J! BUT IT SOUNDS LIKE A Y! AYERS! A FRIEND OF HIS SENT ME!
B

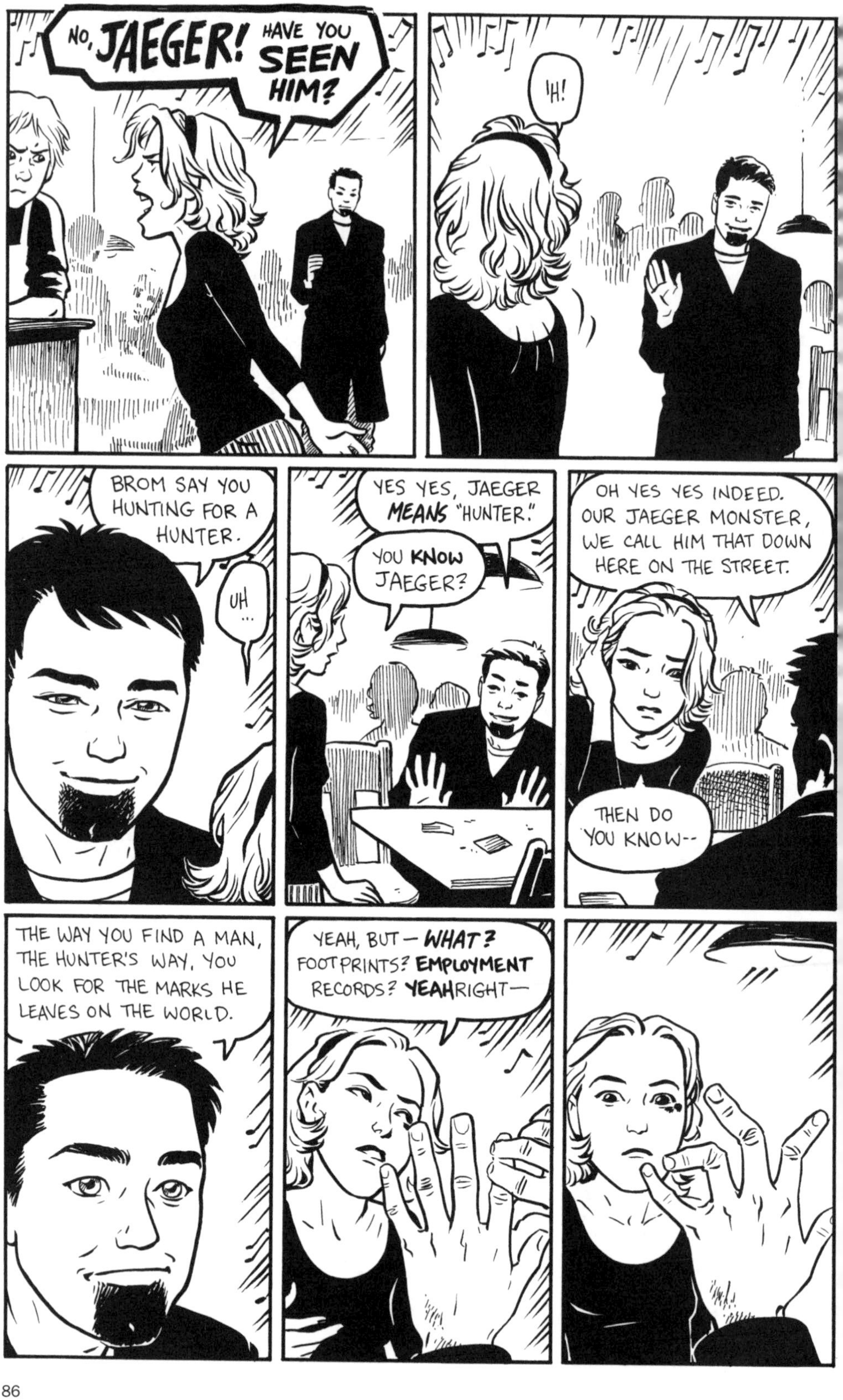
NO, JAEGER! HAVE YOU SEEN HIM?
'H!
BROM SAY YOU HUNTING FOR A HUNTER.
UH ...
YES YES, JAEGER MEANS "HUNTER."
YOU KNOW JAEGER?
OH YES YES INDEED. OUR JAEGER MONSTER, WE CALL HIM THAT DOWN HERE ON THE STREET.
THEN DO YOU KNOW--
THE WAY YOU FIND A MAN, THE HUNTER'S WAY. YOU LOOK FOR THE MARKS HE LEAVES ON THE WORLD.
YEAH, BUT — WHAT? FOOTPRINTS? EMPLOYMENT RECORDS? YEAHRIGHT—

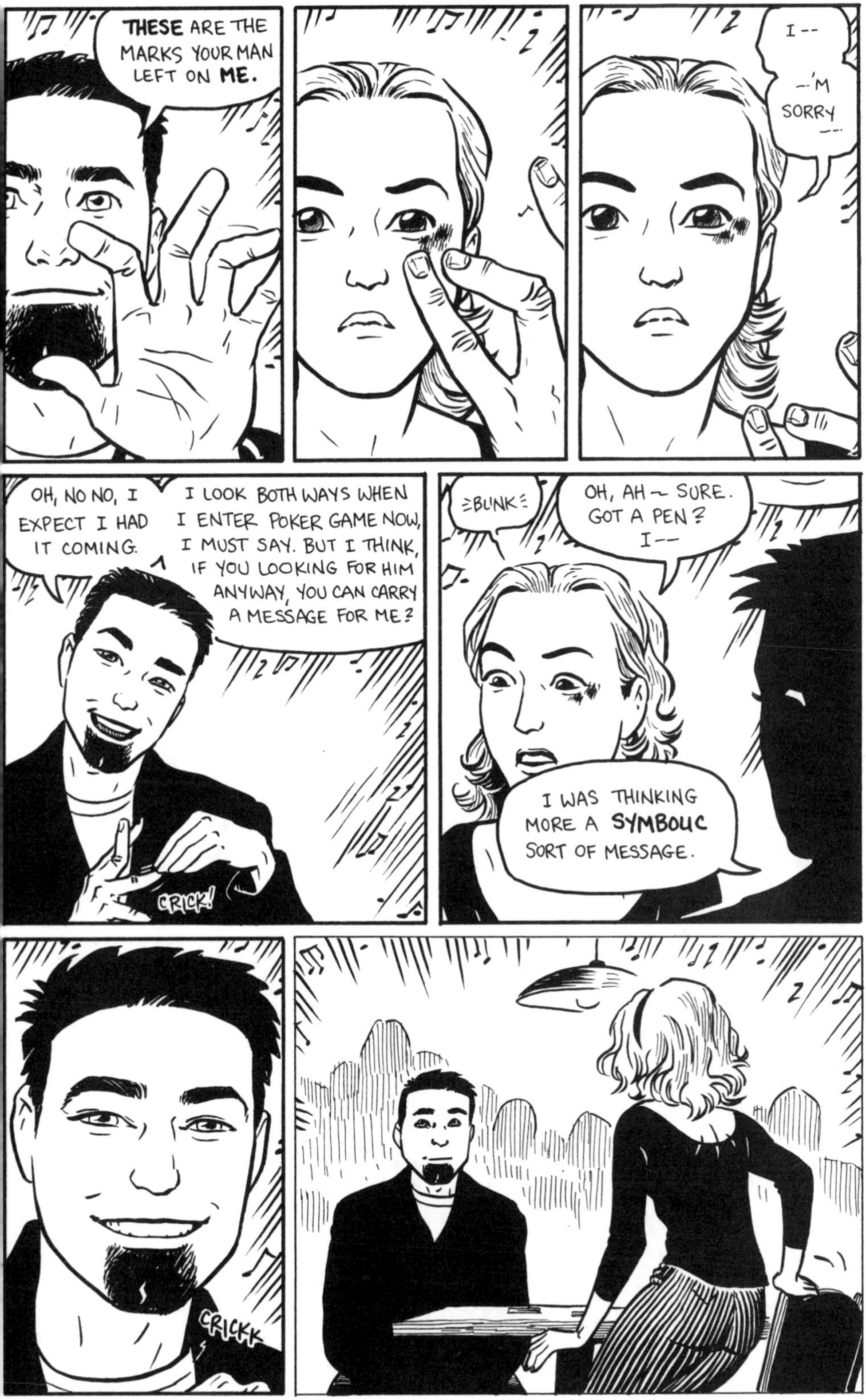
THESE ARE THE MARKS YOUR MAN LEFT ON ME.
I --
--'M SORRY --.
OH, NO NO, I EXPECT I HAD IT COMING.
I LOOK BOTH WAYS WHEN I ENTER POKER GAME NOW, I MUST SAY. BUT I THINK, IF YOU LOOKING FOR HIM ANYWAY, YOU CAN CARRY A MESSAGE FOR ME?
CRICK!
BLINK
OH, AH ~ SURE. GOT A PEN? I--
I WAS THINKING MORE A SYMBOLIC SORT OF MESSAGE.
CRICKK

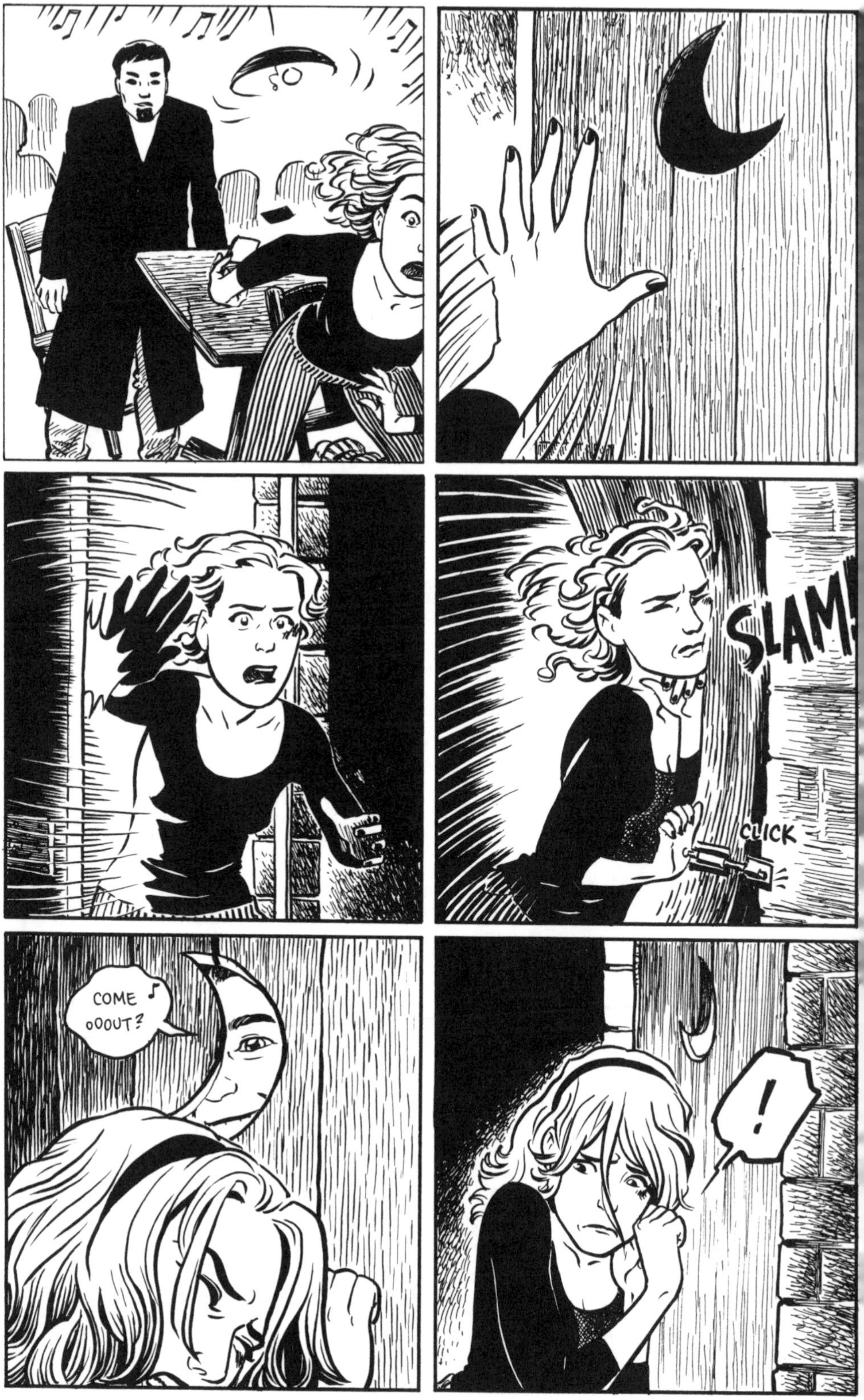
SLAM!
CLICK
COME
OOOUT?
!

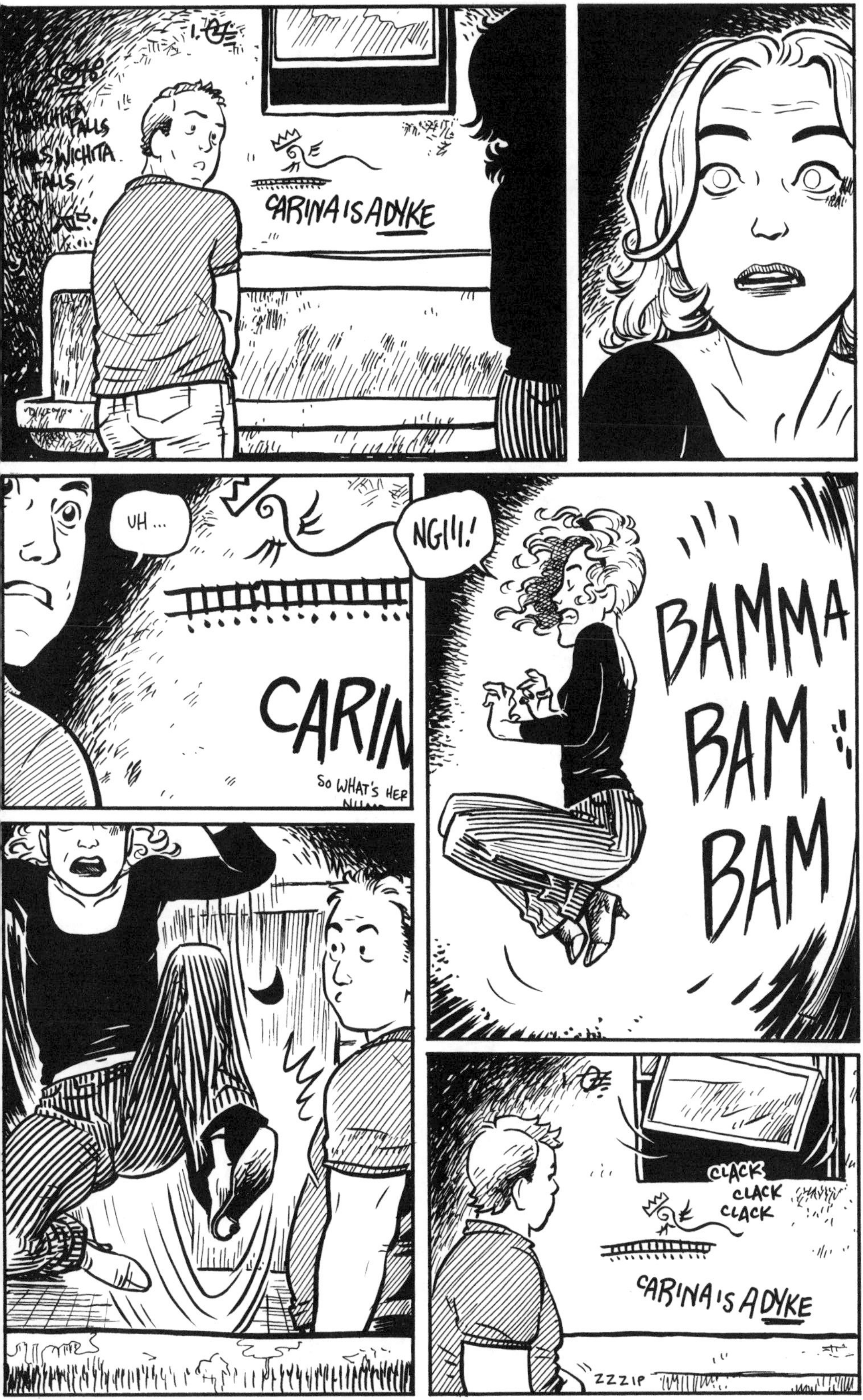

WICHITA FALLS
CARINA IS A DYKE
UH ...
CARIN
SO WHAT'S HER
NGIIII!
BAMMA BAM BAM
CLACK CLACK CLACK
CARINA IS A DYKE
ZZZIP

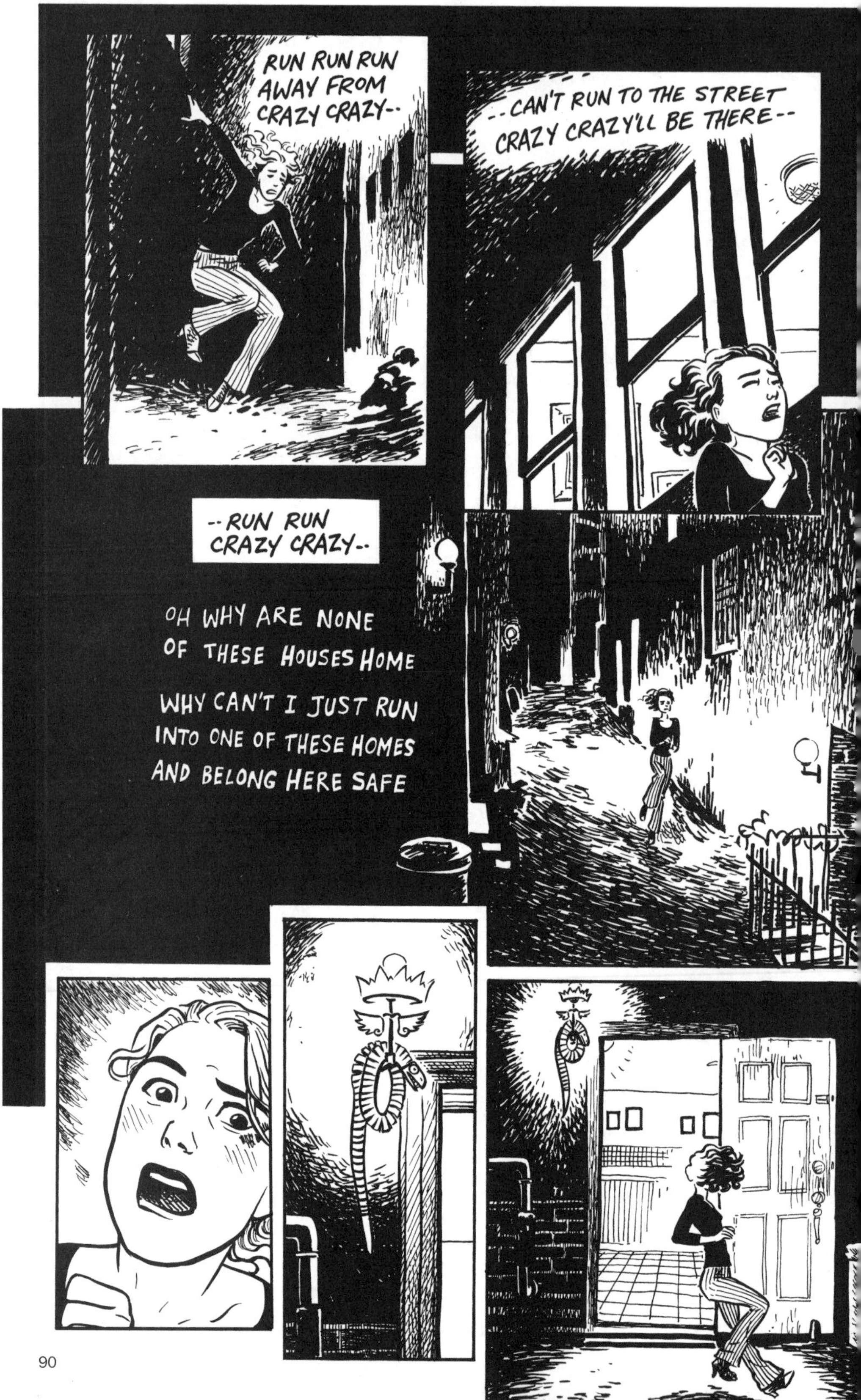
RUN RUN RUN
AWAY FROM
CRAZY CRAZY--
--CAN'T RUN TO THE STREET
CRAZY CRAZY'LL BE THERE--
--RUN RUN
CRAZY CRAZY--
OH WHY ARE NONE
OF THESE HOUSES HOME
WHY CAN'T I JUST RUN
INTO ONE OF THESE HOMES
AND BELONG HERE SAFE

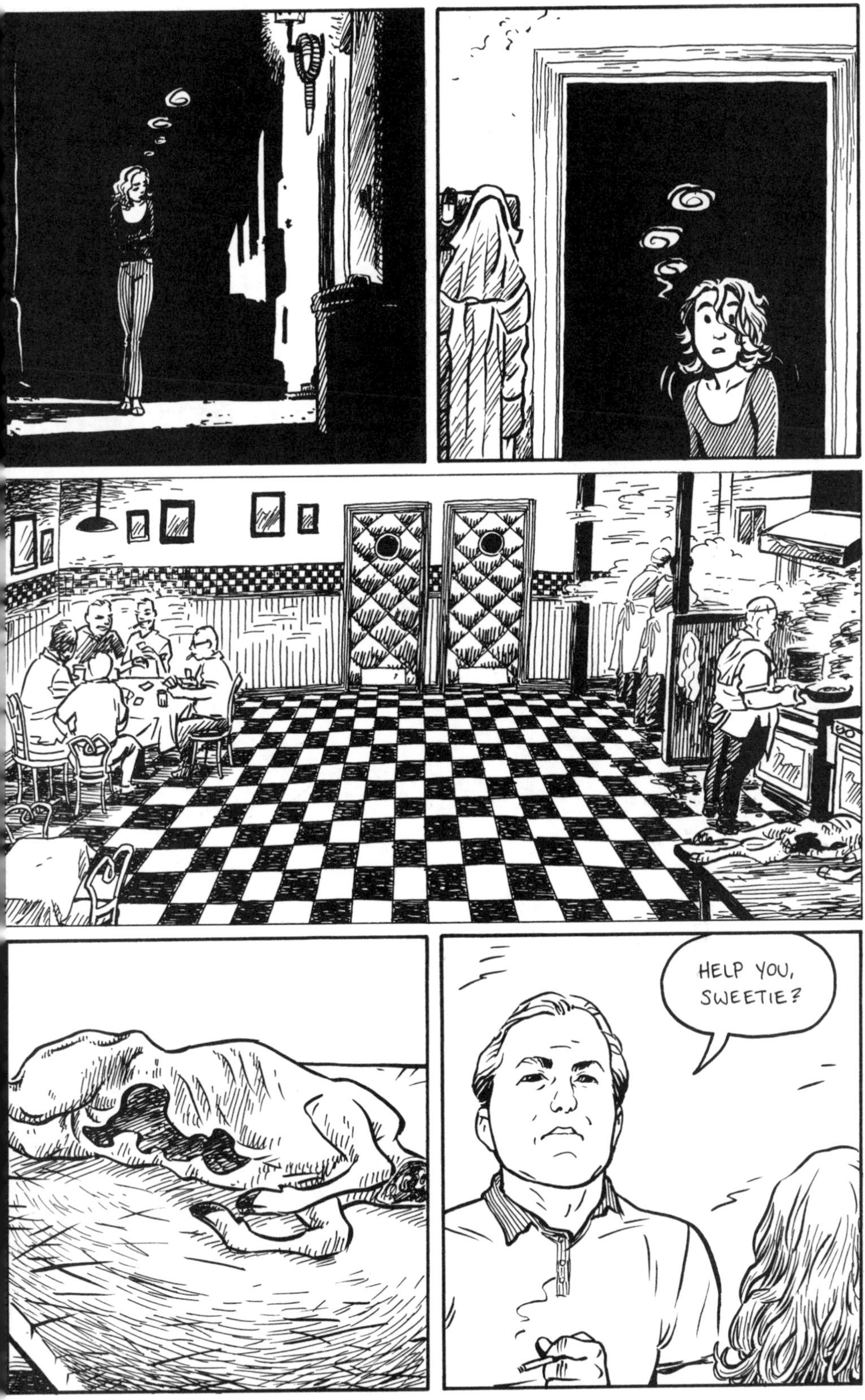
HELP YOU,
SWEETIE?

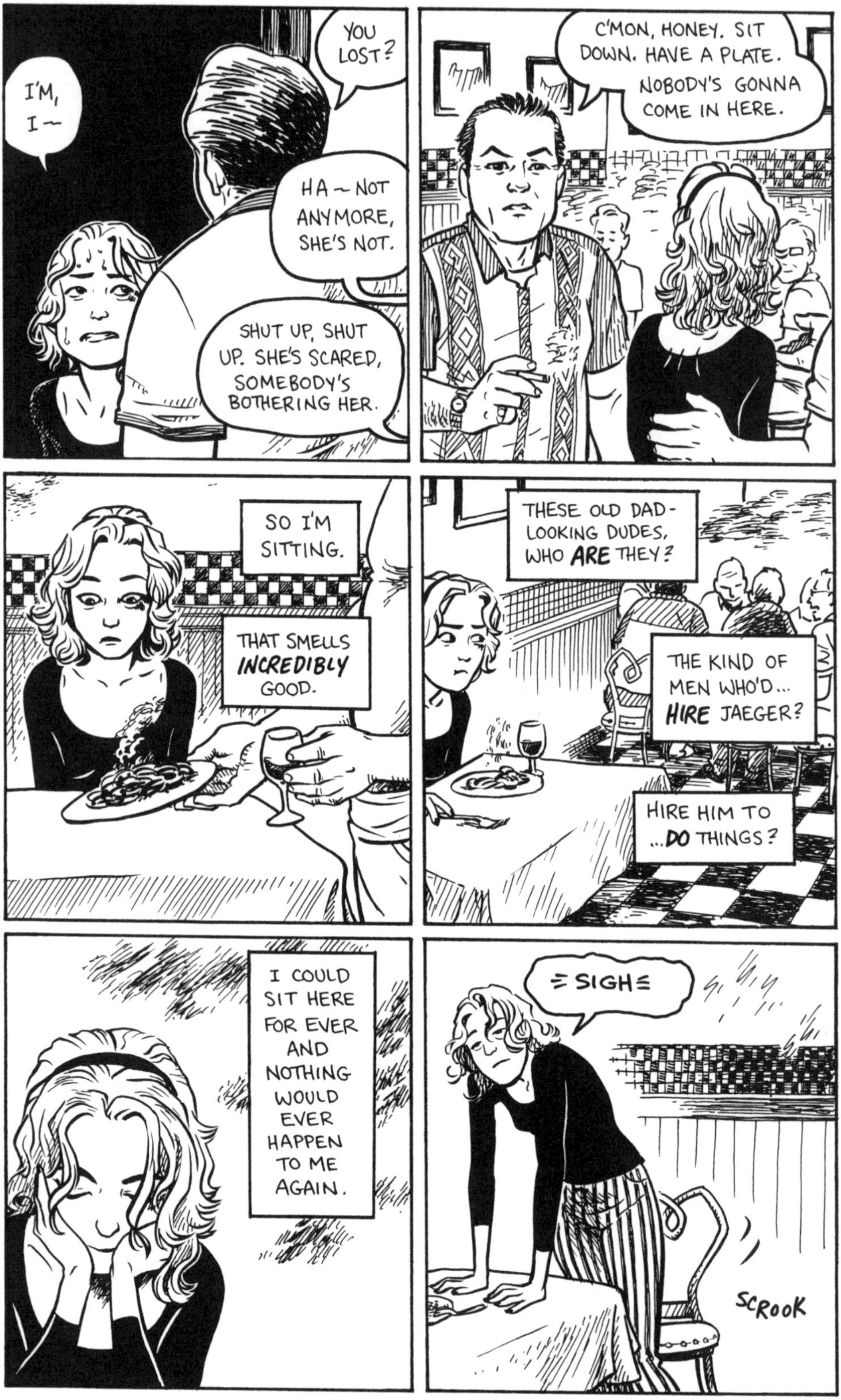

YOU LOST?
I'M, I—
HA—NOT ANYMORE, SHE'S NOT.
SHUT UP, SHUT UP. SHE'S SCARED, SOMEBODY'S BOTHERING HER.
C'MON, HONEY. SIT DOWN. HAVE A PLATE.
NOBODY'S GONNA COME IN HERE.
SO I'M SITTING.
THAT SMELLS INCREDIBLY GOOD.
THESE OLD DAD-LOOKING DUDES, WHO ARE THEY?
THE KIND OF MEN WHO'D... HIRE JAEGER?
HIRE HIM TO ...DO THINGS?
I COULD SIT HERE FOR EVER AND NOTHING WOULD EVER HAPPEN TO ME AGAIN.
SIGH
SCROOK

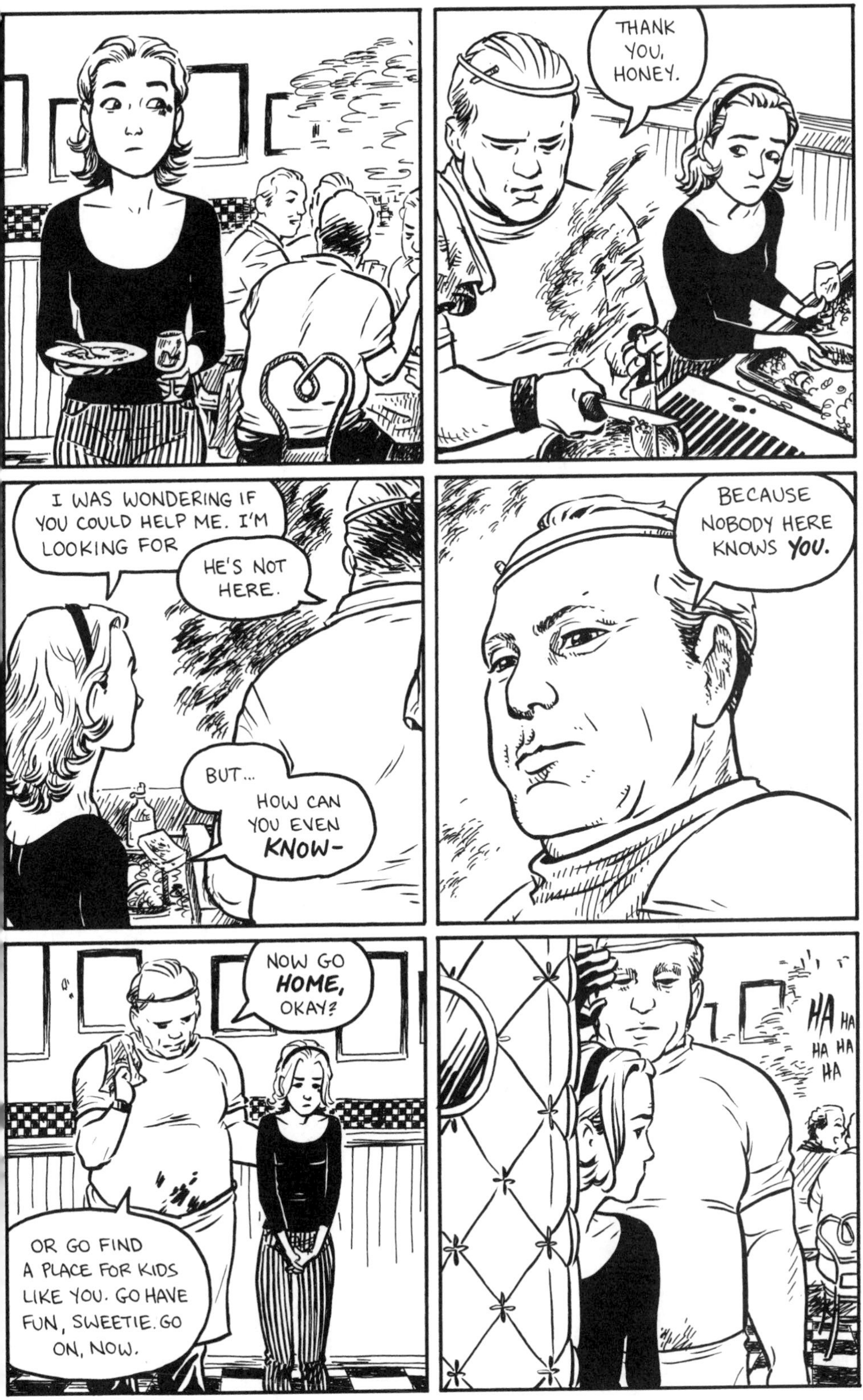
THANK YOU, HONEY.
I WAS WONDERING IF YOU COULD HELP ME. I'M LOOKING FOR
HE'S NOT HERE.
BUT... HOW CAN YOU EVEN KNOW-
BECAUSE NOBODY HERE KNOWS YOU.
NOW GO HOME, OKAY?
OR GO FIND A PLACE FOR KIDS LIKE YOU. GO HAVE FUN, SWEETIE. GO ON, NOW.
HA HA HA HA HA

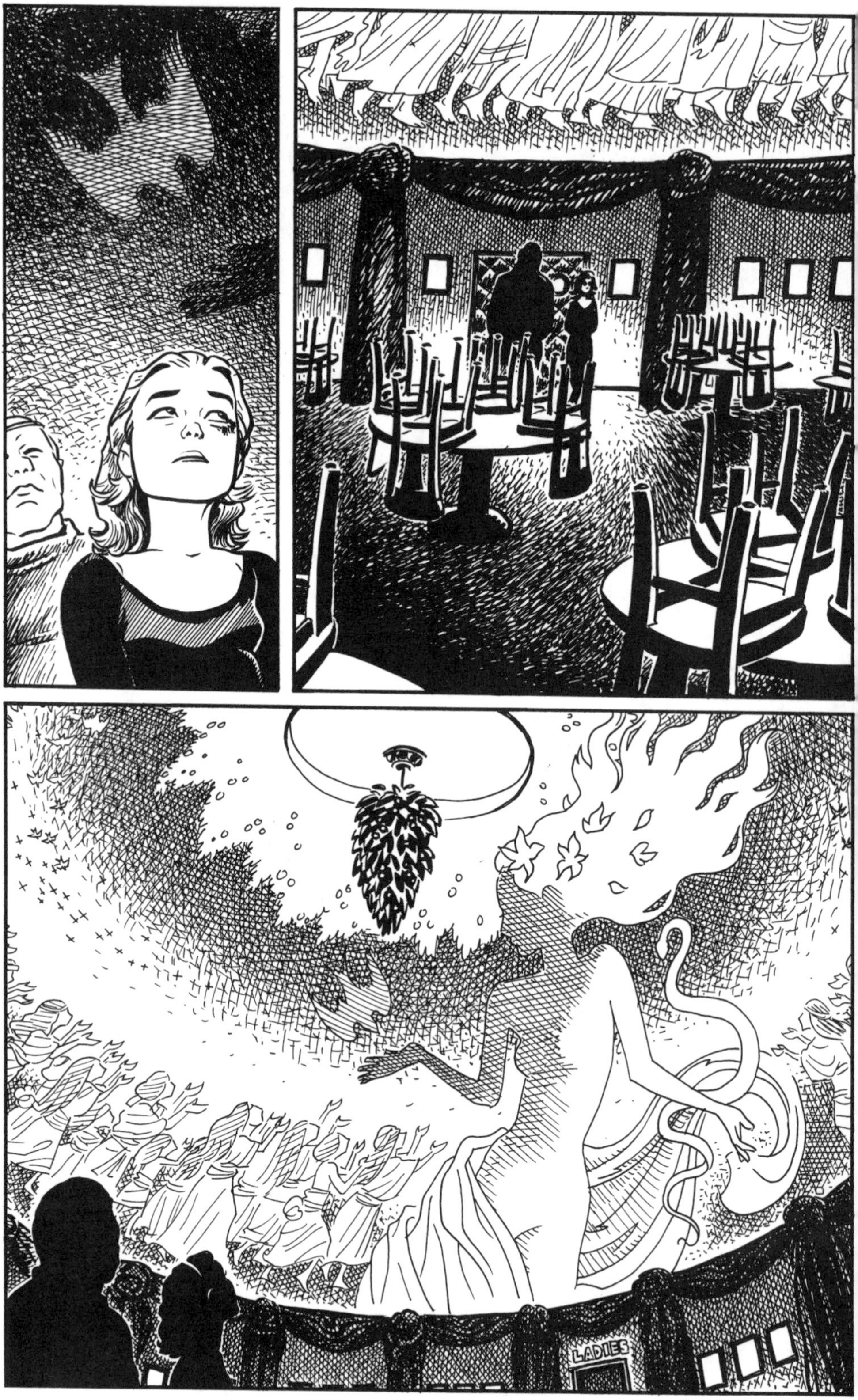
LADIES

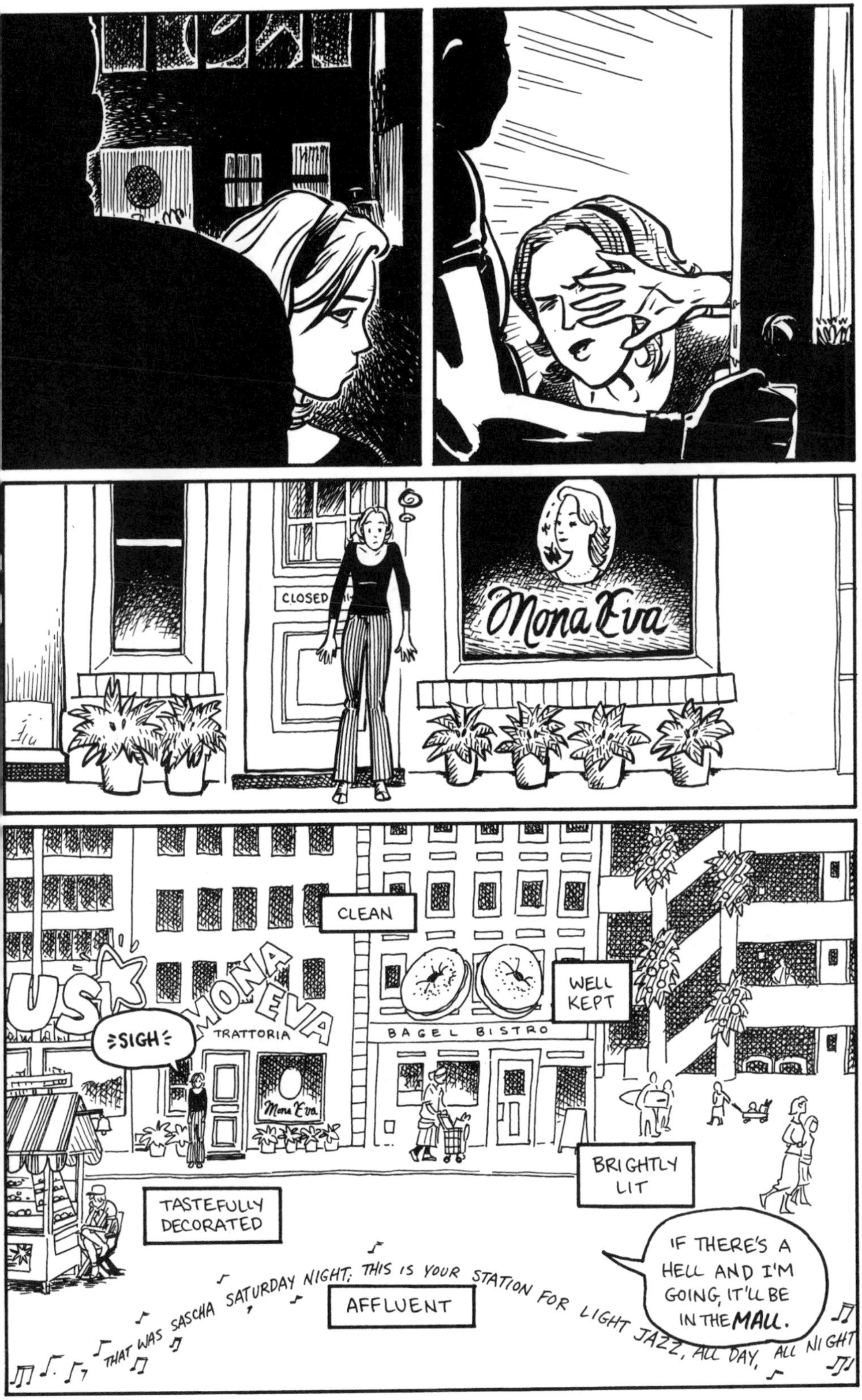
CLOSED
Mona Eva
US
MONA EVA
TRATTORIA
SIGH
Mona Eva
BAGEL BISTRO
CLEAN
WELL KEPT
BRIGHTLY LIT
TASTEFULLY DECORATED
AFFLUENT
THAT WAS SASCHA SATURDAY NIGHT; THIS IS YOUR STATION FOR LIGHT JAZZ, ALL DAY, ALL NIGHT
IF THERE'S A HELL AND I'M GOING, IT'LL BE IN THE MALL.

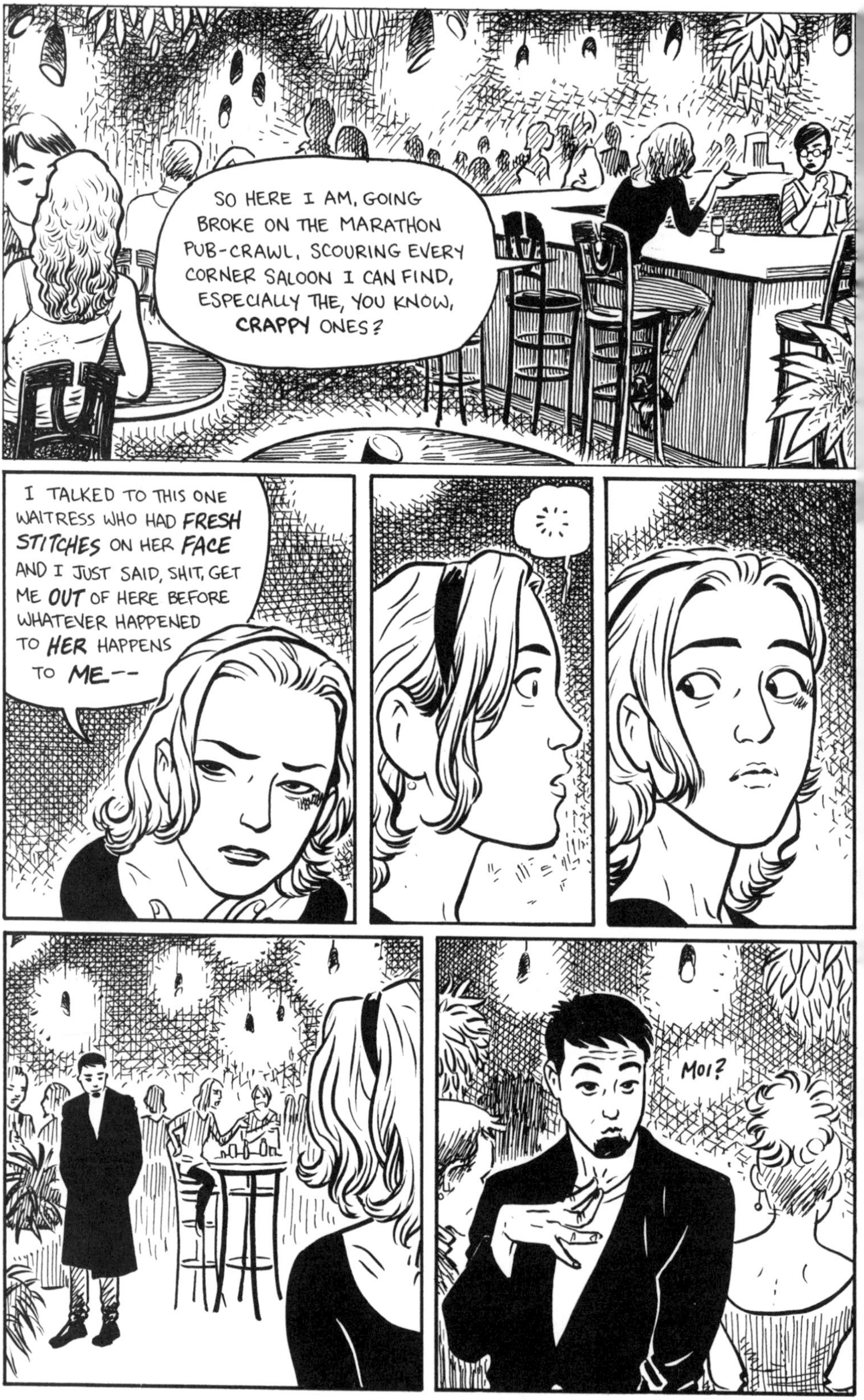
SO HERE I AM, GOING BROKE ON THE MARATHON PUB-CRAWL, SCOURING EVERY CORNER SALOON I CAN FIND, ESPECIALLY THE, YOU KNOW, CRAPPY ONES?
I TALKED TO THIS ONE WAITRESS WHO HAD FRESH STITCHES ON HER FACE AND I JUST SAID, SHIT, GET ME OUT OF HERE BEFORE WHATEVER HAPPENED TO HER HAPPENS TO ME--
Moi?

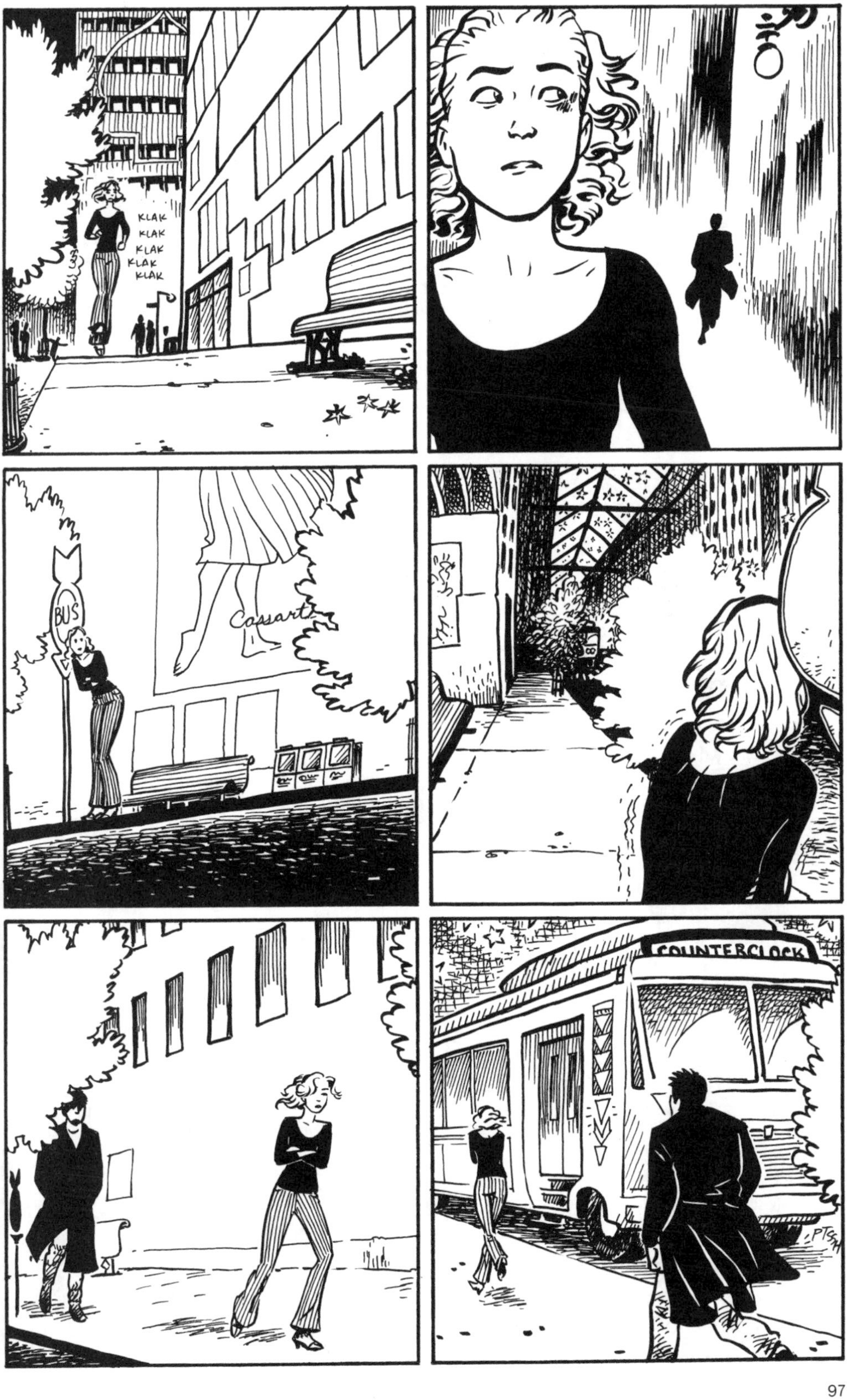
KLAK
KLAK
KLAK
KLAK
KLAK
BUS
Cassart
COUNTERCLOCK
PTSSH

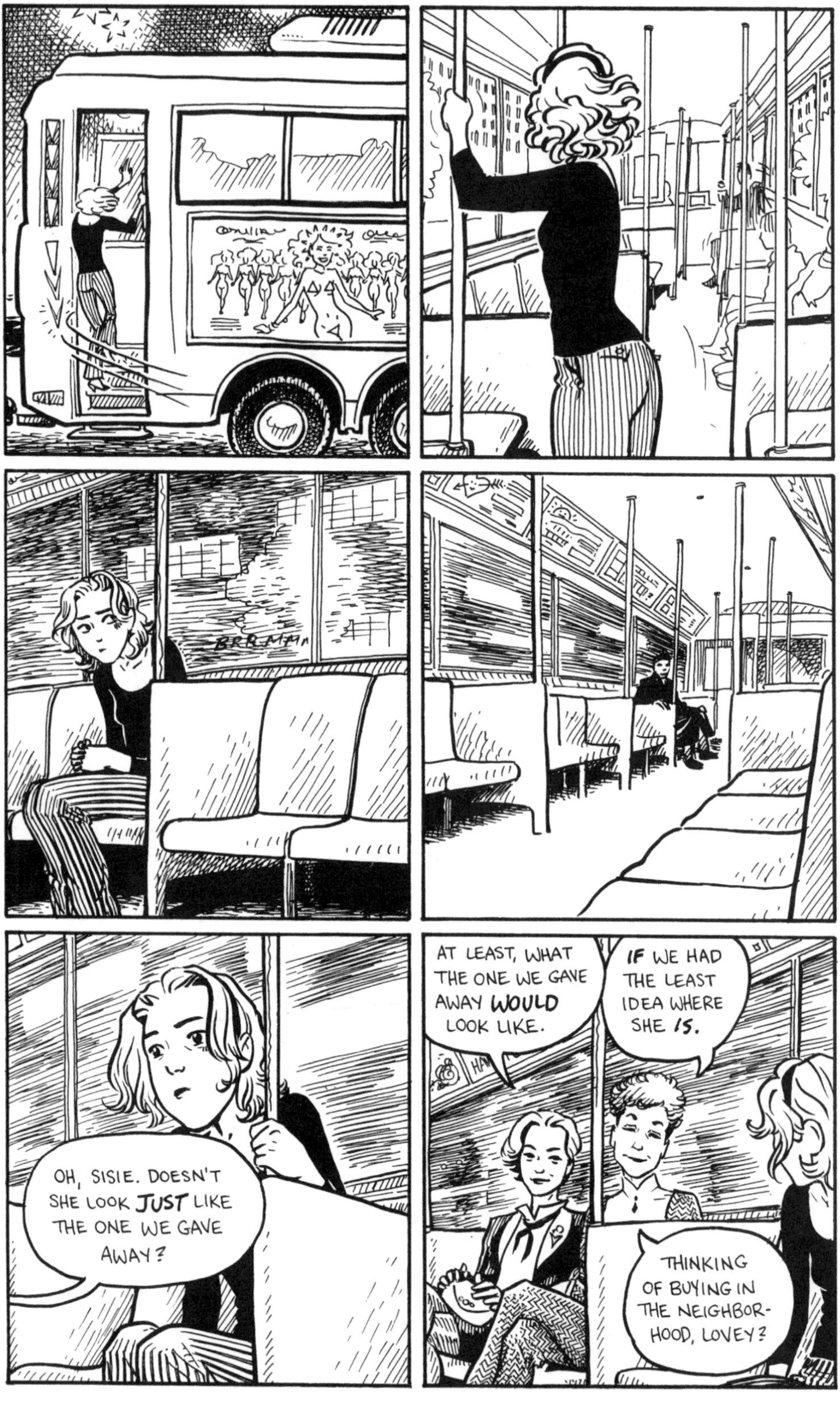
BRRMMM
OH, SISIE. DOESN'T SHE LOOK JUST LIKE THE ONE WE GAVE AWAY?
AT LEAST, WHAT THE ONE WE GAVE AWAY WOULD LOOK LIKE.
IF WE HAD THE LEAST IDEA WHERE SHE IS.
THINKING OF BUYING IN THE NEIGHBOR-HOOD, LOVEY?

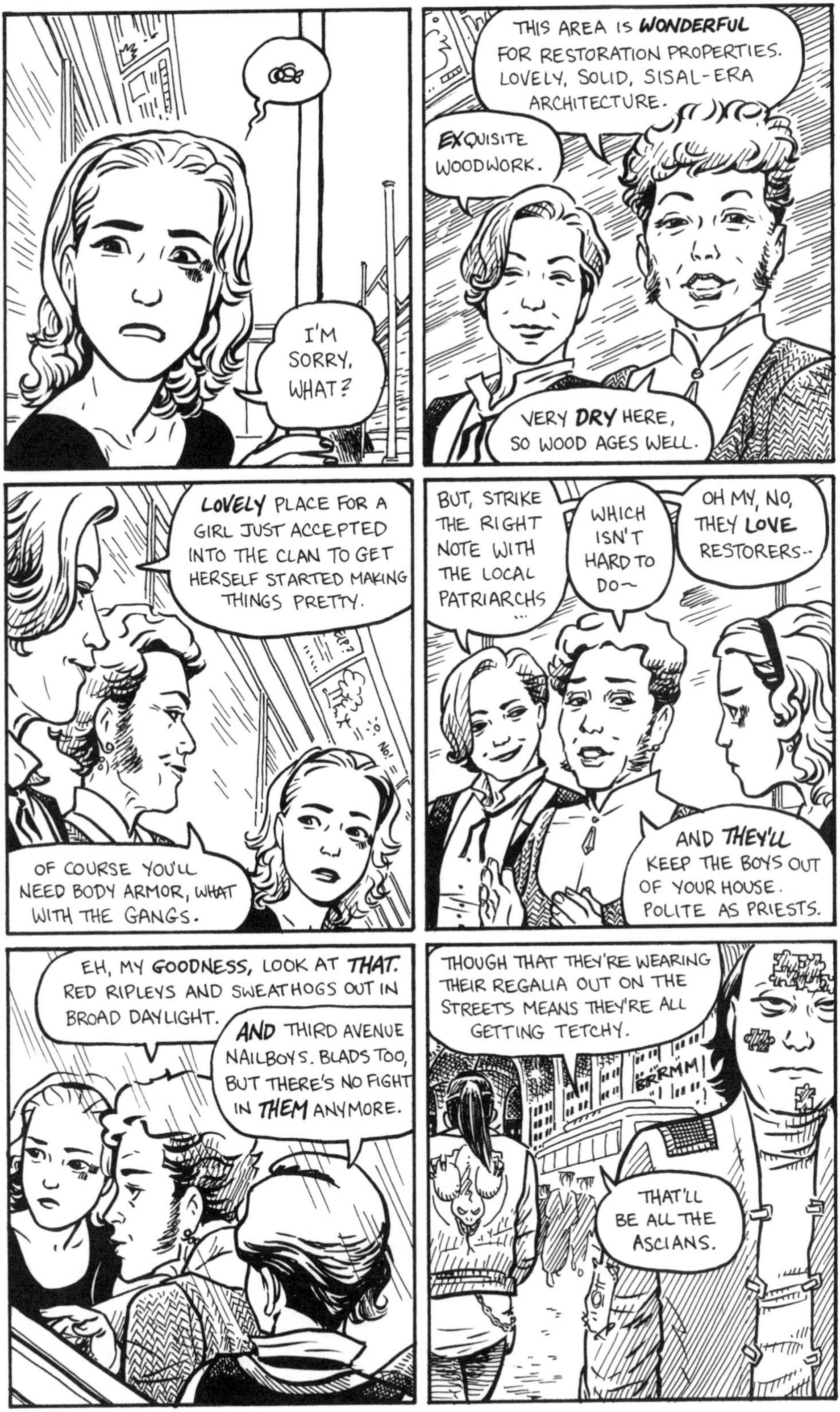
I'M SORRY, WHAT?
THIS AREA IS WONDERFUL FOR RESTORATION PROPERTIES. LOVELY, SOLID, SISAL-ERA ARCHITECTURE.
EXQUISITE WOODWORK.
VERY DRY HERE, SO WOOD AGES WELL.
LOVELY PLACE FOR A GIRL JUST ACCEPTED INTO THE CLAN TO GET HERSELF STARTED MAKING THINGS PRETTY.
OF COURSE YOU'LL NEED BODY ARMOR, WHAT WITH THE GANGS.
BUT, STRIKE THE RIGHT NOTE WITH THE LOCAL PATRIARCHS...
WHICH ISN'T HARD TO DO~
OH MY, NO, THEY LOVE RESTORERS--
AND THEY'LL KEEP THE BOYS OUT OF YOUR HOUSE. POLITE AS PRIESTS.
EH, MY GOODNESS, LOOK AT THAT. RED RIPLEYS AND SWEATHOGS OUT IN BROAD DAYLIGHT.
AND THIRD AVENUE NAILBOYS. BLADS TOO, BUT THERE'S NO FIGHT IN THEM ANYMORE.
THOUGH THAT THEY'RE WEARING THEIR REGALIA OUT ON THE STREETS MEANS THEY'RE ALL GETTING TETCHY.
BRRMM!
THAT'LL BE ALL THE ASCIANS.

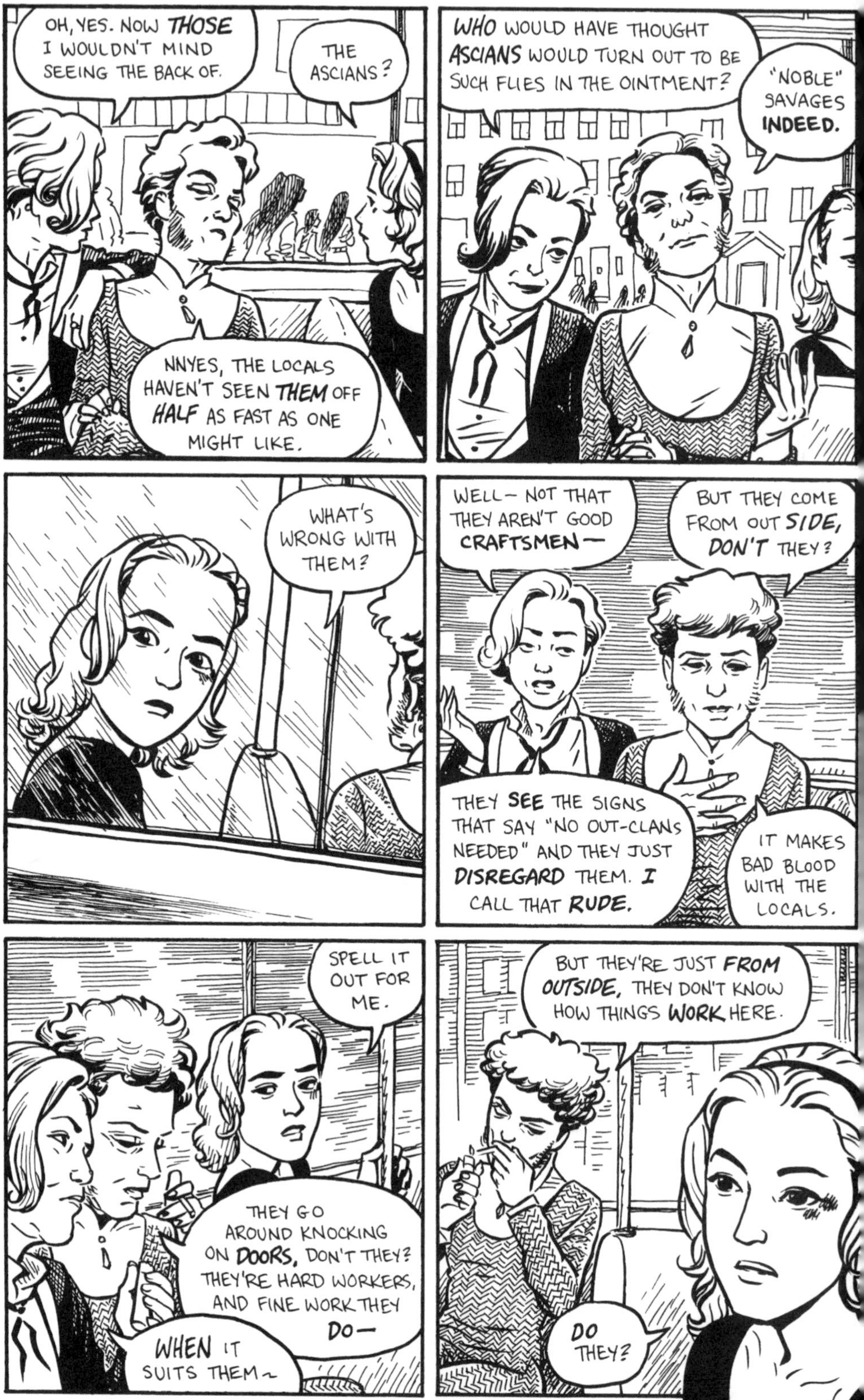
OH, YES. NOW THOSE I WOULDN'T MIND SEEING THE BACK OF.
THE ASCIANS?
NNYES, THE LOCALS HAVEN'T SEEN THEM OFF HALF AS FAST AS ONE MIGHT LIKE.
WHO WOULD HAVE THOUGHT ASCIANS WOULD TURN OUT TO BE SUCH FLIES IN THE OINTMENT?
"NOBLE" SAVAGES INDEED.
WHAT'S WRONG WITH THEM?
WELL— NOT THAT THEY AREN'T GOOD CRAFTSMEN—
BUT THEY COME FROM OUTSIDE, DON'T THEY?
THEY SEE THE SIGNS THAT SAY "NO OUT-CLANS NEEDED" AND THEY JUST DISREGARD THEM. I CALL THAT RUDE.
IT MAKES BAD BLOOD WITH THE LOCALS.
SPELL IT OUT FOR ME.
THEY GO AROUND KNOCKING ON DOORS, DON'T THEY? THEY'RE HARD WORKERS, AND FINE WORK THEY DO—
WHEN IT SUITS THEM~
BUT THEY'RE JUST FROM OUTSIDE, THEY DON'T KNOW HOW THINGS WORK HERE.
DO THEY?

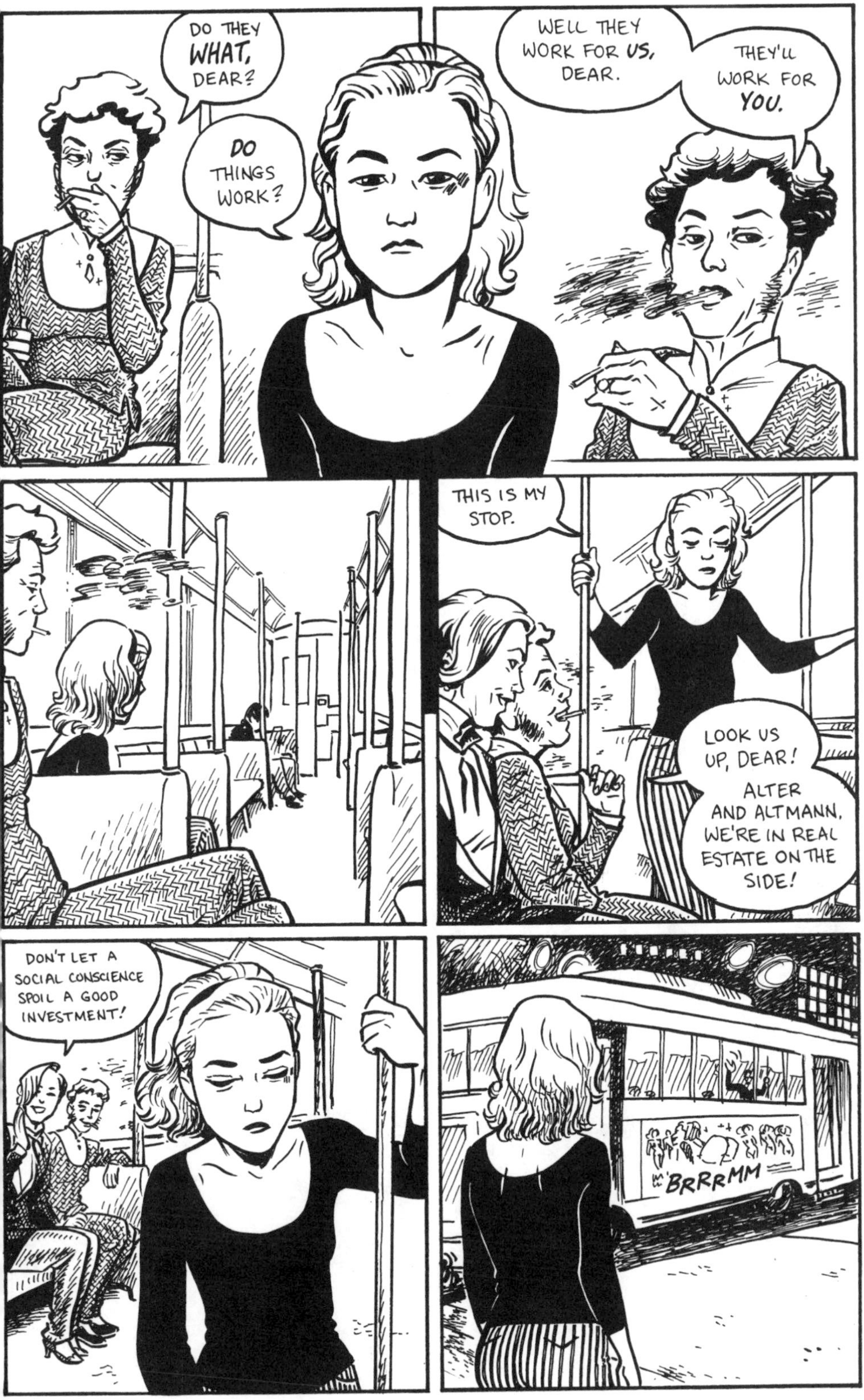
DO THEY WHAT, DEAR?
DO THINGS WORK?
WELL THEY WORK FOR US, DEAR.
THEY'LL WORK FOR YOU.
THIS IS MY STOP.
LOOK US UP, DEAR!
ALTER AND ALTMANN. WE'RE IN REAL ESTATE ON THE SIDE!
DON'T LET A SOCIAL CONSCIENCE SPOIL A GOOD INVESTMENT!
BRRRMM

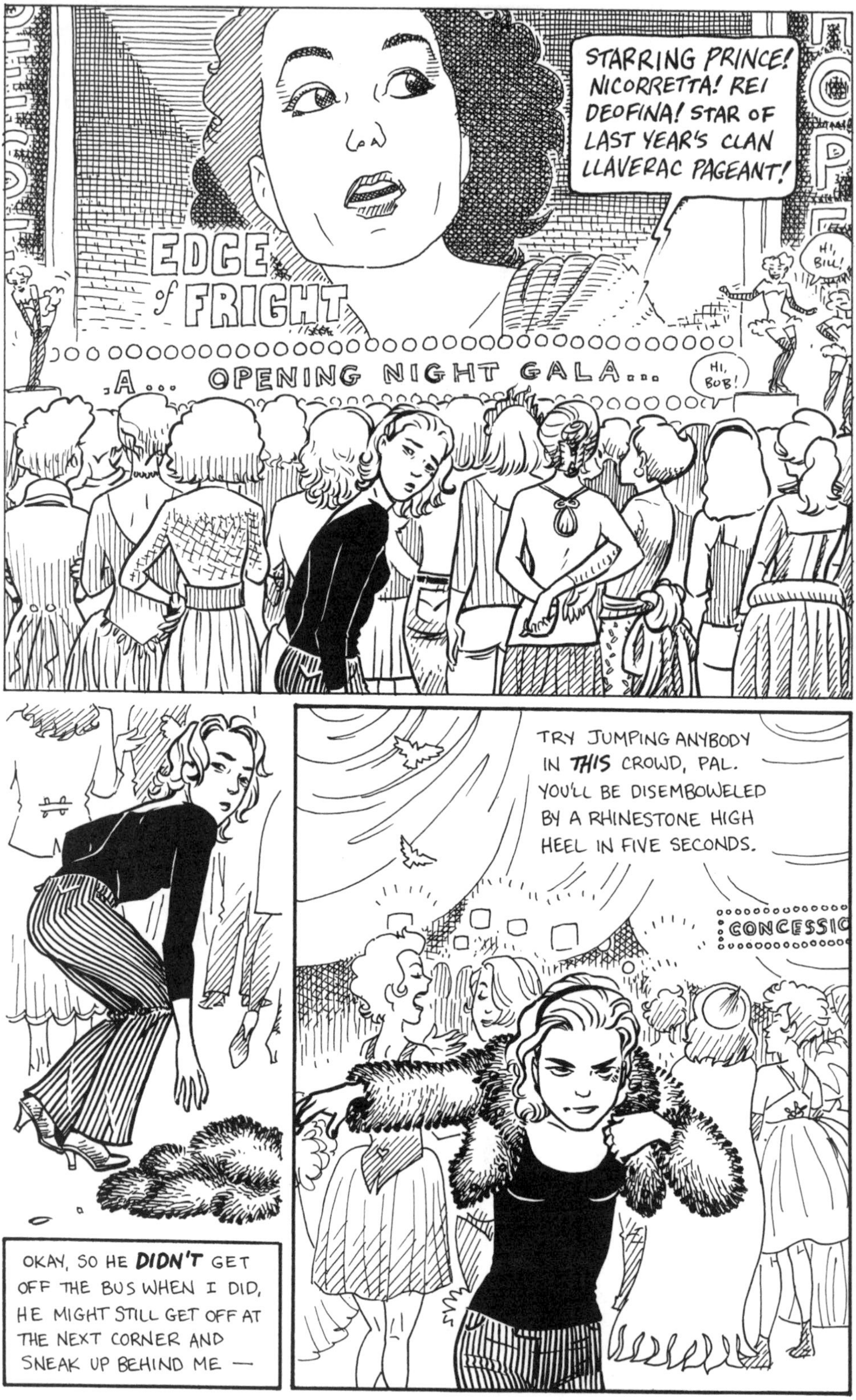
STARRING PRINCE! NICORRETTA! REI DEOFINA! STAR OF LAST YEAR'S CLAN LLAVERAC PAGEANT!
EDGE of FRIGHT
HI, BILL!
A... OPENING NIGHT GALA...
HI, BOB!
OKAY, SO HE DIDN'T GET OFF THE BUS WHEN I DID, HE MIGHT STILL GET OFF AT THE NEXT CORNER AND SNEAK UP BEHIND ME —
TRY JUMPING ANYBODY IN THIS CROWD, PAL. YOU'LL BE DISEMBOWELED BY A RHINESTONE HIGH HEEL IN FIVE SECONDS.

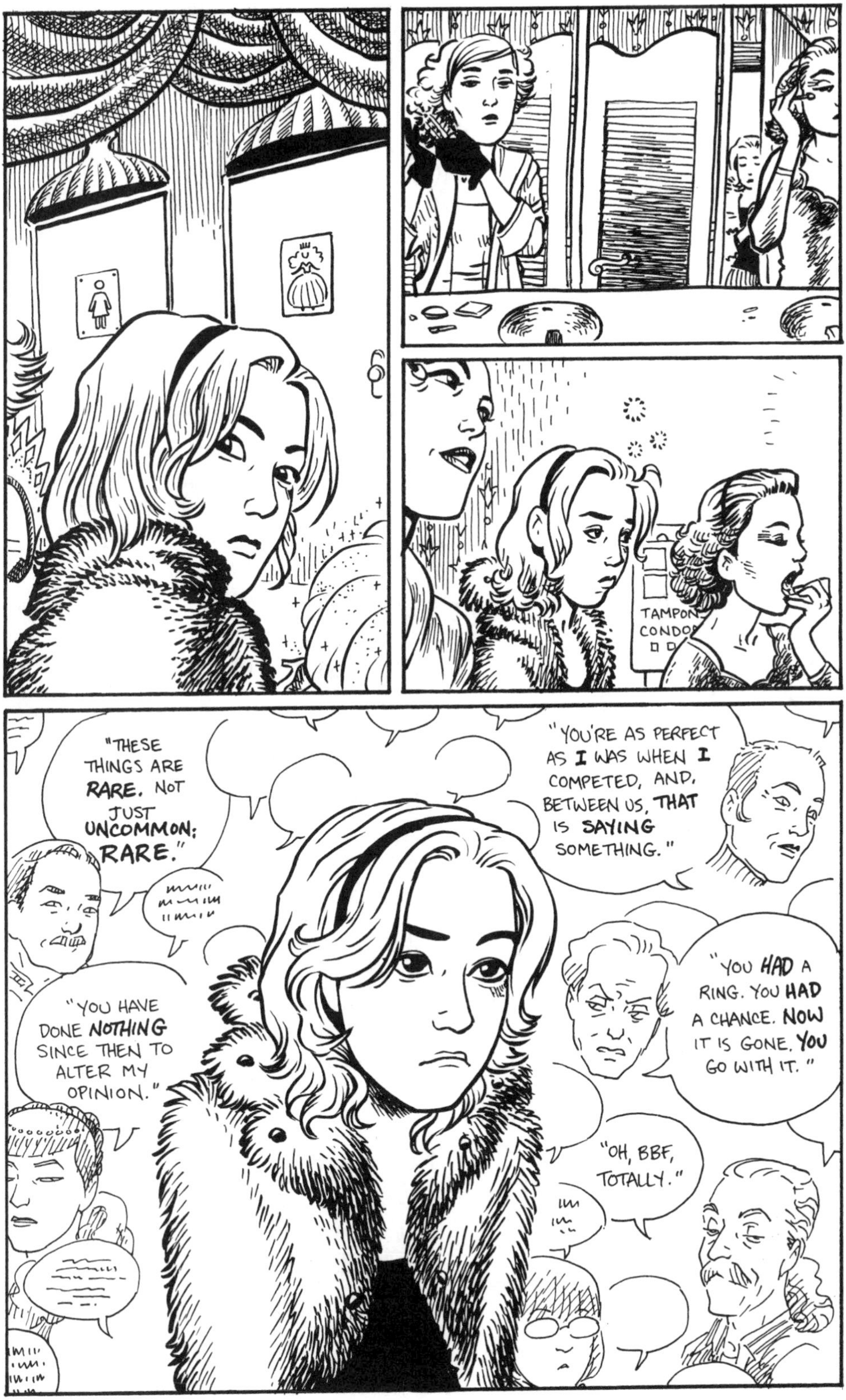
TAMPON
CONDO
"THESE THINGS ARE RARE. NOT JUST UNCOMMON: RARE."
"YOU'RE AS PERFECT AS I WAS WHEN I COMPETED, AND, BETWEEN US, THAT IS SAYING SOMETHING."
"YOU HAVE DONE NOTHING SINCE THEN TO ALTER MY OPINION."
"YOU HAD A RING. YOU HAD A CHANCE. NOW IT IS GONE. YOU GO WITH IT."
"OH, BBF, TOTALLY."

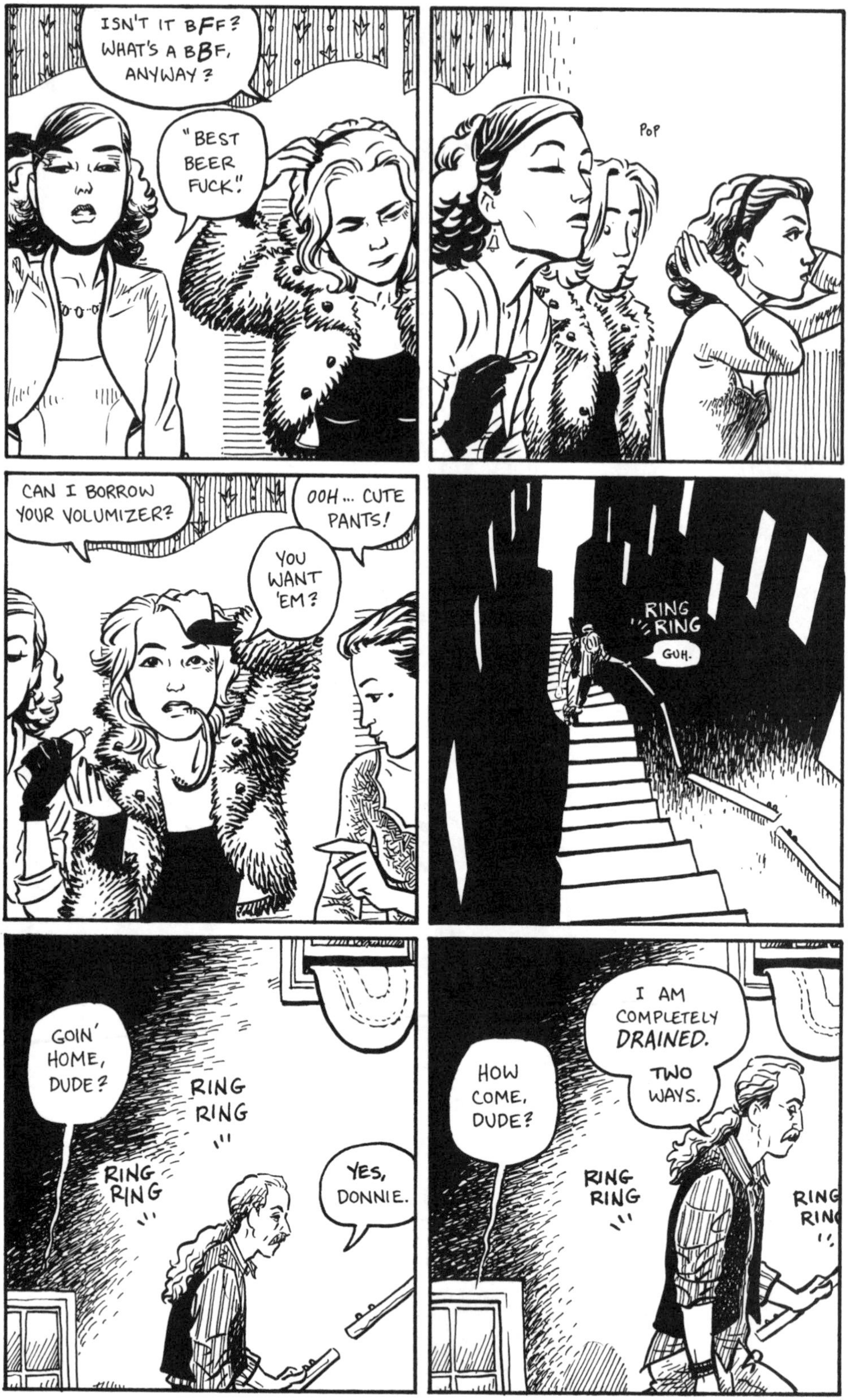
ISN'T IT BFF? WHAT'S A BBF, ANYWAY?
"BEST BEER FUCK!"
POP
CAN I BORROW YOUR VOLUMIZER?
OOH... CUTE PANTS!
YOU WANT 'EM?
RING RING
GUH.
GOIN' HOME, DUDE?
RING RING
RING RING
YES, DONNIE.
I AM COMPLETELY DRAINED.
TWO WAYS.
HOW COME, DUDE?
RING RING
RING RING

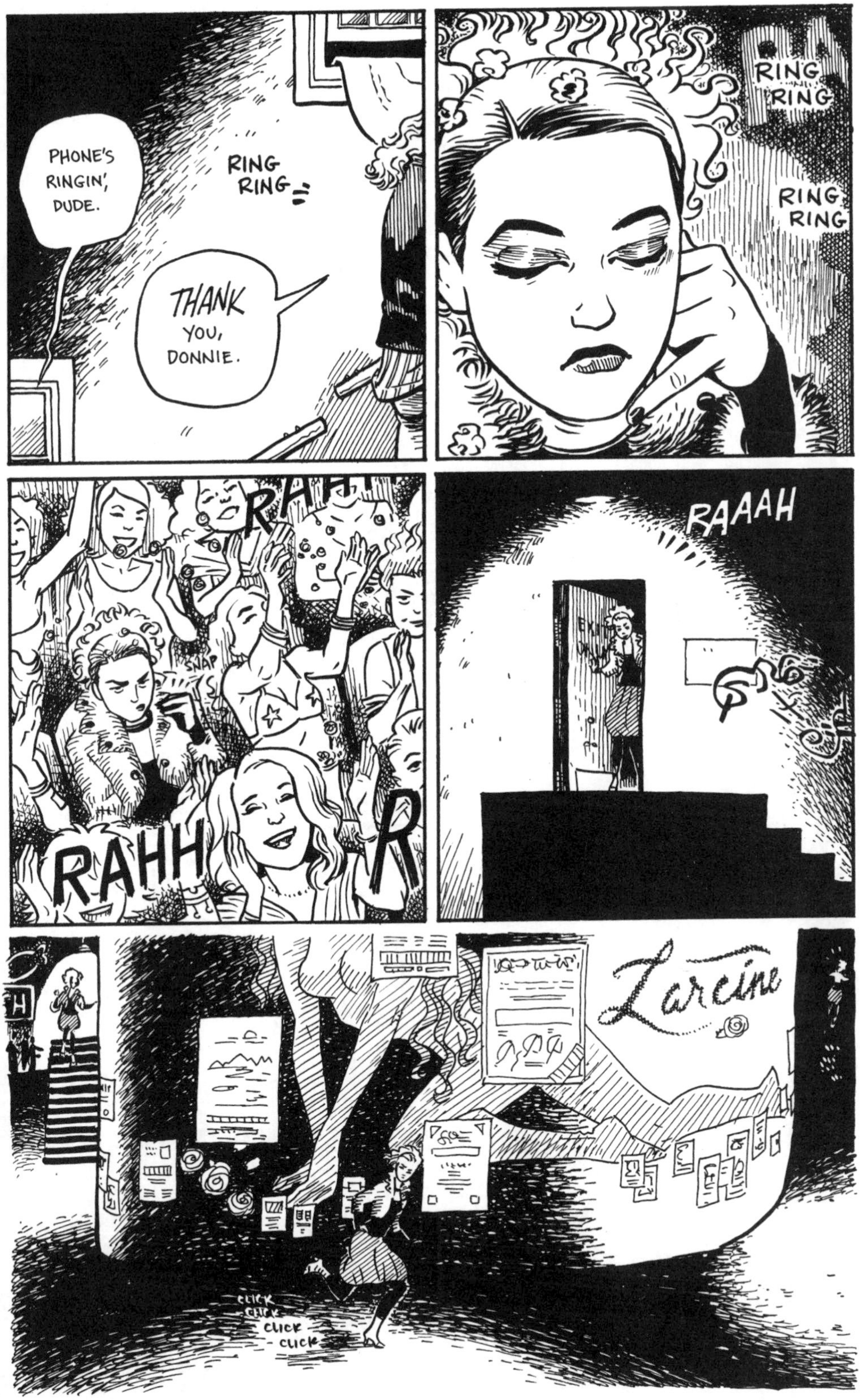

PHONE'S RINGIN', DUDE.
RING RING
THANK YOU, DONNIE.
RING RING
RING RING
SNAP
RAHH
R
RAAAH
Larcine
CLICK CLICK CLICK CLICK

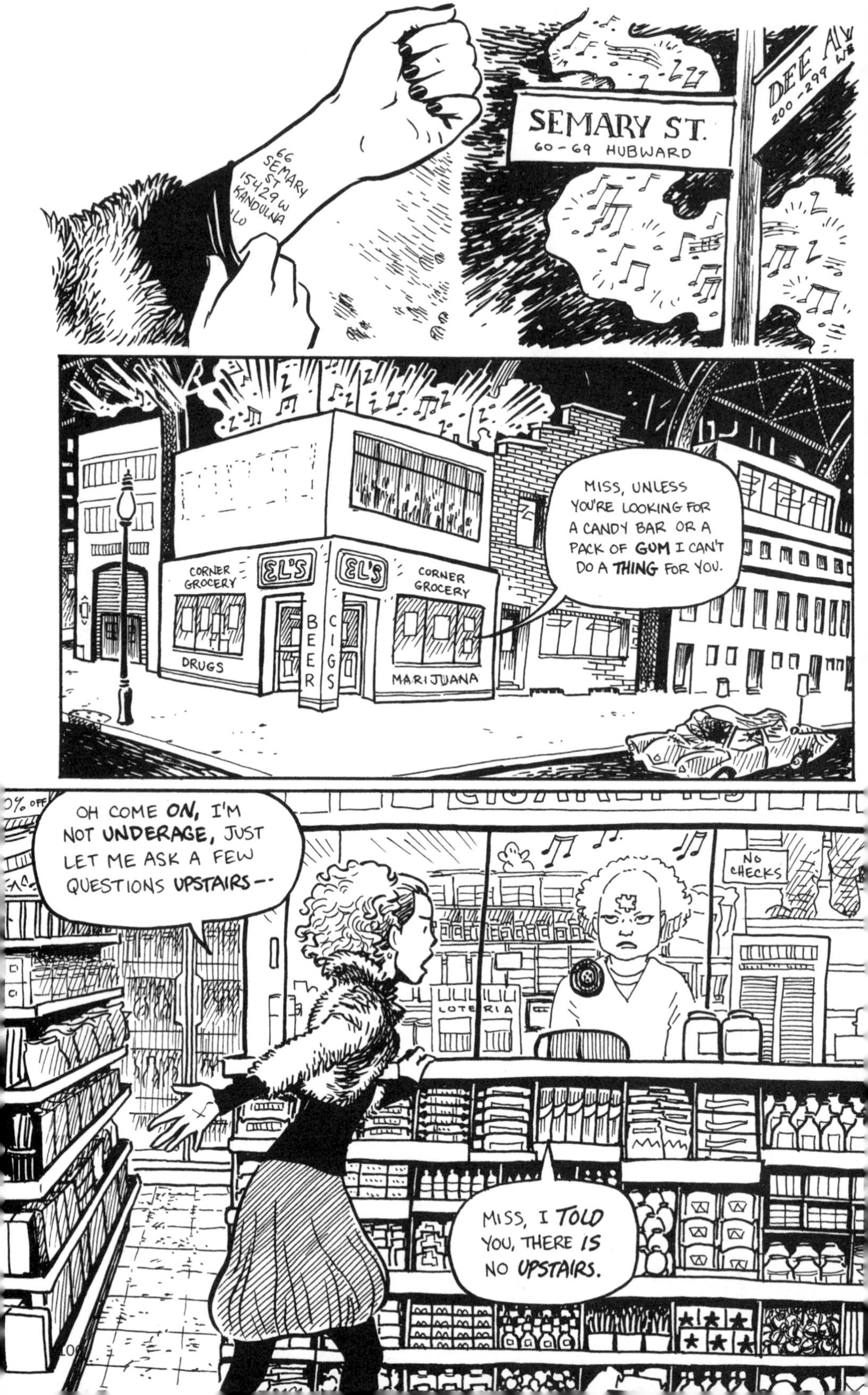
66
SEMARY
ST
15429W
KANDULNA
LO
SEMARY ST.
60-69 HUBWARD
DEE AV
200-299 WE
CORNER GROCERY
EL'S
EL'S
CORNER GROCERY
DRUGS
BEER
CIGS
MARIJUANA
MISS, UNLESS YOU'RE LOOKING FOR A CANDY BAR OR A PACK OF GUM I CAN'T DO A THING FOR YOU.
OH COME ON, I'M NOT UNDERAGE, JUST LET ME ASK A FEW QUESTIONS UPSTAIRS--
NO CHECKS
LOTERIA
MISS, I TOLD YOU, THERE IS NO UPSTAIRS.

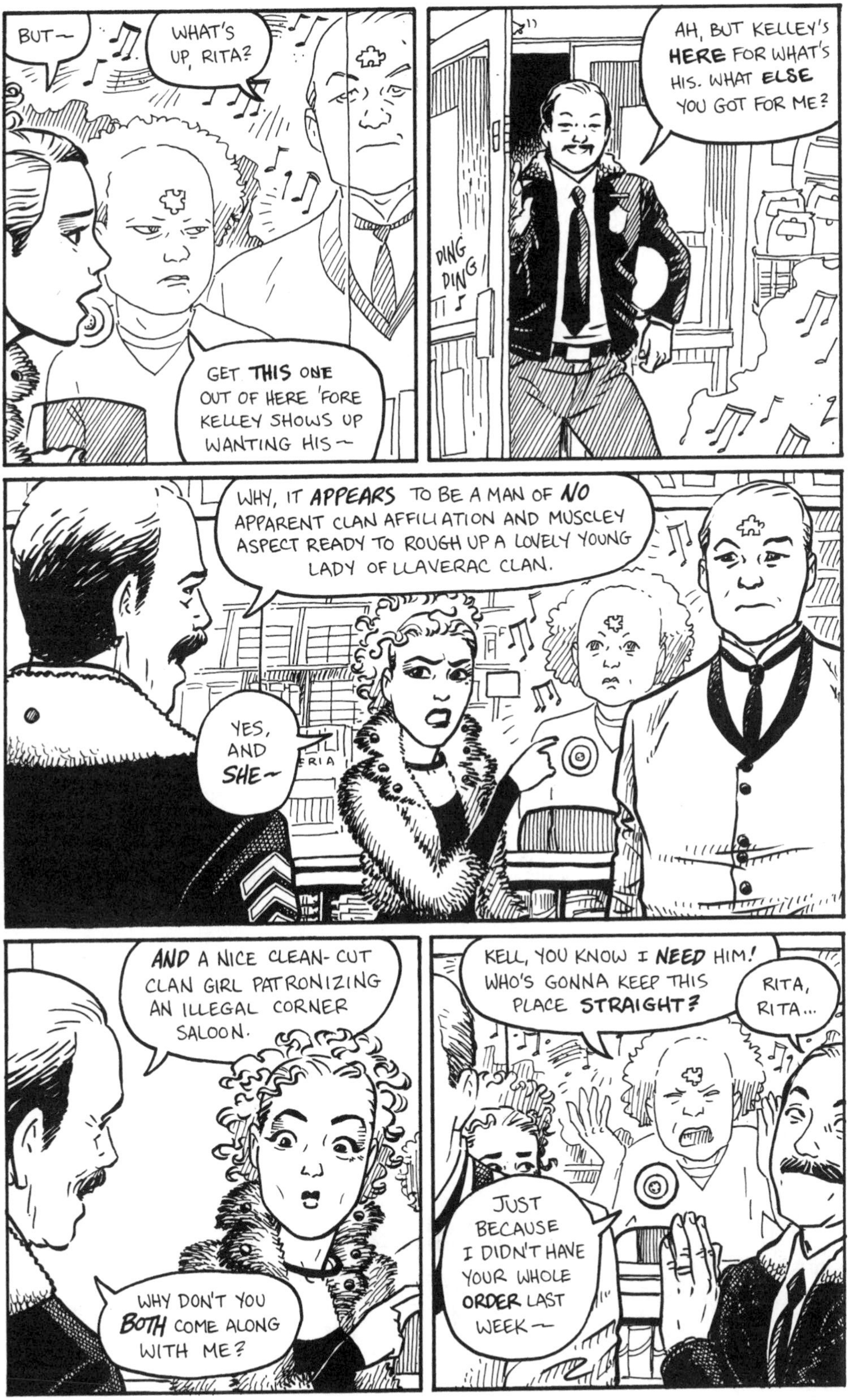

BUT~
WHAT'S UP, RITA?
GET THIS ONE OUT OF HERE 'FORE KELLEY SHOWS UP WANTING HIS~
DING DING
AH, BUT KELLEY'S HERE FOR WHAT'S HIS. WHAT ELSE YOU GOT FOR ME?
WHY, IT APPEARS TO BE A MAN OF NO APPARENT CLAN AFFILIATION AND MUSCLEY ASPECT READY TO ROUGH UP A LOVELY YOUNG LADY OF LLAVERAC CLAN.
YES, AND SHE~
AND A NICE CLEAN-CUT CLAN GIRL PATRONIZING AN ILLEGAL CORNER SALOON.
WHY DON'T YOU BOTH COME ALONG WITH ME?
KELL, YOU KNOW I NEED HIM! WHO'S GONNA KEEP THIS PLACE STRAIGHT?
RITA, RITA...
JUST BECAUSE I DIDN'T HAVE YOUR WHOLE ORDER LAST WEEK~

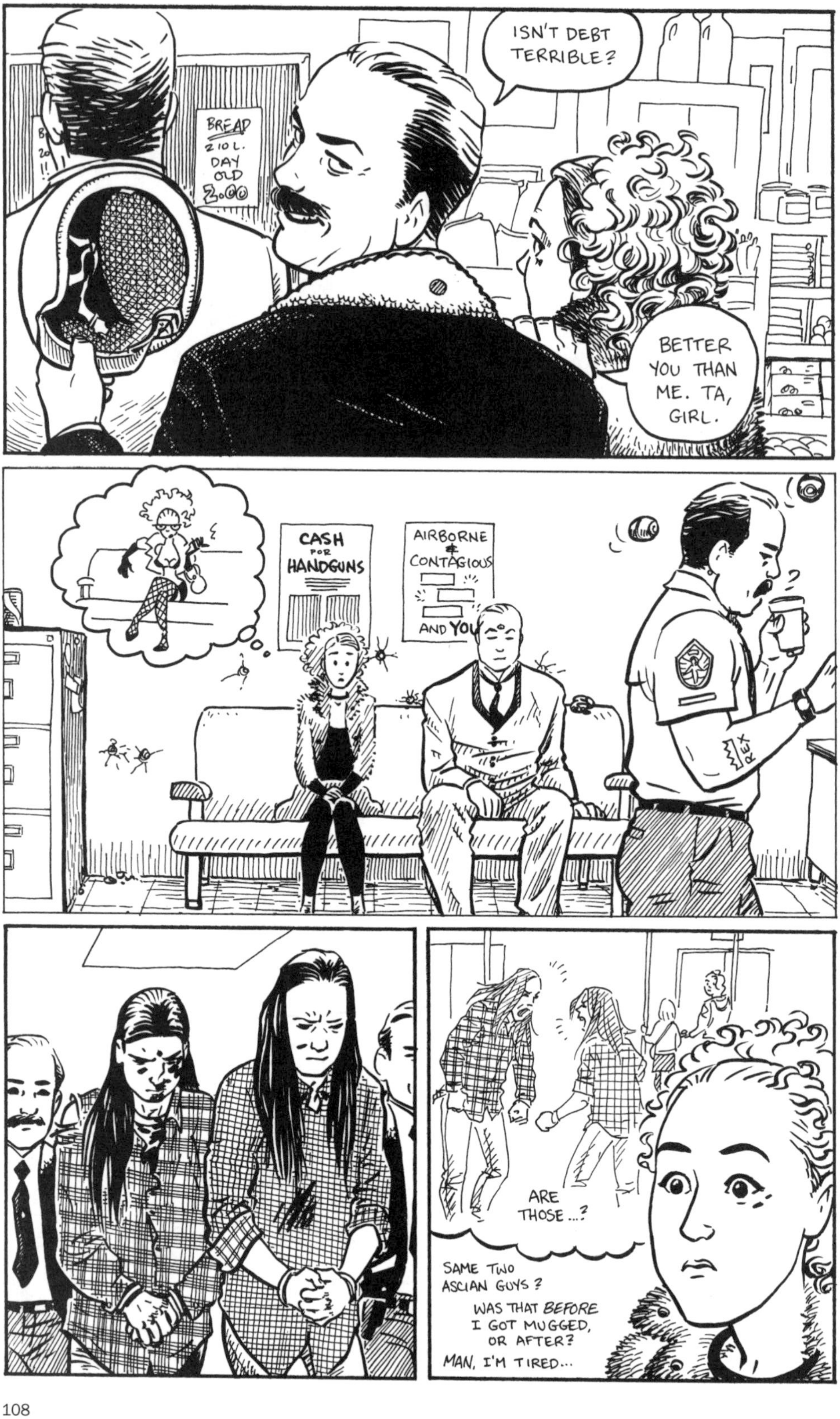
ISN'T DEBT TERRIBLE?
BREAD
DAY OLD
BETTER YOU THAN ME. TA, GIRL.
CASH FOR HANDGUNS
AIRBORNE & CONTAGIOUS
AND YOU
REX
ARE THOSE...?
SAME TWO ASCIAN GUYS?
WAS THAT *BEFORE* I GOT MUGGED, OR AFTER?
MAN, I'M TIRED...

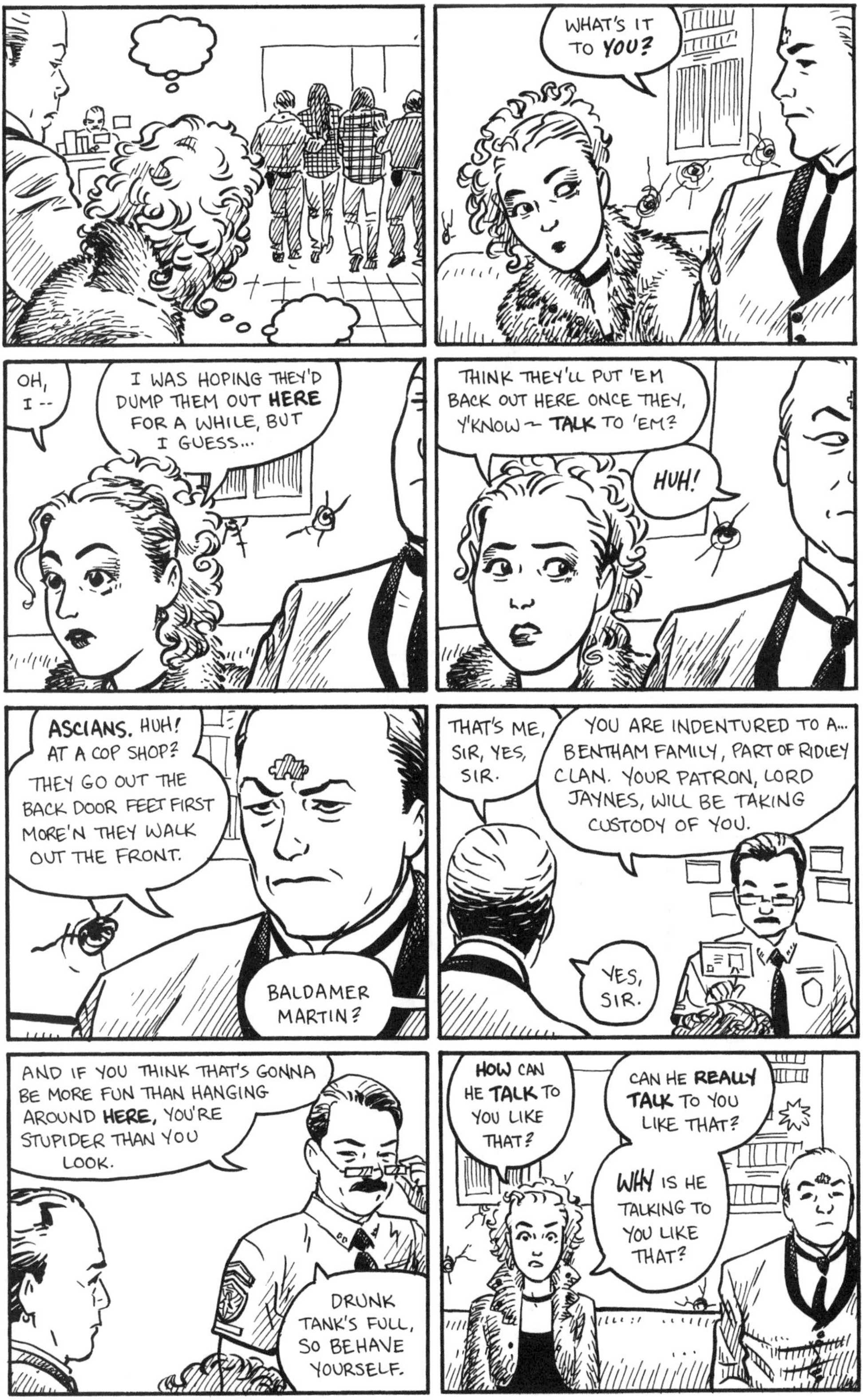
WHAT'S IT TO YOU?
OH, I --
I WAS HOPING THEY'D DUMP THEM OUT HERE FOR A WHILE, BUT I GUESS...
THINK THEY'LL PUT 'EM BACK OUT HERE ONCE THEY, Y'KNOW -- TALK TO 'EM?
HUH!
ASCIANS. HUH! AT A COP SHOP?
THEY GO OUT THE BACK DOOR FEET FIRST MORE'N THEY WALK OUT THE FRONT.
BALDAMER MARTIN?
THAT'S ME, SIR, YES, SIR.
YOU ARE INDENTURED TO A... BENTHAM FAMILY, PART OF RIDLEY CLAN. YOUR PATRON, LORD JAYNES, WILL BE TAKING CUSTODY OF YOU.
YES, SIR.
AND IF YOU THINK THAT'S GONNA BE MORE FUN THAN HANGING AROUND HERE, YOU'RE STUPIDER THAN YOU LOOK.
DRUNK TANK'S FULL, SO BEHAVE YOURSELF.
HOW CAN HE TALK TO YOU LIKE THAT?
CAN HE REALLY TALK TO YOU LIKE THAT?
WHY IS HE TALKING TO YOU LIKE THAT?

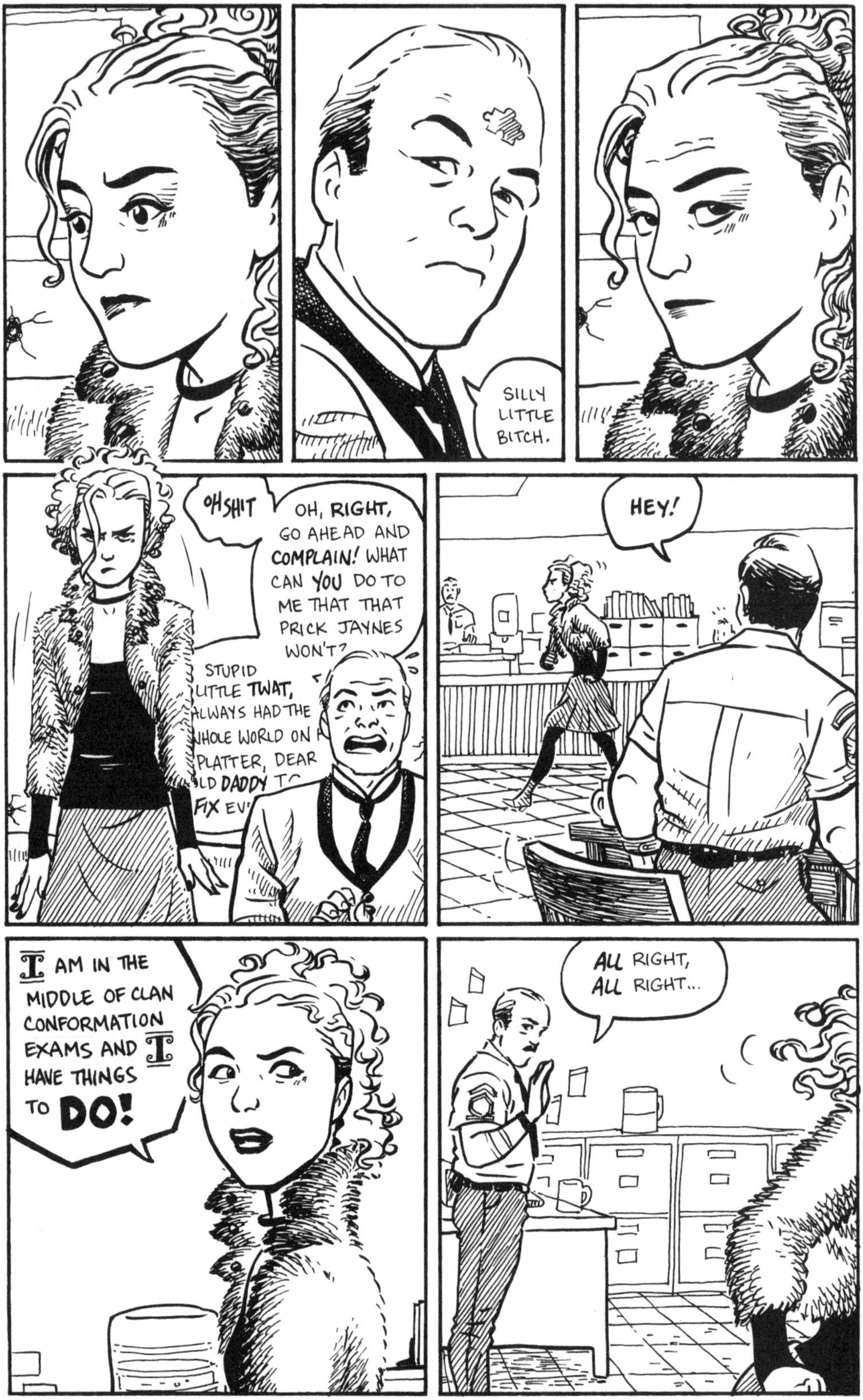
SILLY LITTLE BITCH.
OH SHIT
OH, RIGHT, GO AHEAD AND COMPLAIN! WHAT CAN YOU DO TO ME THAT THAT PRICK JAYNES WON'T?
STUPID LITTLE TWAT, ALWAYS HAD THE WHOLE WORLD ON A PLATTER, DEAR OLD DADDY TO FIX EV
HEY!
I AM IN THE MIDDLE OF CLAN CONFORMATION EXAMS AND I HAVE THINGS TO DO!
ALL RIGHT, ALL RIGHT...

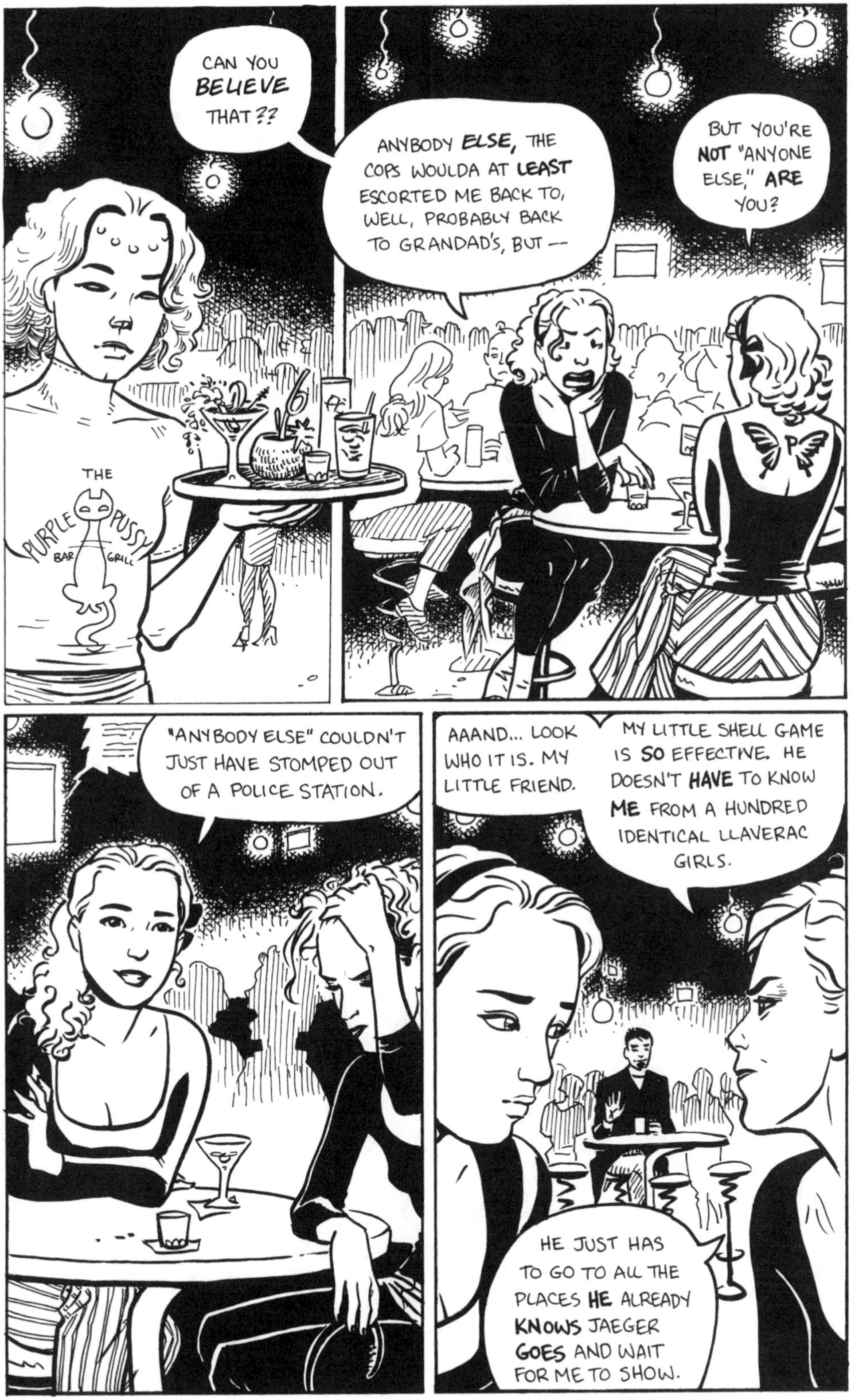
CAN YOU BELIEVE THAT??
ANYBODY ELSE, THE COPS WOULDA AT LEAST ESCORTED ME BACK TO, WELL, PROBABLY BACK TO GRANDAD'S, BUT --
BUT YOU'RE NOT "ANYONE ELSE," ARE YOU?
THE PURPLE PUSSY BAR GRILL
"ANYBODY ELSE" COULDN'T JUST HAVE STOMPED OUT OF A POLICE STATION.
AAAND... LOOK WHO IT IS. MY LITTLE FRIEND.
MY LITTLE SHELL GAME IS SO EFFECTIVE. HE DOESN'T HAVE TO KNOW ME FROM A HUNDRED IDENTICAL LLAVERAC GIRLS.
HE JUST HAS TO GO TO ALL THE PLACES HE ALREADY KNOWS JAEGER GOES AND WAIT FOR ME TO SHOW.

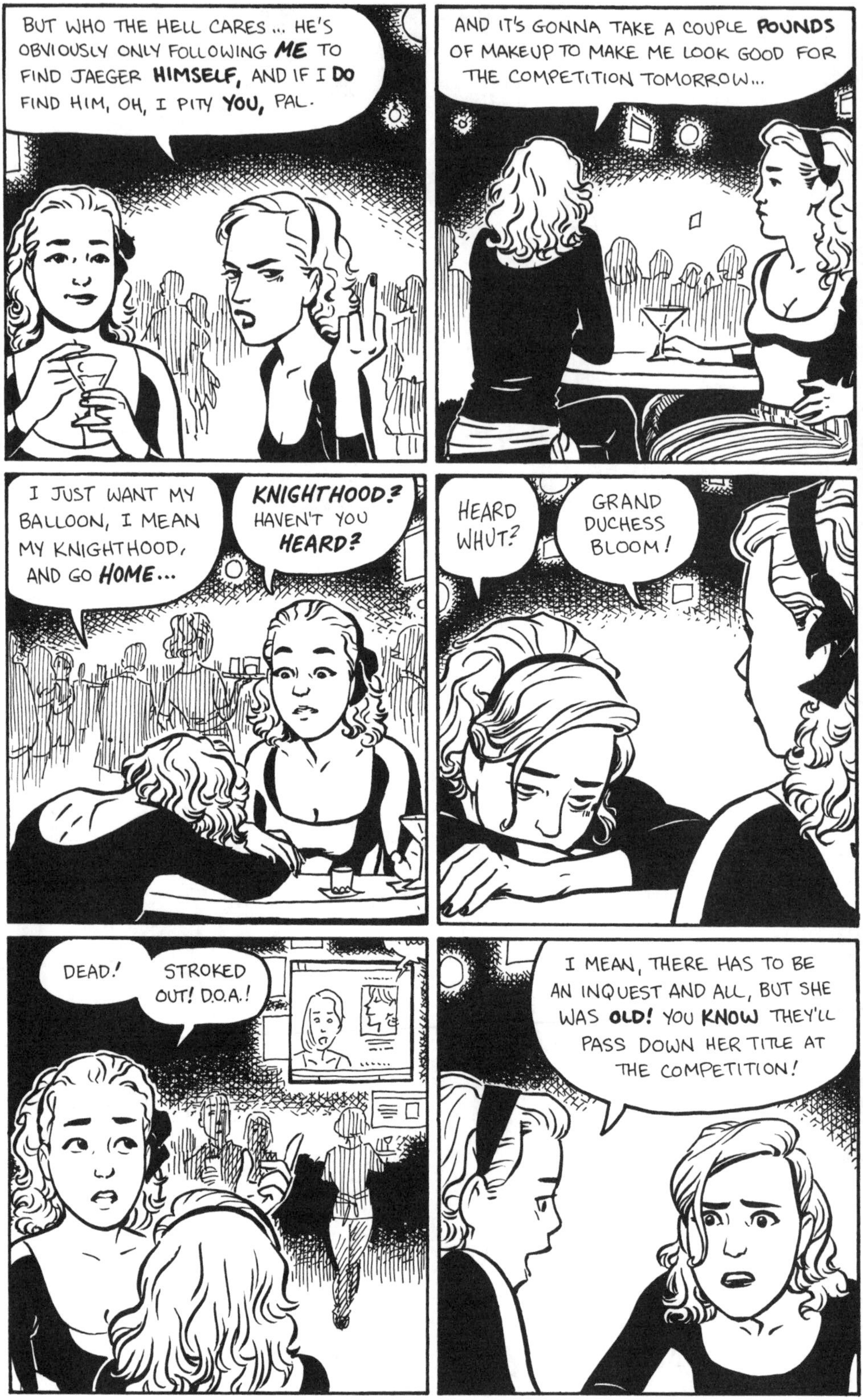
BUT WHO THE HELL CARES... HE'S OBVIOUSLY ONLY FOLLOWING ME TO FIND JAEGER HIMSELF, AND IF I DO FIND HIM, OH, I PITY YOU, PAL.
AND IT'S GONNA TAKE A COUPLE POUNDS OF MAKEUP TO MAKE ME LOOK GOOD FOR THE COMPETITION TOMORROW...
I JUST WANT MY BALLOON, I MEAN MY KNIGHTHOOD, AND GO HOME...
KNIGHTHOOD? HAVEN'T YOU HEARD?
HEARD WHUT?
GRAND DUCHESS BLOOM!
DEAD!
STROKED OUT! D.O.A.!
I MEAN, THERE HAS TO BE AN INQUEST AND ALL, BUT SHE WAS OLD! YOU KNOW THEY'LL PASS DOWN HER TITLE AT THE COMPETITION!

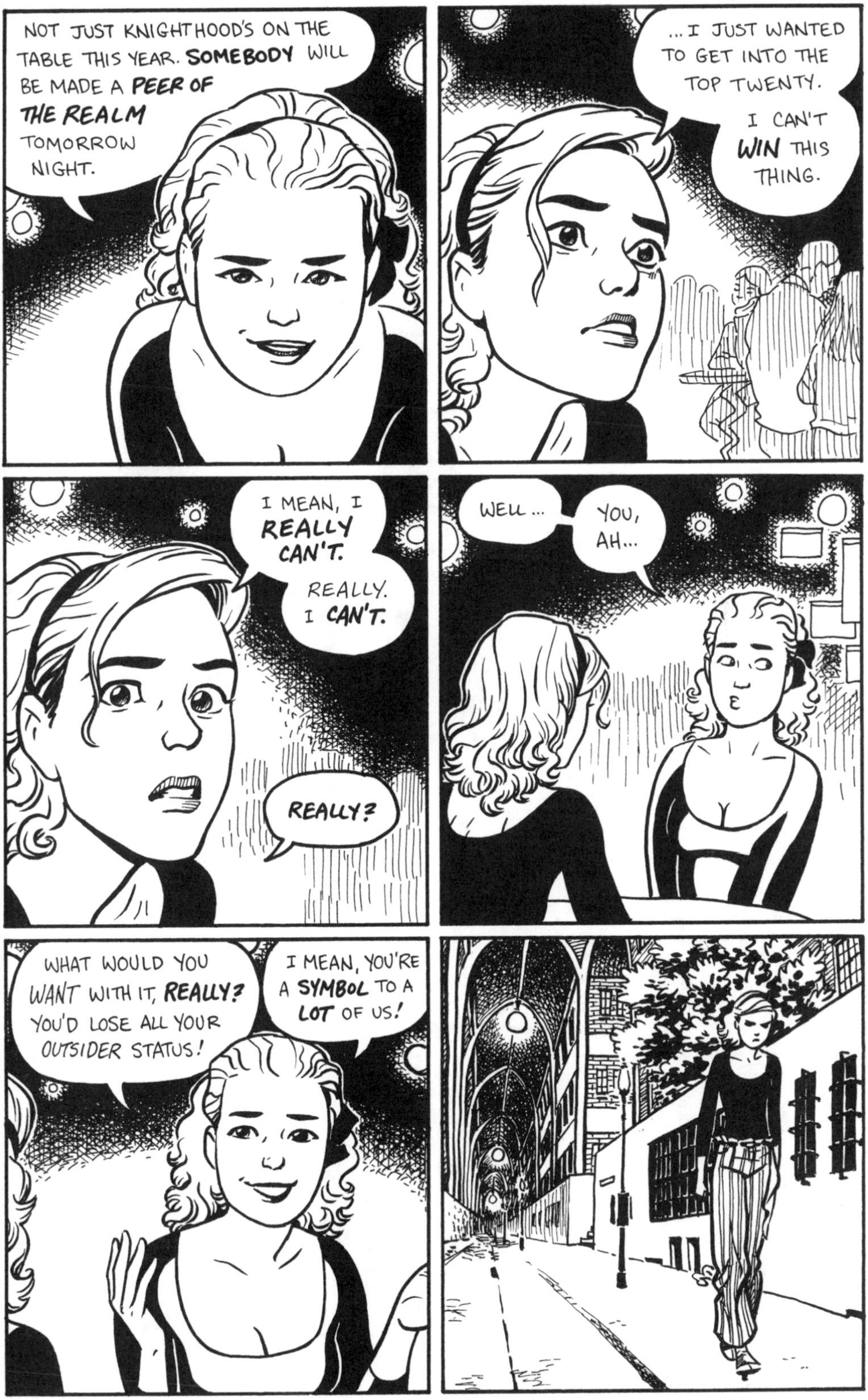
NOT JUST KNIGHTHOOD'S ON THE TABLE THIS YEAR. SOMEBODY WILL BE MADE A PEER OF THE REALM TOMORROW NIGHT.
...I JUST WANTED TO GET INTO THE TOP TWENTY.
I CAN'T WIN THIS THING.
I MEAN, I REALLY CAN'T.
REALLY. I CAN'T.
REALLY?
WELL...
YOU, AH...
WHAT WOULD YOU WANT WITH IT, REALLY? YOU'D LOSE ALL YOUR OUTSIDER STATUS!
I MEAN, YOU'RE A SYMBOL TO A LOT OF US!

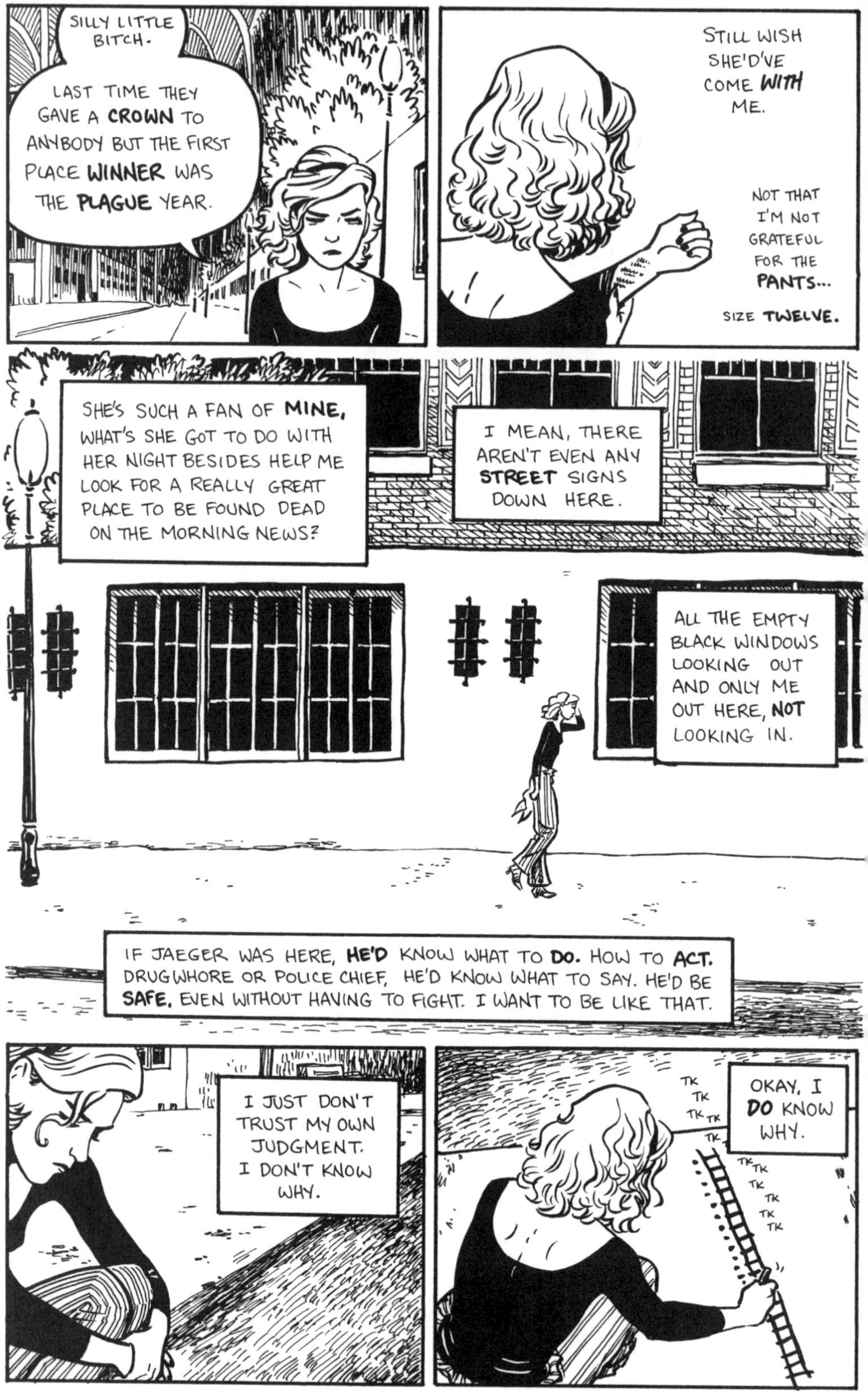
SILLY LITTLE BITCH.
LAST TIME THEY GAVE A CROWN TO ANYBODY BUT THE FIRST PLACE WINNER WAS THE PLAGUE YEAR.
STILL WISH SHE'D'VE COME WITH ME.
NOT THAT I'M NOT GRATEFUL FOR THE PANTS...
SIZE TWELVE.
SHE'S SUCH A FAN OF MINE, WHAT'S SHE GOT TO DO WITH HER NIGHT BESIDES HELP ME LOOK FOR A REALLY GREAT PLACE TO BE FOUND DEAD ON THE MORNING NEWS?
I MEAN, THERE AREN'T EVEN ANY STREET SIGNS DOWN HERE.
ALL THE EMPTY BLACK WINDOWS LOOKING OUT AND ONLY ME OUT HERE, NOT LOOKING IN.
IF JAEGER WAS HERE, HE'D KNOW WHAT TO DO. HOW TO ACT. DRUGWHORE OR POLICE CHIEF, HE'D KNOW WHAT TO SAY. HE'D BE SAFE, EVEN WITHOUT HAVING TO FIGHT. I WANT TO BE LIKE THAT.
I JUST DON'T TRUST MY OWN JUDGMENT. I DON'T KNOW WHY.
TK TK TK TK TK
OKAY, I DO KNOW WHY.
TK TK TK TK TK TK

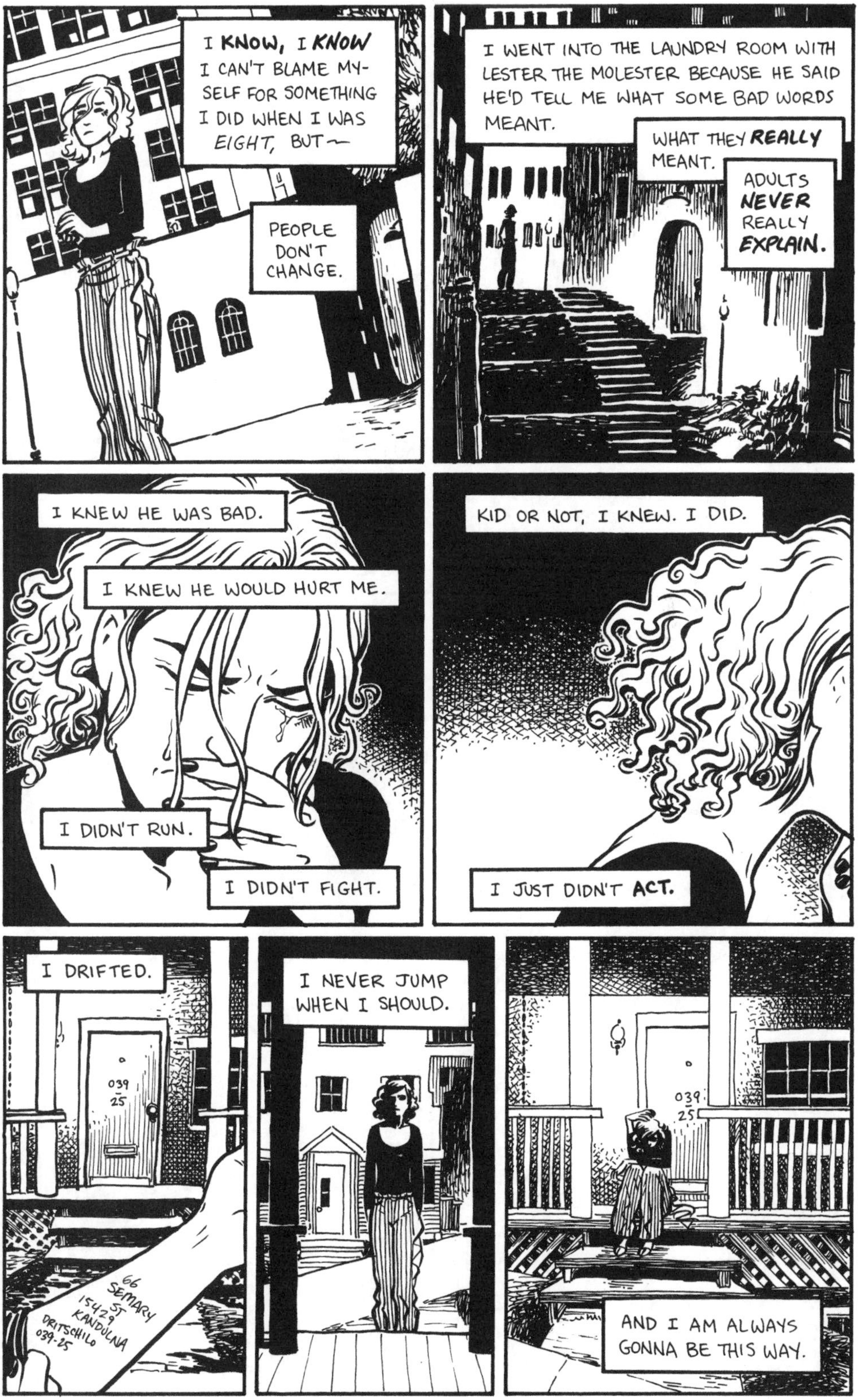
I KNOW, I KNOW I CAN'T BLAME MYSELF FOR SOMETHING I DID WHEN I WAS EIGHT, BUT—
PEOPLE DON'T CHANGE.
I WENT INTO THE LAUNDRY ROOM WITH LESTER THE MOLESTER BECAUSE HE SAID HE'D TELL ME WHAT SOME BAD WORDS MEANT.
WHAT THEY REALLY MEANT.
ADULTS NEVER REALLY EXPLAIN.
I KNEW HE WAS BAD.
I KNEW HE WOULD HURT ME.
I DIDN'T RUN.
I DIDN'T FIGHT.
KID OR NOT, I KNEW. I DID.
I JUST DIDN'T ACT.
I DRIFTED.
039 25
66 SEMARY ST 15429 KANDULNA DRITSCHILO 039-25
I NEVER JUMP WHEN I SHOULD.
039 25
AND I AM ALWAYS GONNA BE THIS WAY.

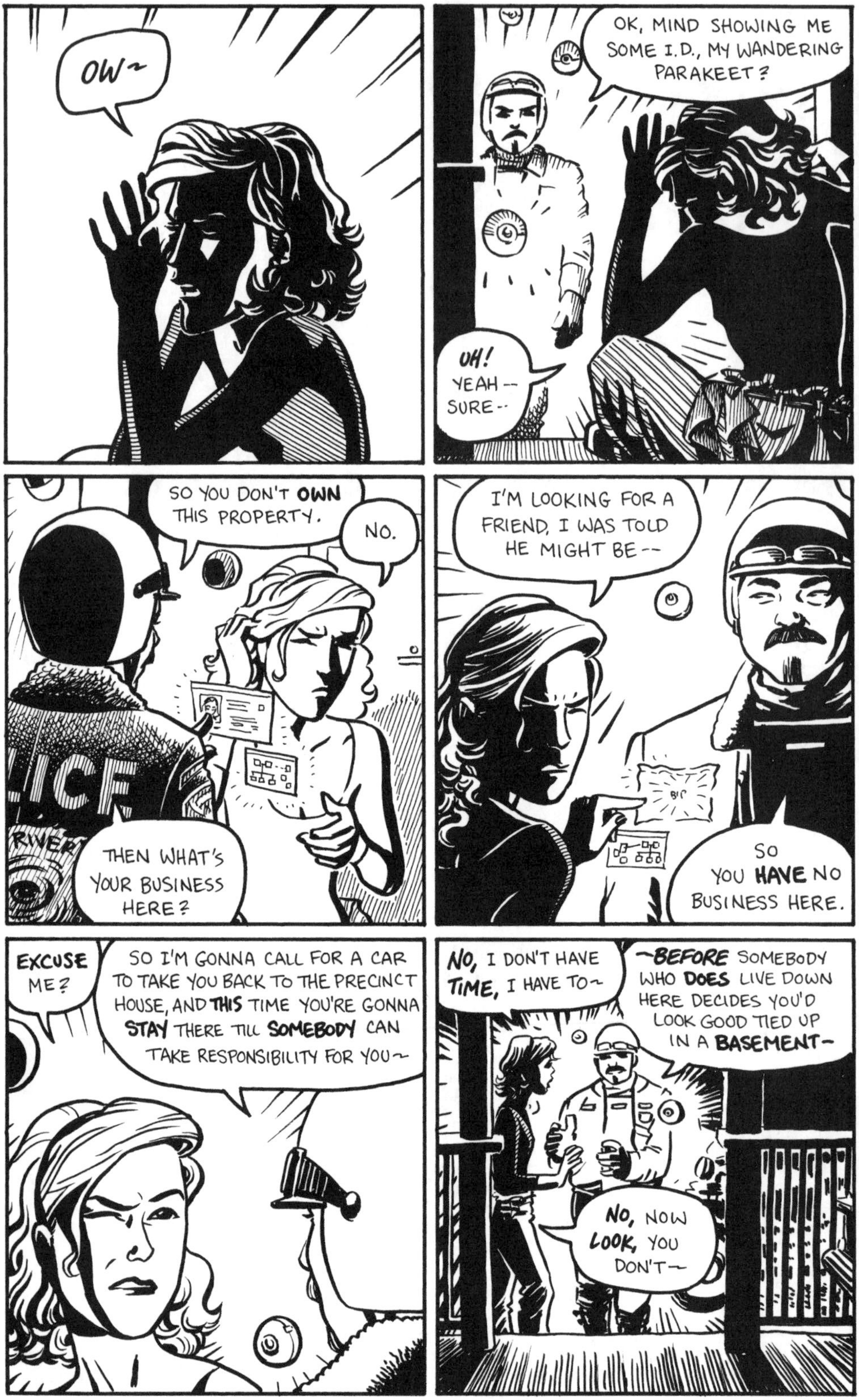
OW~
OK, MIND SHOWING ME SOME I.D., MY WANDERING PARAKEET?
UH! YEAH -- SURE --
SO YOU DON'T **OWN** THIS PROPERTY.
NO.
THEN WHAT'S YOUR BUSINESS HERE?
I'M LOOKING FOR A FRIEND, I WAS TOLD HE MIGHT BE --
SO YOU **HAVE** NO BUSINESS HERE.
EXCUSE ME?
SO I'M GONNA CALL FOR A CAR TO TAKE YOU BACK TO THE PRECINCT HOUSE, AND **THIS** TIME YOU'RE GONNA **STAY** THERE TILL **SOMEBODY** CAN TAKE RESPONSIBILITY FOR YOU~
NO, I DON'T HAVE **TIME,** I HAVE TO~
~**BEFORE** SOMEBODY WHO **DOES** LIVE DOWN HERE DECIDES YOU'D LOOK GOOD TIED UP IN A **BASEMENT**~
NO, NOW **LOOK,** YOU DON'T~

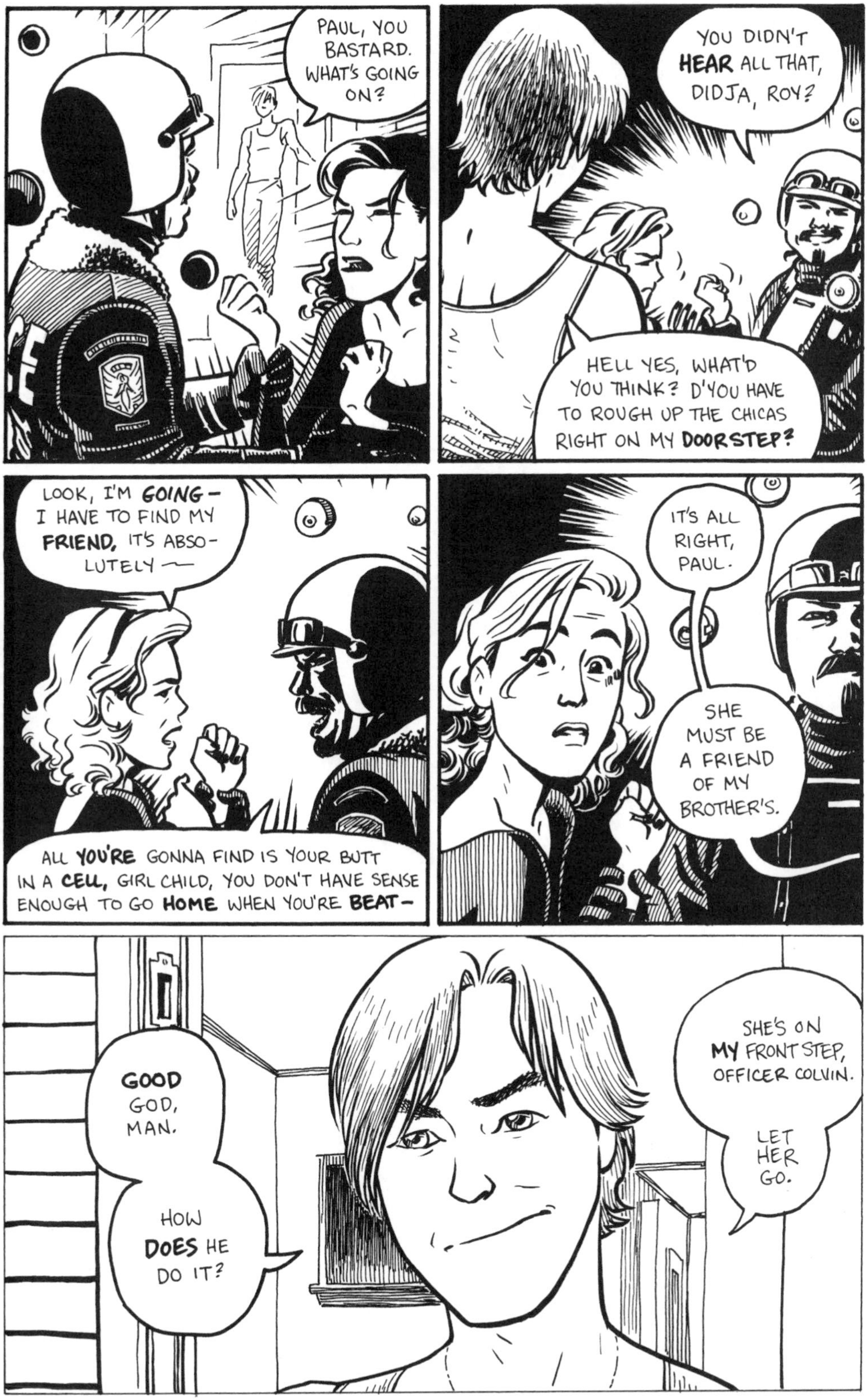
PAUL, YOU BASTARD. WHAT'S GOING ON?
YOU DIDN'T HEAR ALL THAT, DIDJA, ROY?
HELL YES, WHAT'D YOU THINK? D'YOU HAVE TO ROUGH UP THE CHICAS RIGHT ON MY DOORSTEP?
LOOK, I'M GOING— I HAVE TO FIND MY FRIEND, IT'S ABSOLUTELY—
ALL YOU'RE GONNA FIND IS YOUR BUTT IN A CELL, GIRL CHILD, YOU DON'T HAVE SENSE ENOUGH TO GO HOME WHEN YOU'RE BEAT—
IT'S ALL RIGHT, PAUL.
SHE MUST BE A FRIEND OF MY BROTHER'S.
GOOD GOD, MAN.
HOW DOES HE DO IT?
SHE'S ON MY FRONT STEP, OFFICER COLVIN.
LET HER GO.

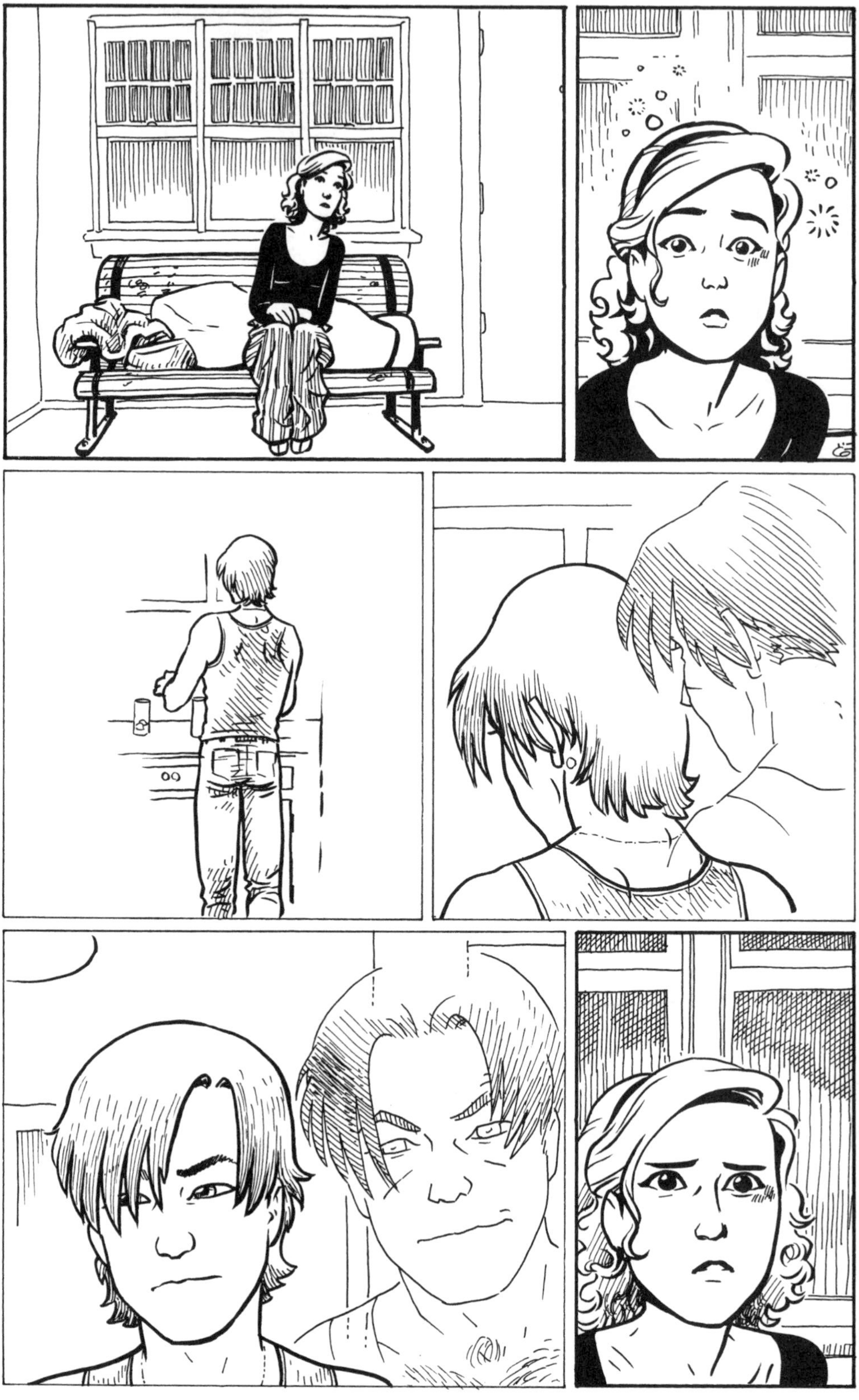

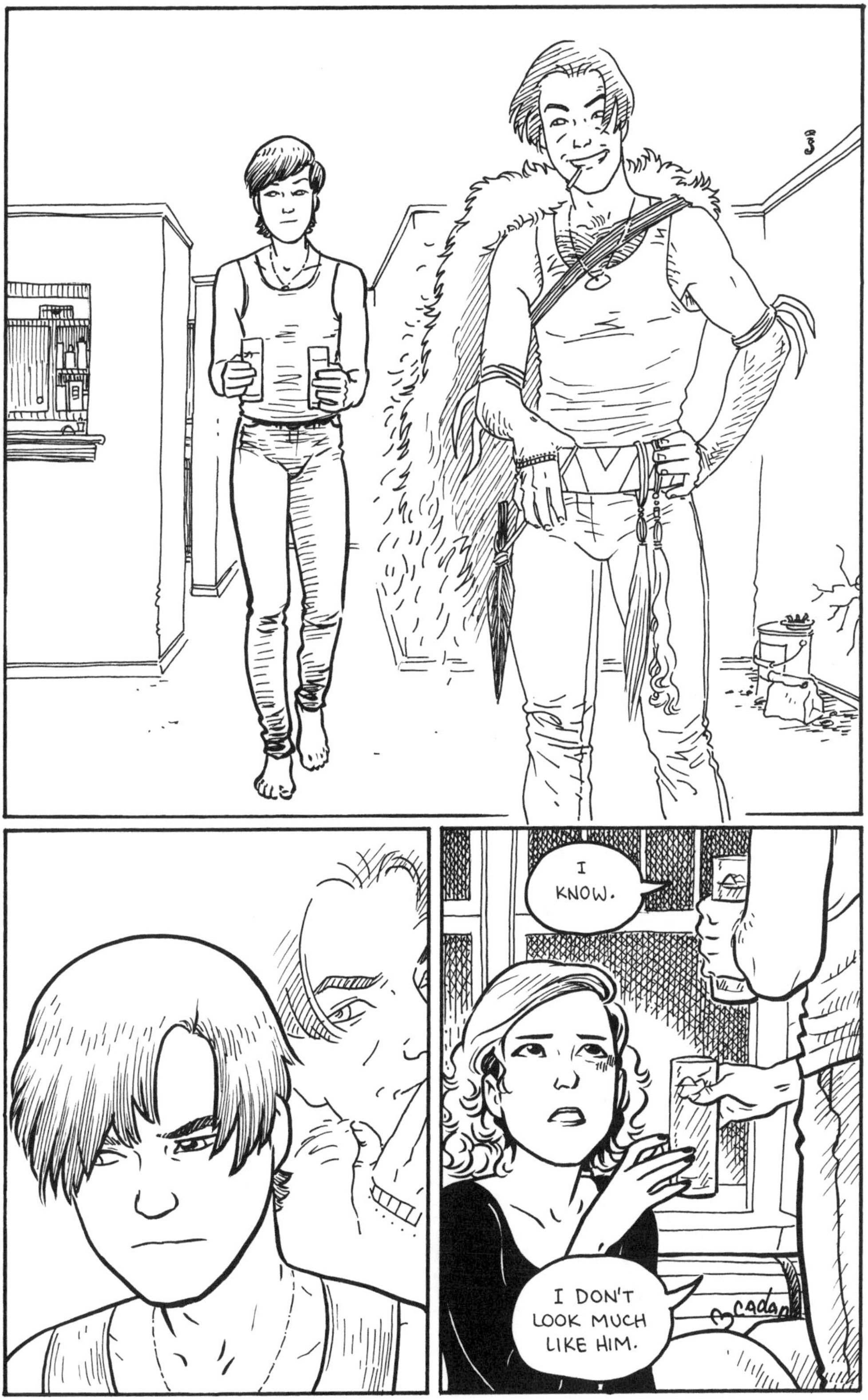
I KNOW.
I DON'T LOOK MUCH LIKE HIM.

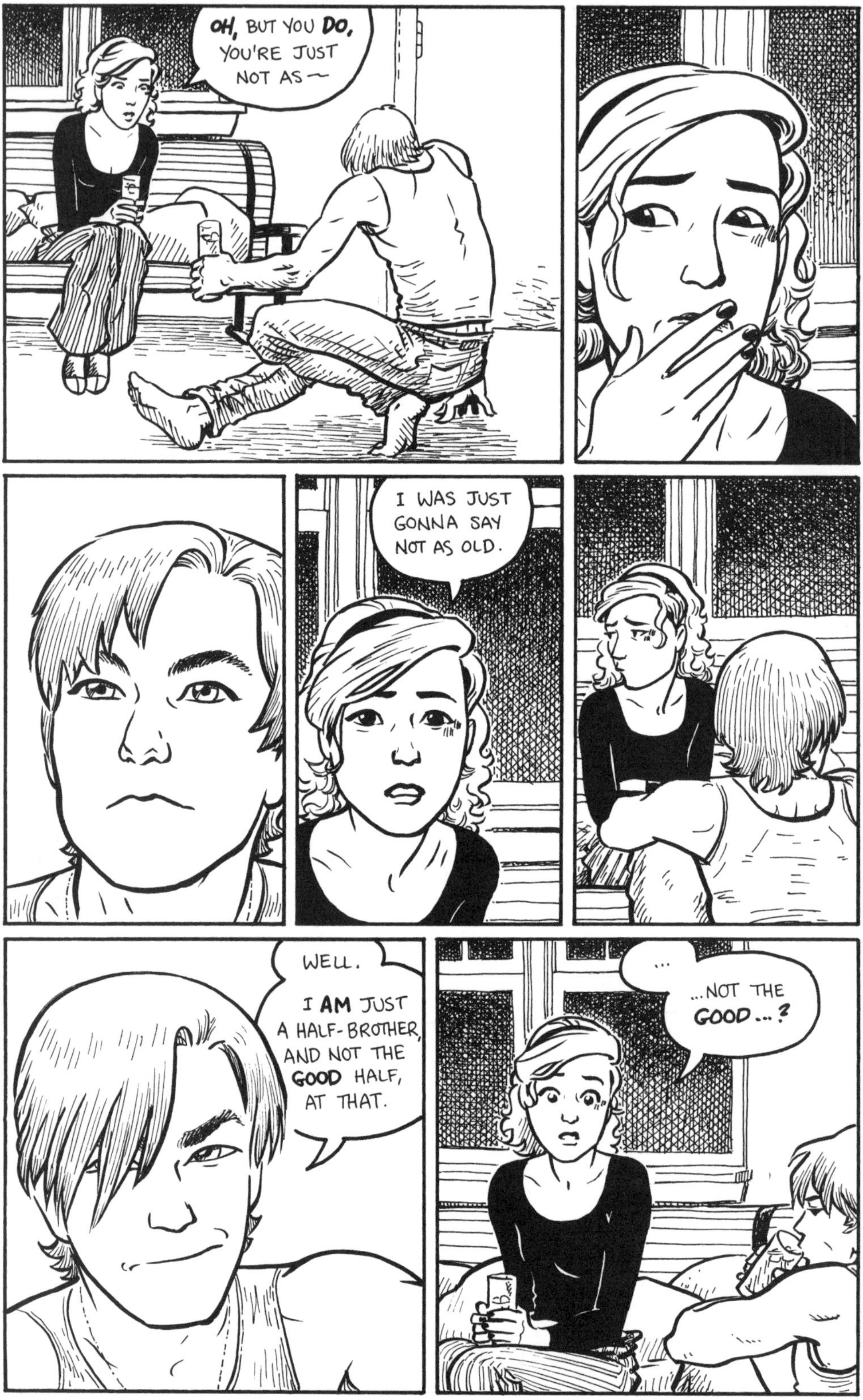
OH, BUT YOU DO, YOU'RE JUST NOT AS~
I WAS JUST GONNA SAY NOT AS OLD.
WELL.
I AM JUST A HALF-BROTHER, AND NOT THE GOOD HALF, AT THAT.
...
...NOT THE GOOD...?

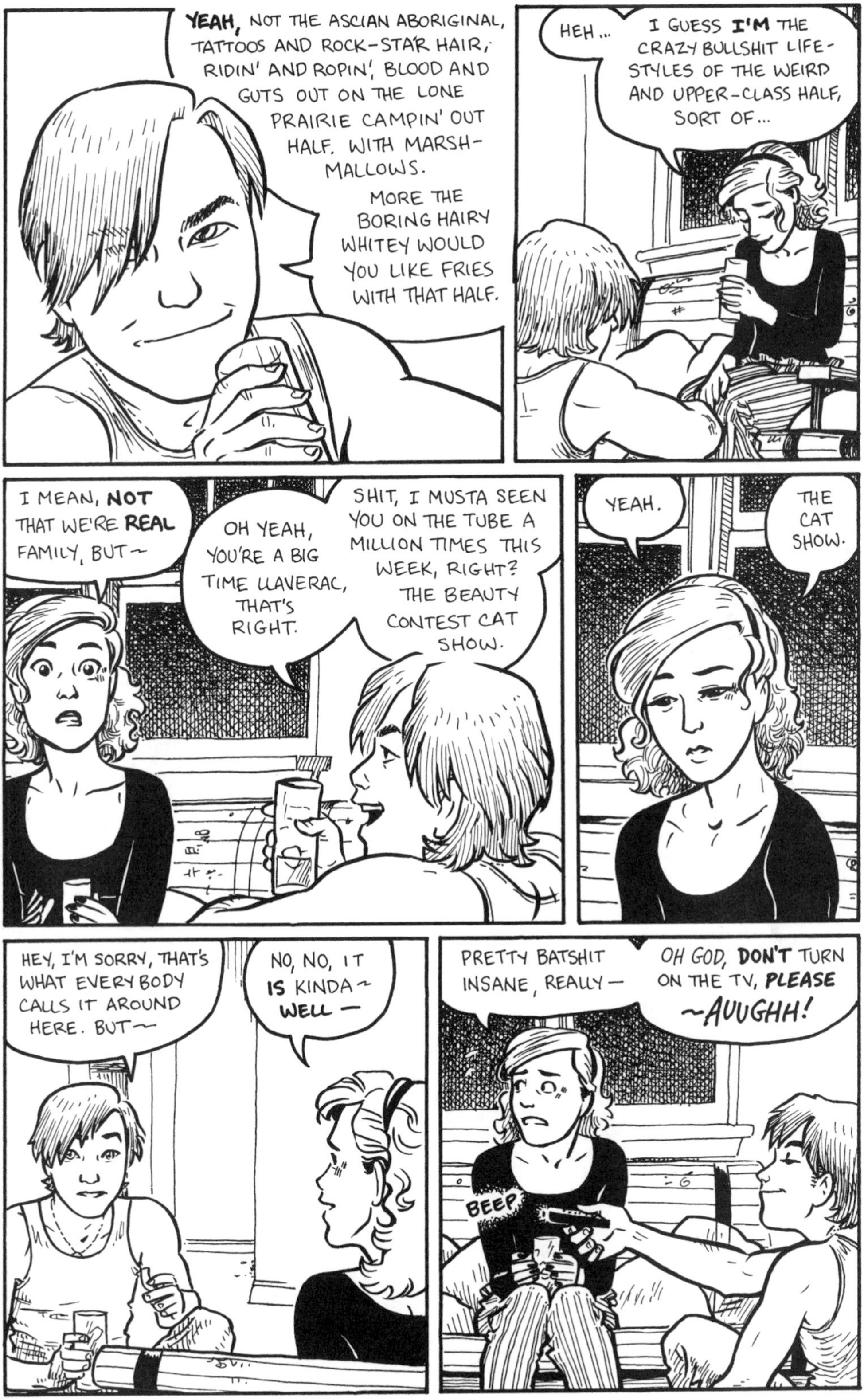
YEAH, NOT THE ASCIAN ABORIGINAL, TATTOOS AND ROCK-STAR HAIR, RIDIN' AND ROPIN', BLOOD AND GUTS OUT ON THE LONE PRAIRIE CAMPIN' OUT HALF. WITH MARSH-MALLOWS.
MORE THE BORING HAIRY WHITEY WOULD YOU LIKE FRIES WITH THAT HALF.
HEH...
I GUESS I'M THE CRAZY BULLSHIT LIFE-STYLES OF THE WEIRD AND UPPER-CLASS HALF, SORT OF...
I MEAN, NOT THAT WE'RE REAL FAMILY, BUT~
OH YEAH, YOU'RE A BIG TIME LLAVERAC, THAT'S RIGHT.
SHIT, I MUSTA SEEN YOU ON THE TUBE A MILLION TIMES THIS WEEK, RIGHT? THE BEAUTY CONTEST CAT SHOW.
YEAH.
THE CAT SHOW.
HEY, I'M SORRY, THAT'S WHAT EVERYBODY CALLS IT AROUND HERE. BUT~
NO, NO, IT IS KINDA~ WELL —
PRETTY BATSHIT INSANE, REALLY —
OH GOD, DON'T TURN ON THE TV, PLEASE ~AUUGHH!
BEEP

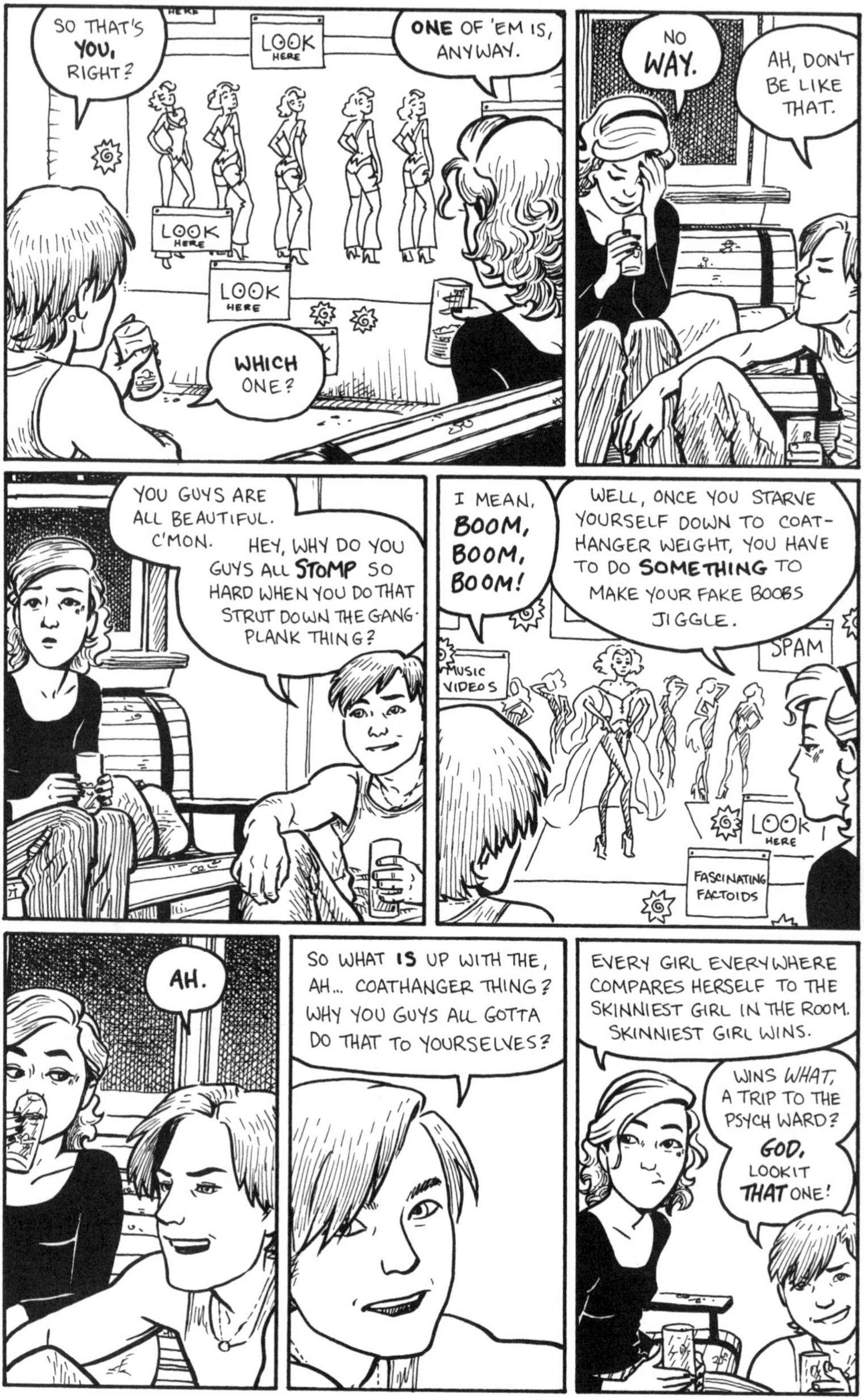
HERE
SO THAT'S **YOU,** RIGHT?
LOOK HERE
ONE OF 'EM IS, ANYWAY.
LOOK HERE
LOOK HERE
WHICH ONE?
NO **WAY.**
AH, DON'T BE LIKE THAT.
YOU GUYS ARE ALL BEAUTIFUL. C'MON.
HEY, WHY DO YOU GUYS ALL **STOMP** SO HARD WHEN YOU DO THAT STRUT DOWN THE GANG-PLANK THING?
I MEAN, **BOOM, BOOM, BOOM!**
WELL, ONCE YOU STARVE YOURSELF DOWN TO COAT-HANGER WEIGHT, YOU HAVE TO DO **SOMETHING** TO MAKE YOUR FAKE BOOBS JIGGLE.
SPAM
MUSIC VIDEOS
LOOK HERE
FASCINATING FACTOIDS
AH.
SO WHAT **IS** UP WITH THE, AH... COATHANGER THING? WHY YOU GUYS ALL GOTTA DO THAT TO YOURSELVES?
EVERY GIRL EVERYWHERE COMPARES HERSELF TO THE SKINNIEST GIRL IN THE ROOM. SKINNIEST GIRL WINS.
WINS *WHAT,* A TRIP TO THE PSYCH WARD? **GOD,** LOOKIT **THAT** ONE!

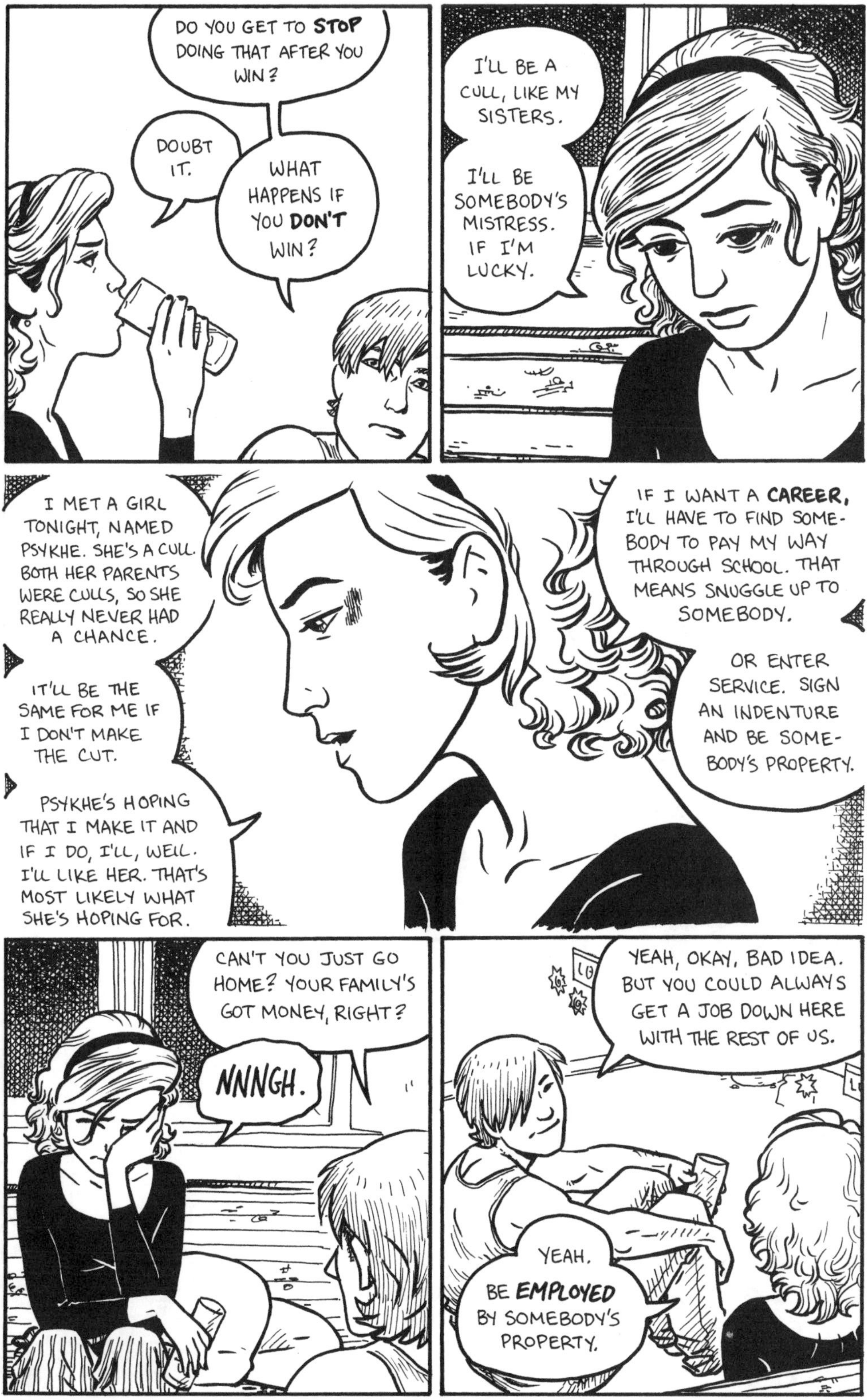
DO YOU GET TO **STOP** DOING THAT AFTER YOU WIN?
DOUBT IT.
WHAT HAPPENS IF YOU **DON'T** WIN?
I'LL BE A CULL, LIKE MY SISTERS.
I'LL BE SOMEBODY'S MISTRESS. IF I'M LUCKY.
I MET A GIRL TONIGHT, NAMED PSYKHE. SHE'S A CULL. BOTH HER PARENTS WERE CULLS, SO SHE REALLY NEVER HAD A CHANCE.
IT'LL BE THE SAME FOR ME IF I DON'T MAKE THE CUT.
PSYKHE'S HOPING THAT I MAKE IT AND IF I DO, I'LL, WELL. I'LL LIKE HER. THAT'S MOST LIKELY WHAT SHE'S HOPING FOR.
IF I WANT A **CAREER,** I'LL HAVE TO FIND SOMEBODY TO PAY MY WAY THROUGH SCHOOL. THAT MEANS SNUGGLE UP TO SOMEBODY.
OR ENTER SERVICE. SIGN AN INDENTURE AND BE SOMEBODY'S PROPERTY.
CAN'T YOU JUST GO HOME? YOUR FAMILY'S GOT MONEY, RIGHT?
NNNGH.
YEAH, OKAY, BAD IDEA. BUT YOU COULD ALWAYS GET A JOB DOWN HERE WITH THE REST OF US.
YEAH.
BE **EMPLOYED** BY SOMEBODY'S PROPERTY.

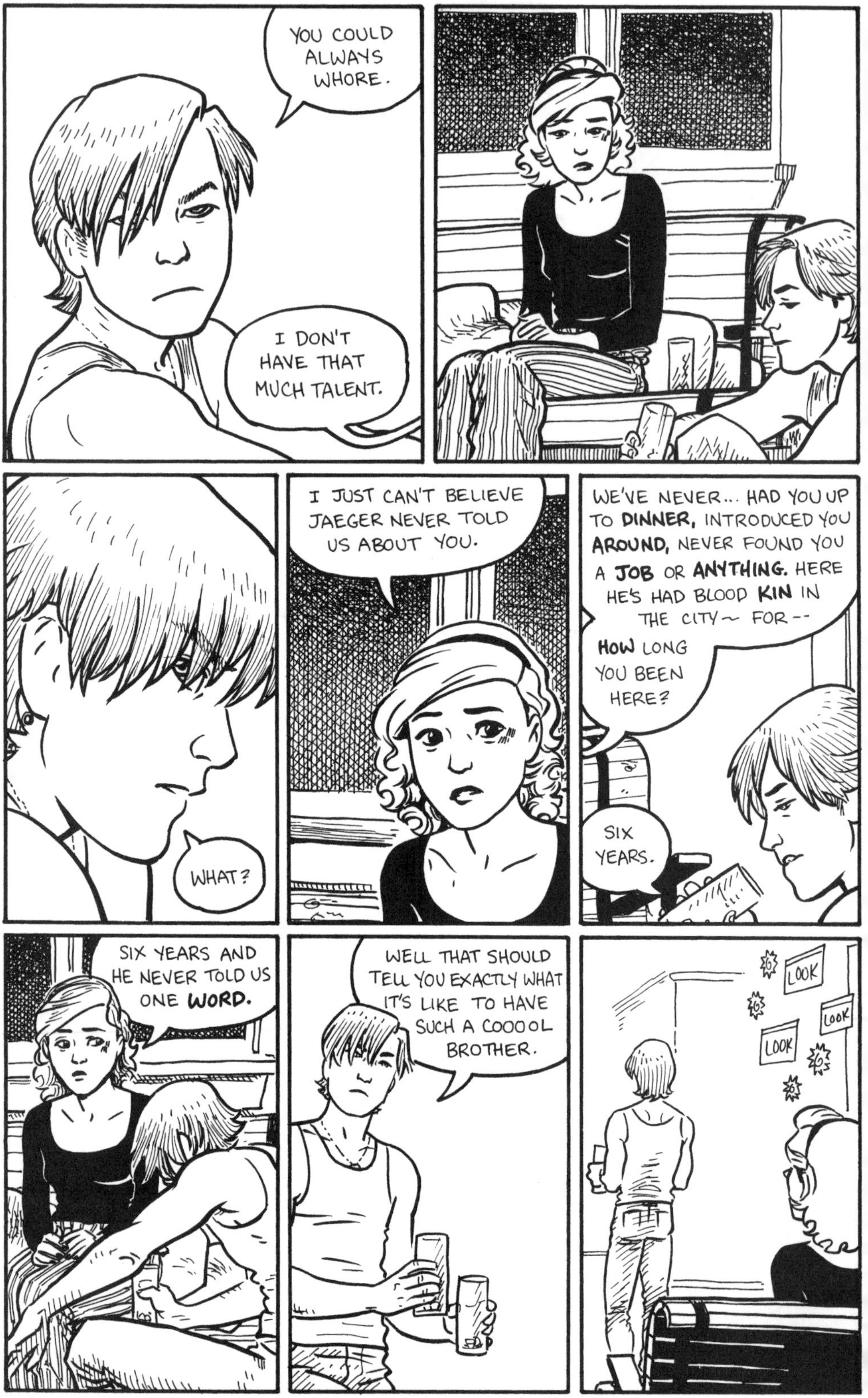
YOU COULD ALWAYS WHORE.
I DON'T HAVE THAT MUCH TALENT.
WHAT?
I JUST CAN'T BELIEVE JAEGER NEVER TOLD US ABOUT YOU.
WE'VE NEVER... HAD YOU UP TO DINNER, INTRODUCED YOU AROUND, NEVER FOUND YOU A JOB OR ANYTHING. HERE HE'S HAD BLOOD KIN IN THE CITY~ FOR--
HOW LONG YOU BEEN HERE?
SIX YEARS.
SIX YEARS AND HE NEVER TOLD US ONE WORD.
WELL THAT SHOULD TELL YOU EXACTLY WHAT IT'S LIKE TO HAVE SUCH A COOOOL BROTHER.
LOOK
LOOK
LOOK

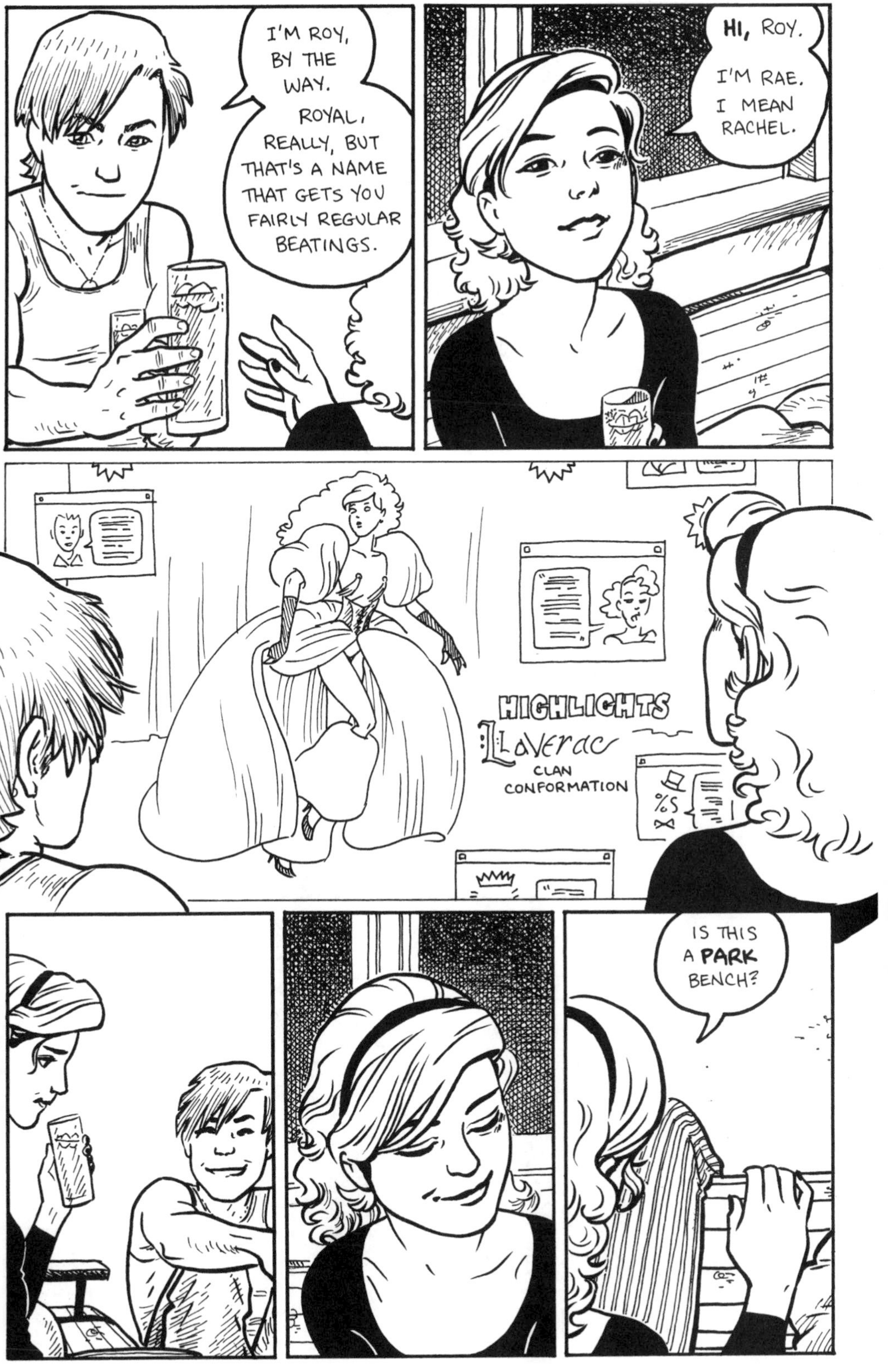
I'M ROY, BY THE WAY.
ROYAL, REALLY, BUT THAT'S A NAME THAT GETS YOU FAIRLY REGULAR BEATINGS.
HI, ROY.
I'M RAE. I MEAN RACHEL.
HIGHLIGHTS
Laverac
CLAN CONFORMATION
IS THIS A PARK BENCH?

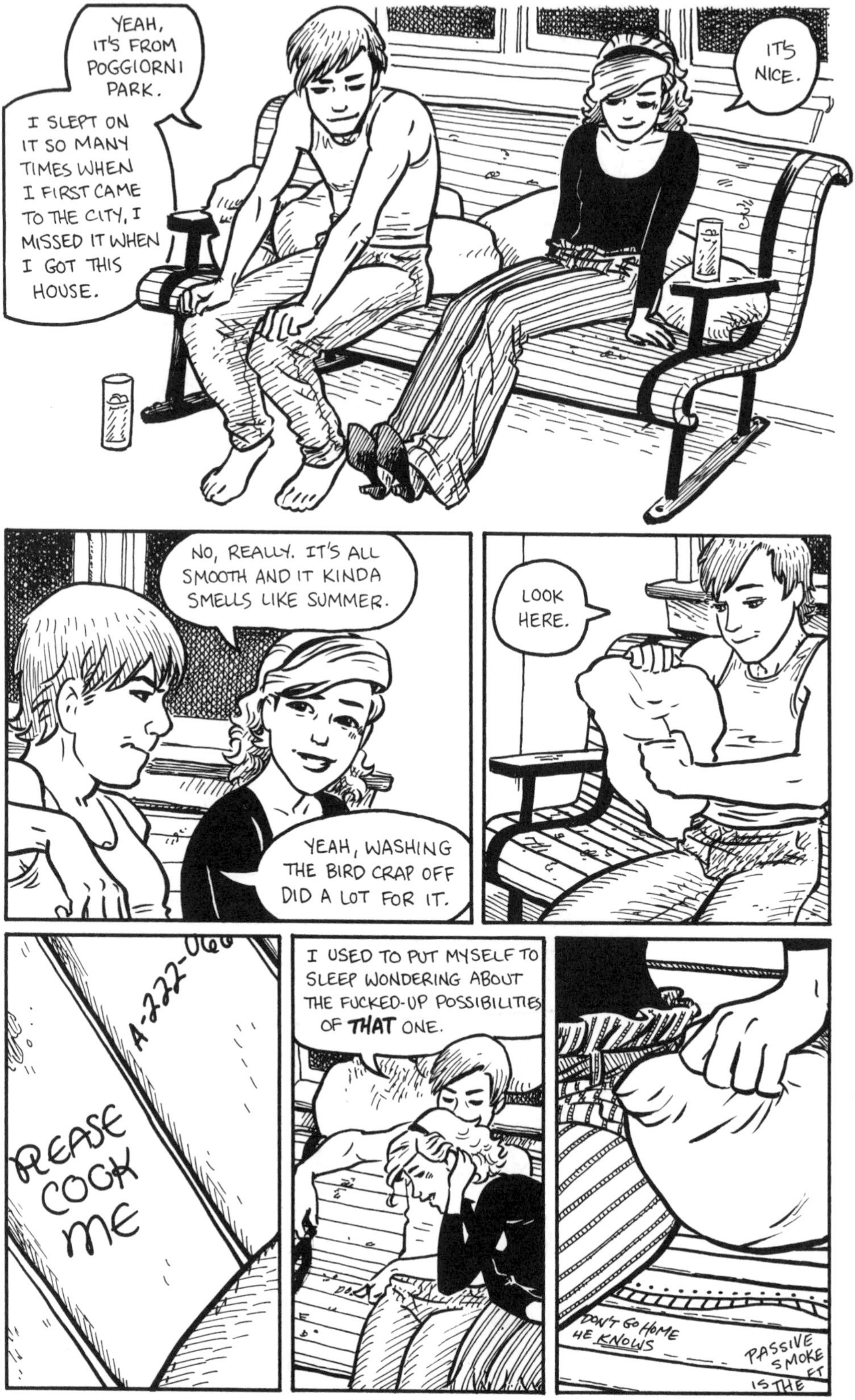
YEAH, IT'S FROM POGGIORNI PARK.
I SLEPT ON IT SO MANY TIMES WHEN I FIRST CAME TO THE CITY, I MISSED IT WHEN I GOT THIS HOUSE.
IT'S NICE.
NO, REALLY. IT'S ALL SMOOTH AND IT KINDA SMELLS LIKE SUMMER.
YEAH, WASHING THE BIRD CRAP OFF DID A LOT FOR IT.
LOOK HERE.
PLEASE COOK ME
I USED TO PUT MYSELF TO SLEEP WONDERING ABOUT THE FUCKED-UP POSSIBILITIES OF **THAT** ONE.
DON'T GO HOME HE KNOWS
PASSIVE SMOKE IS THE

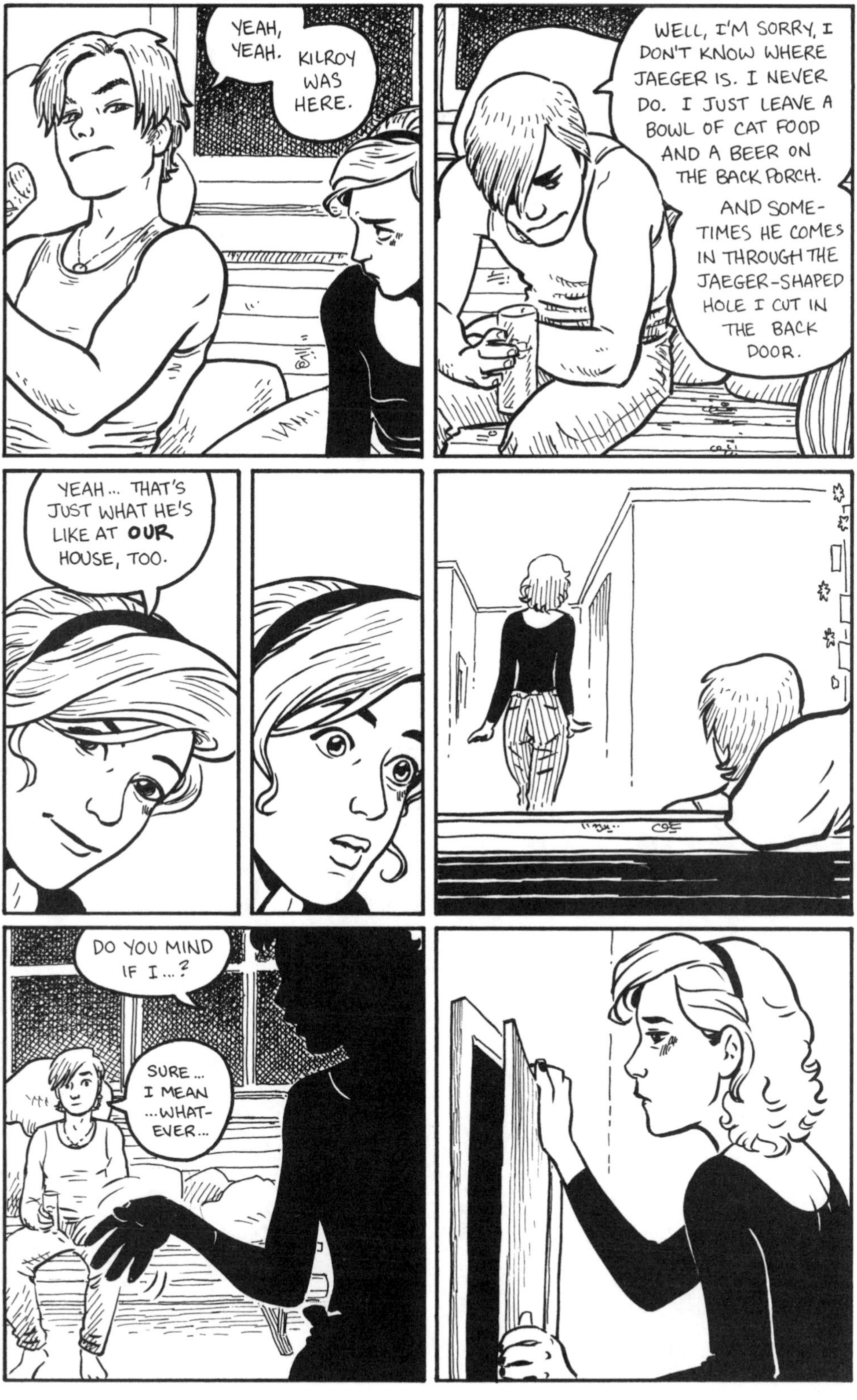
YEAH, YEAH.
KILROY WAS HERE.
WELL, I'M SORRY, I DON'T KNOW WHERE JAEGER IS. I NEVER DO. I JUST LEAVE A BOWL OF CAT FOOD AND A BEER ON THE BACK PORCH.
AND SOMETIMES HE COMES IN THROUGH THE JAEGER-SHAPED HOLE I CUT IN THE BACK DOOR.
YEAH... THAT'S JUST WHAT HE'S LIKE AT **OUR** HOUSE, TOO.
DO YOU MIND IF I...?
SURE... I MEAN ...WHATEVER...

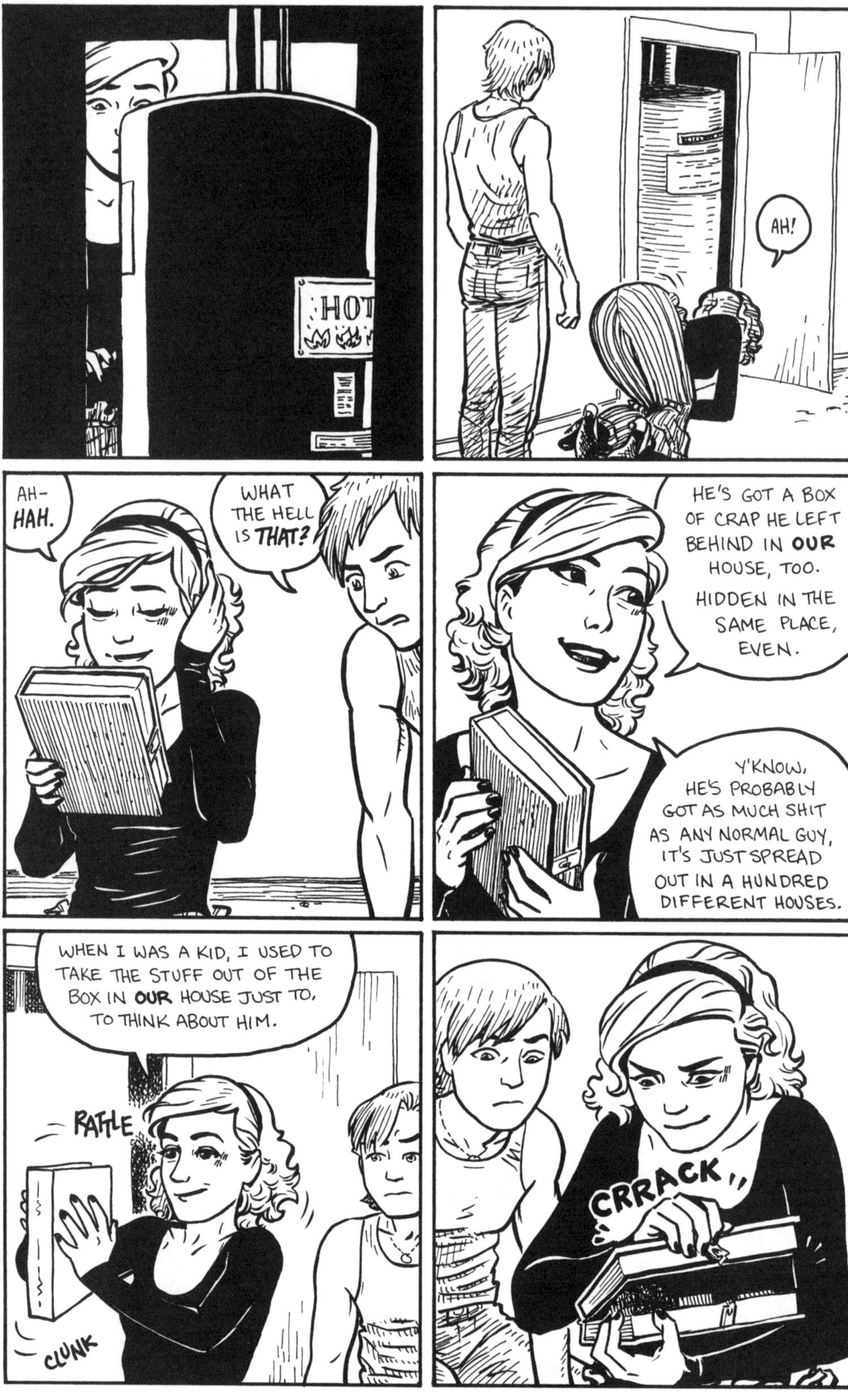
HOT
AH!
AH- HAH.
WHAT THE HELL IS THAT?
HE'S GOT A BOX OF CRAP HE LEFT BEHIND IN OUR HOUSE, TOO.
HIDDEN IN THE SAME PLACE, EVEN.
Y'KNOW, HE'S PROBABLY GOT AS MUCH SHIT AS ANY NORMAL GUY, IT'S JUST SPREAD OUT IN A HUNDRED DIFFERENT HOUSES.
WHEN I WAS A KID, I USED TO TAKE THE STUFF OUT OF THE BOX IN OUR HOUSE JUST TO, TO THINK ABOUT HIM.
RATTLE
CLUNK
CRRACK

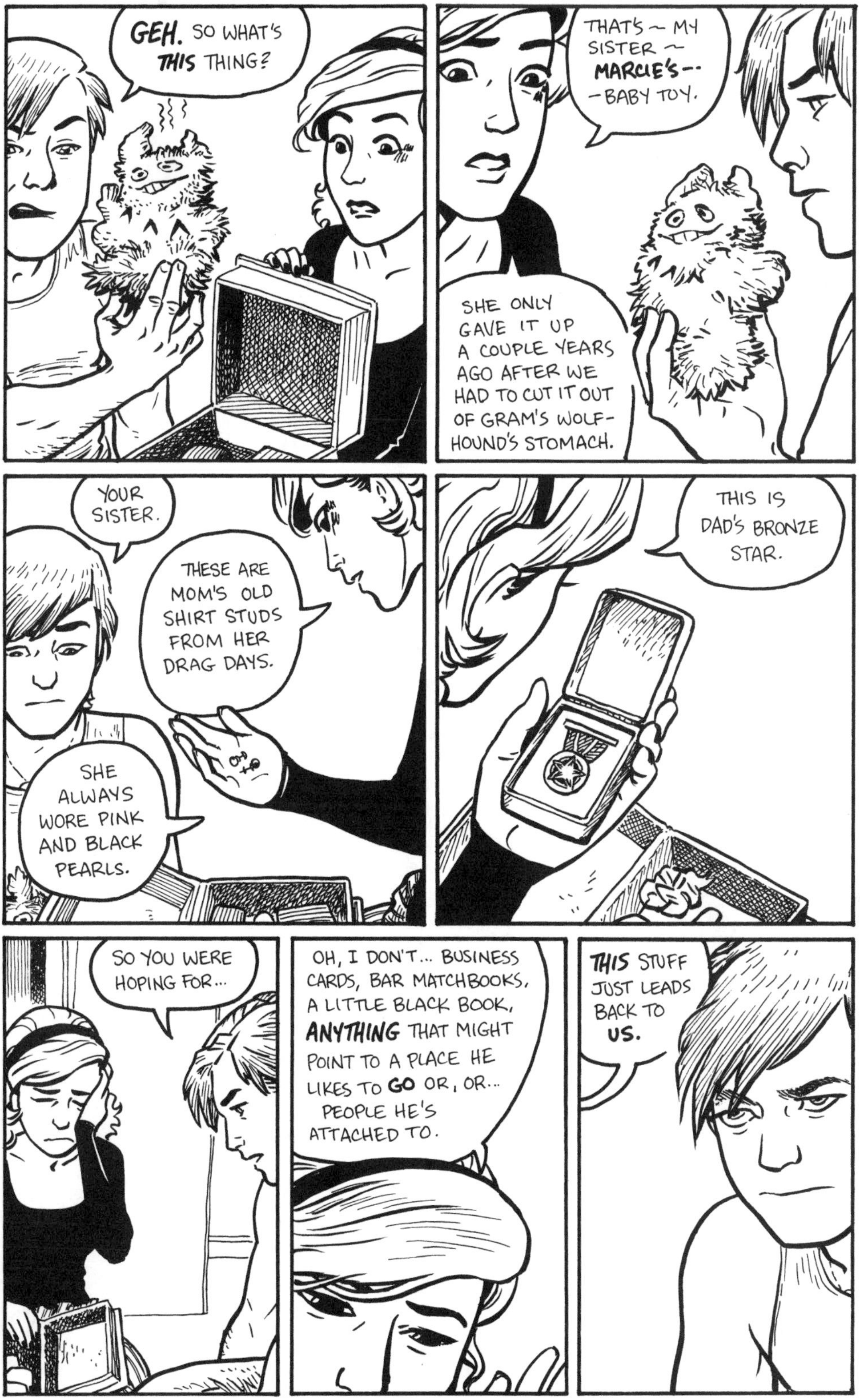
GEH. SO WHAT'S THIS THING?
THAT'S ~ MY SISTER ~ MARCIE'S -- -BABY TOY.
SHE ONLY GAVE IT UP A COUPLE YEARS AGO AFTER WE HAD TO CUT IT OUT OF GRAM'S WOLF-HOUND'S STOMACH.
YOUR SISTER.
THESE ARE MOM'S OLD SHIRT STUDS FROM HER DRAG DAYS.
SHE ALWAYS WORE PINK AND BLACK PEARLS.
THIS IS DAD'S BRONZE STAR.
SO YOU WERE HOPING FOR...
OH, I DON'T... BUSINESS CARDS, BAR MATCHBOOKS, A LITTLE BLACK BOOK, ANYTHING THAT MIGHT POINT TO A PLACE HE LIKES TO GO OR, OR... PEOPLE HE'S ATTACHED TO.
THIS STUFF JUST LEADS BACK TO US.

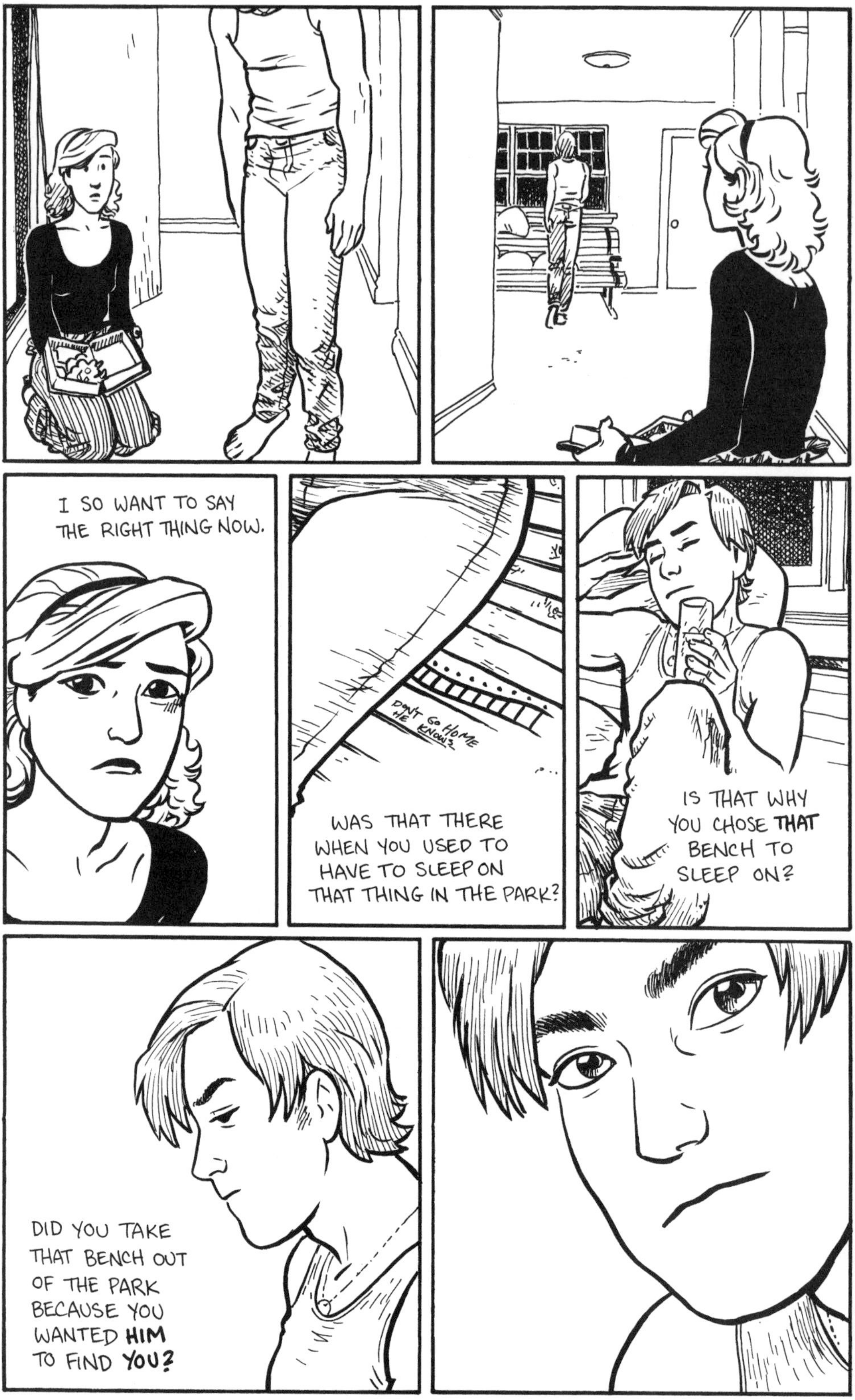
I SO WANT TO SAY THE RIGHT THING NOW.
DON'T GO HOME HE KNOWS
WAS THAT THERE WHEN YOU USED TO HAVE TO SLEEP ON THAT THING IN THE PARK?
IS THAT WHY YOU CHOSE **THAT** BENCH TO SLEEP ON?
DID YOU TAKE THAT BENCH OUT OF THE PARK BECAUSE YOU WANTED **HIM** TO FIND **YOU**?

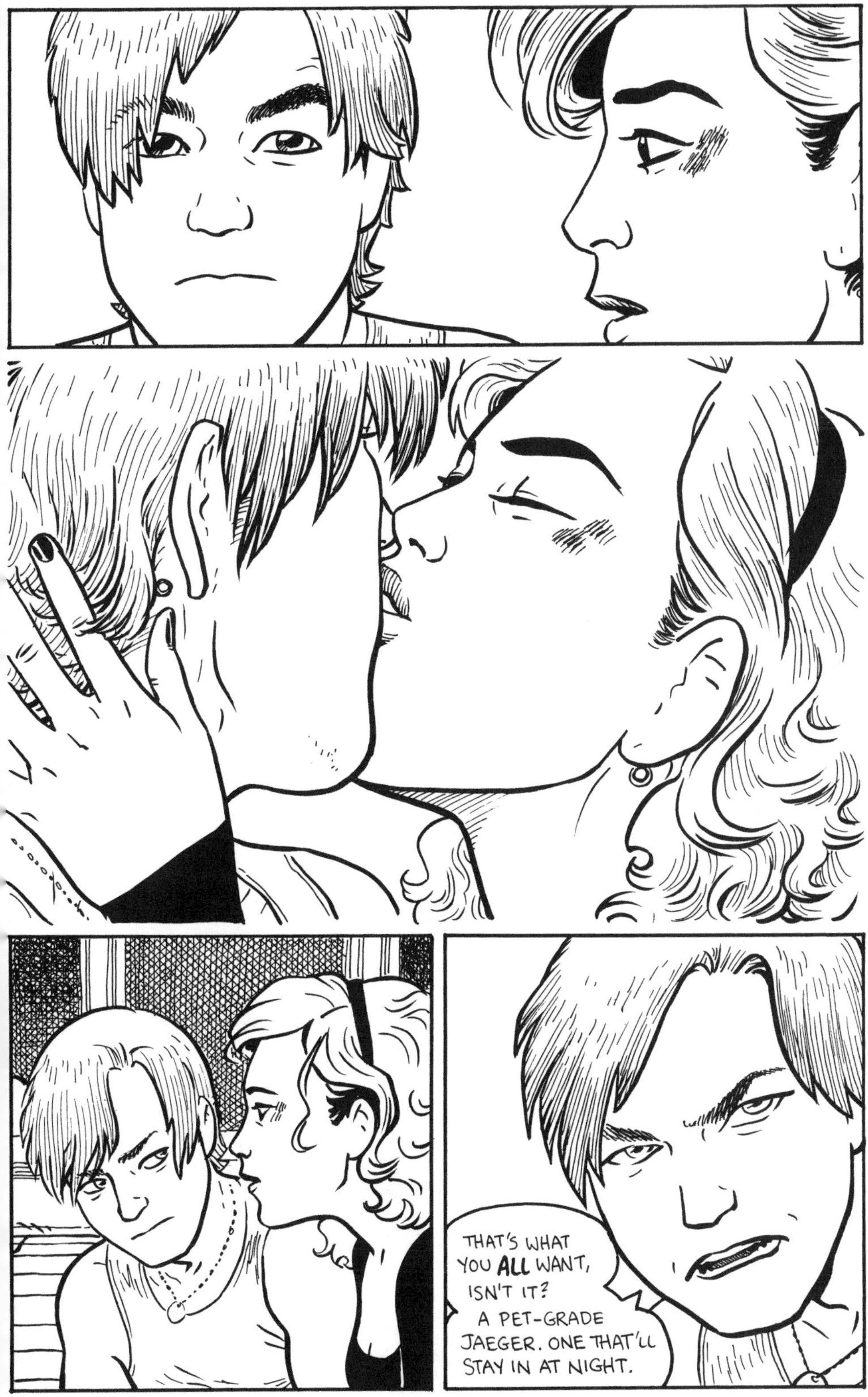
THAT'S WHAT YOU ALL WANT, ISN'T IT? A PET-GRADE JAEGER. ONE THAT'LL STAY IN AT NIGHT.

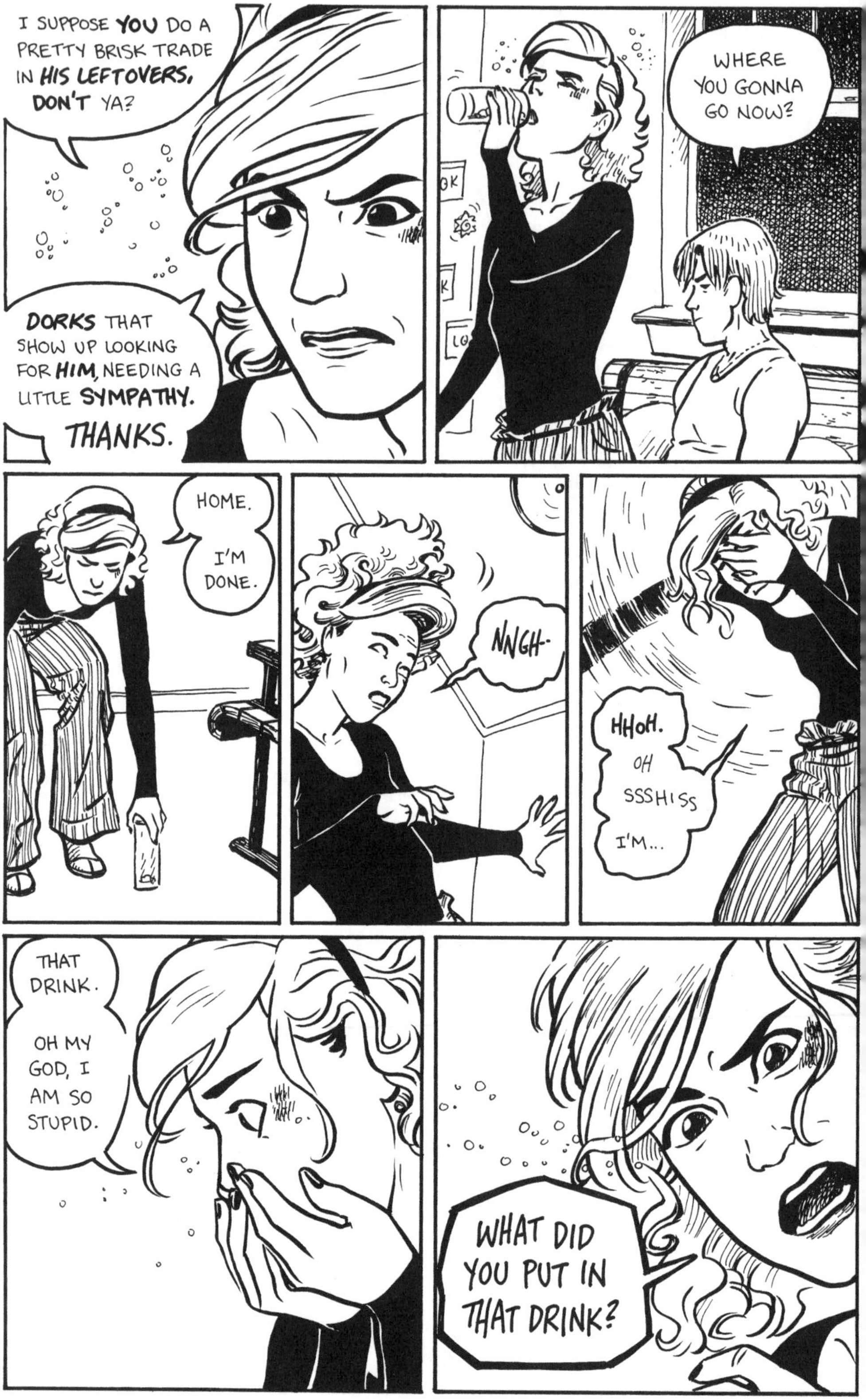
I SUPPOSE YOU DO A PRETTY BRISK TRADE IN HIS LEFTOVERS, DON'T YA?
DORKS THAT SHOW UP LOOKING FOR HIM, NEEDING A LITTLE SYMPATHY.
THANKS.
WHERE YOU GONNA GO NOW?
HOME.
I'M DONE.
NNGH-
HHOH.
OH
SSSHISS
I'M...
THAT DRINK.
OH MY GOD, I AM SO STUPID.
WHAT DID YOU PUT IN THAT DRINK?

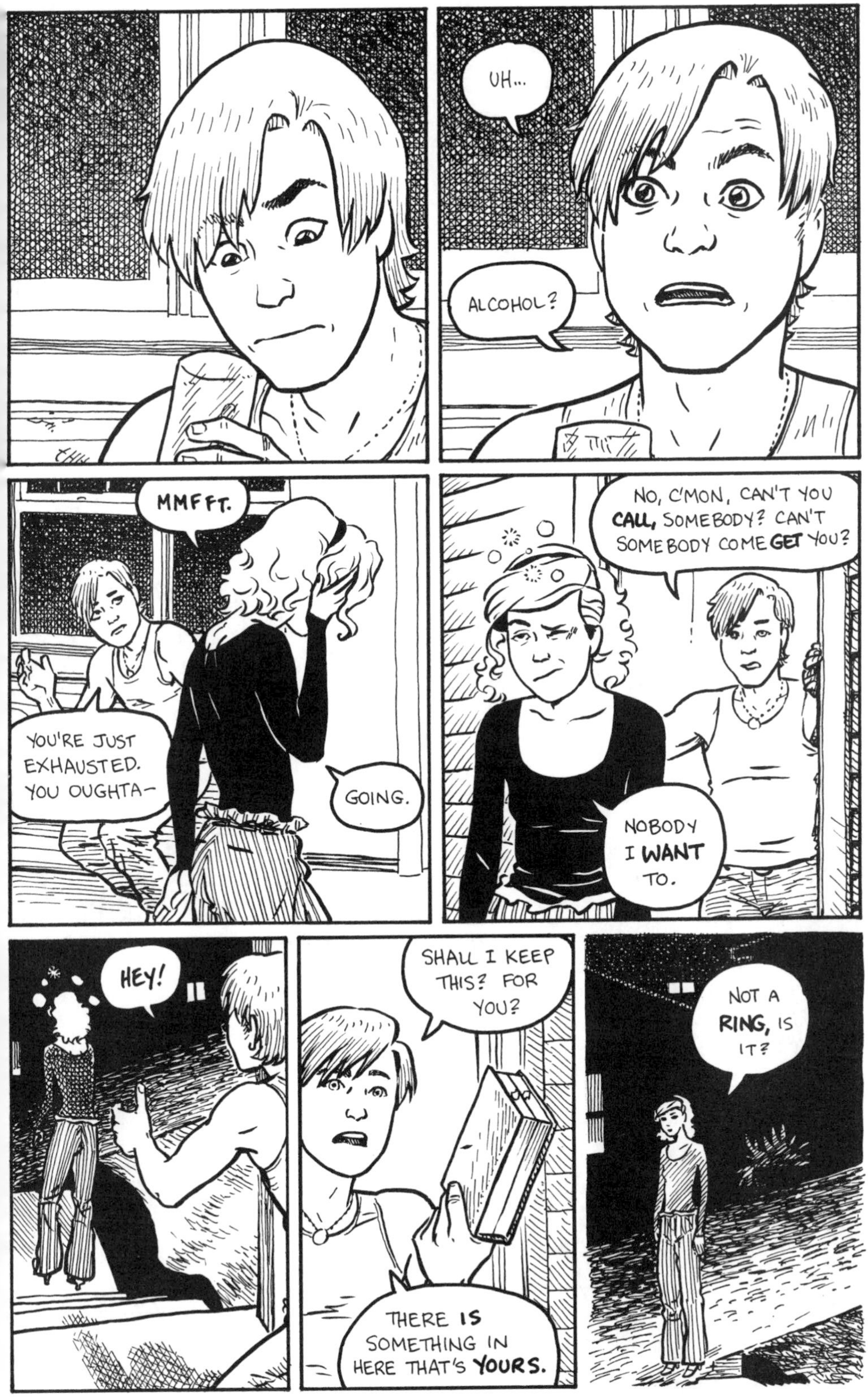
UH...
ALCOHOL?
MMFFT.
YOU'RE JUST EXHAUSTED. YOU OUGHTA-
GOING.
NO, C'MON, CAN'T YOU CALL, SOMEBODY? CAN'T SOMEBODY COME GET YOU?
NOBODY I WANT TO.
HEY!
SHALL I KEEP THIS? FOR YOU?
THERE IS SOMETHING IN HERE THAT'S YOURS.
NOT A RING, IS IT?

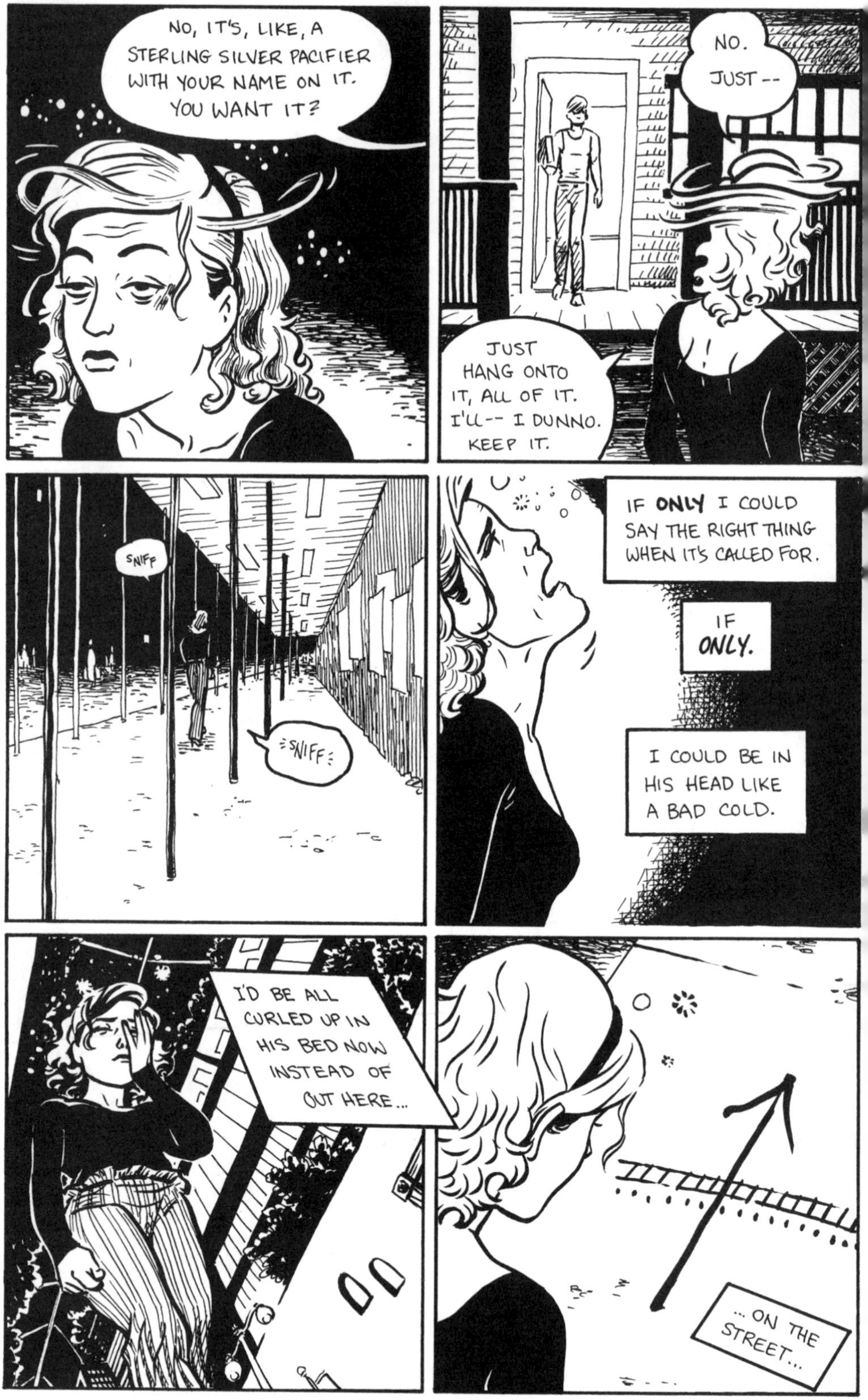
NO, IT'S, LIKE, A STERLING SILVER PACIFIER WITH YOUR NAME ON IT. YOU WANT IT?
NO. JUST --
JUST HANG ONTO IT, ALL OF IT. I'LL-- I DUNNO. KEEP IT.
SNIFF
SNIFF
IF ONLY I COULD SAY THE RIGHT THING WHEN IT'S CALLED FOR.
IF ONLY.
I COULD BE IN HIS HEAD LIKE A BAD COLD.
I'D BE ALL CURLED UP IN HIS BED NOW INSTEAD OF OUT HERE...
... ON THE STREET...

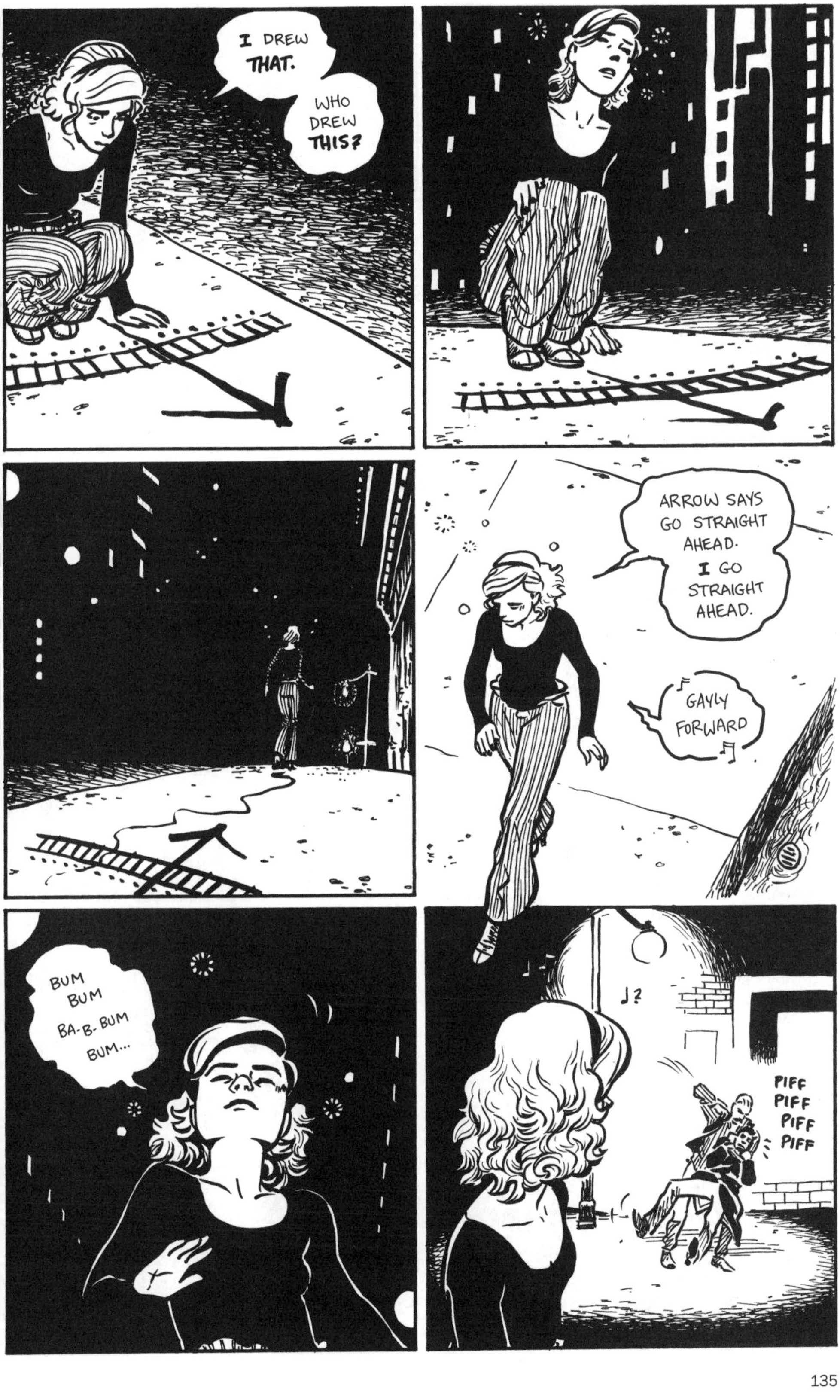
I DREW THAT.
WHO DREW THIS?
ARROW SAYS GO STRAIGHT AHEAD. I GO STRAIGHT AHEAD.
GAYLY FORWARD
BUM BUM BA-B-BUM BUM...
PIFF PIFF PIFF PIFF

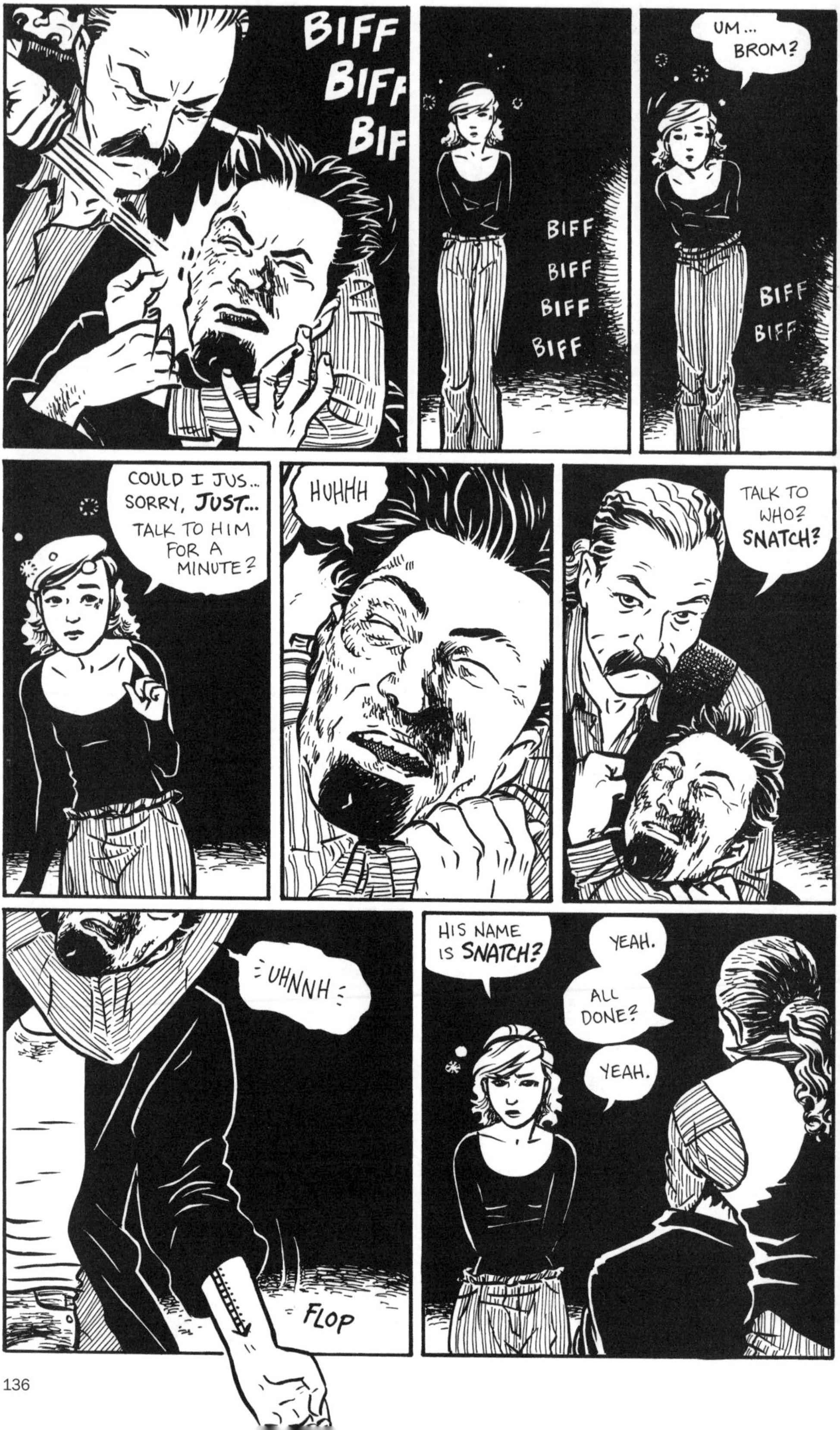
BIFF
BIFF
BIF
BIFF
BIFF
BIFF
BIFF
UM... BROM?
BIFF
BIFF
COULD I JUS... SORRY, JUST... TALK TO HIM FOR A MINUTE?
HUHHH
TALK TO WHO? SNATCH?
UHNNH
FLOP
HIS NAME IS SNATCH?
YEAH.
ALL DONE?
YEAH.

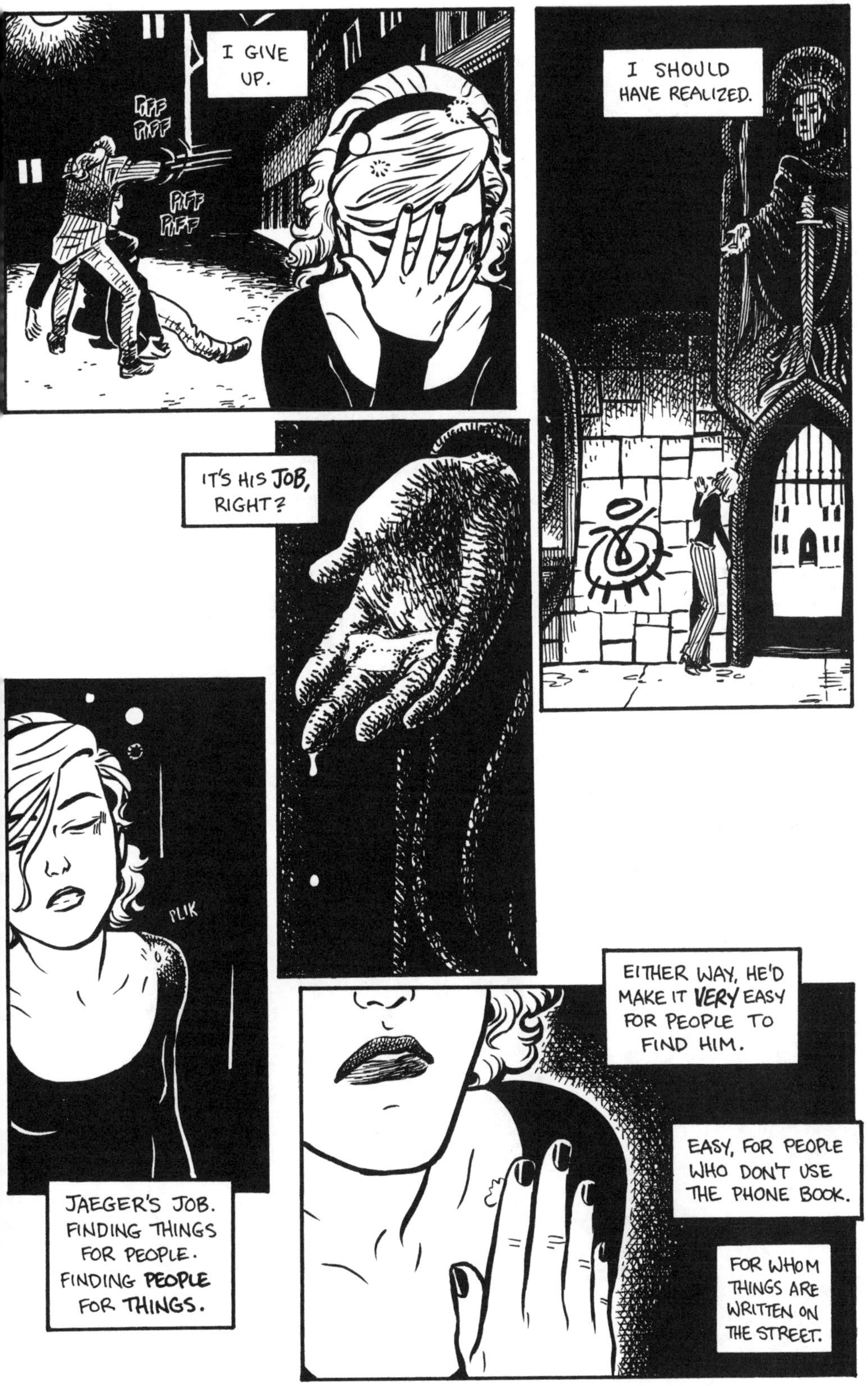
I GIVE UP.
PIFF PIFF
PIFF PIFF
I SHOULD HAVE REALIZED.
IT'S HIS JOB, RIGHT?
PLIK
JAEGER'S JOB. FINDING THINGS FOR PEOPLE. FINDING PEOPLE FOR THINGS.
EITHER WAY, HE'D MAKE IT VERY EASY FOR PEOPLE TO FIND HIM.
EASY, FOR PEOPLE WHO DON'T USE THE PHONE BOOK.
FOR WHOM THINGS ARE WRITTEN ON THE STREET.

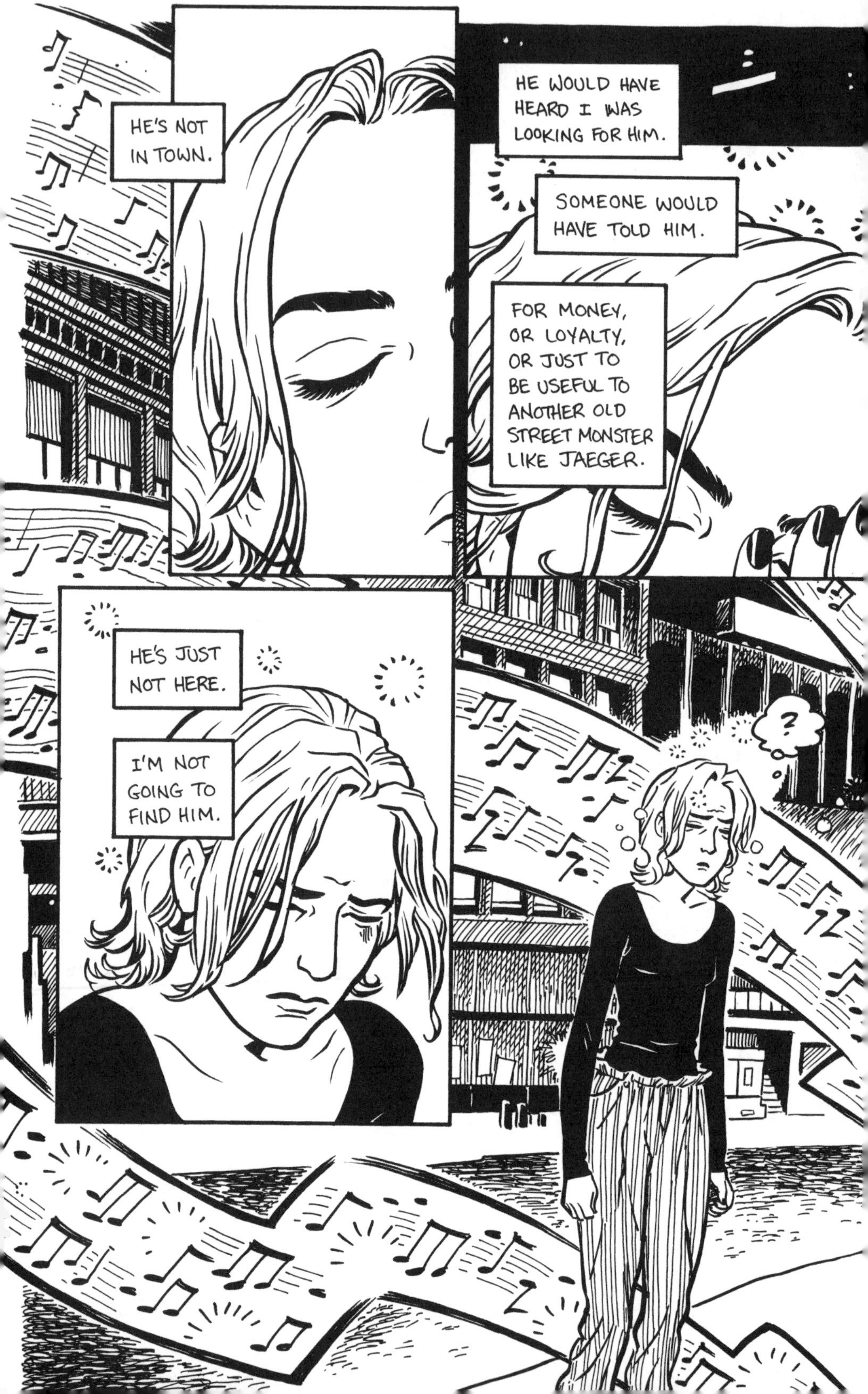
HE'S NOT IN TOWN.
HE WOULD HAVE HEARD I WAS LOOKING FOR HIM.
SOMEONE WOULD HAVE TOLD HIM.
FOR MONEY, OR LOYALTY, OR JUST TO BE USEFUL TO ANOTHER OLD STREET MONSTER LIKE JAEGER.
HE'S JUST NOT HERE.
I'M NOT GOING TO FIND HIM.
?

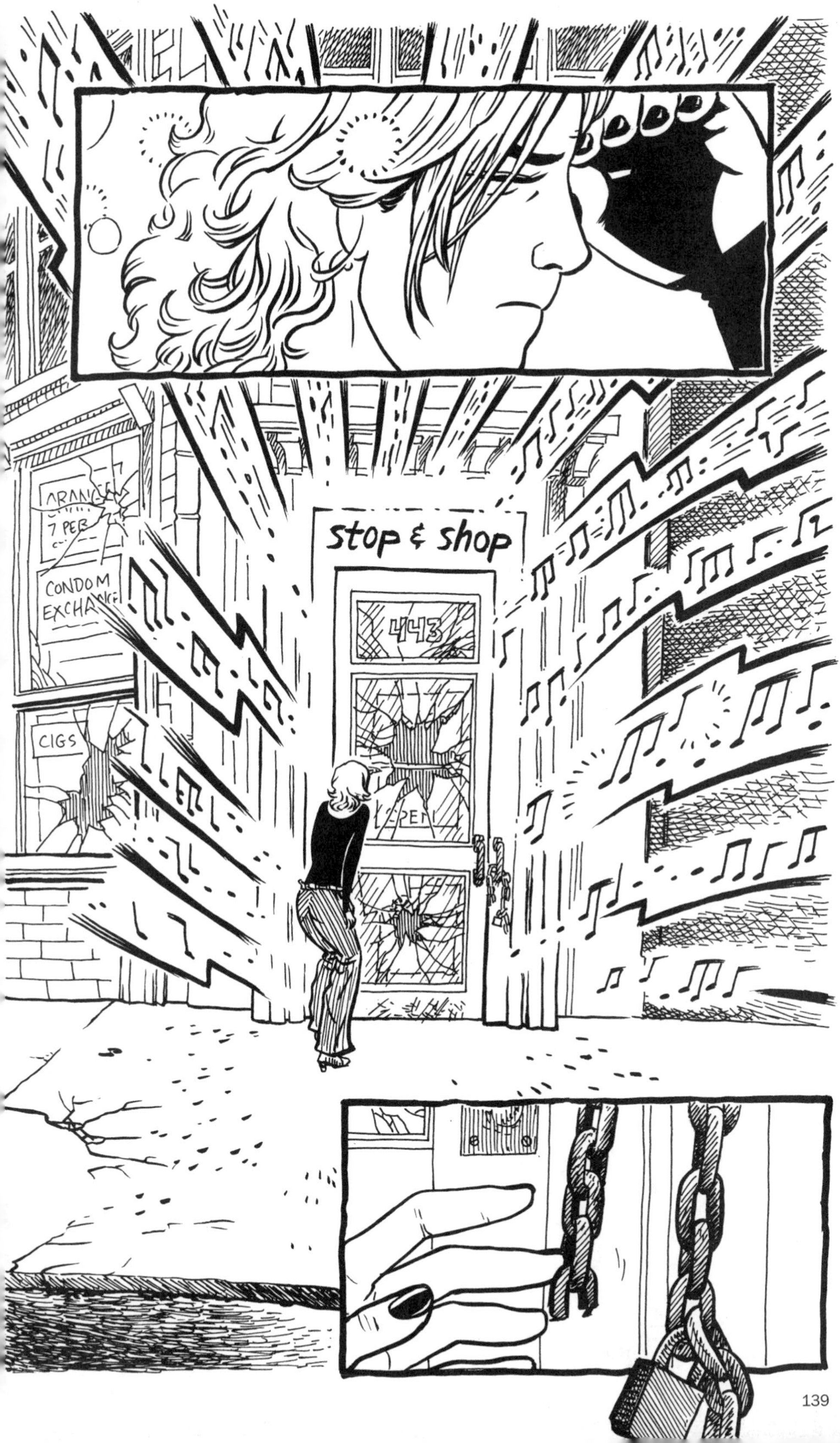
stop & shop
443
CONDOM
CIGS

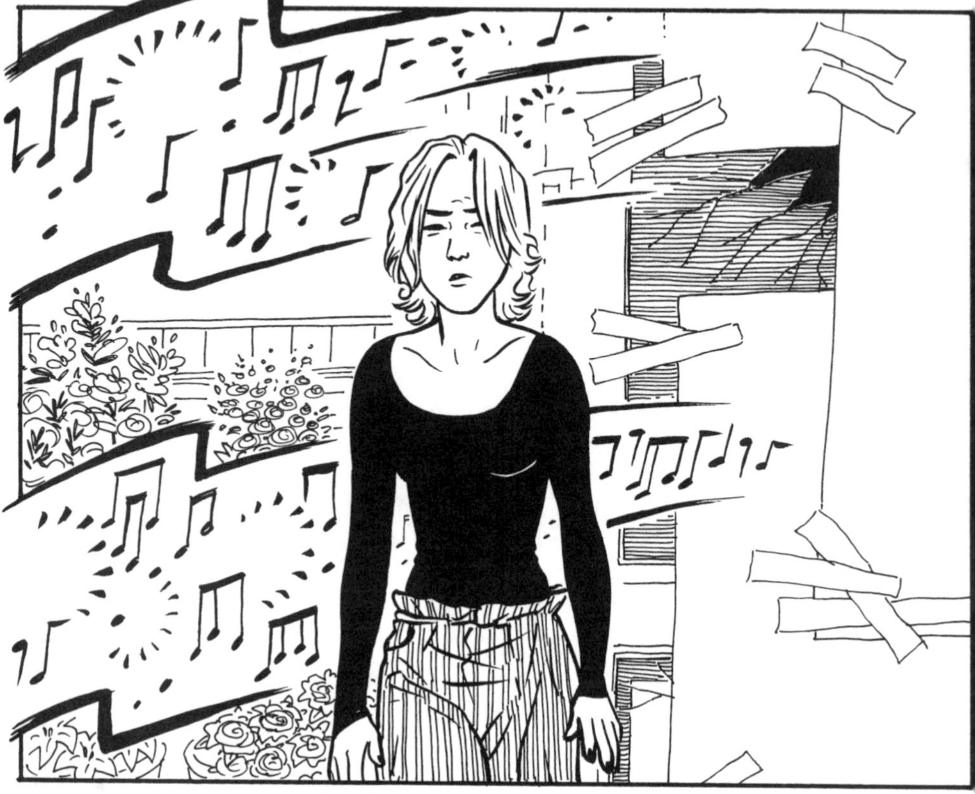

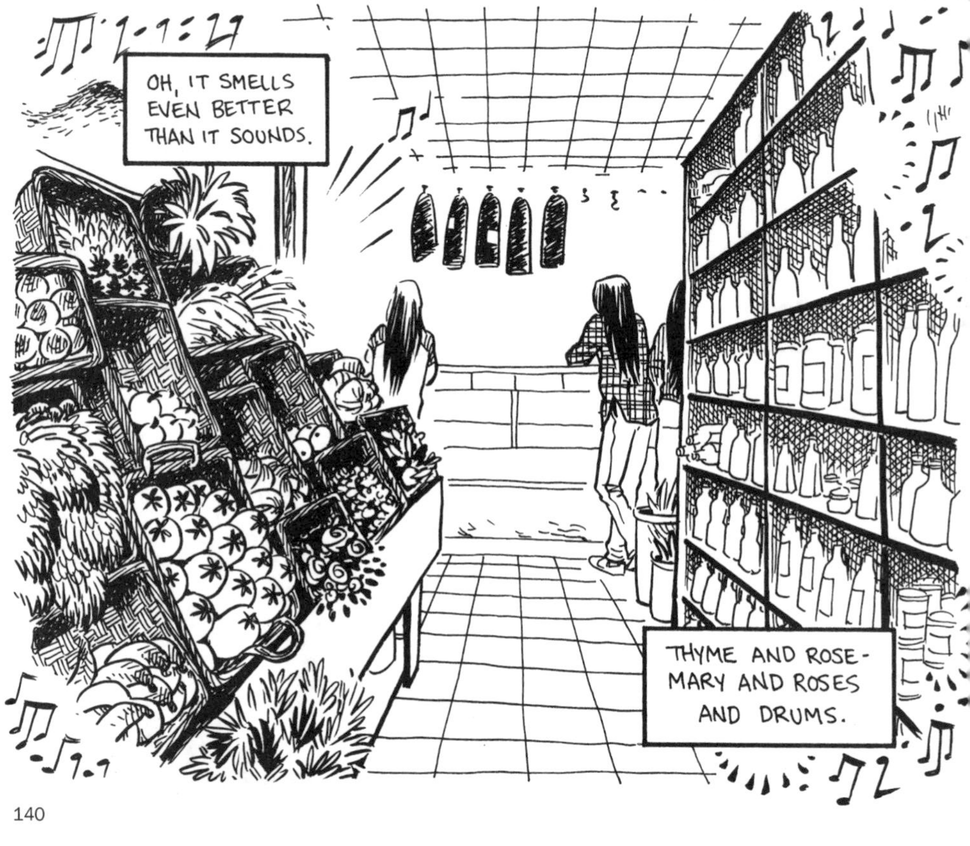
OH, IT SMELLS EVEN BETTER THAN IT SOUNDS.
THYME AND ROSE-MARY AND ROSES AND DRUMS.

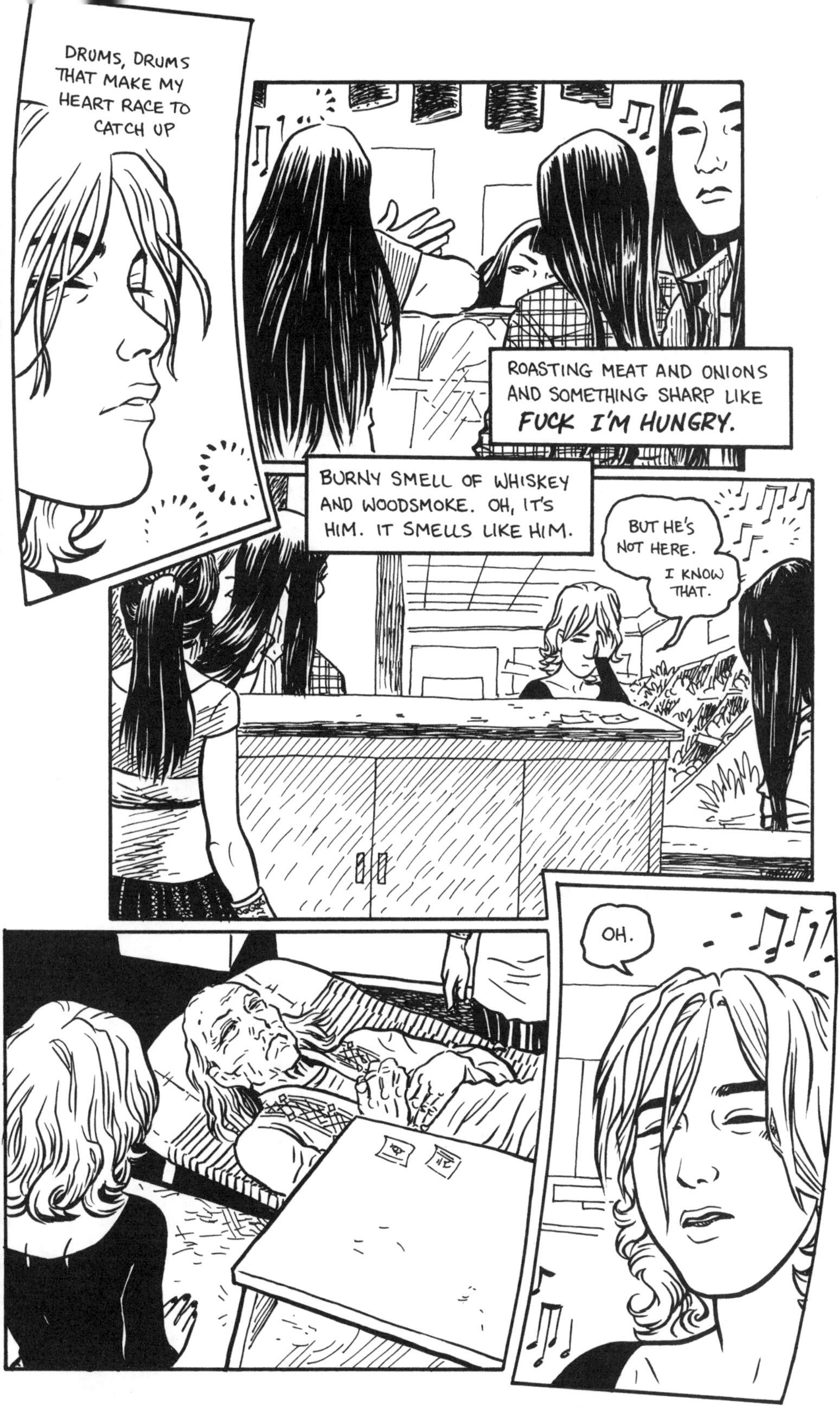
DRUMS, DRUMS THAT MAKE MY HEART RACE TO CATCH UP
ROASTING MEAT AND ONIONS AND SOMETHING SHARP LIKE FUCK I'M HUNGRY.
BURNY SMELL OF WHISKEY AND WOODSMOKE. OH, IT'S HIM. IT SMELLS LIKE HIM.
BUT HE'S NOT HERE.
I KNOW THAT.
OH.

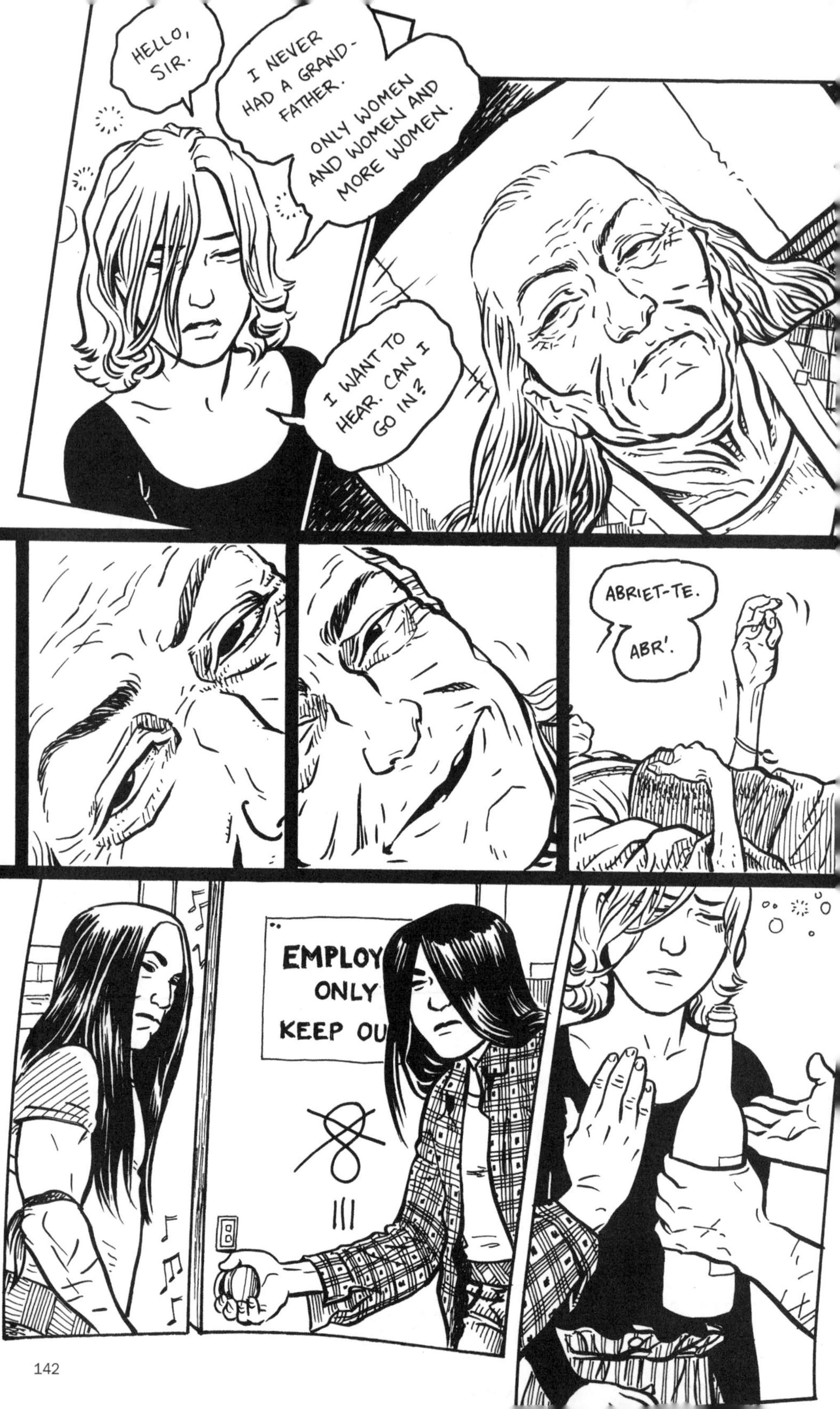
HELLO, SIR.
I NEVER HAD A GRAND-FATHER.
ONLY WOMEN AND WOMEN AND MORE WOMEN.
I WANT TO HEAR. CAN I GO IN?
ABRIET-TE.
ABR'.
EMPLOY
ONLY
KEEP OU

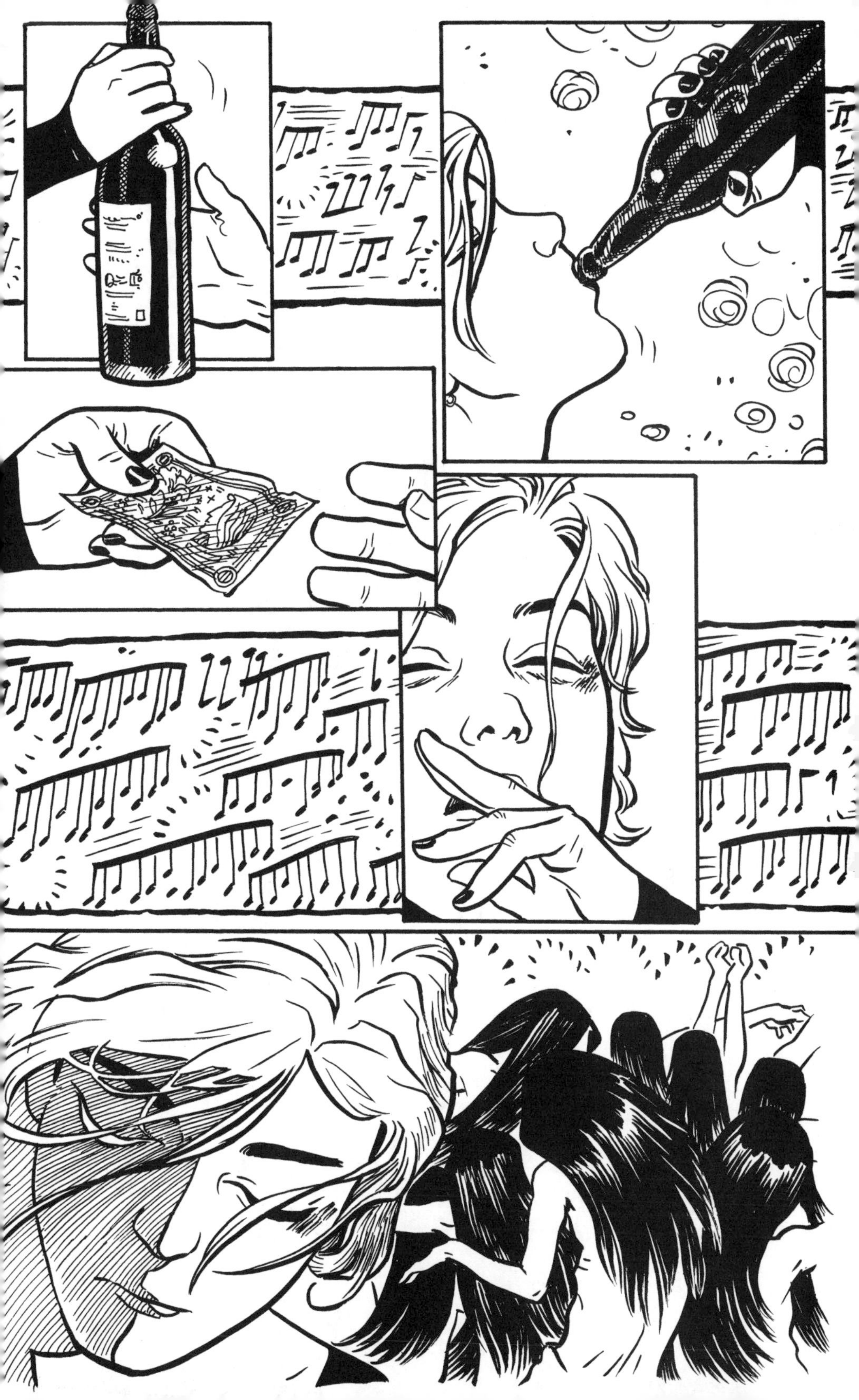

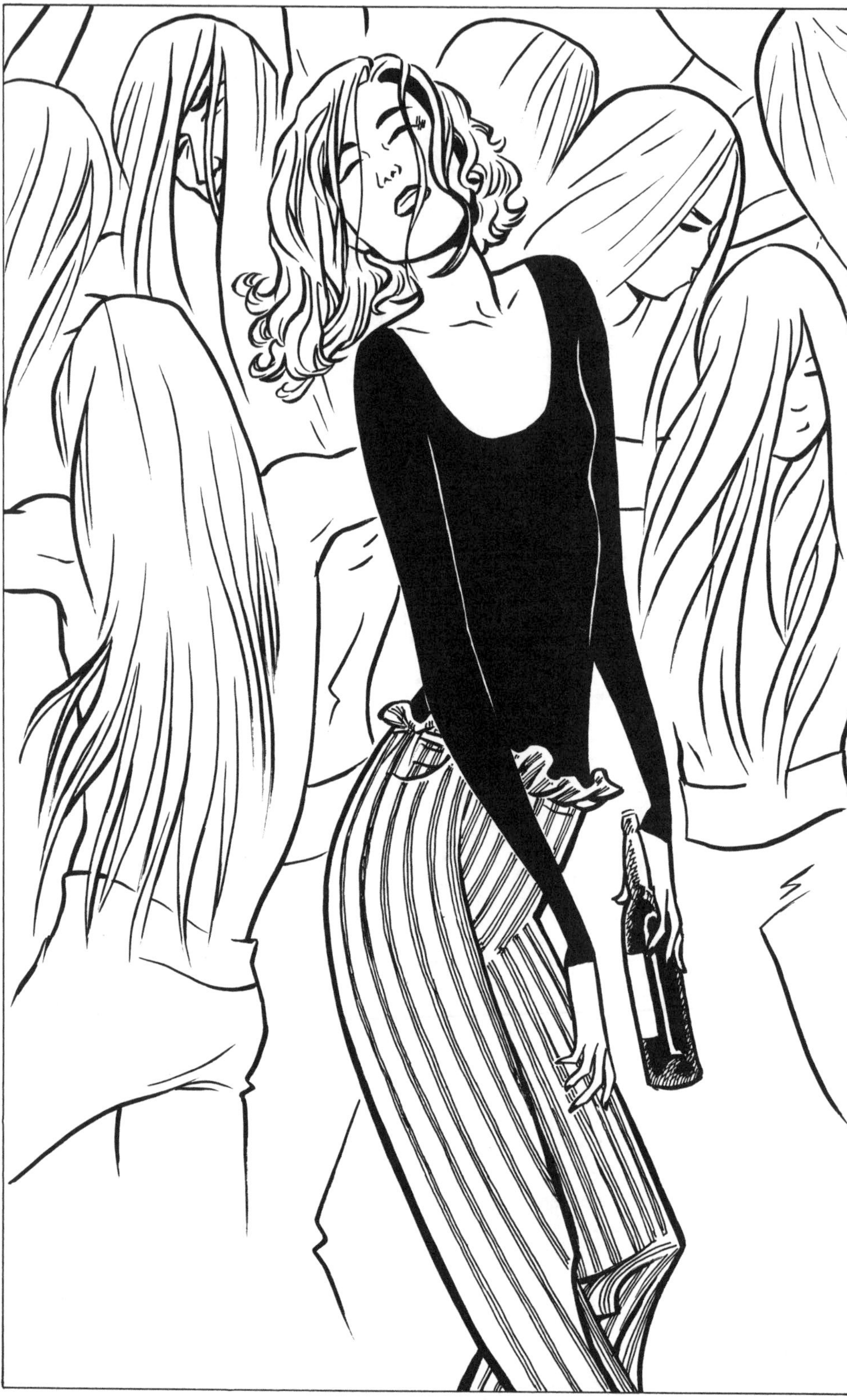

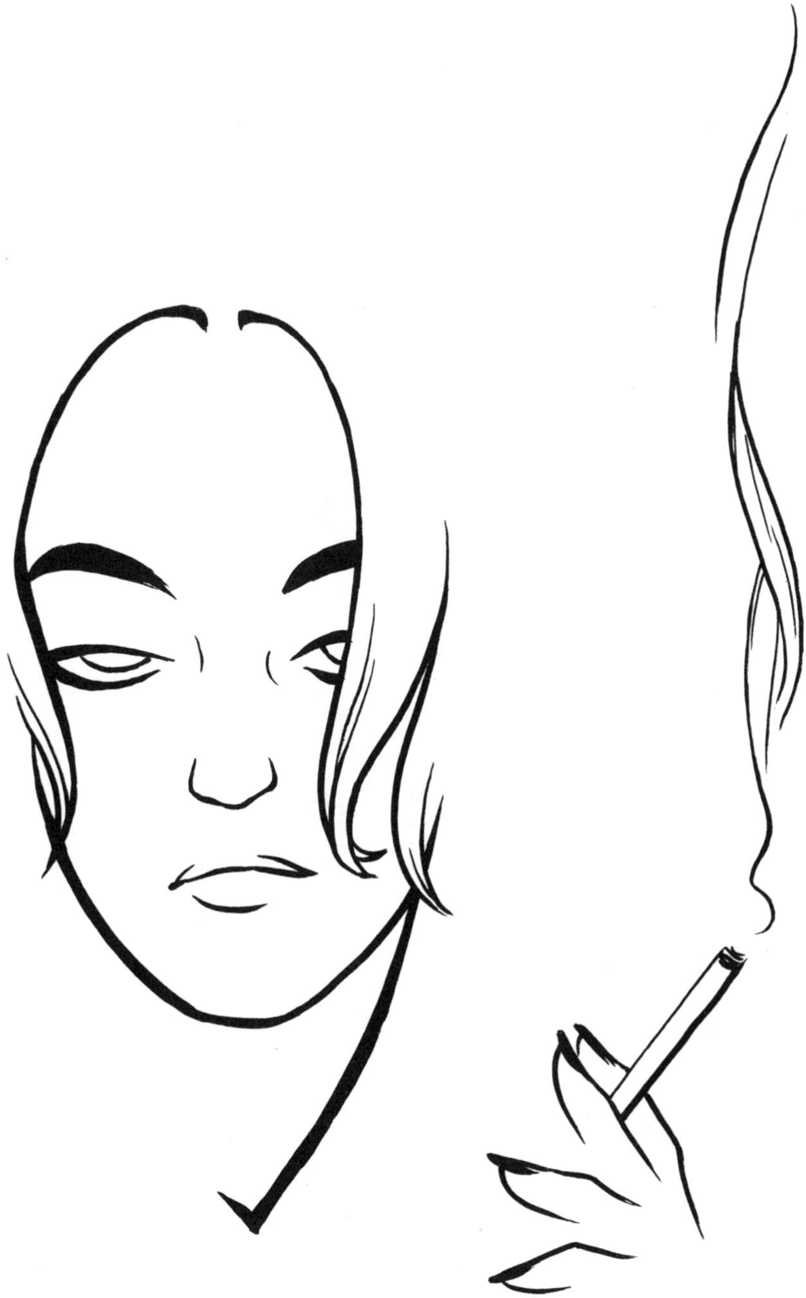

four:

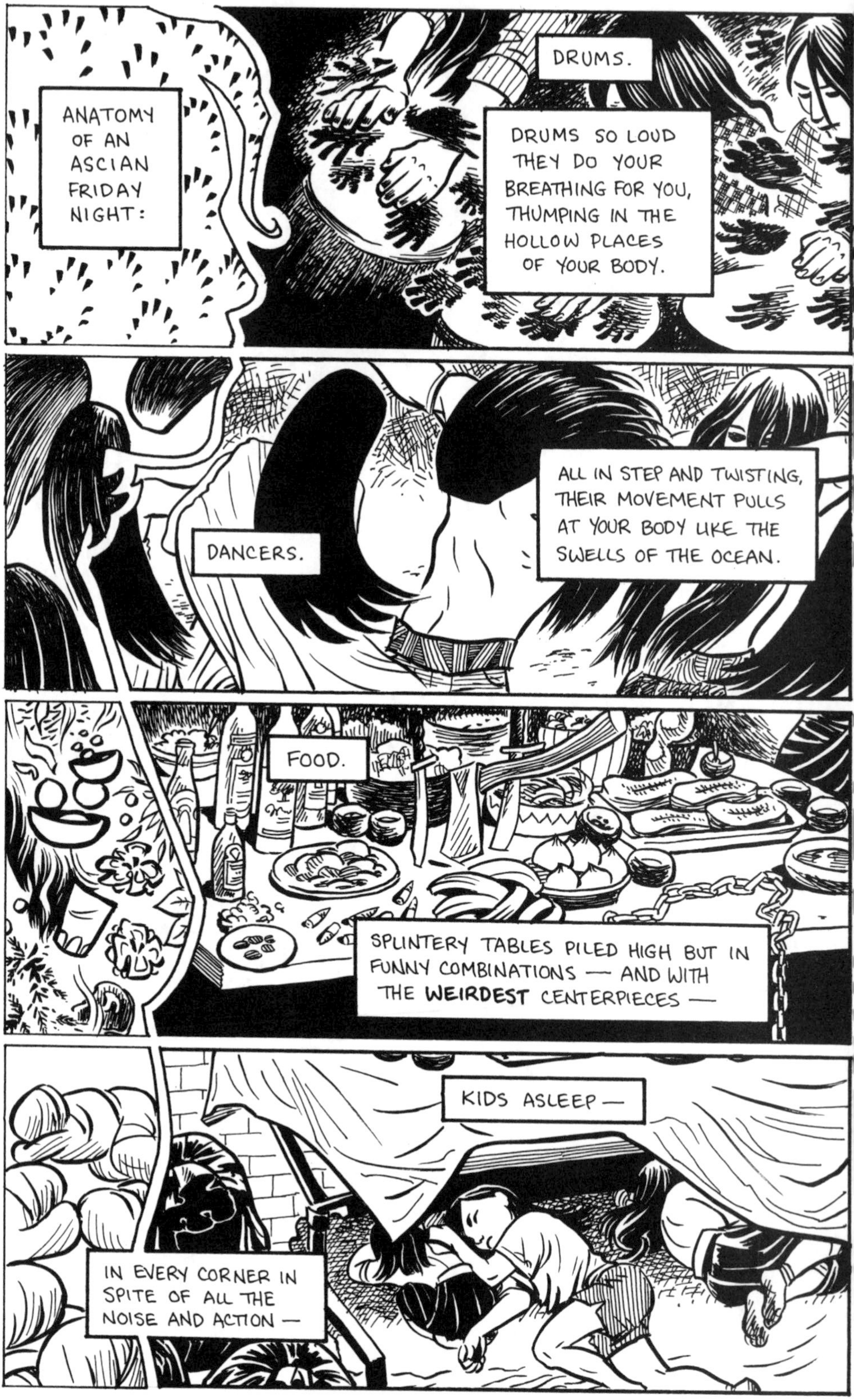
ANATOMY OF AN ASCIAN FRIDAY NIGHT:
DRUMS.
DRUMS SO LOUD THEY DO YOUR BREATHING FOR YOU, THUMPING IN THE HOLLOW PLACES OF YOUR BODY.
DANCERS.
ALL IN STEP AND TWISTING, THEIR MOVEMENT PULLS AT YOUR BODY LIKE THE SWELLS OF THE OCEAN.
FOOD.
SPLINTERY TABLES PILED HIGH BUT IN FUNNY COMBINATIONS — AND WITH THE WEIRDEST CENTERPIECES —
KIDS ASLEEP —
IN EVERY CORNER IN SPITE OF ALL THE NOISE AND ACTION —

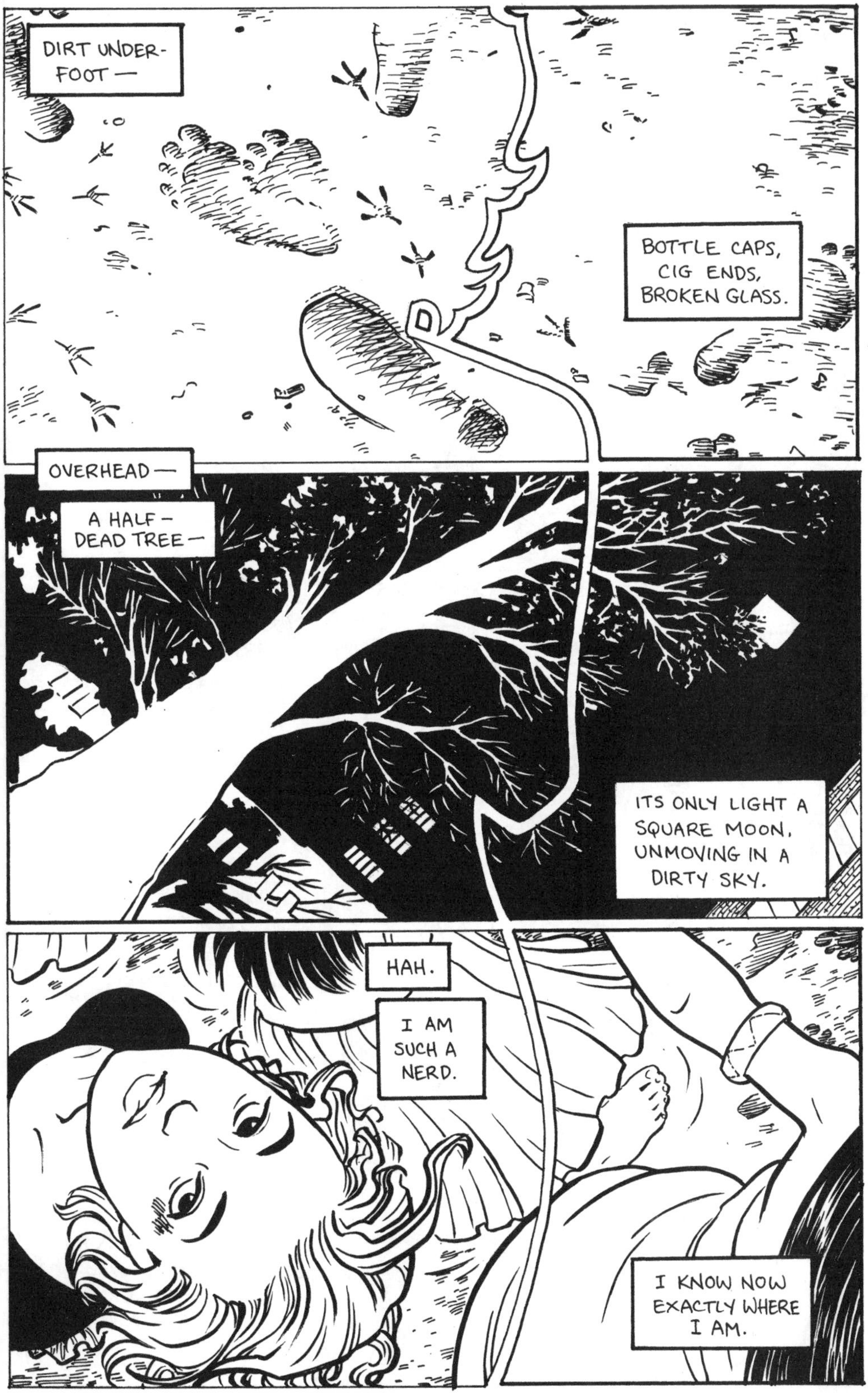
DIRT UNDER-FOOT —
BOTTLE CAPS, CIG ENDS, BROKEN GLASS.
OVERHEAD —
A HALF-DEAD TREE —
ITS ONLY LIGHT A SQUARE MOON, UNMOVING IN A DIRTY SKY.
HAH.
I AM SUCH A NERD.
I KNOW NOW EXACTLY WHERE I AM.

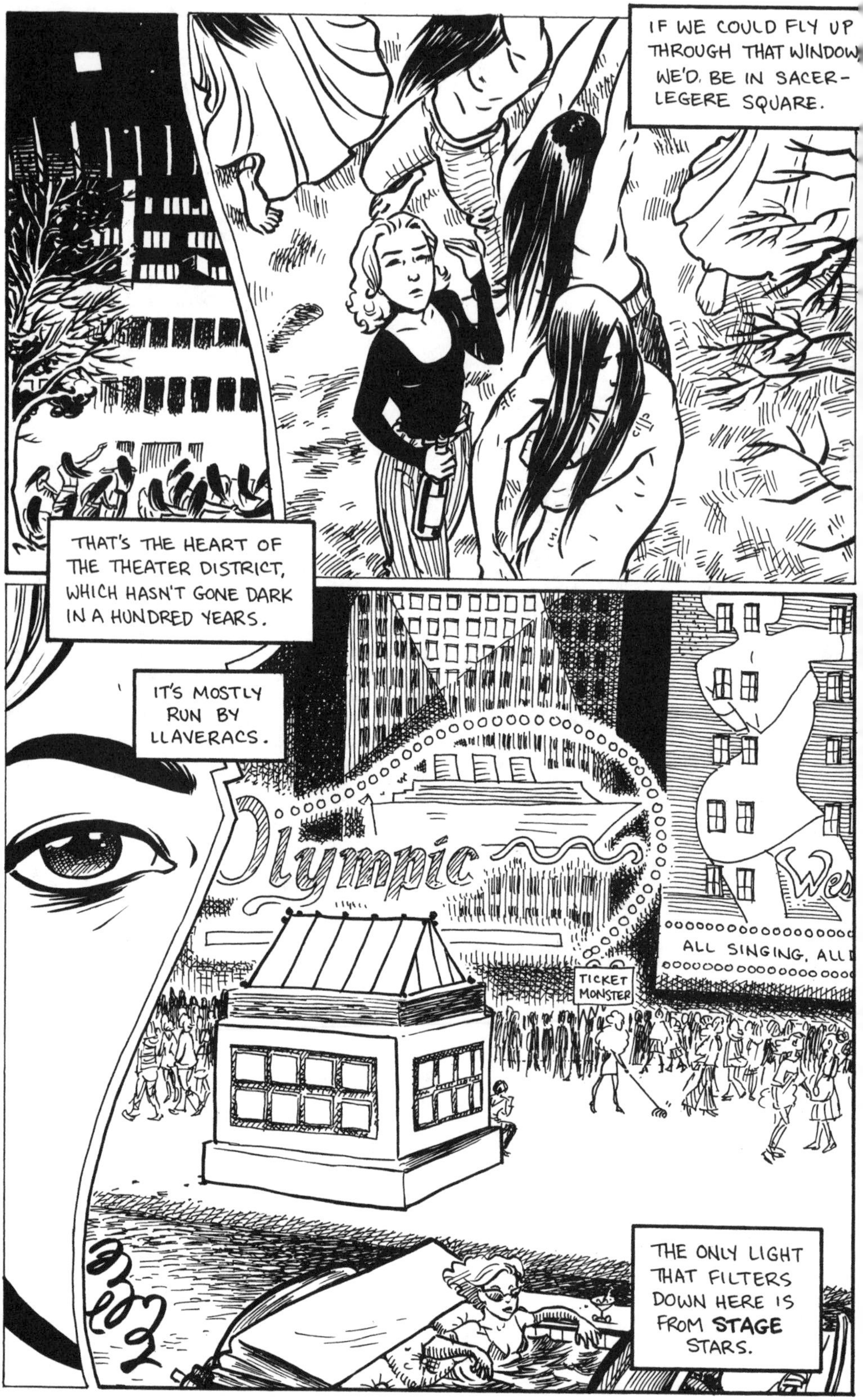
IF WE COULD FLY UP THROUGH THAT WINDOW WE'D BE IN SACER-LEGERE SQUARE.
THAT'S THE HEART OF THE THEATER DISTRICT, WHICH HASN'T GONE DARK IN A HUNDRED YEARS.
IT'S MOSTLY RUN BY LLAVERACS.
Olympic
TICKET MONSTER
ALL SINGING, ALL
THE ONLY LIGHT THAT FILTERS DOWN HERE IS FROM STAGE STARS.

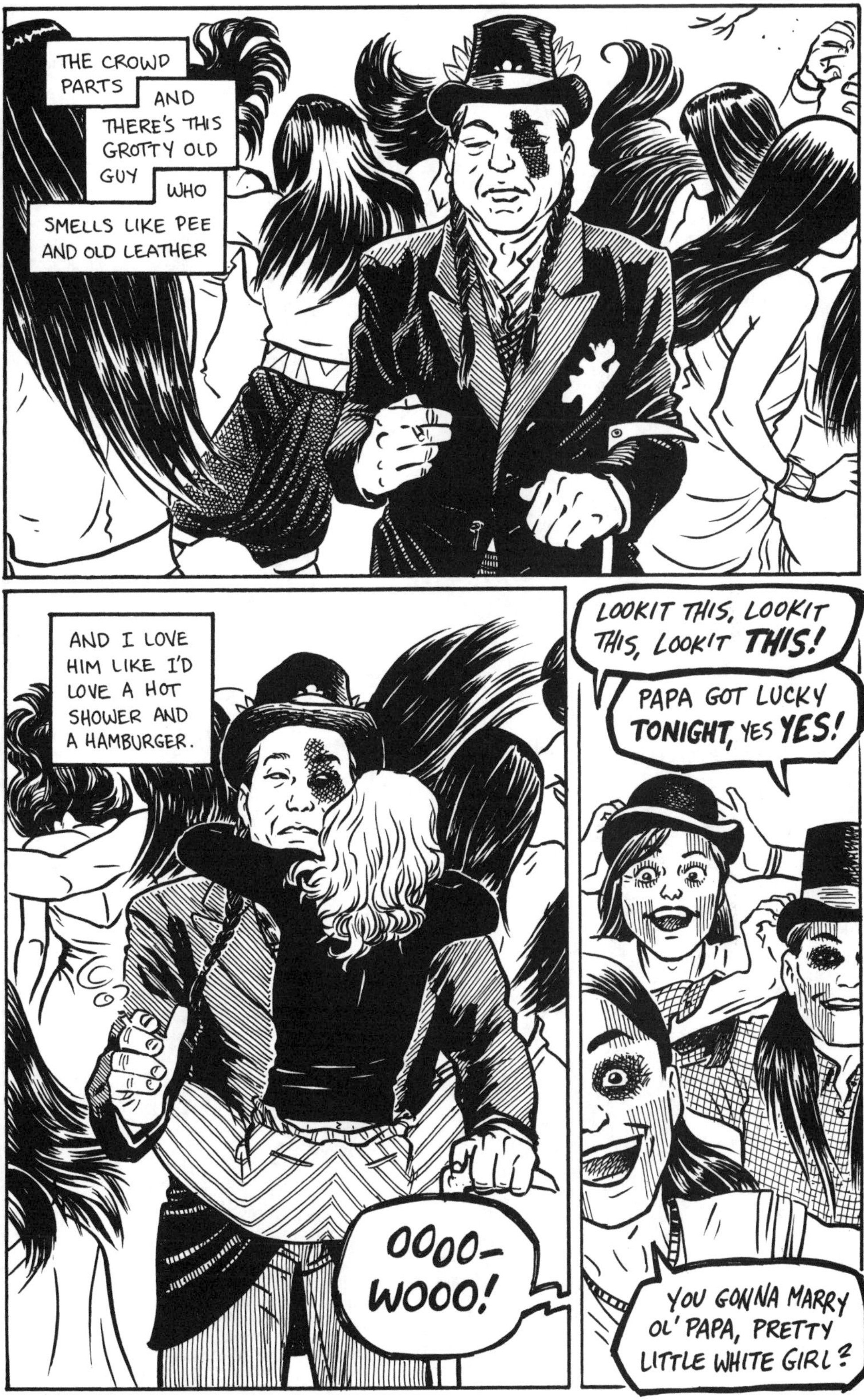
THE CROWD PARTS
AND THERE'S THIS GROTTY OLD GUY
WHO
SMELLS LIKE PEE AND OLD LEATHER
AND I LOVE HIM LIKE I'D LOVE A HOT SHOWER AND A HAMBURGER.
OOOO-WOOO!
LOOKIT THIS, LOOKIT THIS, LOOKIT THIS!
PAPA GOT LUCKY TONIGHT, YES YES!
YOU GONNA MARRY OL' PAPA, PRETTY LITTLE WHITE GIRL?

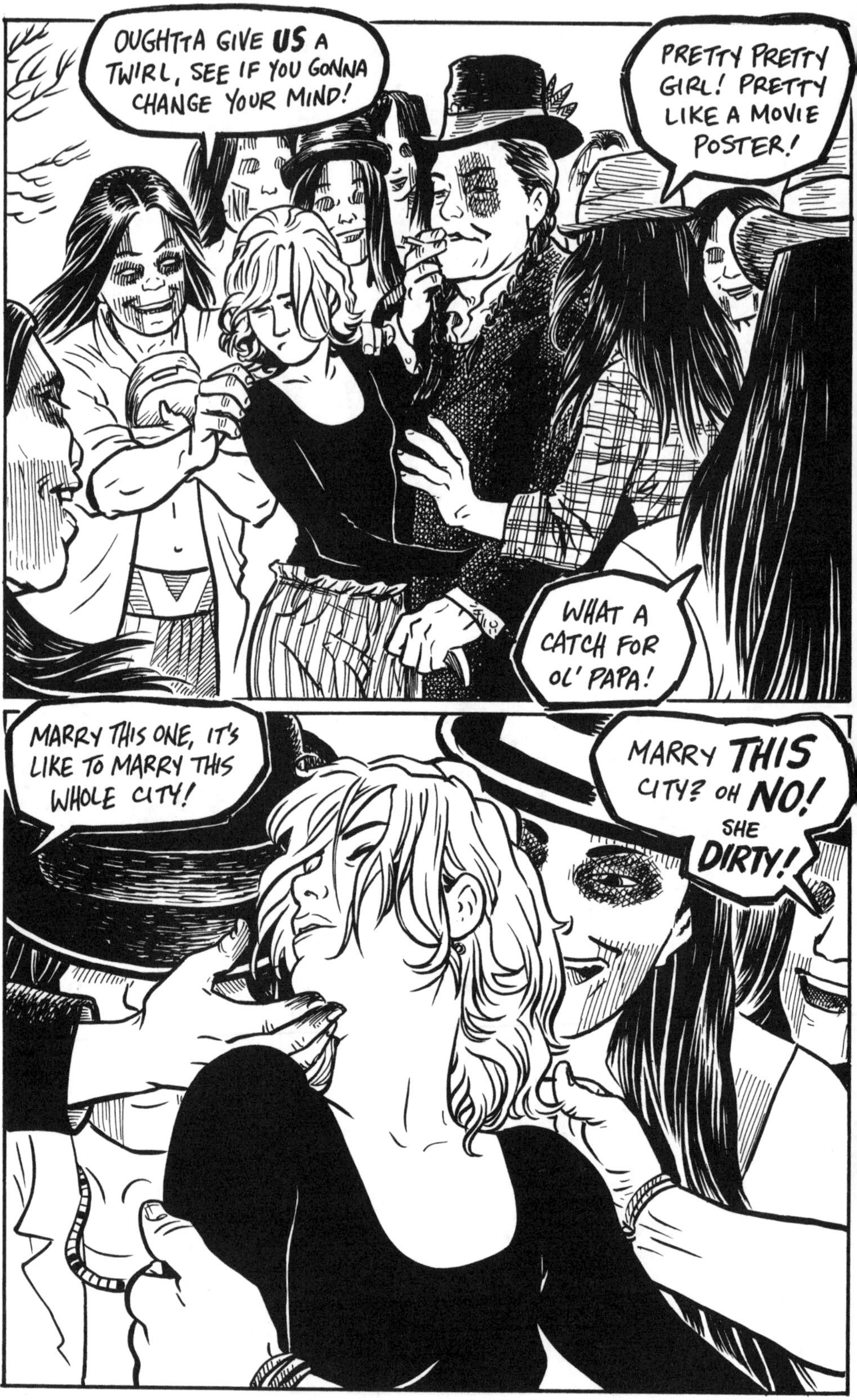
OUGHTTA GIVE US A TWIRL, SEE IF YOU GONNA CHANGE YOUR MIND!
PRETTY PRETTY GIRL! PRETTY LIKE A MOVIE POSTER!
WHAT A CATCH FOR OL' PAPA!
MARRY THIS ONE, IT'S LIKE TO MARRY THIS WHOLE CITY!
MARRY THIS CITY? OH NO! SHE DIRTY!

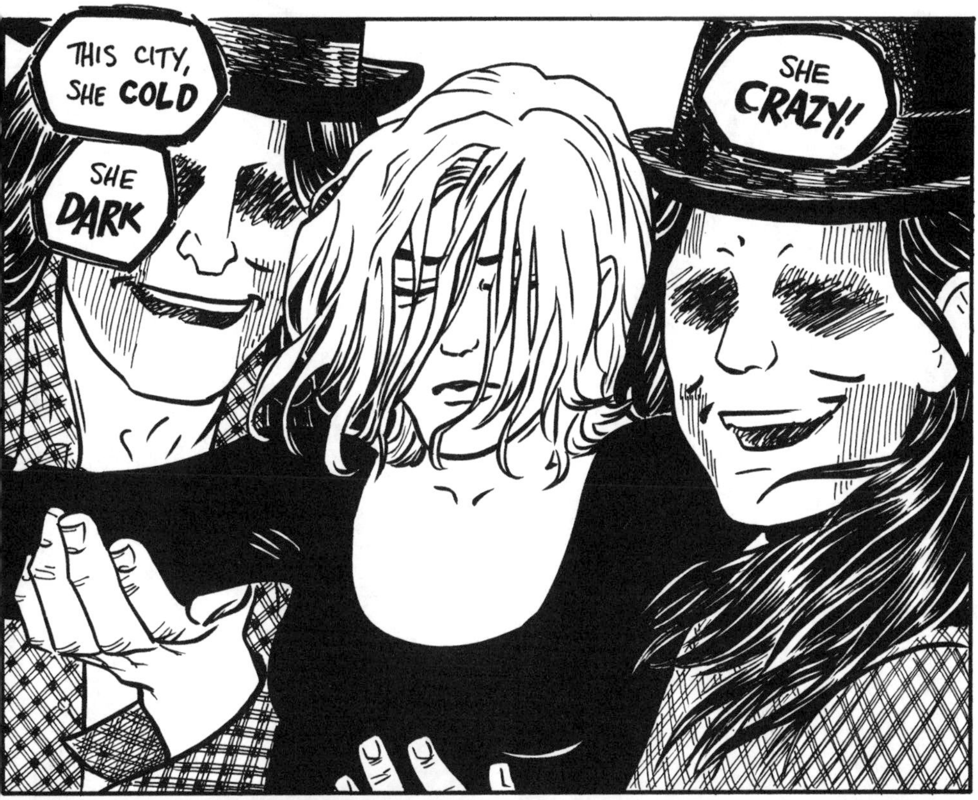
THIS CITY, SHE COLD
SHE DARK
SHE CRAZY!

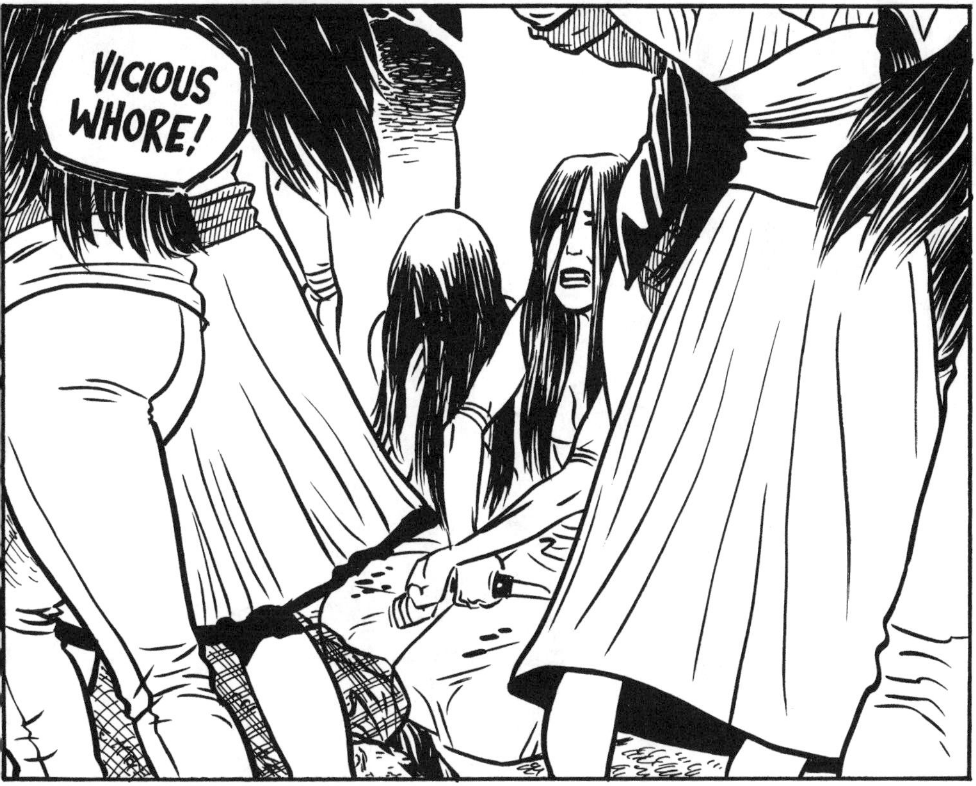
VICIOUS WHORE!

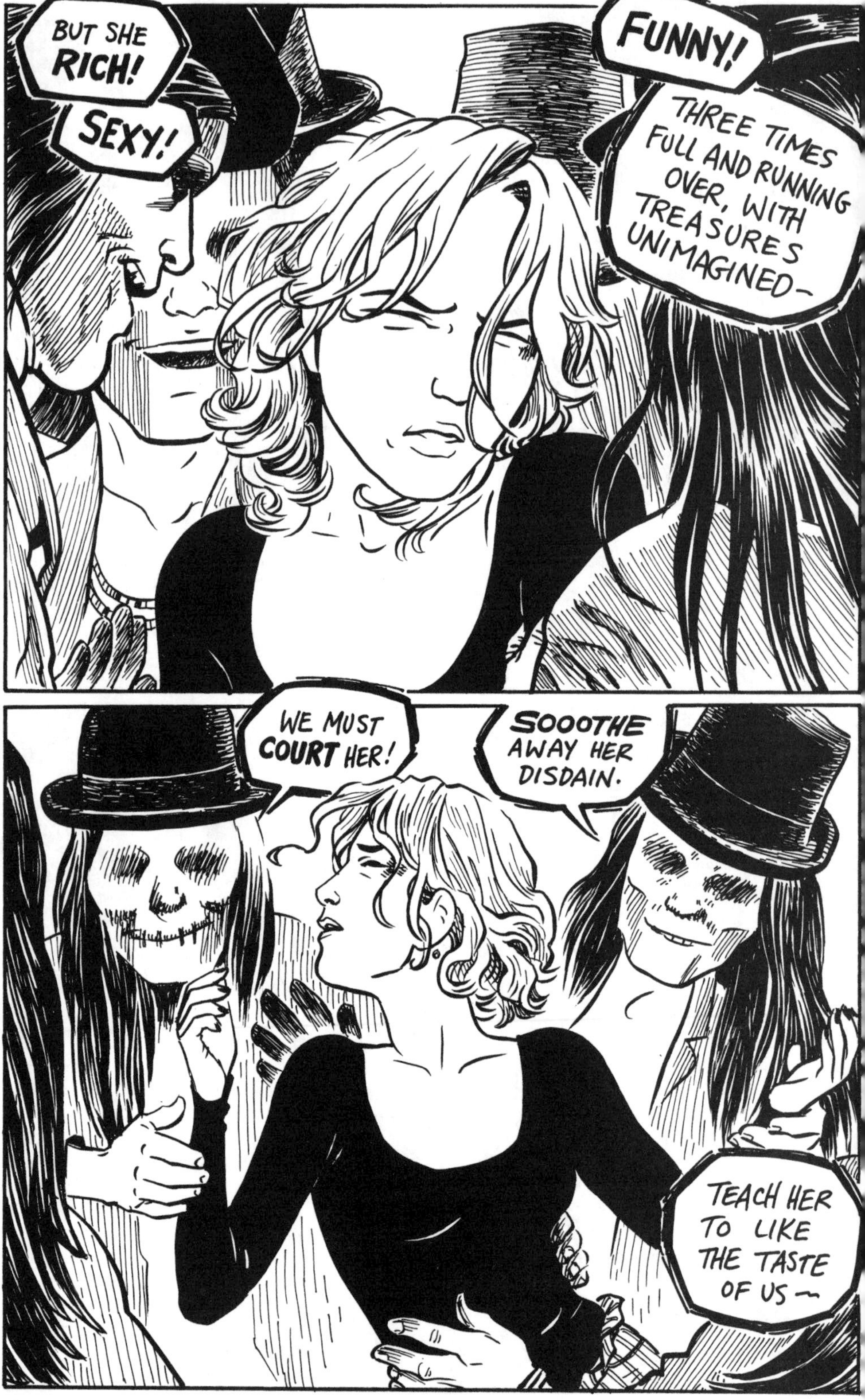
BUT SHE RICH!
SEXY!
FUNNY!
THREE TIMES FULL AND RUNNING OVER, WITH TREASURES UNIMAGINED–
WE MUST COURT HER!
SOOOTHE AWAY HER DISDAIN.
TEACH HER TO LIKE THE TASTE OF US–

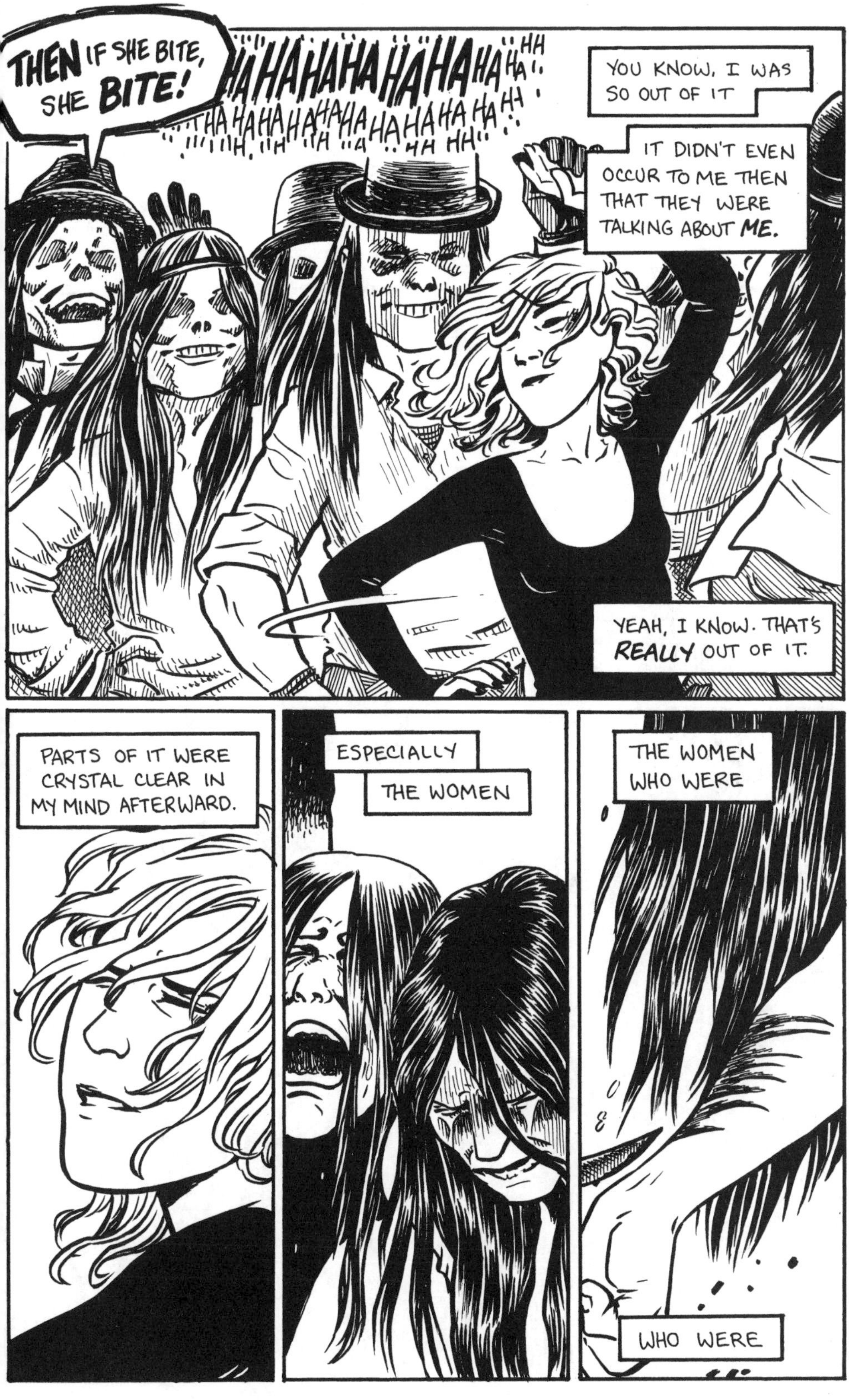
THEN IF SHE BITE, SHE BITE!
HAHAHAHAHAHAHAHA
YOU KNOW, I WAS SO OUT OF IT
IT DIDN'T EVEN OCCUR TO ME THEN THAT THEY WERE TALKING ABOUT ME.
YEAH, I KNOW. THAT'S REALLY OUT OF IT.
PARTS OF IT WERE CRYSTAL CLEAR IN MY MIND AFTERWARD.
ESPECIALLY
THE WOMEN
THE WOMEN WHO WERE
WHO WERE

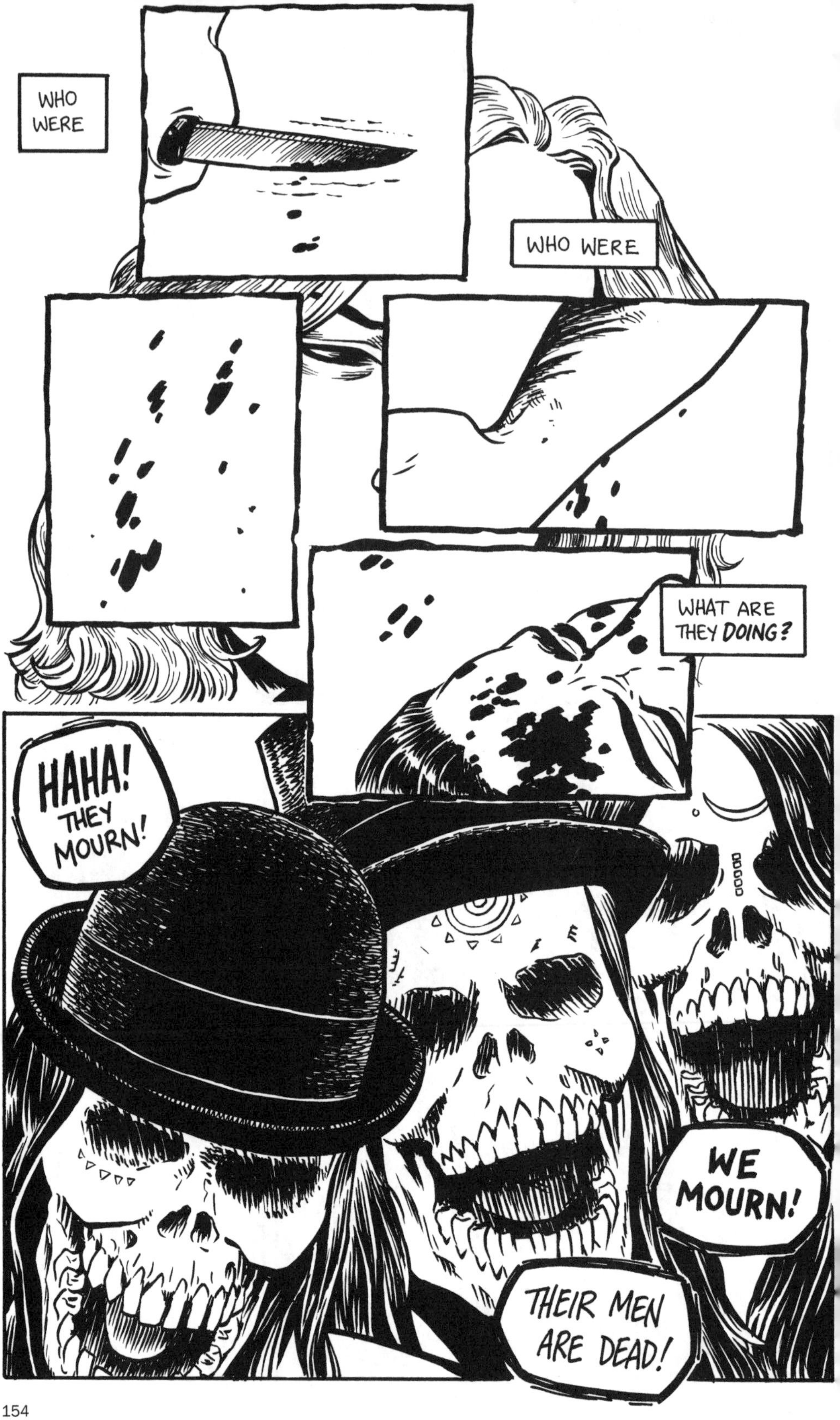
WHO WERE
WHO WERE
WHAT ARE THEY DOING?
HAHA! THEY MOURN!
WE MOURN!
THEIR MEN ARE DEAD!

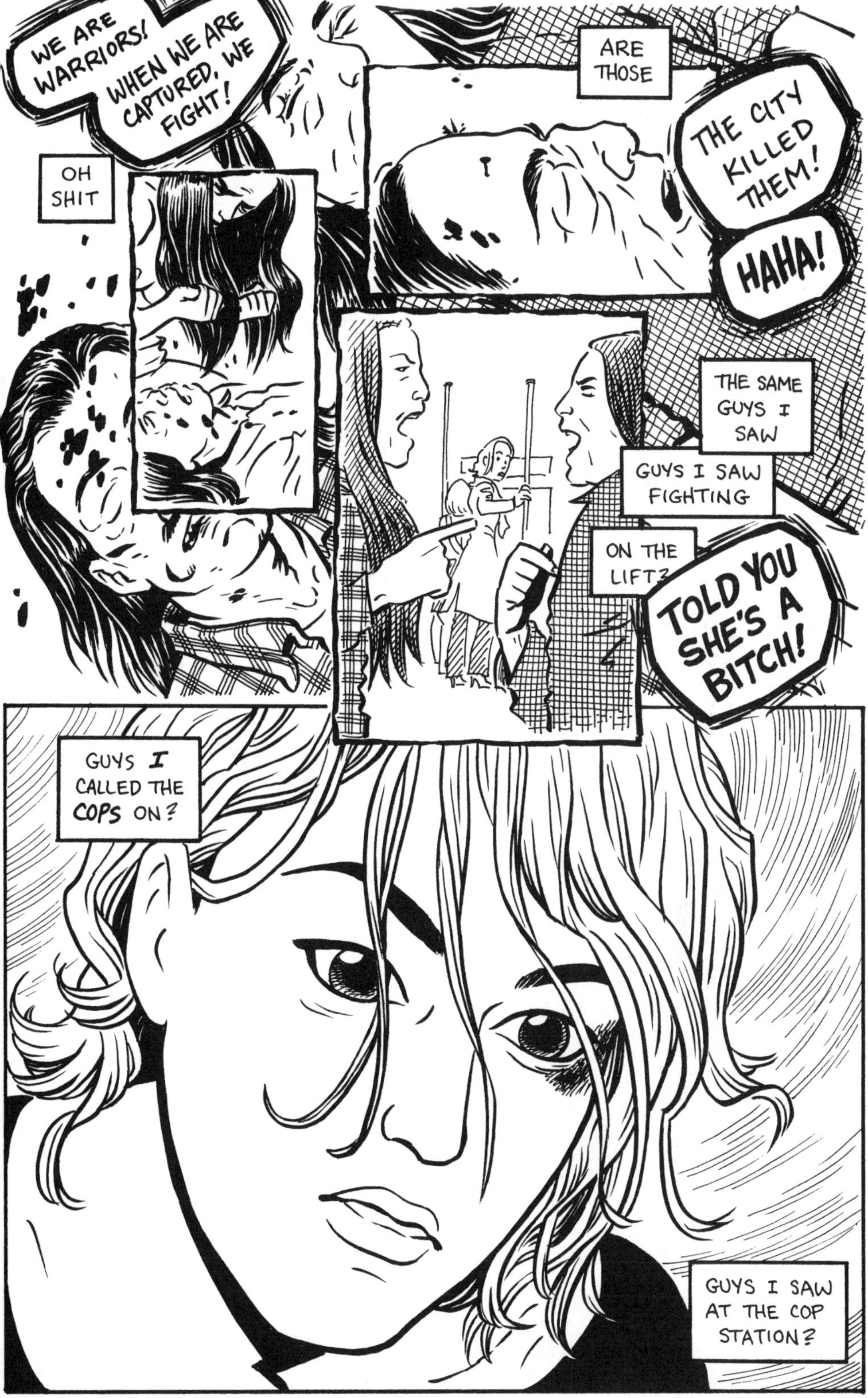
WE ARE WARRIORS!
WHEN WE ARE CAPTURED, WE FIGHT!
OH SHIT
ARE THOSE
THE CITY KILLED THEM!
HAHA!
THE SAME GUYS I SAW
GUYS I SAW FIGHTING
ON THE LIFT?
TOLD YOU SHE'S A BITCH!
GUYS I CALLED THE COPS ON?
GUYS I SAW AT THE COP STATION?

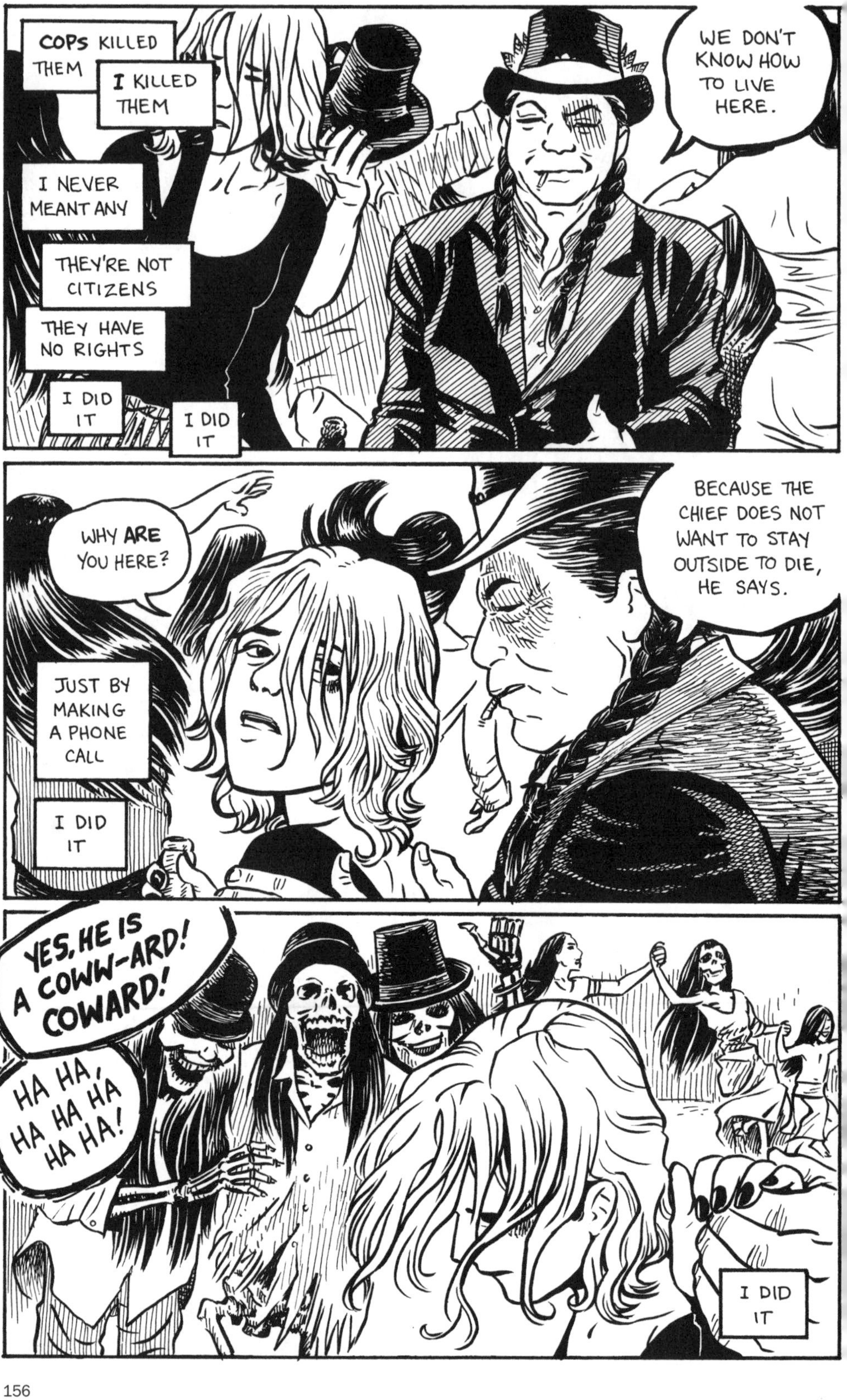
COPS KILLED THEM
I KILLED THEM
I NEVER MEANT ANY
THEY'RE NOT CITIZENS
THEY HAVE NO RIGHTS
I DID IT
I DID IT
WE DON'T KNOW HOW TO LIVE HERE.
WHY ARE YOU HERE?
BECAUSE THE CHIEF DOES NOT WANT TO STAY OUTSIDE TO DIE, HE SAYS.
JUST BY MAKING A PHONE CALL
I DID IT
YES, HE IS A COWW-ARD! COWARD!
HA HA, HA HA HA HA HA!
I DID IT

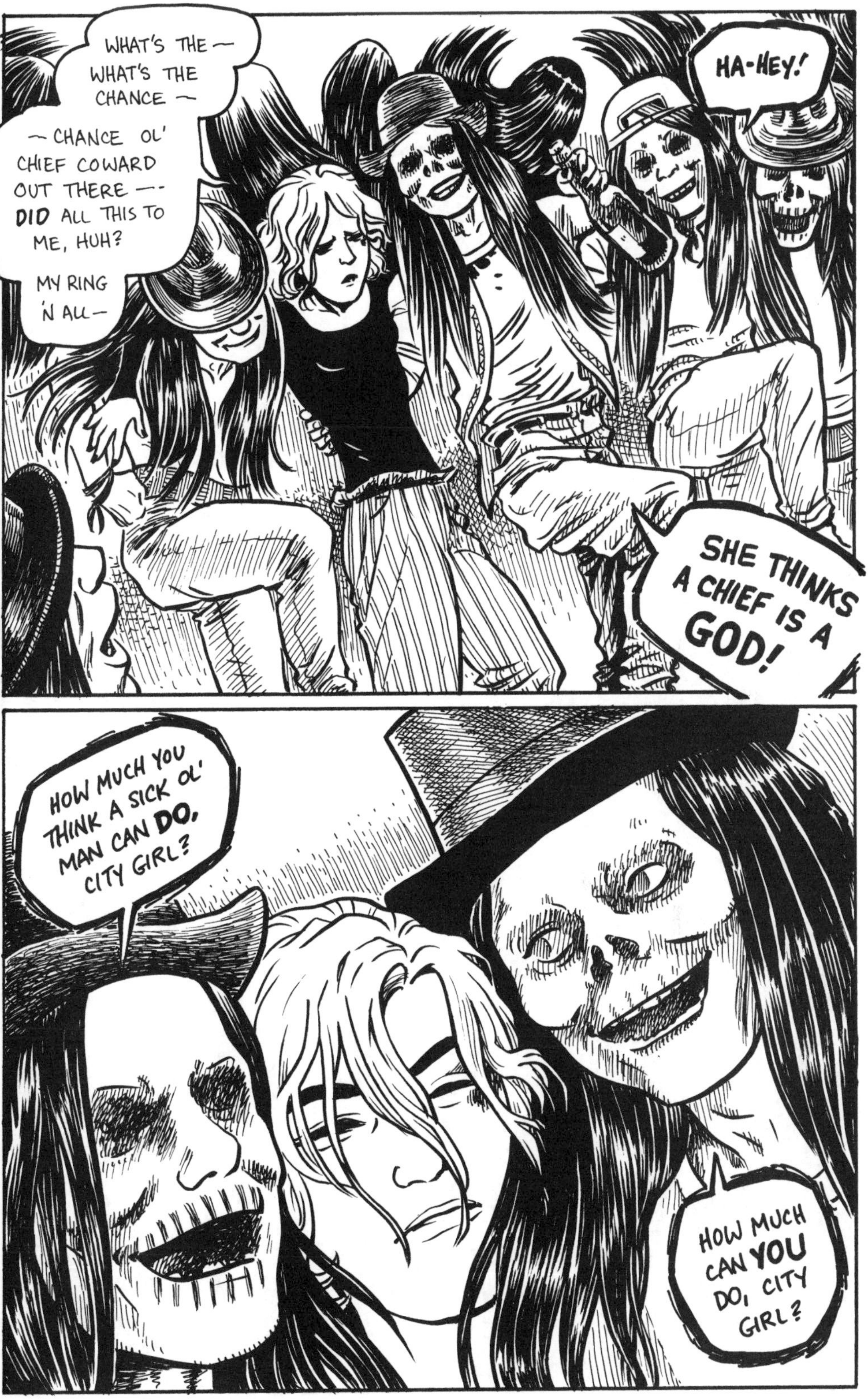
WHAT'S THE — WHAT'S THE CHANCE —
— CHANCE OL' CHIEF COWARD OUT THERE — DID ALL THIS TO ME, HUH?
MY RING 'N ALL—
HA-HEY!
SHE THINKS A CHIEF IS A GOD!
HOW MUCH YOU THINK A SICK OL' MAN CAN DO, CITY GIRL?
HOW MUCH CAN YOU DO, CITY GIRL?

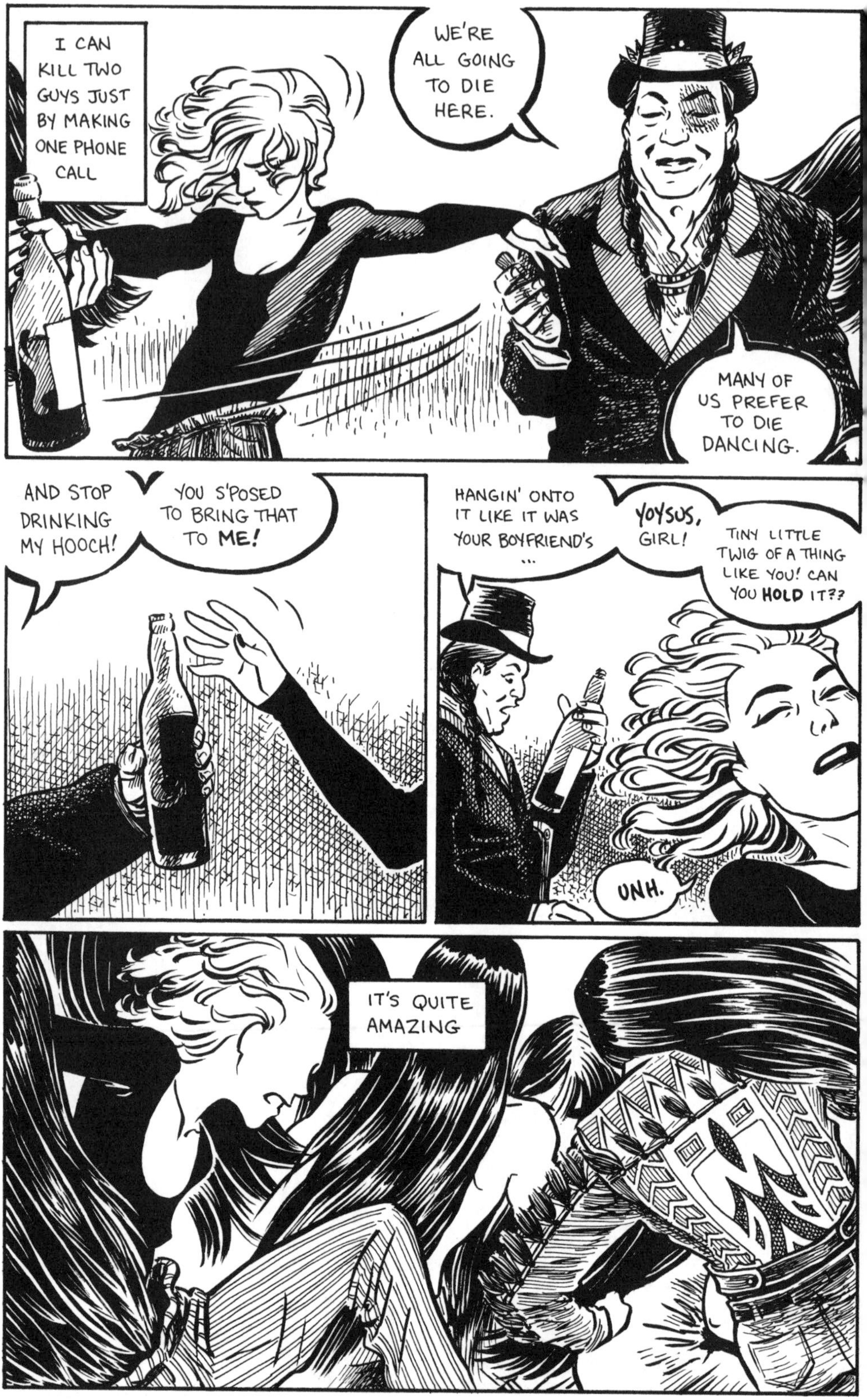
I CAN KILL TWO GUYS JUST BY MAKING ONE PHONE CALL
WE'RE ALL GOING TO DIE HERE.
MANY OF US PREFER TO DIE DANCING.
AND STOP DRINKING MY HOOCH!
YOU S'POSED TO BRING THAT TO **ME!**
HANGIN' ONTO IT LIKE IT WAS YOUR BOYFRIEND'S ...
YOYSUS, GIRL!
TINY LITTLE TWIG OF A THING LIKE YOU! CAN YOU **HOLD** IT??
UNH.
IT'S QUITE AMAZING

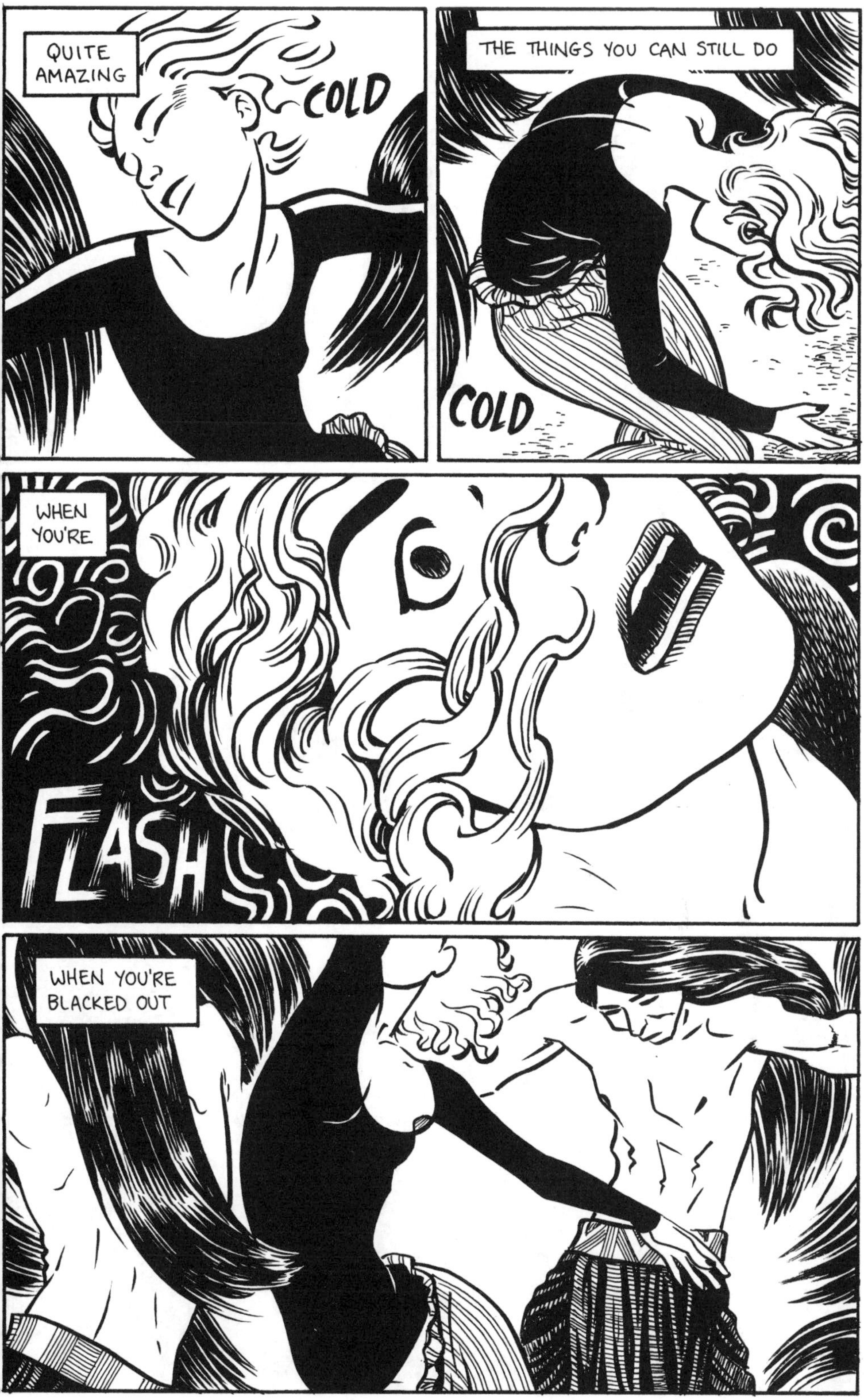
QUITE AMAZING
COLD
THE THINGS YOU CAN STILL DO
COLD
WHEN YOU'RE
FLASH
WHEN YOU'RE BLACKED OUT

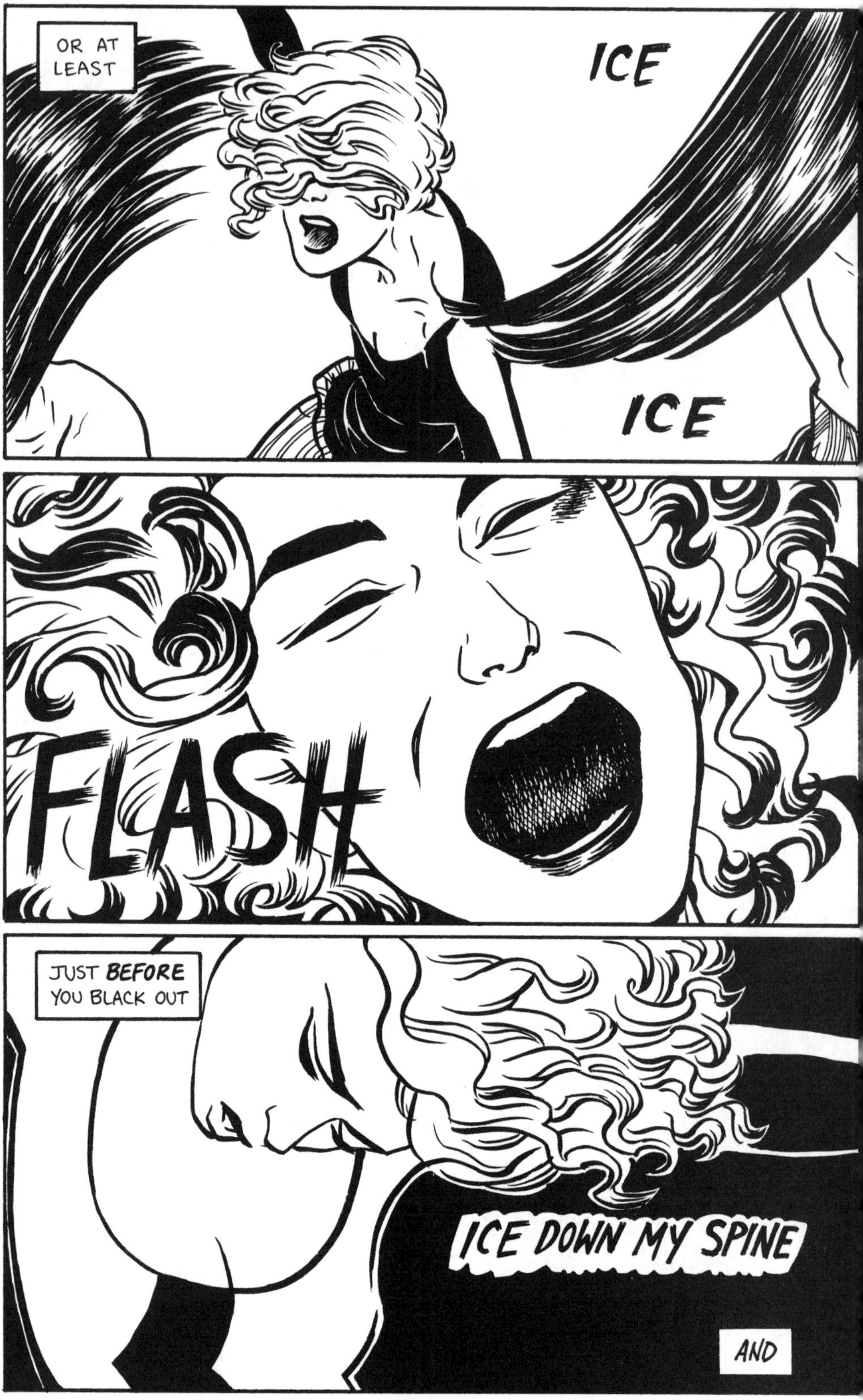
OR AT LEAST
ICE
ICE
FLASH
JUST BEFORE YOU BLACK OUT
ICE DOWN MY SPINE
AND

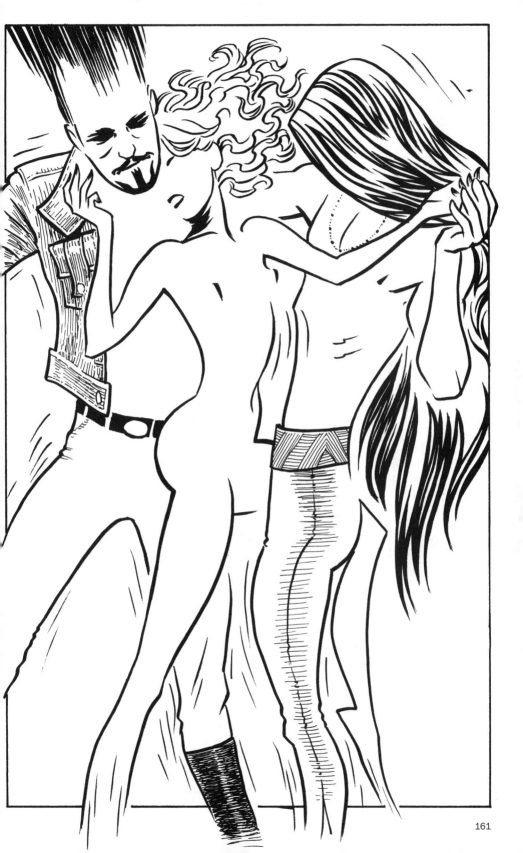

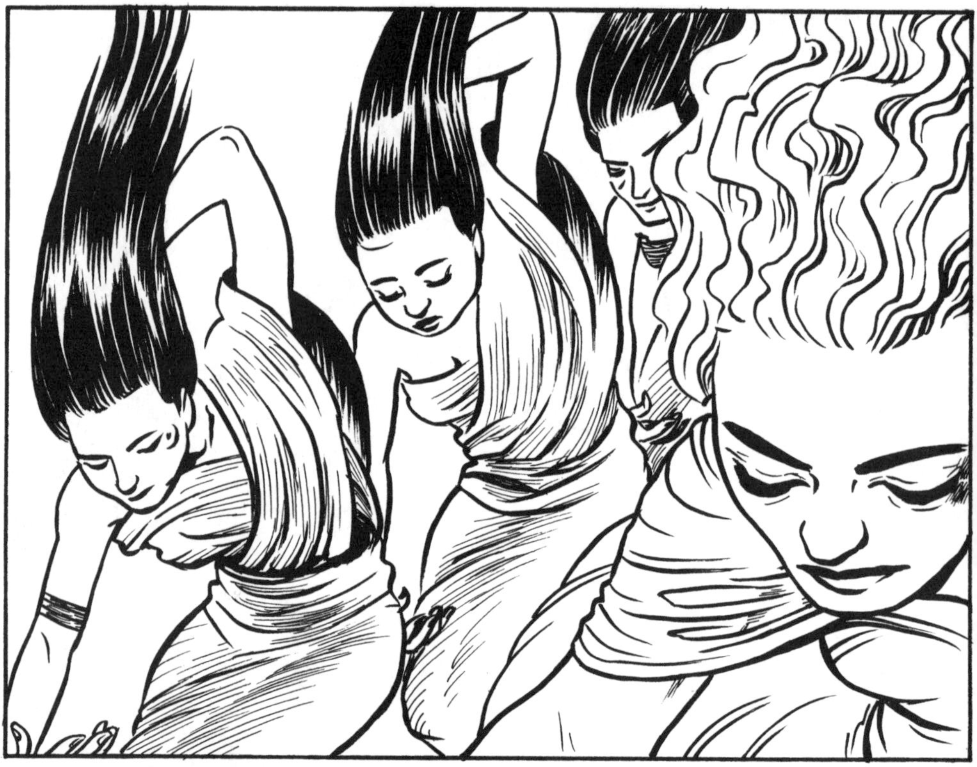

AFTER THAT

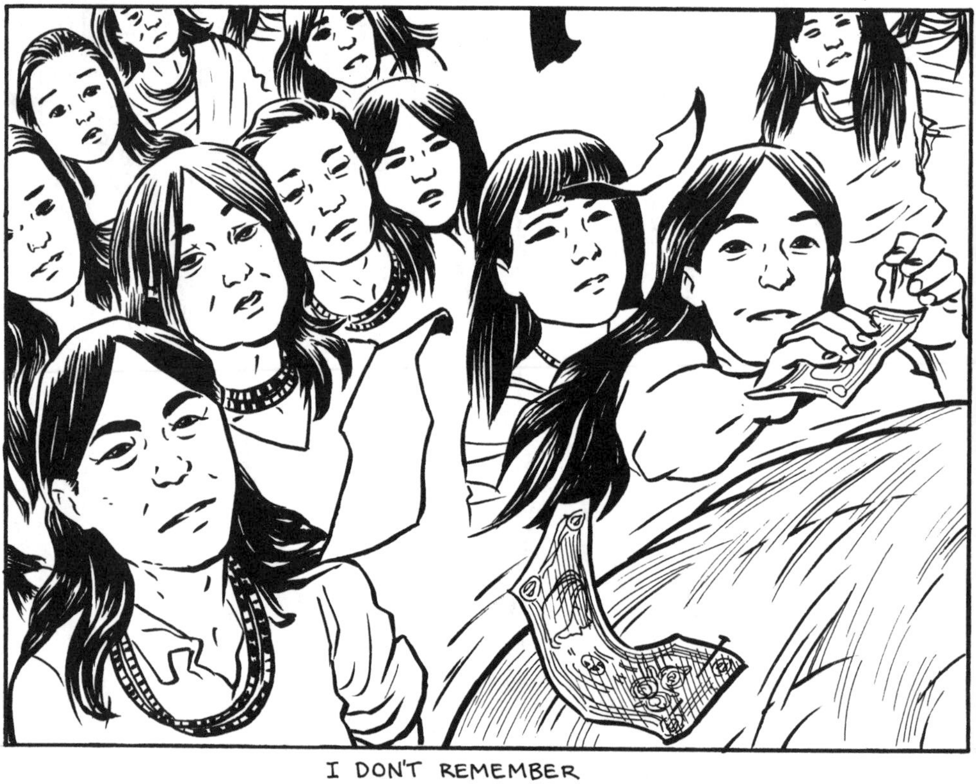

I DON'T REMEMBER

MUCH OF ANYTHING.

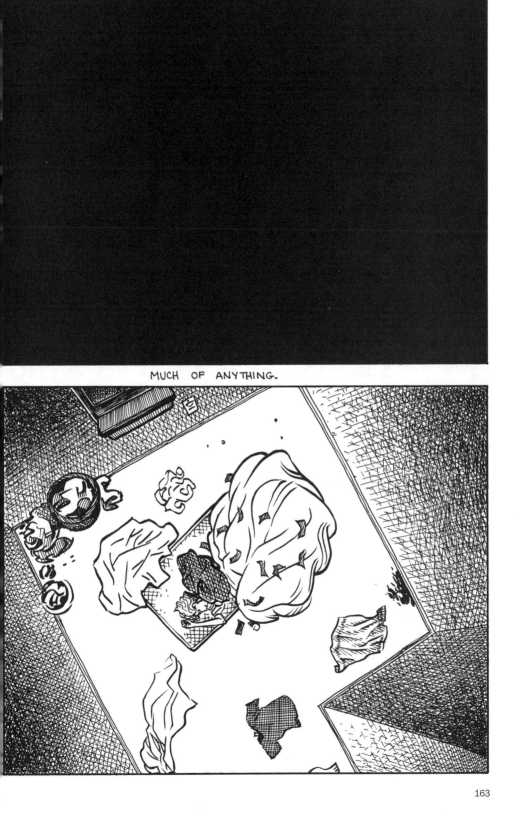

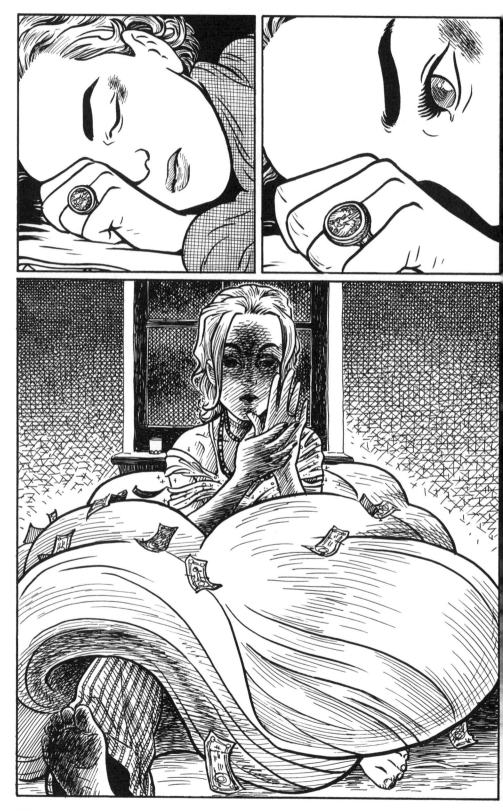

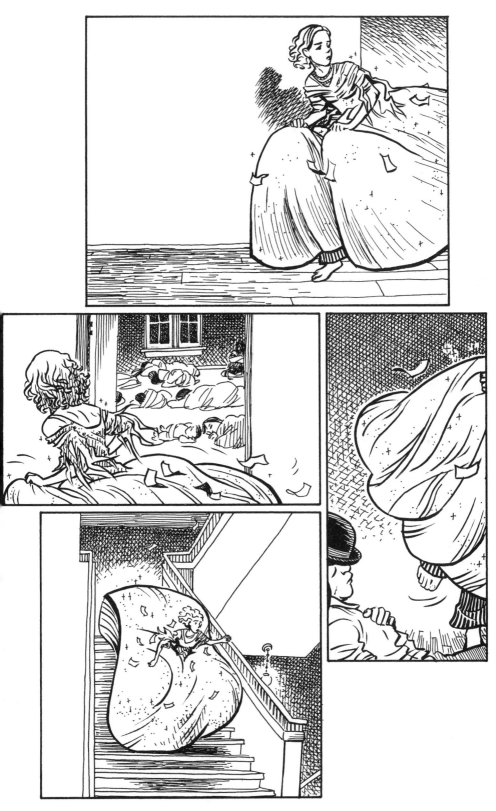

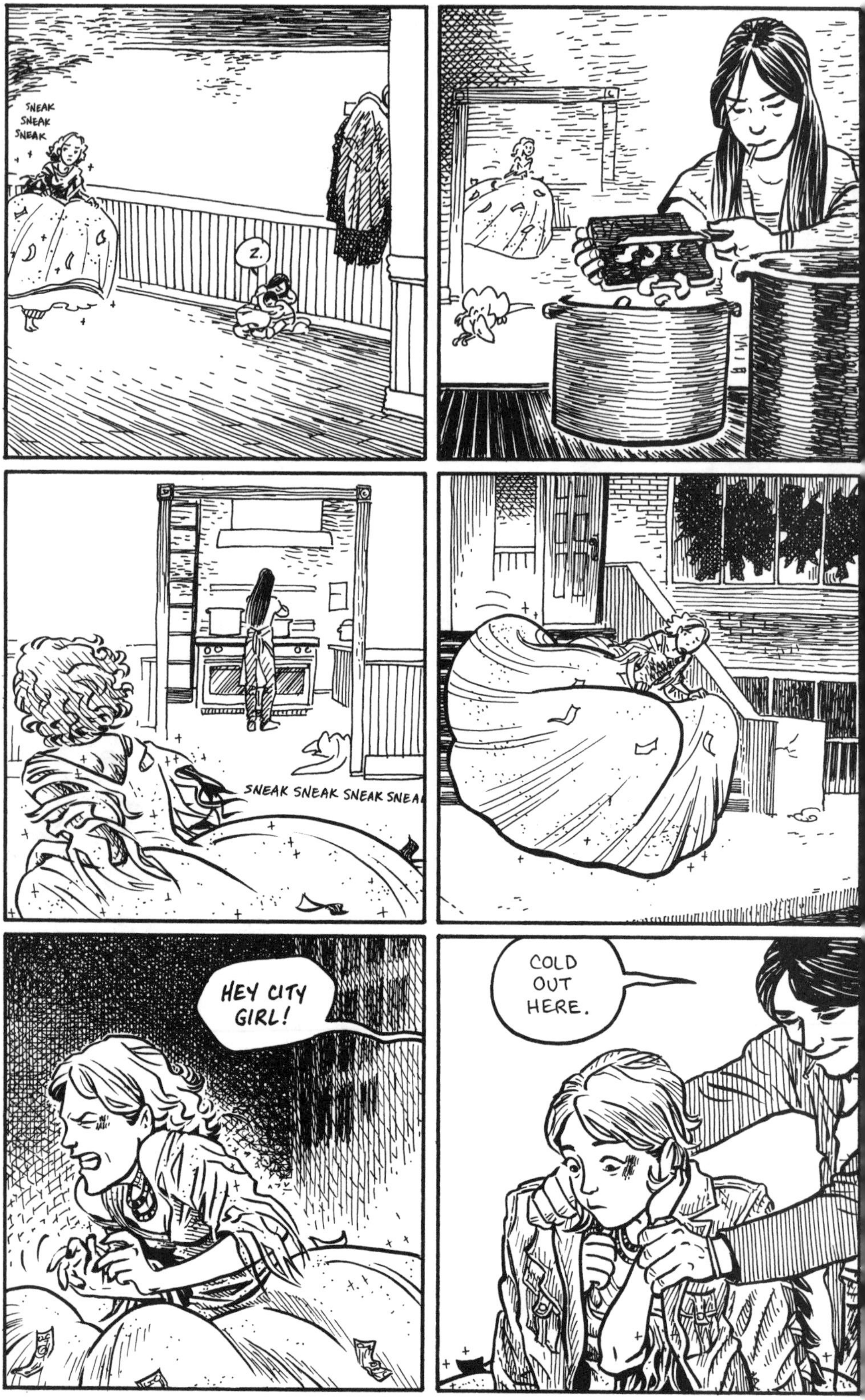
SNEAK
SNEAK
SNEAK
Z.
SNEAK SNEAK SNEAK SNEA
HEY CITY GIRL!
COLD OUT HERE.

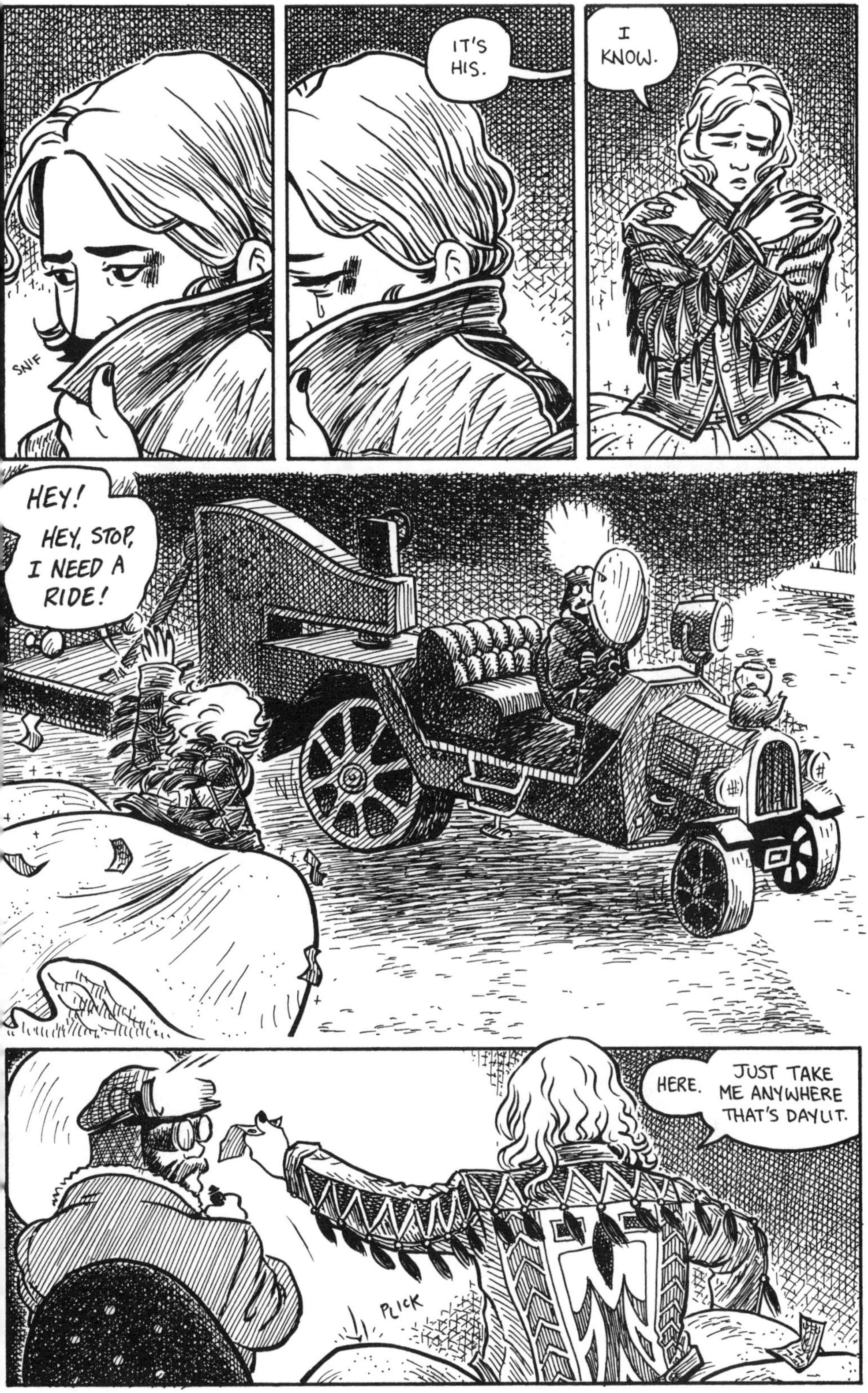
SNIF
IT'S HIS.
I KNOW.
HEY!
HEY, STOP, I NEED A RIDE!
HERE.
JUST TAKE ME ANYWHERE THAT'S DAYLIT.
PLICK

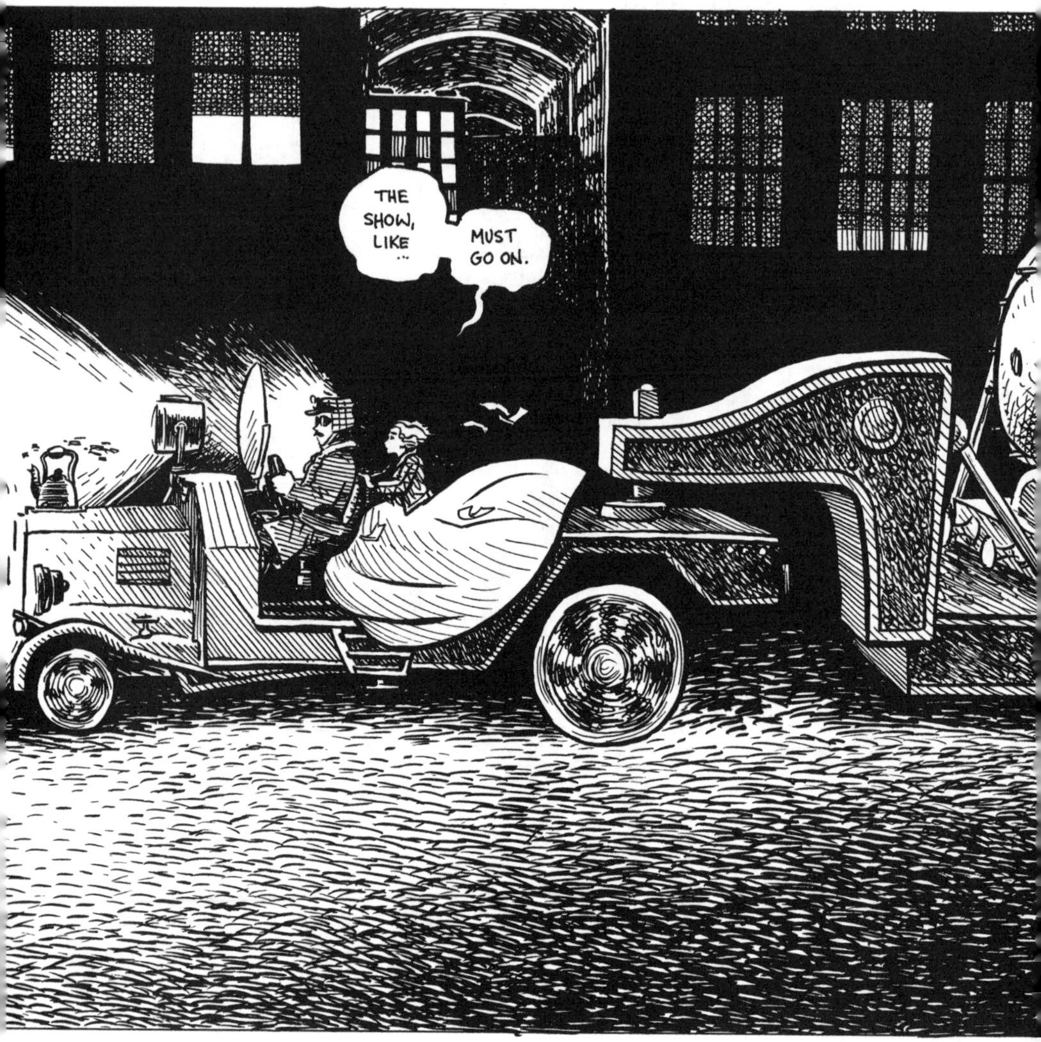
THE SHOW, LIKE ...
MUST GO ON.

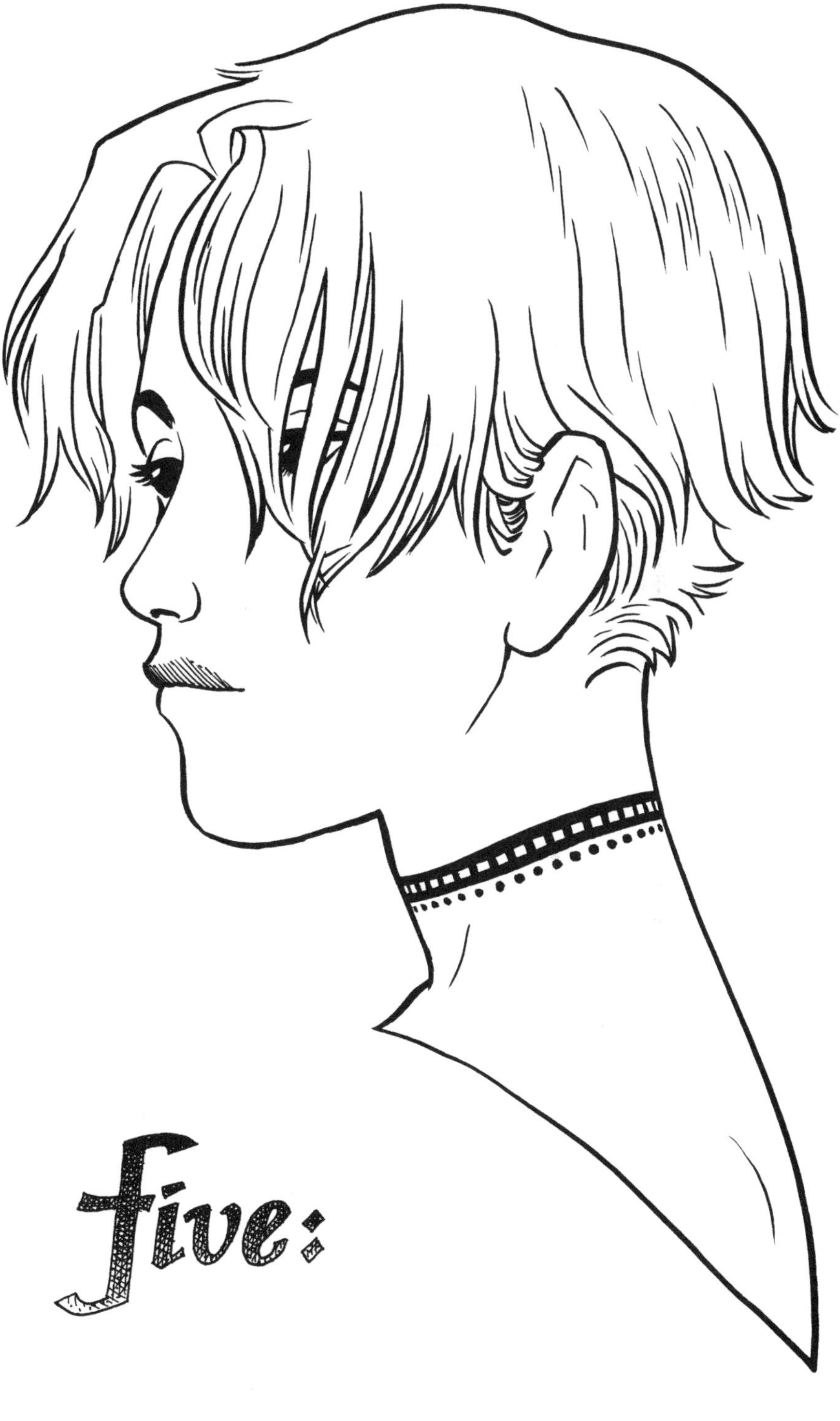

five:

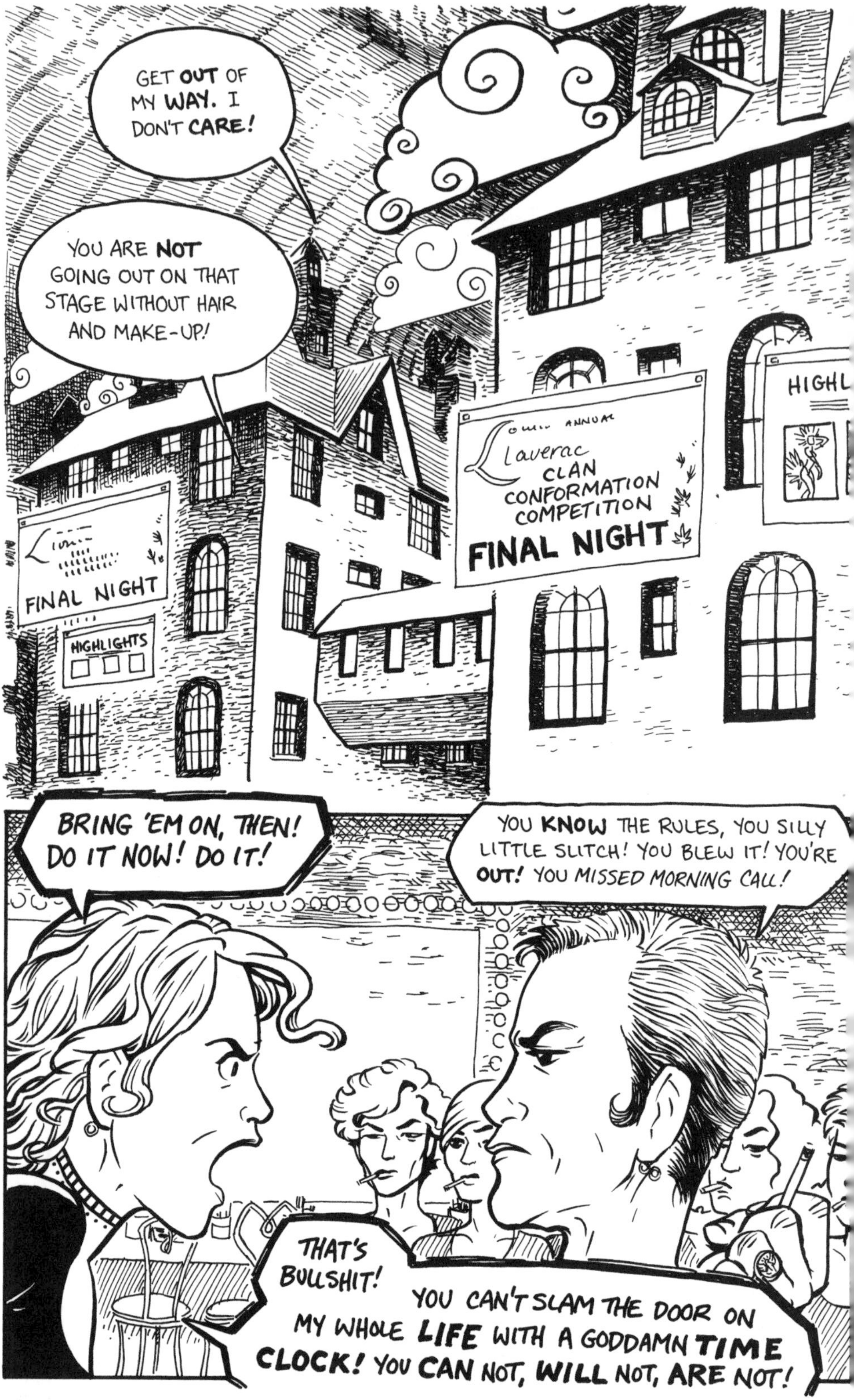

GET **OUT** OF MY **WAY.** I DON'T **CARE!**
YOU ARE **NOT** GOING OUT ON THAT STAGE WITHOUT HAIR AND MAKE-UP!
FINAL NIGHT
HIGHLIGHTS
ANNUAL
Llaverac CLAN CONFORMATION COMPETITION
FINAL NIGHT
BRING 'EM ON, THEN! DO IT NOW! DO IT!
YOU **KNOW** THE RULES, YOU SILLY LITTLE SLITCH! YOU BLEW IT! YOU'RE **OUT!** YOU MISSED MORNING CALL!
THAT'S BULLSHIT!
YOU CAN'T SLAM THE DOOR ON MY WHOLE **LIFE** WITH A GODDAMN **TIME CLOCK!** YOU **CAN** NOT, **WILL** NOT, **ARE** NOT!

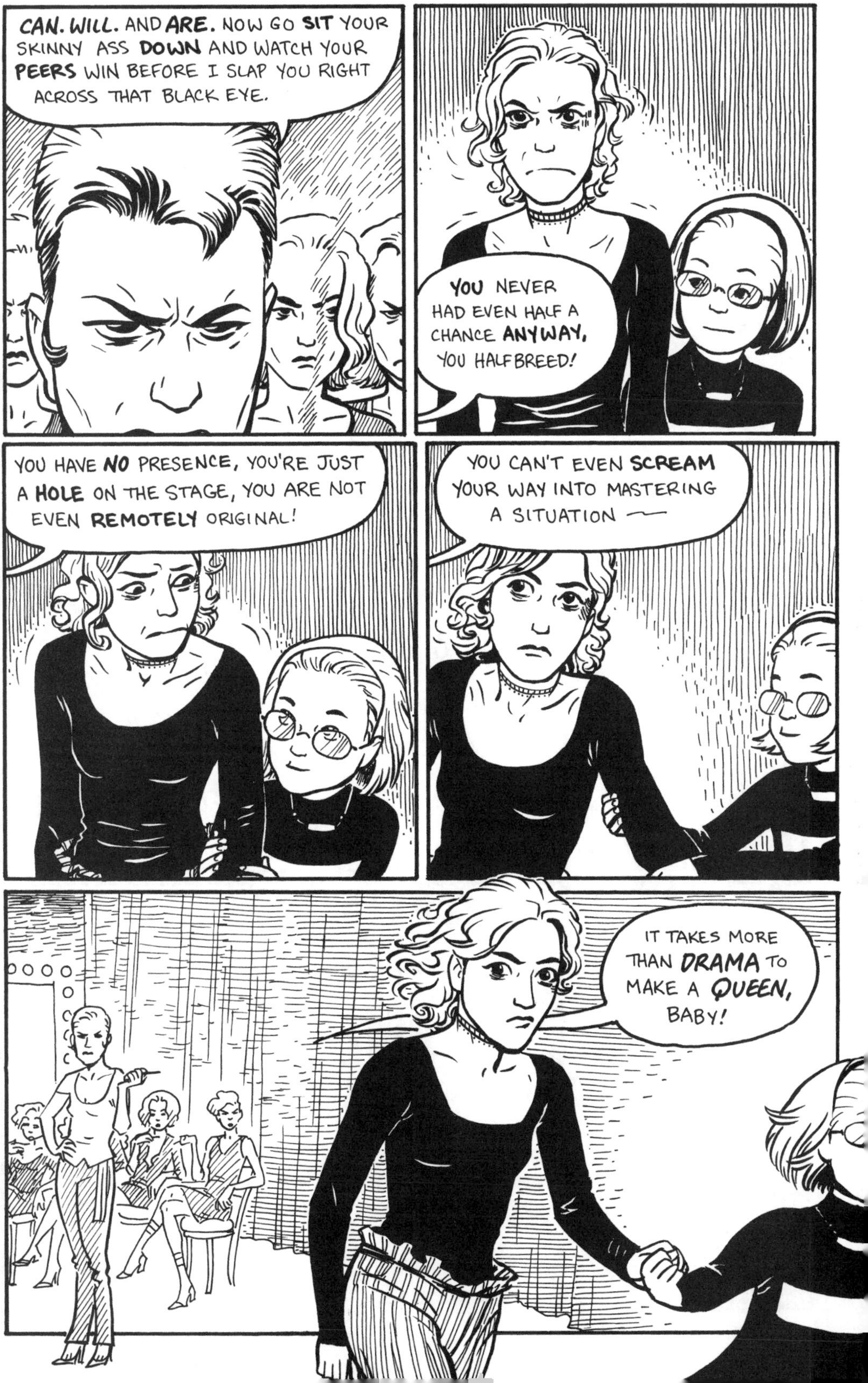
CAN. WILL. AND ARE. NOW GO SIT YOUR SKINNY ASS DOWN AND WATCH YOUR PEERS WIN BEFORE I SLAP YOU RIGHT ACROSS THAT BLACK EYE.
YOU NEVER HAD EVEN HALF A CHANCE ANYWAY, YOU HALFBREED!
YOU HAVE NO PRESENCE, YOU'RE JUST A HOLE ON THE STAGE, YOU ARE NOT EVEN REMOTELY ORIGINAL!
YOU CAN'T EVEN SCREAM YOUR WAY INTO MASTERING A SITUATION —
IT TAKES MORE THAN DRAMA TO MAKE A QUEEN, BABY!

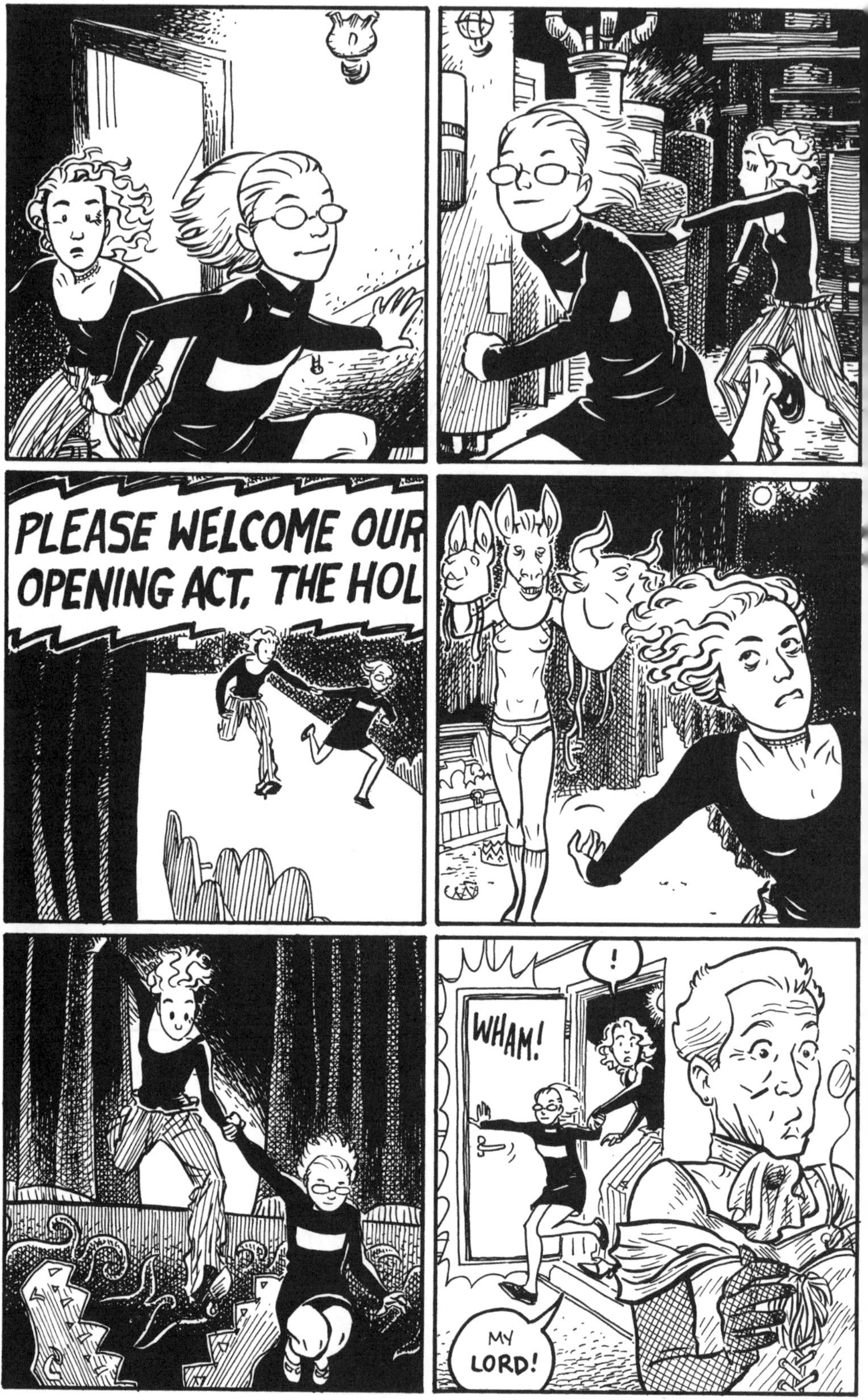
PLEASE WELCOME OUR OPENING ACT, THE HOL
!
WHAM!
MY LORD!

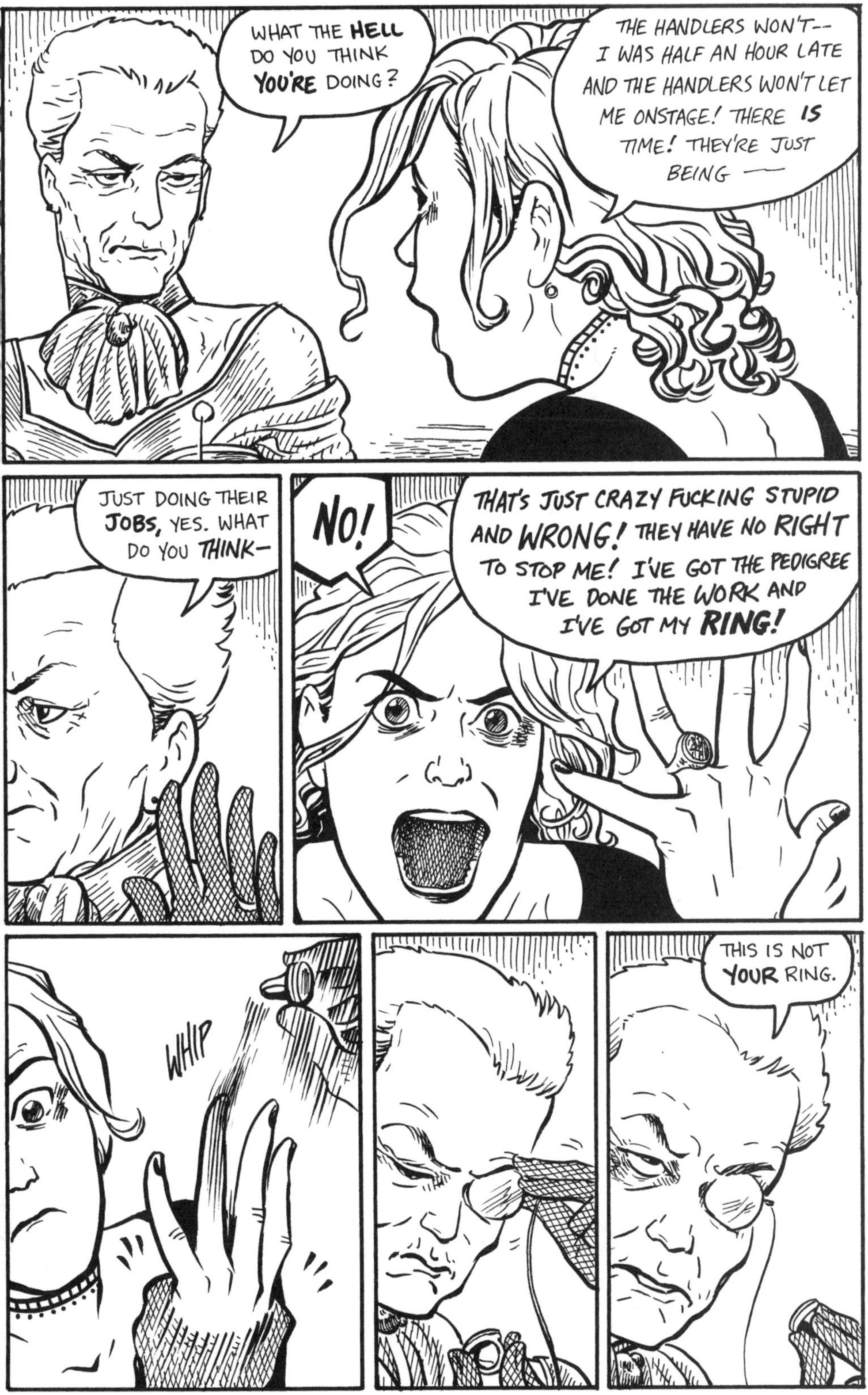
WHAT THE HELL DO YOU THINK YOU'RE DOING?
THE HANDLERS WON'T-- I WAS HALF AN HOUR LATE AND THE HANDLERS WON'T LET ME ONSTAGE! THERE IS TIME! THEY'RE JUST BEING —
JUST DOING THEIR JOBS, YES. WHAT DO YOU THINK—
NO!
THAT'S JUST CRAZY FUCKING STUPID AND WRONG! THEY HAVE NO RIGHT TO STOP ME! I'VE GOT THE PEDIGREE I'VE DONE THE WORK AND I'VE GOT MY RING!
WHIP
THIS IS NOT YOUR RING.

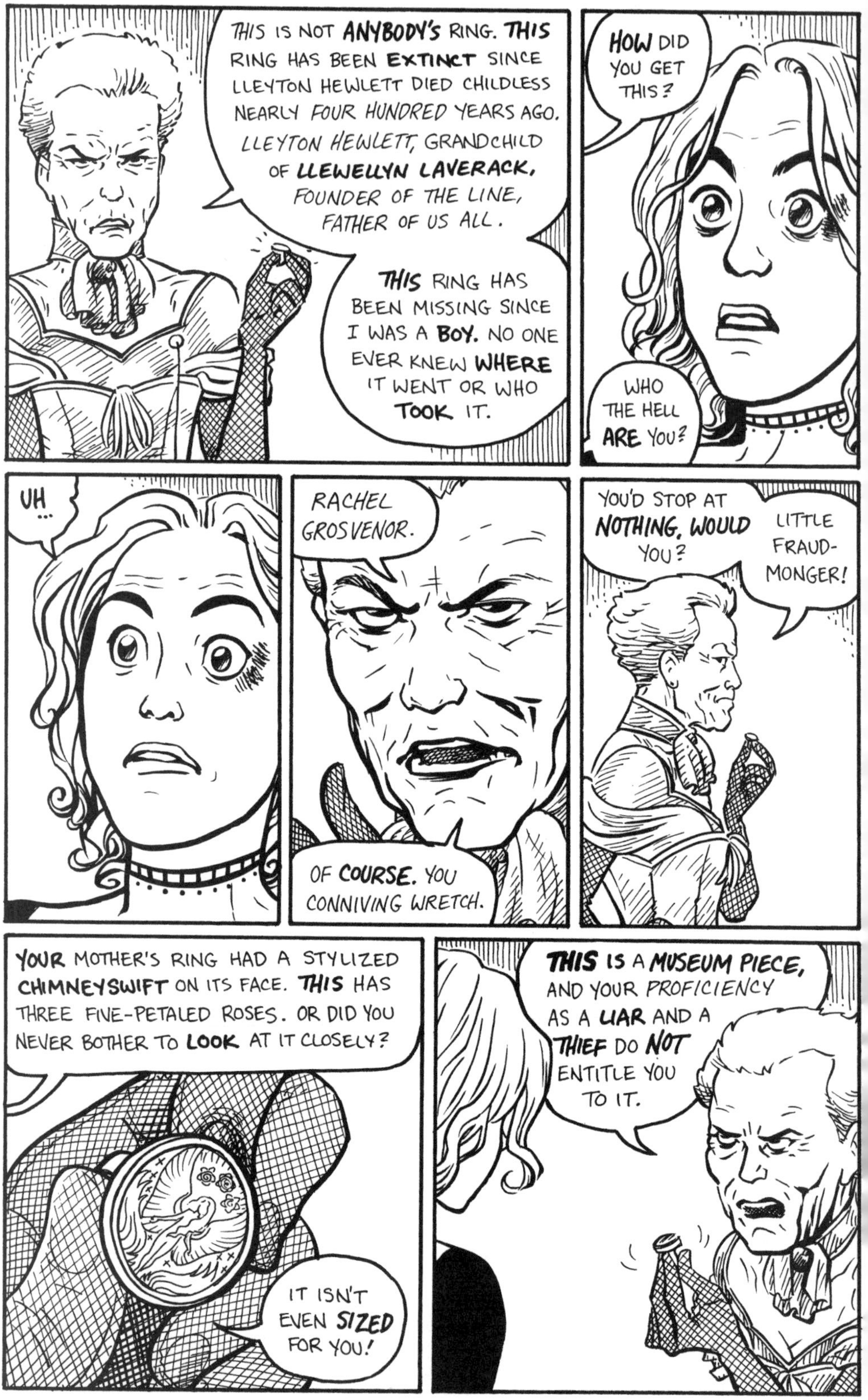
THIS IS NOT ANYBODY'S RING. THIS RING HAS BEEN EXTINCT SINCE LLEYTON HEWLETT DIED CHILDLESS NEARLY FOUR HUNDRED YEARS AGO. LLEYTON HEWLETT, GRANDCHILD OF LLEWELLYN LAVERACK, FOUNDER OF THE LINE, FATHER OF US ALL.
THIS RING HAS BEEN MISSING SINCE I WAS A BOY. NO ONE EVER KNEW WHERE IT WENT OR WHO TOOK IT.
HOW DID YOU GET THIS?
WHO THE HELL ARE YOU?
UH ...
RACHEL GROSVENOR.
OF COURSE. YOU CONNIVING WRETCH.
YOU'D STOP AT NOTHING, WOULD YOU?
LITTLE FRAUD-MONGER!
YOUR MOTHER'S RING HAD A STYLIZED CHIMNEYSWIFT ON ITS FACE. THIS HAS THREE FIVE-PETALED ROSES. OR DID YOU NEVER BOTHER TO LOOK AT IT CLOSELY?
IT ISN'T EVEN SIZED FOR YOU!
THIS IS A MUSEUM PIECE, AND YOUR PROFICIENCY AS A LIAR AND A THIEF DO NOT ENTITLE YOU TO IT.

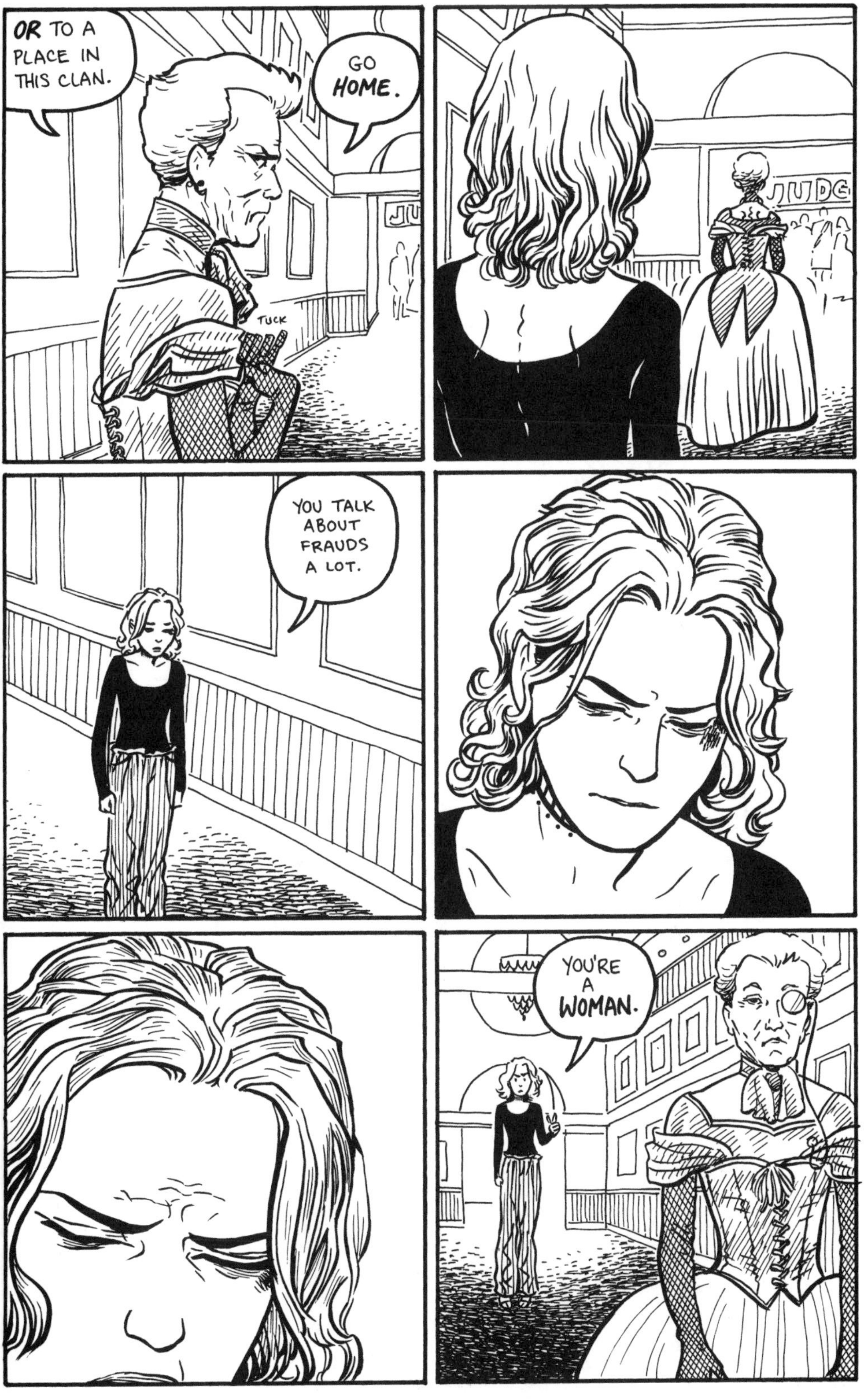
OR TO A PLACE IN THIS CLAN.
GO HOME.
TUCK
JU
JUDG
YOU TALK ABOUT FRAUDS A LOT.
YOU'RE A WOMAN.

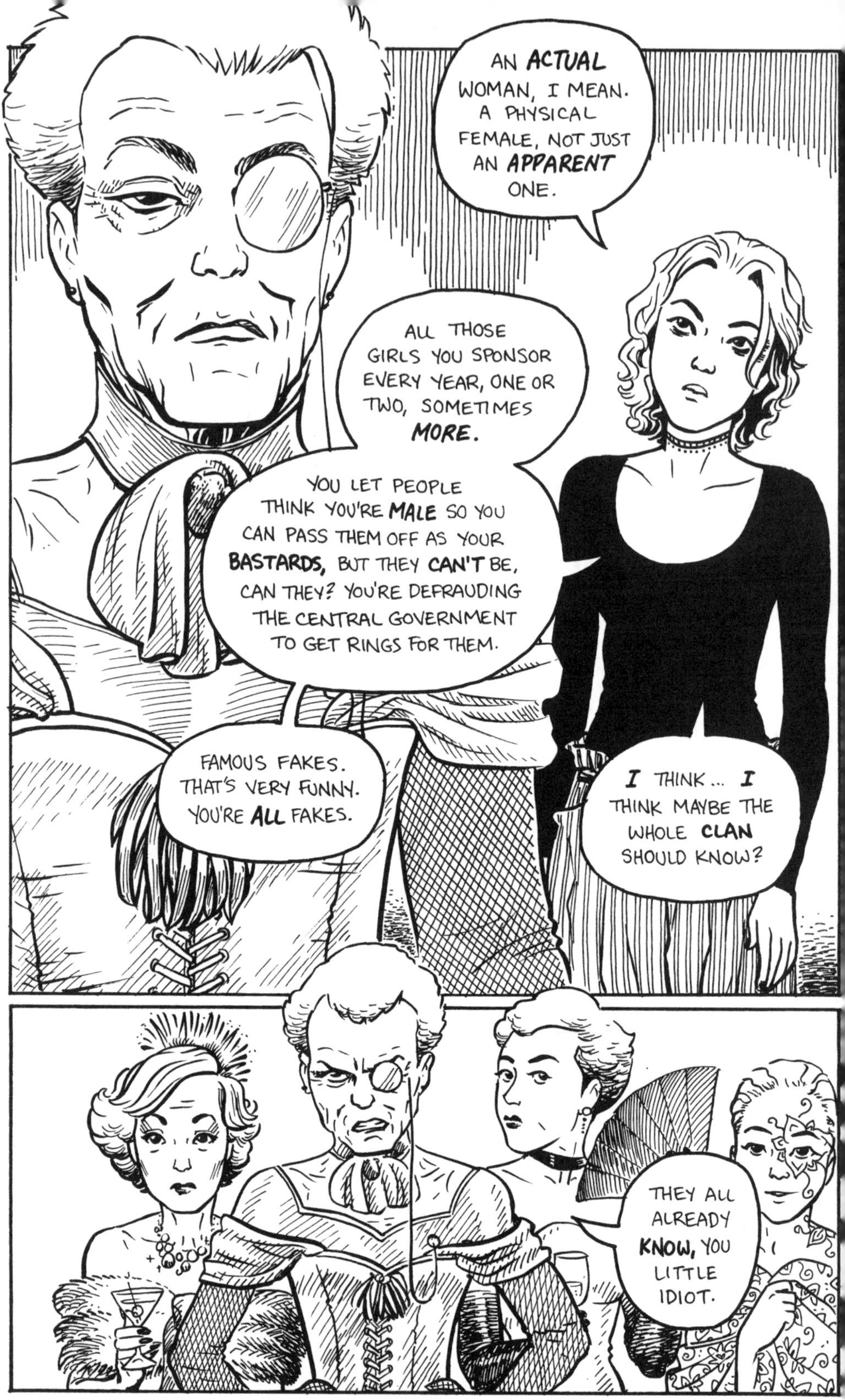
AN ACTUAL WOMAN, I MEAN. A PHYSICAL FEMALE, NOT JUST AN APPARENT ONE.
ALL THOSE GIRLS YOU SPONSOR EVERY YEAR, ONE OR TWO, SOMETIMES MORE.
YOU LET PEOPLE THINK YOU'RE MALE SO YOU CAN PASS THEM OFF AS YOUR BASTARDS, BUT THEY CAN'T BE, CAN THEY? YOU'RE DEFRAUDING THE CENTRAL GOVERNMENT TO GET RINGS FOR THEM.
FAMOUS FAKES. THAT'S VERY FUNNY. YOU'RE ALL FAKES.
I THINK... I THINK MAYBE THE WHOLE CLAN SHOULD KNOW?
THEY ALL ALREADY KNOW, YOU LITTLE IDIOT.

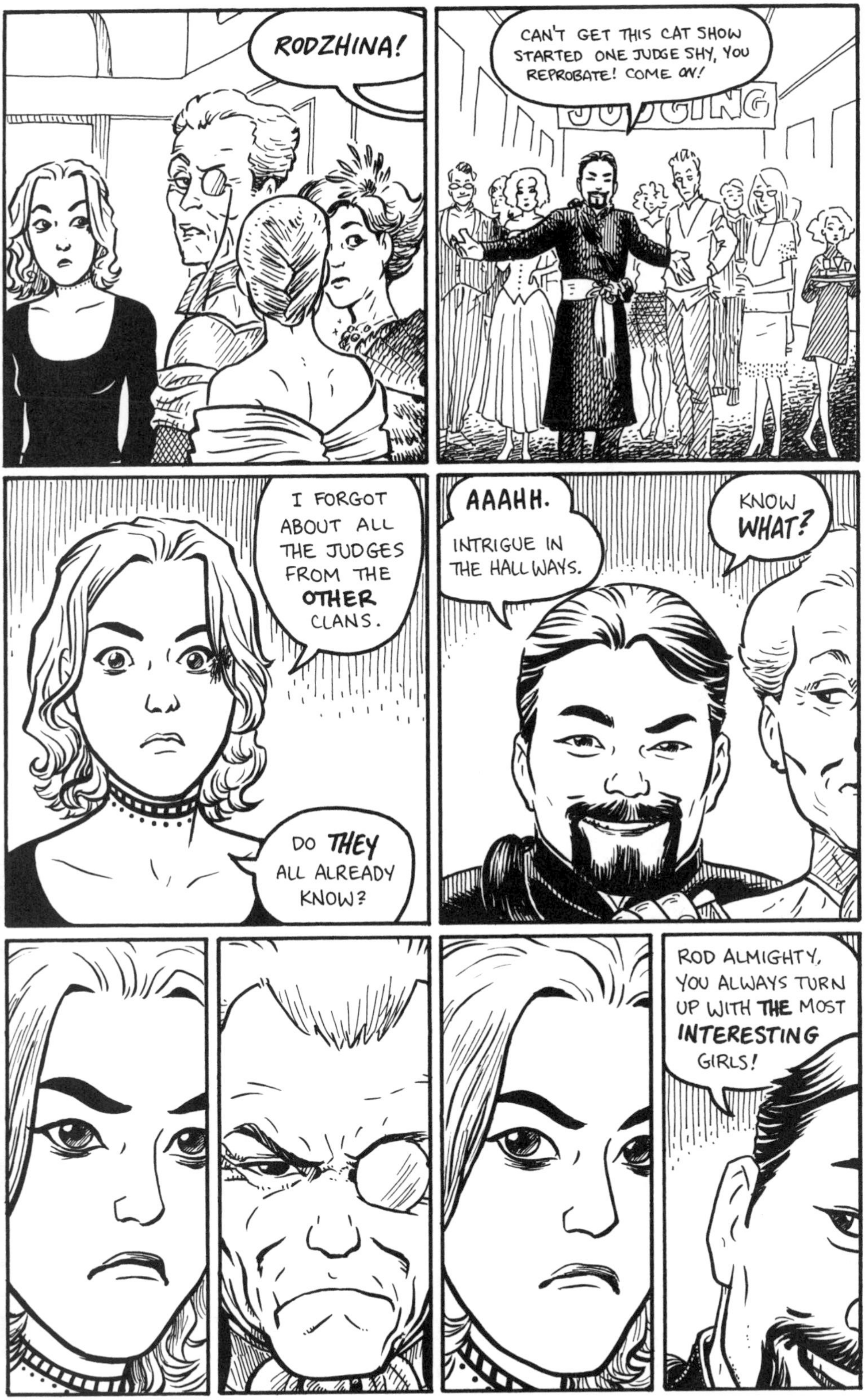
RODZHINA!
CAN'T GET THIS CAT SHOW STARTED ONE JUDGE SHY, YOU REPROBATE! COME ON!
JUDGING
I FORGOT ABOUT ALL THE JUDGES FROM THE OTHER CLANS.
DO THEY ALL ALREADY KNOW?
AAAHH.
INTRIGUE IN THE HALLWAYS.
KNOW WHAT?
ROD ALMIGHTY, YOU ALWAYS TURN UP WITH THE MOST INTERESTING GIRLS!

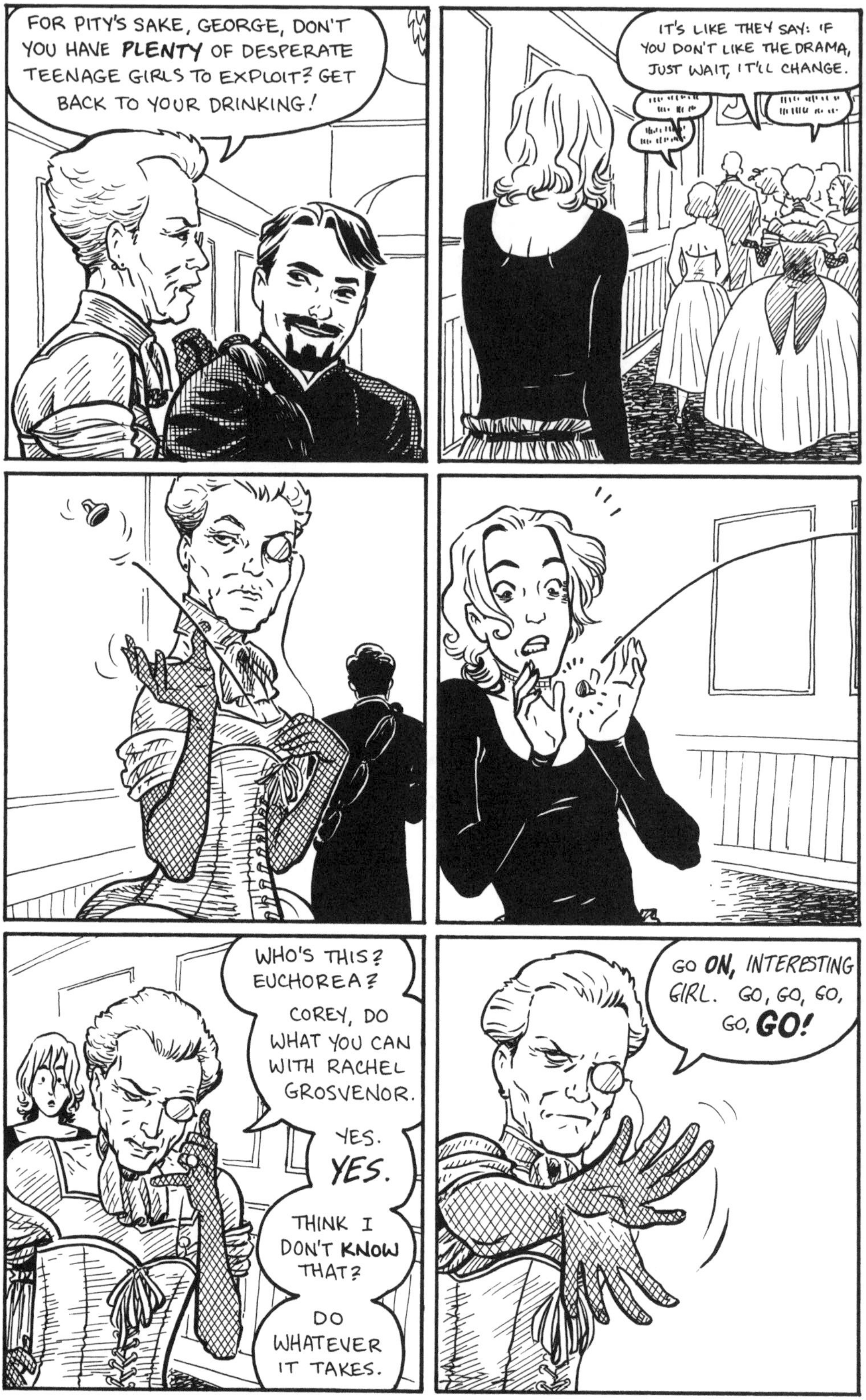
FOR PITY'S SAKE, GEORGE, DON'T YOU HAVE PLENTY OF DESPERATE TEENAGE GIRLS TO EXPLOIT? GET BACK TO YOUR DRINKING!
IT'S LIKE THEY SAY: IF YOU DON'T LIKE THE DRAMA, JUST WAIT, IT'LL CHANGE.
WHO'S THIS? EUCHOREA?
COREY, DO WHAT YOU CAN WITH RACHEL GROSVENOR.
YES. YES.
THINK I DON'T KNOW THAT?
DO WHATEVER IT TAKES.
GO ON, INTERESTING GIRL. GO, GO, GO, GO, GO!

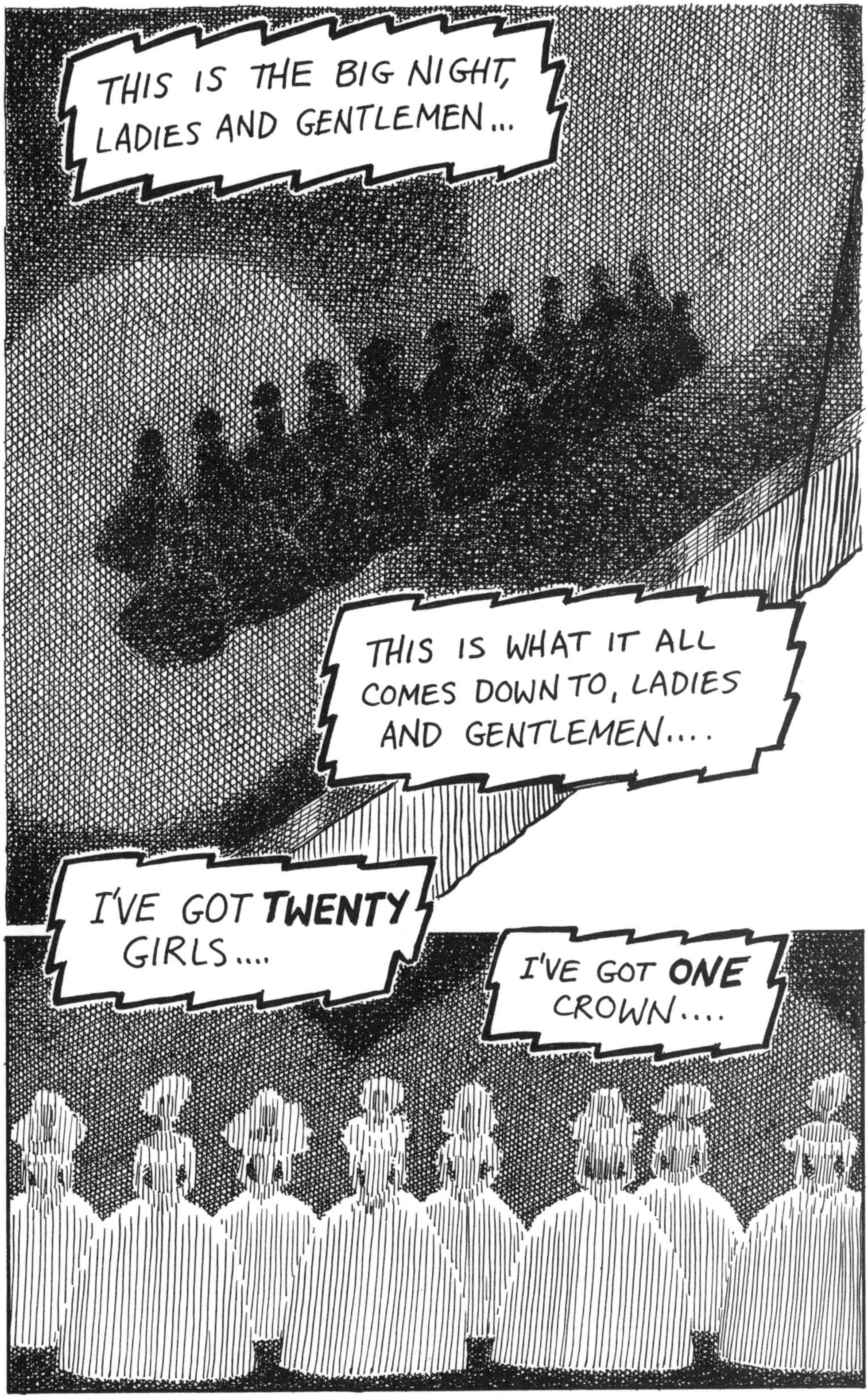
THIS IS THE BIG NIGHT, LADIES AND GENTLEMEN...
THIS IS WHAT IT ALL COMES DOWN TO, LADIES AND GENTLEMEN....
I'VE GOT **TWENTY** GIRLS....
I'VE GOT **ONE** CROWN....

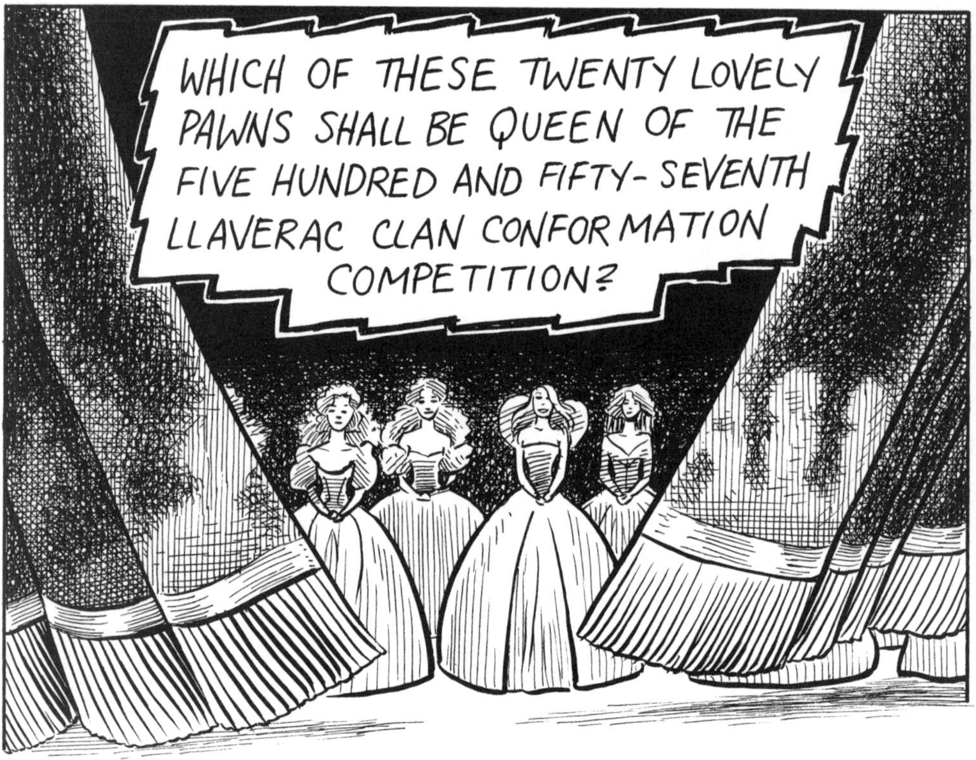
WHICH OF THESE TWENTY LOVELY PAWNS SHALL BE QUEEN OF THE FIVE HUNDRED AND FIFTY-SEVENTH LLAVERAC CLAN CONFORMATION COMPETITION?

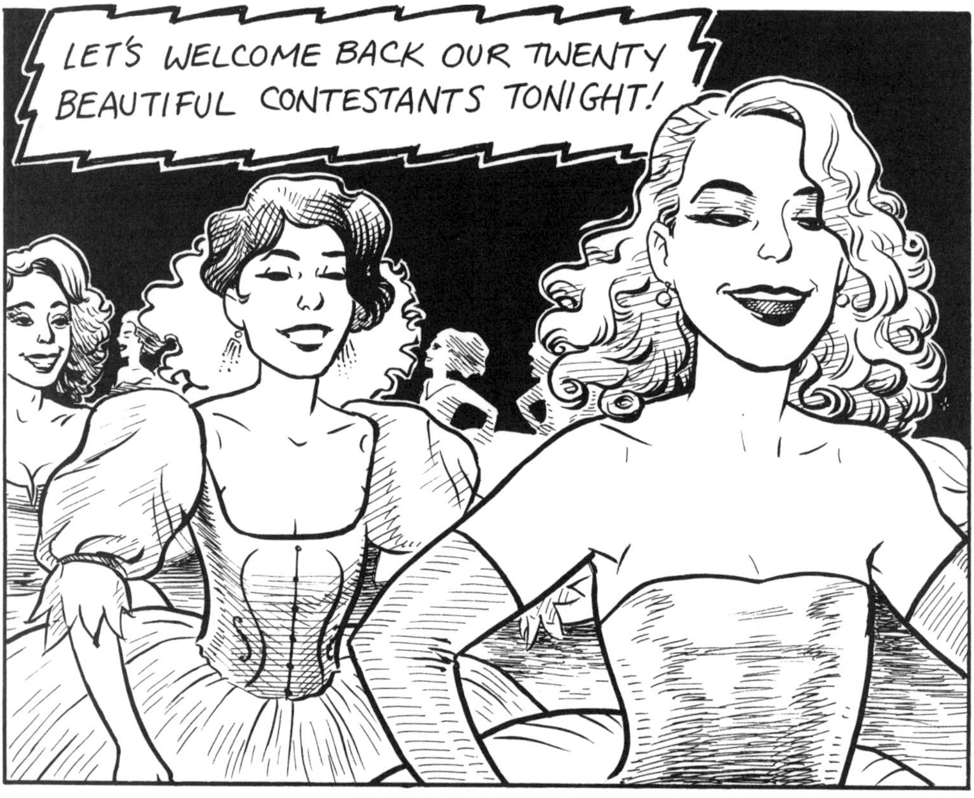
LET'S WELCOME BACK OUR TWENTY BEAUTIFUL CONTESTANTS TONIGHT!

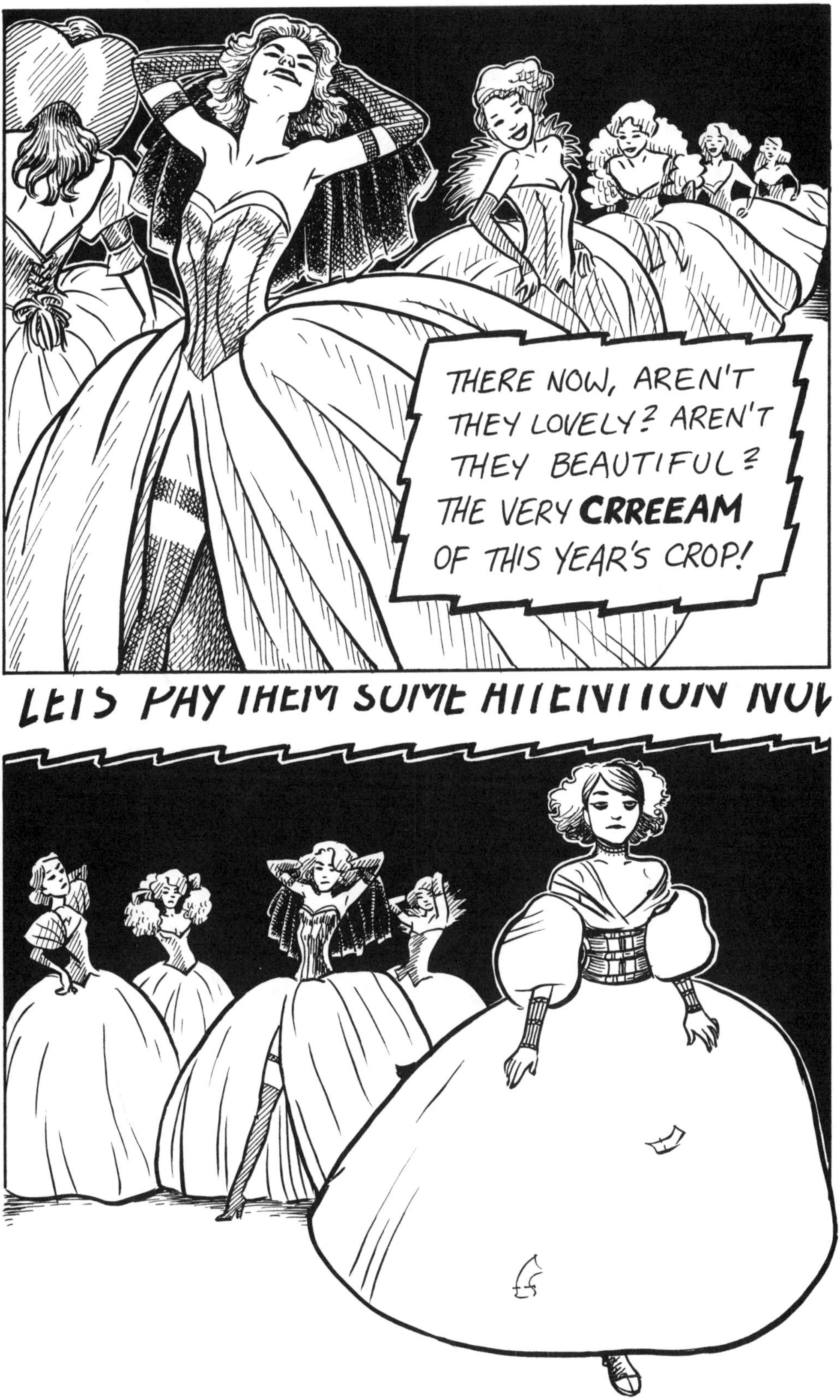
THERE NOW, AREN'T THEY LOVELY? AREN'T THEY BEAUTIFUL? THE VERY **CRREEAM** OF THIS YEAR'S CROP!
LETS PAY THEM SOME ATTENTION NOW

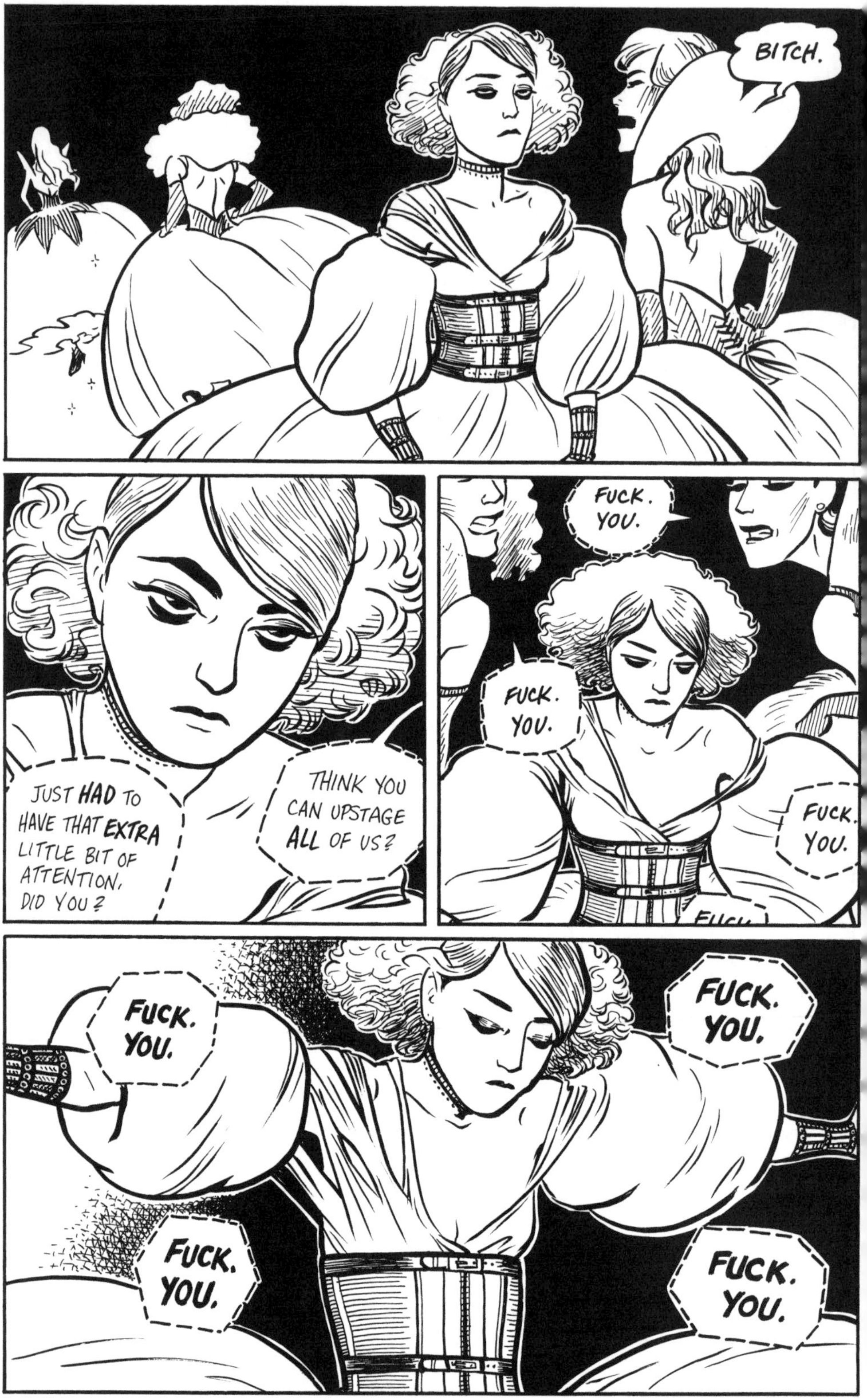
BITCH.
JUST HAD TO HAVE THAT EXTRA LITTLE BIT OF ATTENTION, DID YOU?
THINK YOU CAN UPSTAGE ALL OF US?
FUCK. YOU.
FUCK. YOU.
FUCK. YOU.
FUCK. YOU.
FUCK. YOU.
FUCK. YOU.
FUCK. YOU.

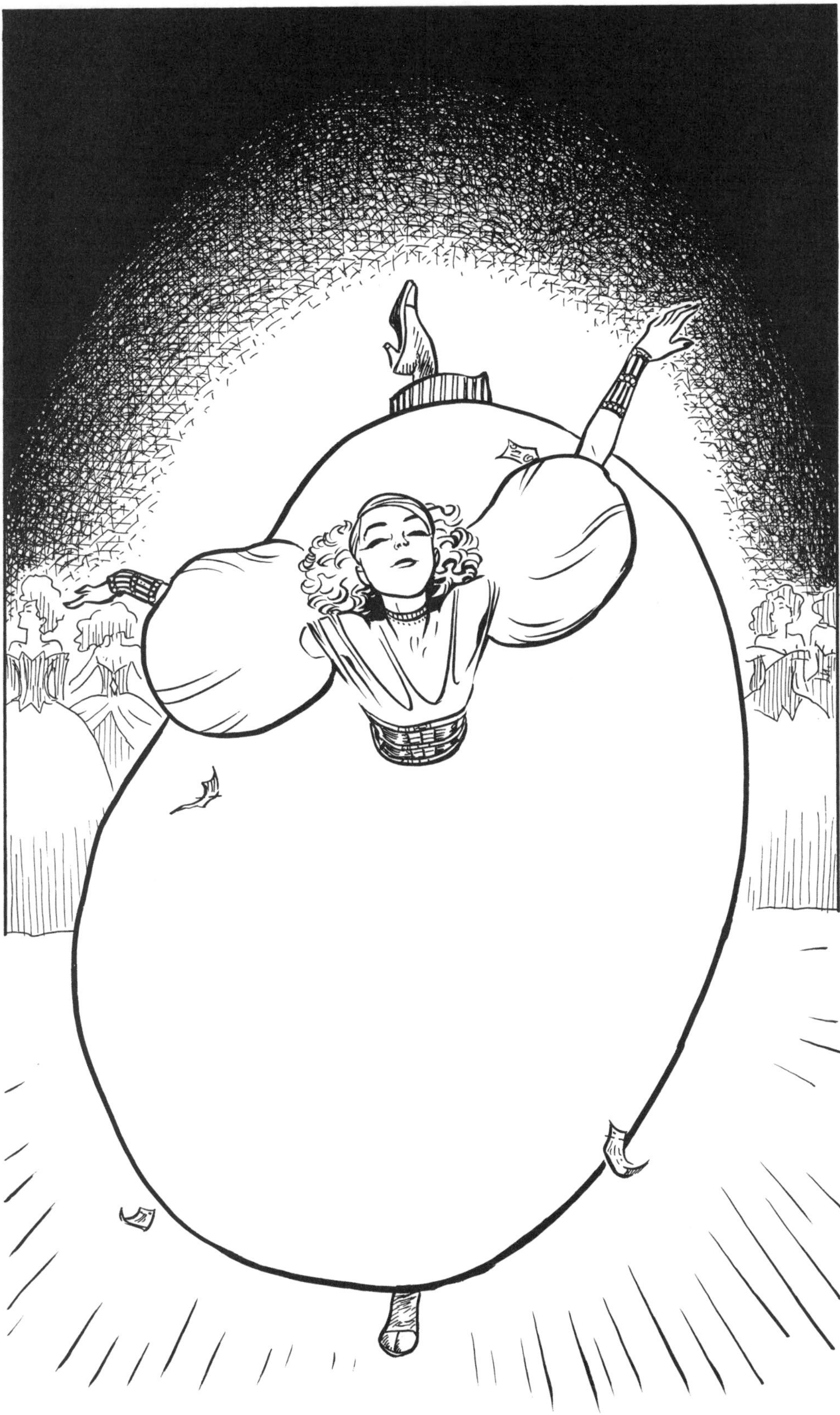

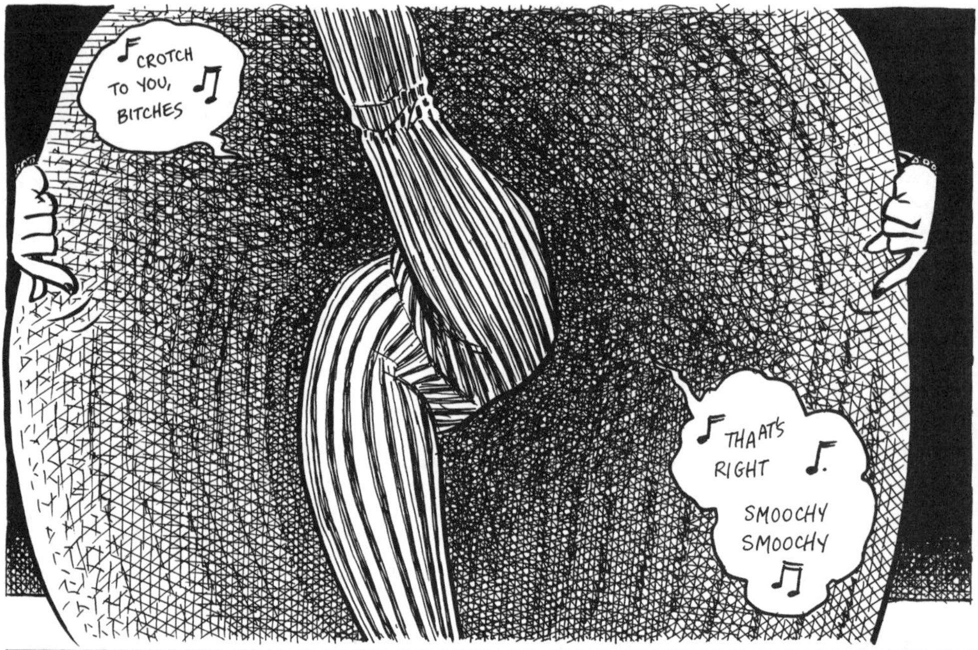
CROTCH TO YOU, BITCHES
THAAT'S RIGHT SMOOCHY SMOOCHY

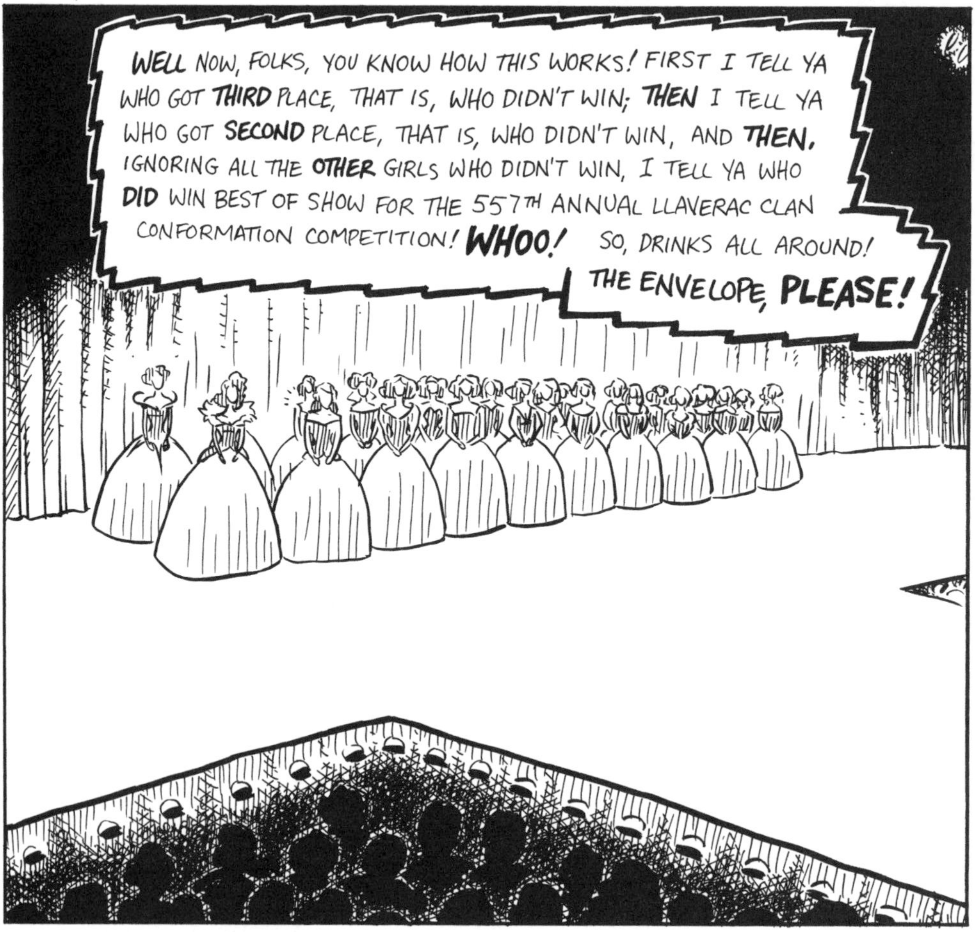
WELL NOW, FOLKS, YOU KNOW HOW THIS WORKS! FIRST I TELL YA WHO GOT THIRD PLACE, THAT IS, WHO DIDN'T WIN; THEN I TELL YA WHO GOT SECOND PLACE, THAT IS, WHO DIDN'T WIN, AND THEN, IGNORING ALL THE OTHER GIRLS WHO DIDN'T WIN, I TELL YA WHO DID WIN BEST OF SHOW FOR THE 557TH ANNUAL LLAVERAC CLAN CONFORMATION COMPETITION! WHOO! SO, DRINKS ALL AROUND! THE ENVELOPE, PLEASE!

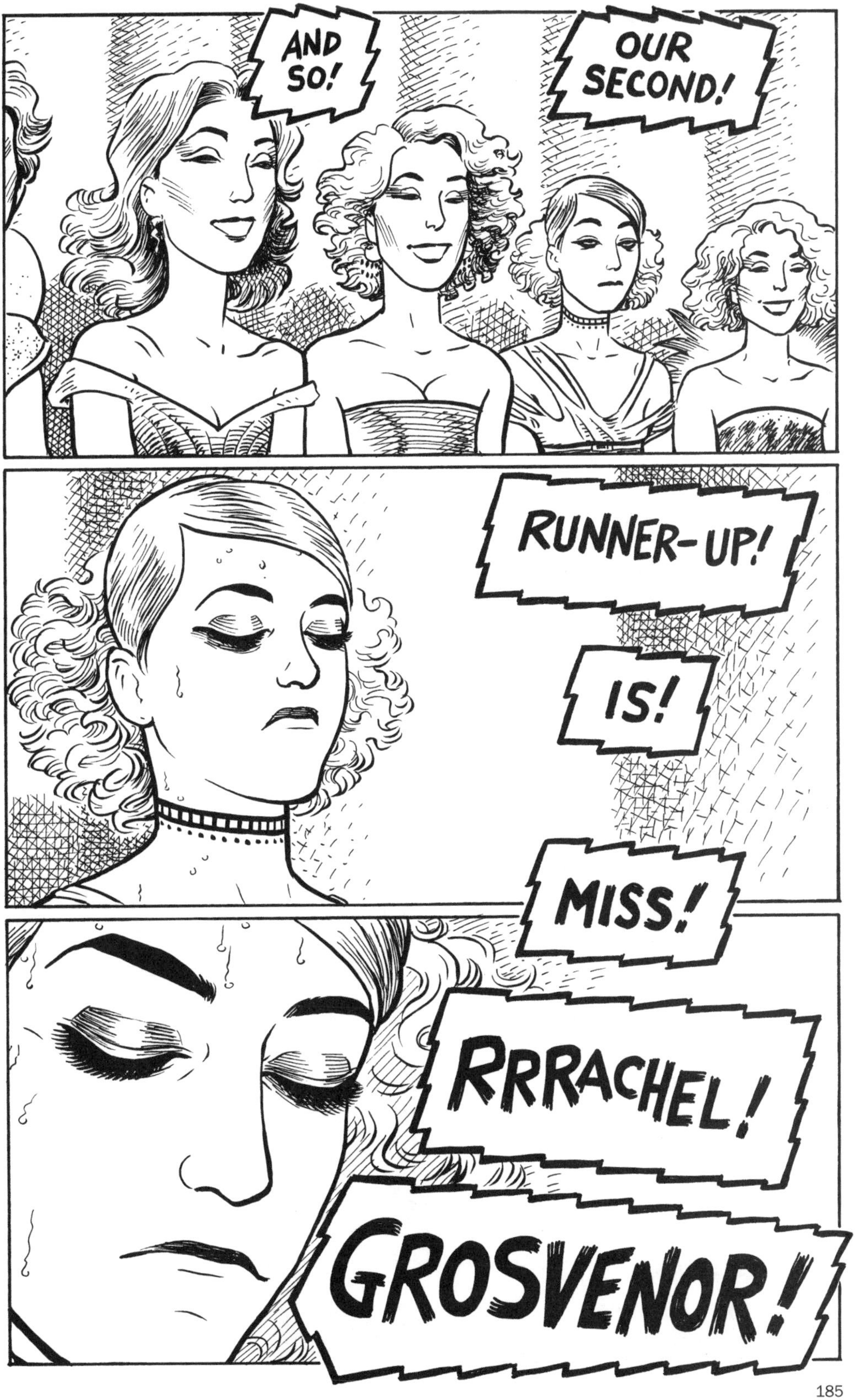
AND SO!
OUR SECOND!
RUNNER-UP!
IS!
MISS!
RRRACHEL!
GROSVENOR!

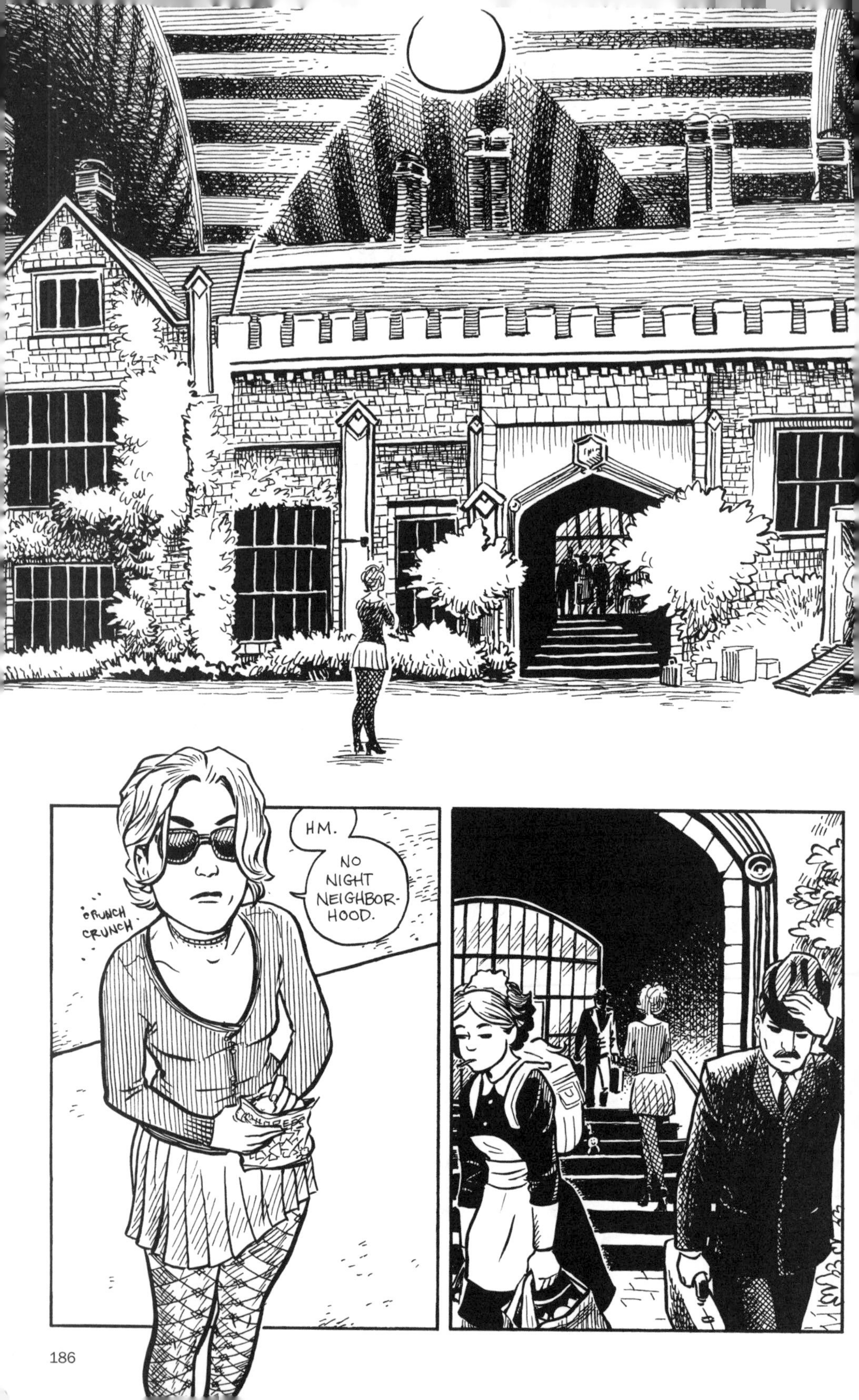
CRUNCH
CRUNCH
HM.
NO NIGHT NEIGHBOR-HOOD.

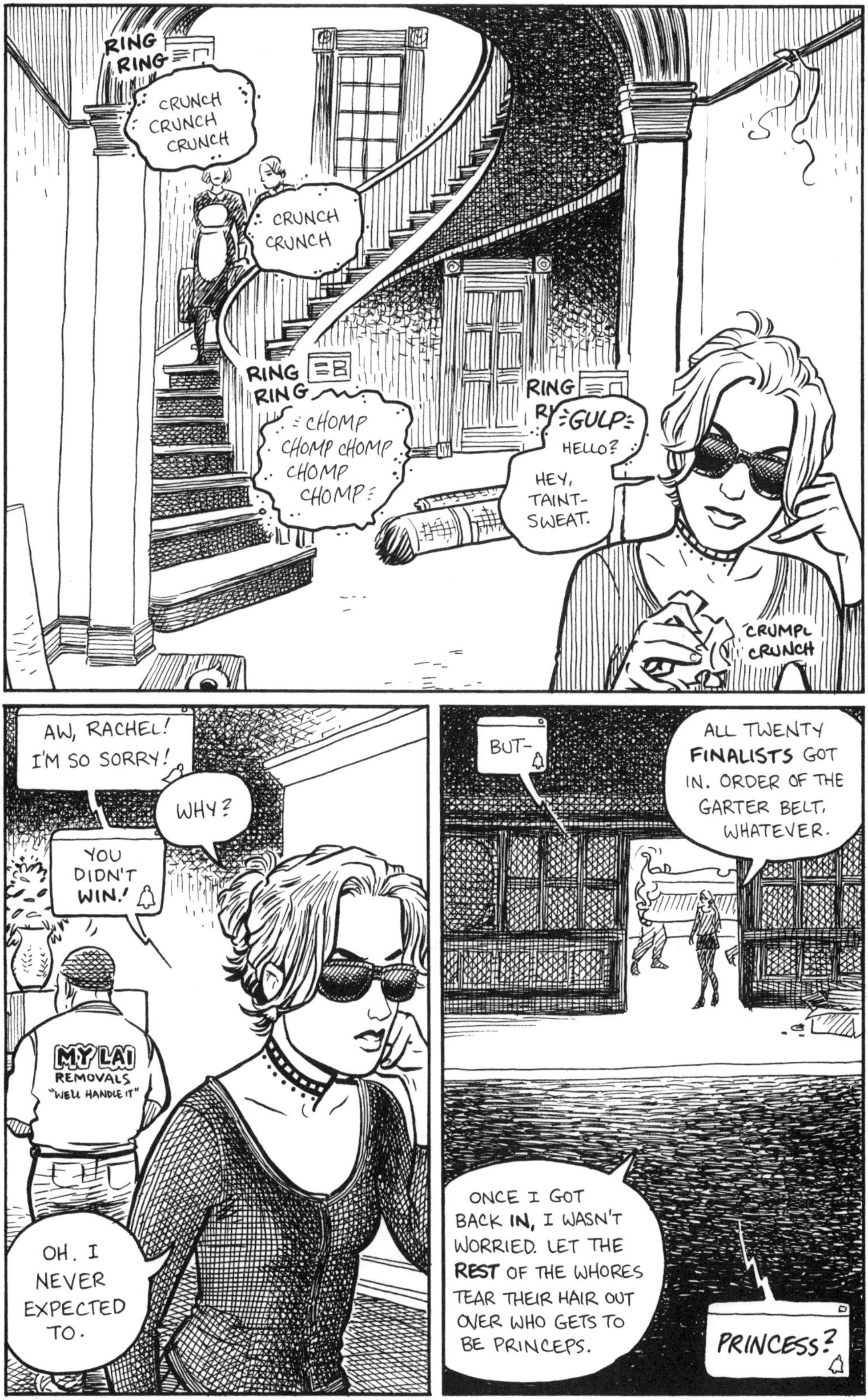

RING RING
CRUNCH CRUNCH CRUNCH
CRUNCH CRUNCH
RING RING
CHOMP CHOMP CHOMP CHOMP CHOMP
RING
GULP
HELLO?
HEY, TAINT-SWEAT.
CRUMPL CRUNCH
AW, RACHEL! I'M SO SORRY!
WHY?
YOU DIDN'T WIN!
MY LAI REMOVALS "WE'LL HANDLE IT"
OH. I NEVER EXPECTED TO.
BUT-
ALL TWENTY FINALISTS GOT IN. ORDER OF THE GARTER BELT. WHATEVER.
ONCE I GOT BACK IN, I WASN'T WORRIED. LET THE REST OF THE WHORES TEAR THEIR HAIR OUT OVER WHO GETS TO BE PRINCEPS.
PRINCESS?

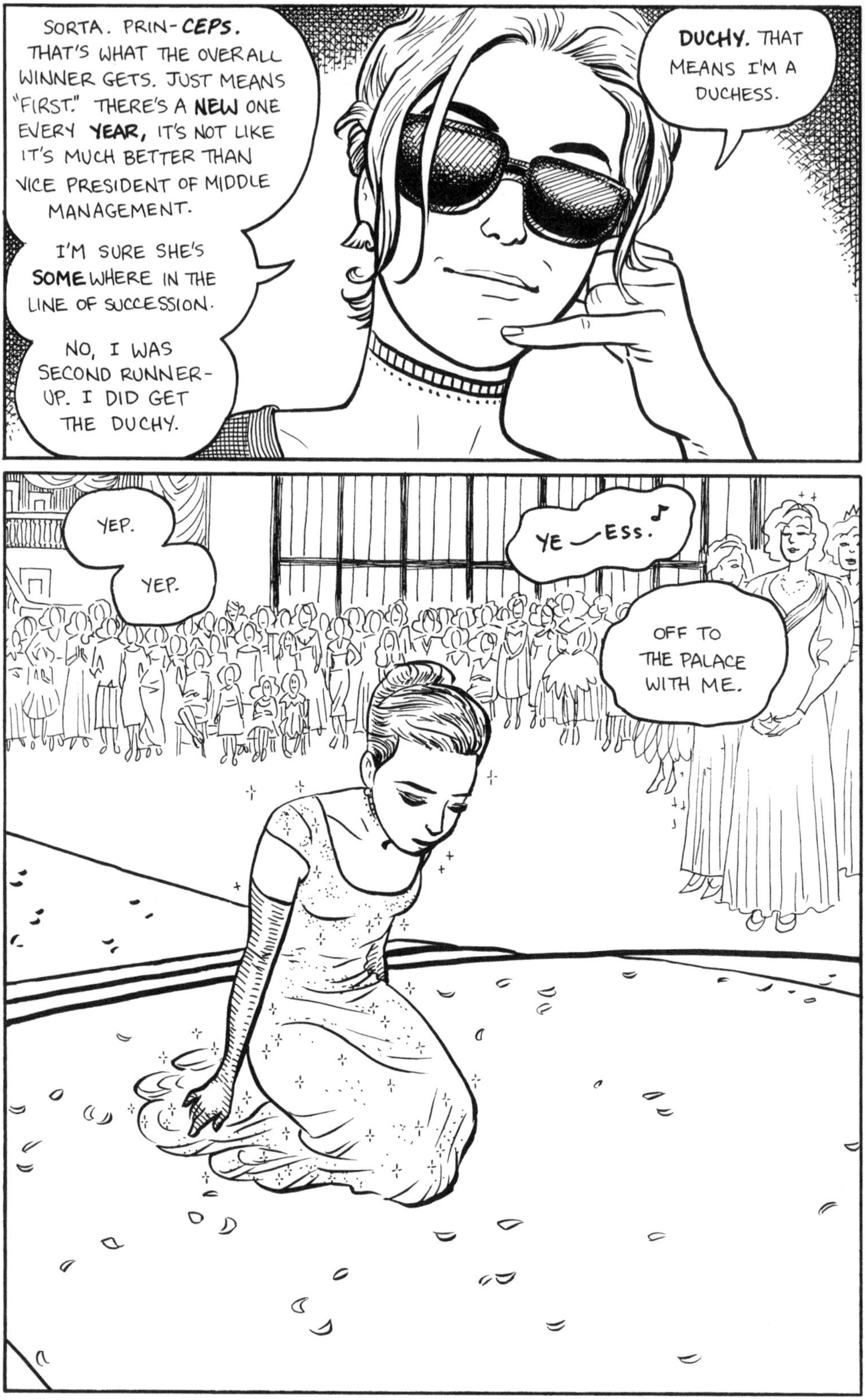
SORTA. PRIN-**CEPS.** THAT'S WHAT THE OVERALL WINNER GETS. JUST MEANS "FIRST." THERE'S A **NEW** ONE EVERY **YEAR,** IT'S NOT LIKE IT'S MUCH BETTER THAN VICE PRESIDENT OF MIDDLE MANAGEMENT.
I'M SURE SHE'S **SOME**WHERE IN THE LINE OF SUCCESSION.
NO, I WAS SECOND RUNNER-UP. I DID GET THE DUCHY.
DUCHY. THAT MEANS I'M A DUCHESS.
YEP.
YEP.
YE—ESS.
OFF TO THE PALACE WITH ME.

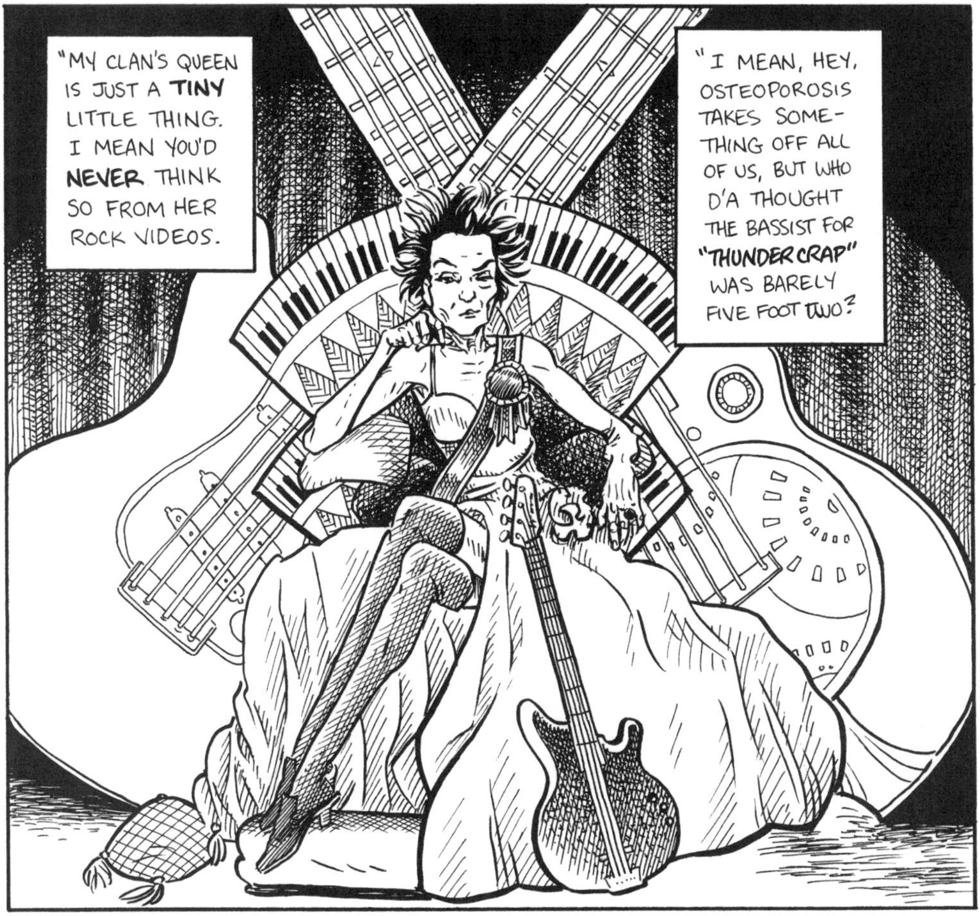
"MY CLAN'S QUEEN IS JUST A TINY LITTLE THING. I MEAN YOU'D NEVER THINK SO FROM HER ROCK VIDEOS.
"I MEAN, HEY, OSTEOPOROSIS TAKES SOMETHING OFF ALL OF US, BUT WHO D'A THOUGHT THE BASSIST FOR "THUNDERCRAP" WAS BARELY FIVE FOOT TWO?

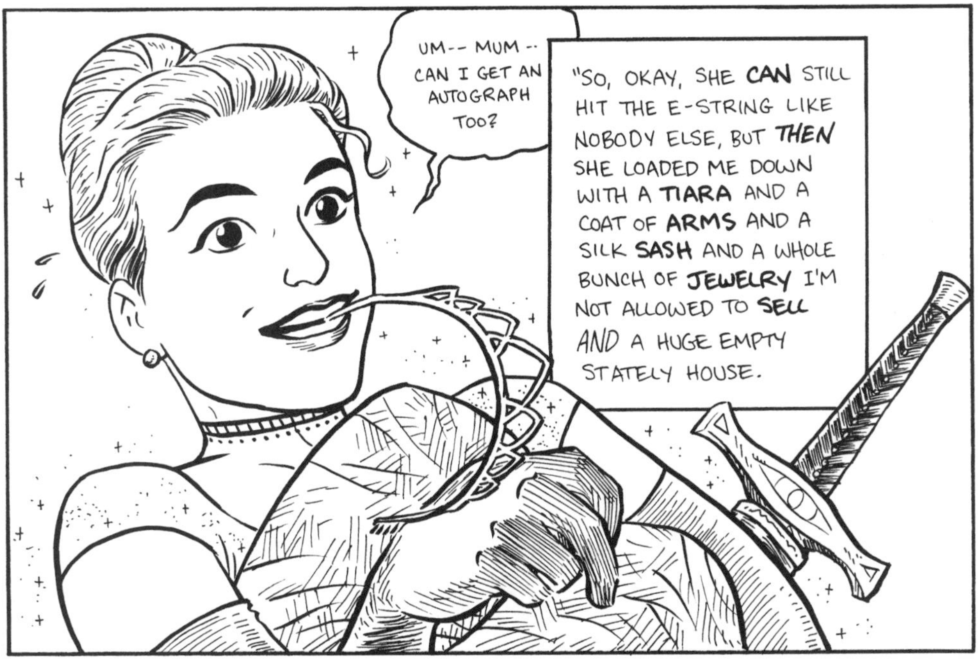
UM-- MUM-- CAN I GET AN AUTOGRAPH TOO?
"SO, OKAY, SHE CAN STILL HIT THE E-STRING LIKE NOBODY ELSE, BUT THEN SHE LOADED ME DOWN WITH A TIARA AND A COAT OF ARMS AND A SILK SASH AND A WHOLE BUNCH OF JEWELRY I'M NOT ALLOWED TO SELL AND A HUGE EMPTY STATELY HOUSE.

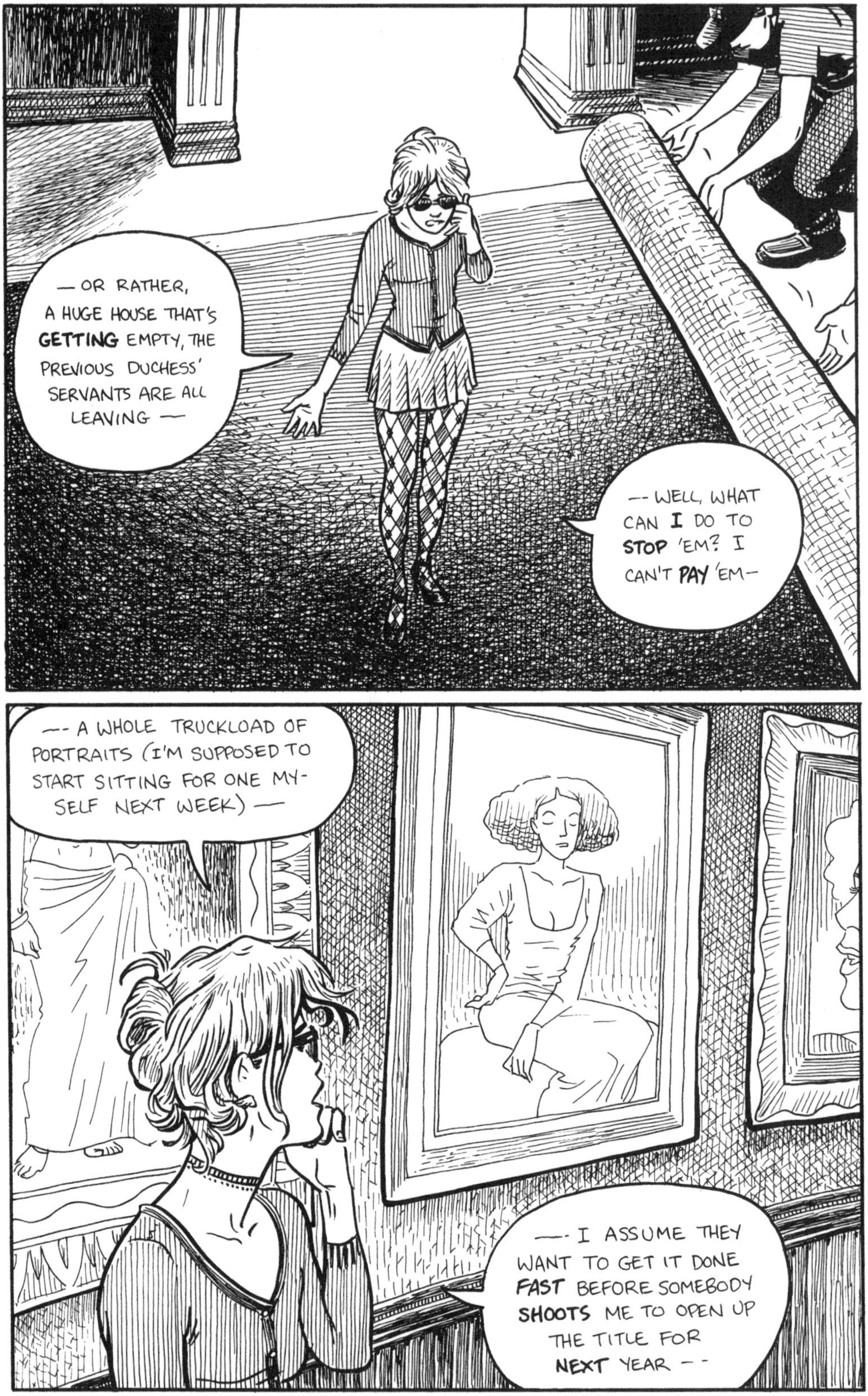
— OR RATHER, A HUGE HOUSE THAT'S GETTING EMPTY, THE PREVIOUS DUCHESS' SERVANTS ARE ALL LEAVING —
-- WELL, WHAT CAN I DO TO STOP 'EM? I CAN'T PAY 'EM—
-- A WHOLE TRUCKLOAD OF PORTRAITS (I'M SUPPOSED TO START SITTING FOR ONE MY-SELF NEXT WEEK) —
— I ASSUME THEY WANT TO GET IT DONE FAST BEFORE SOMEBODY SHOOTS ME TO OPEN UP THE TITLE FOR NEXT YEAR --

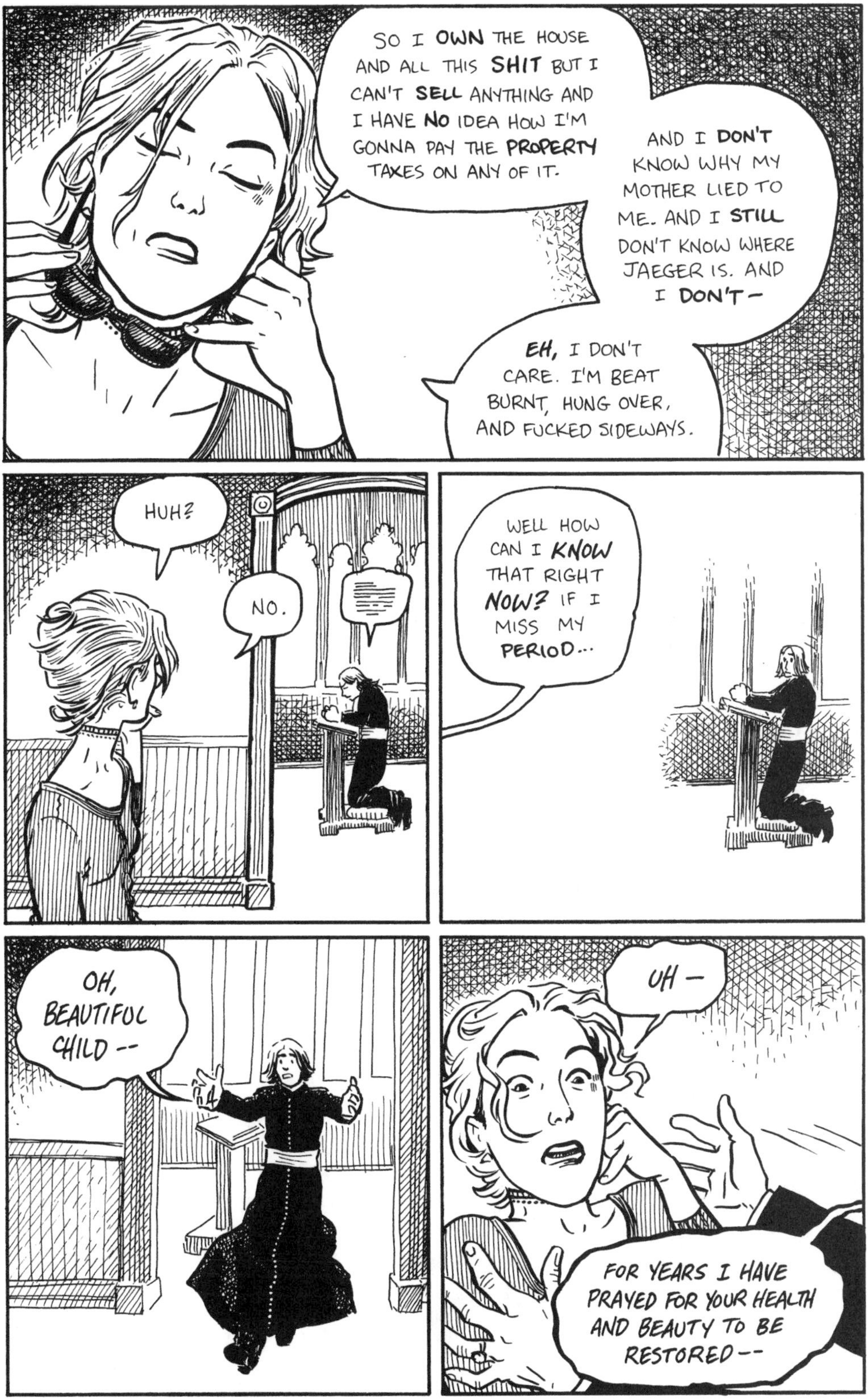
SO I OWN THE HOUSE AND ALL THIS SHIT BUT I CAN'T SELL ANYTHING AND I HAVE NO IDEA HOW I'M GONNA PAY THE PROPERTY TAXES ON ANY OF IT.
AND I DON'T KNOW WHY MY MOTHER LIED TO ME. AND I STILL DON'T KNOW WHERE JAEGER IS. AND I DON'T –
EH, I DON'T CARE. I'M BEAT BURNT, HUNG OVER, AND FUCKED SIDEWAYS.
HUH?
NO.
WELL HOW CAN I KNOW THAT RIGHT NOW? IF I MISS MY PERIOD...
OH, BEAUTIFUL CHILD --
UH –
FOR YEARS I HAVE PRAYED FOR YOUR HEALTH AND BEAUTY TO BE RESTORED --

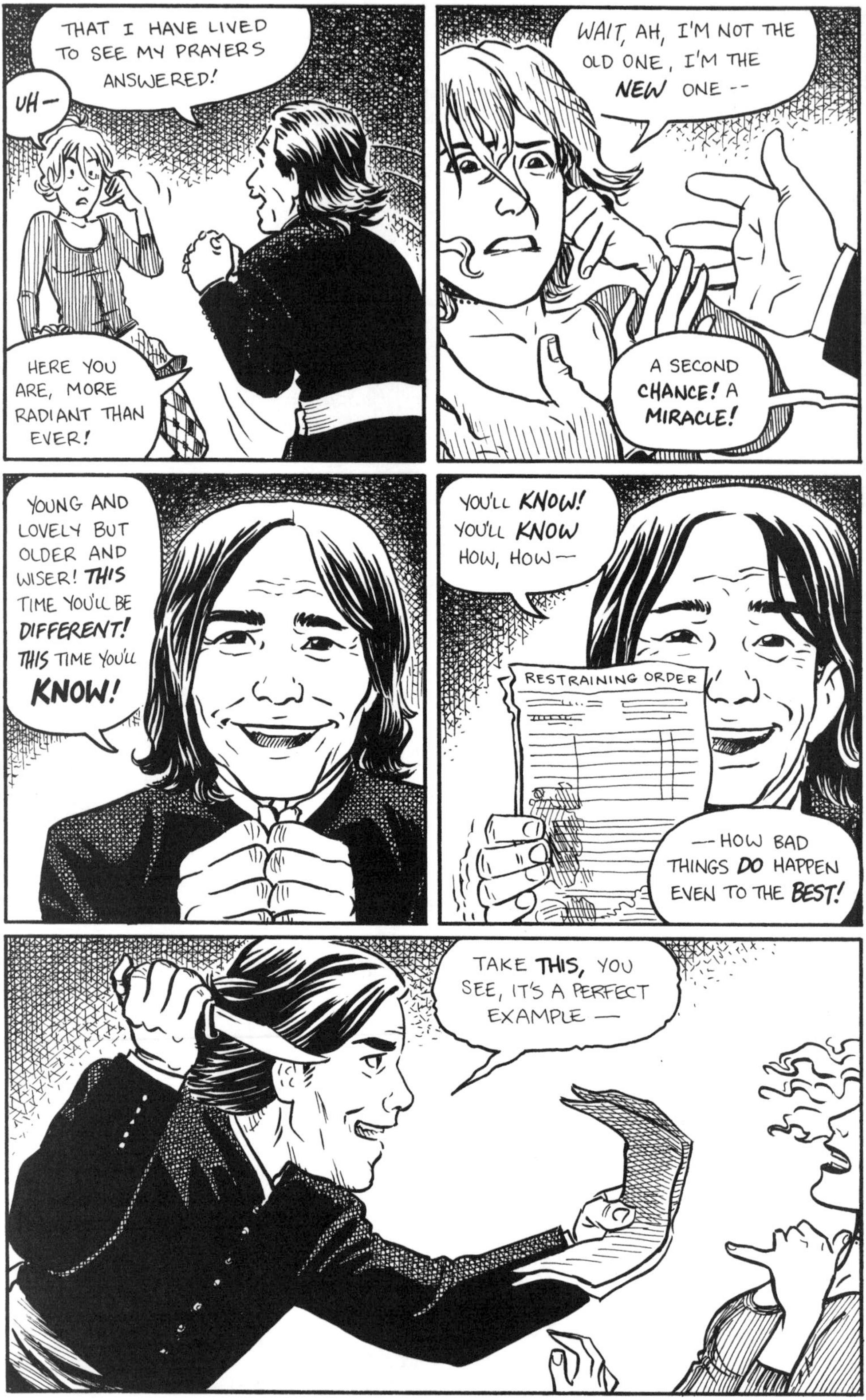
THAT I HAVE LIVED TO SEE MY PRAYERS ANSWERED!
UH—
HERE YOU ARE, MORE RADIANT THAN EVER!
WAIT, AH, I'M NOT THE OLD ONE, I'M THE NEW ONE --
A SECOND CHANCE! A MIRACLE!
YOUNG AND LOVELY BUT OLDER AND WISER! THIS TIME YOU'LL BE DIFFERENT! THIS TIME YOU'LL KNOW!
YOU'LL KNOW! YOU'LL KNOW HOW, HOW—
RESTRAINING ORDER
—HOW BAD THINGS DO HAPPEN EVEN TO THE BEST!
TAKE THIS, YOU SEE, IT'S A PERFECT EXAMPLE —

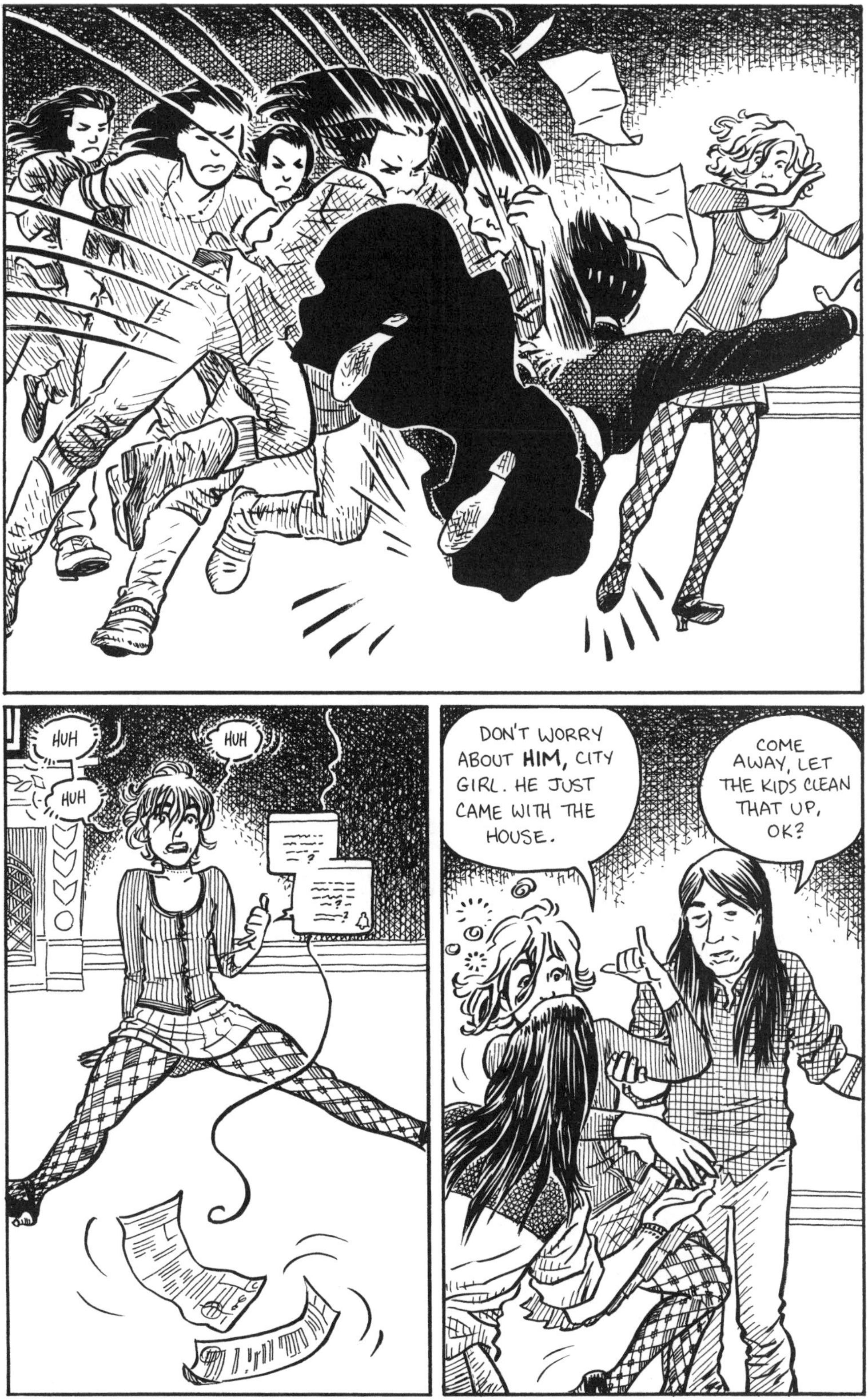
HUH
HUH
HUH
DON'T WORRY ABOUT HIM, CITY GIRL. HE JUST CAME WITH THE HOUSE.
COME AWAY, LET THE KIDS CLEAN THAT UP, OK?

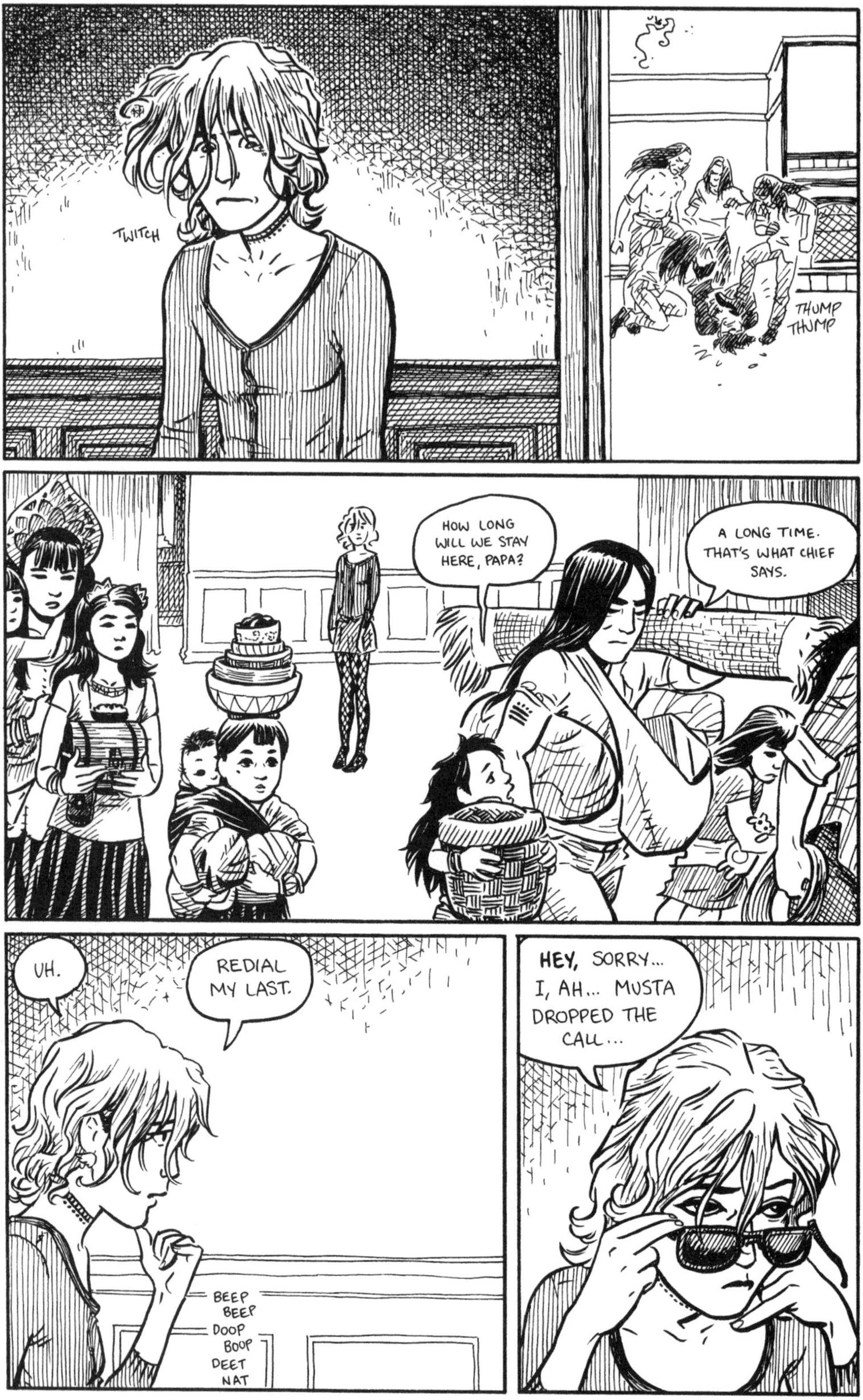
TWITCH
THUMP THUMP
HOW LONG WILL WE STAY HERE, PAPA?
A LONG TIME. THAT'S WHAT CHIEF SAYS.
UH.
REDIAL MY LAST.
BEEP BEEP DOOP BOOP DEET NAT
HEY, SORRY... I, AH... MUSTA DROPPED THE CALL...

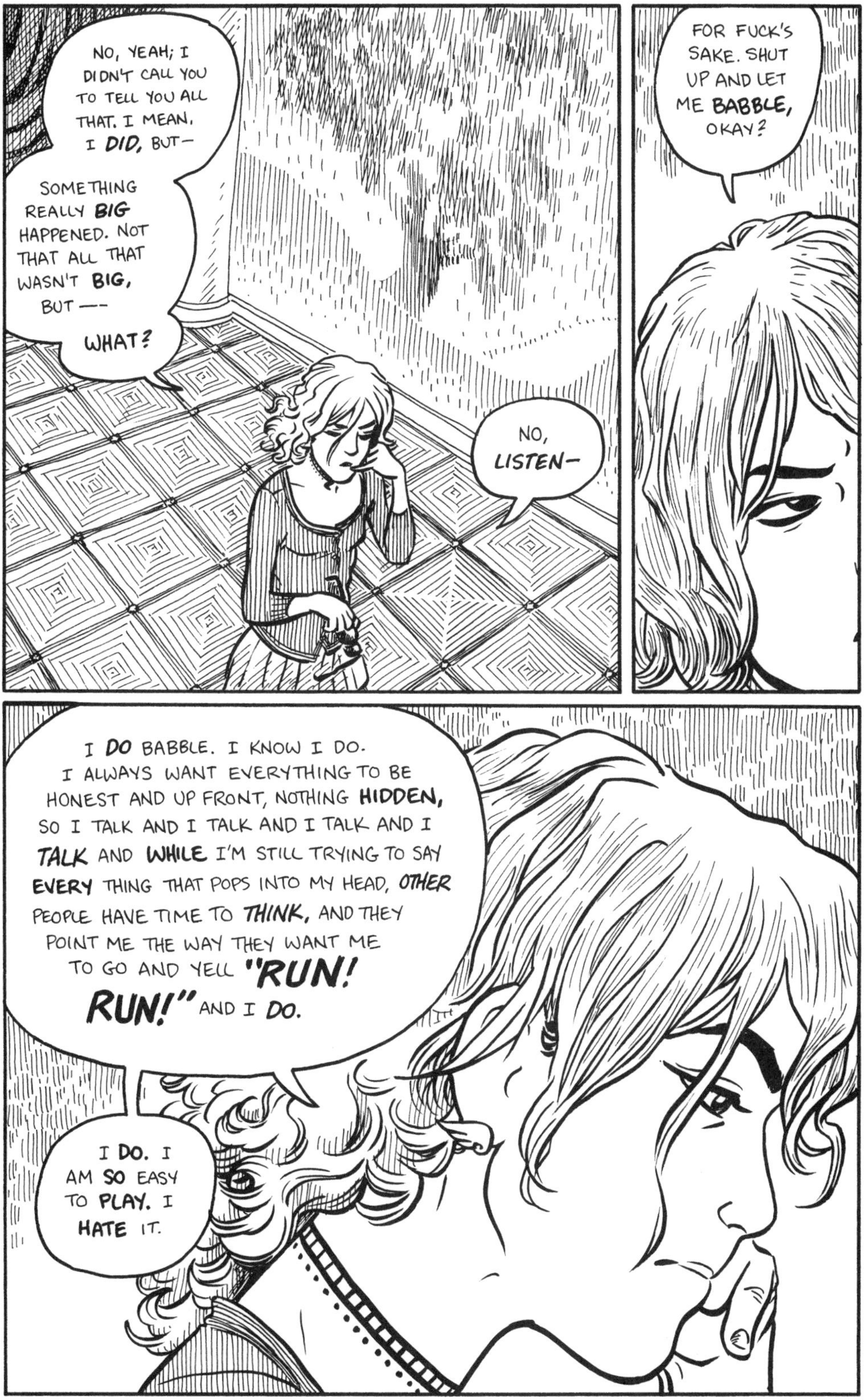
NO, YEAH; I DIDN'T CALL YOU TO TELL YOU ALL THAT. I MEAN, I DID, BUT—
SOMETHING REALLY BIG HAPPENED. NOT THAT ALL THAT WASN'T BIG, BUT ——
WHAT?
NO, LISTEN—
FOR FUCK'S SAKE. SHUT UP AND LET ME BABBLE, OKAY?
I DO BABBLE. I KNOW I DO. I ALWAYS WANT EVERYTHING TO BE HONEST AND UP FRONT, NOTHING HIDDEN, SO I TALK AND I TALK AND I TALK AND I TALK AND WHILE I'M STILL TRYING TO SAY EVERY THING THAT POPS INTO MY HEAD, OTHER PEOPLE HAVE TIME TO THINK, AND THEY POINT ME THE WAY THEY WANT ME TO GO AND YELL "RUN! RUN!" AND I DO.
I DO. I AM SO EASY TO PLAY. I HATE IT.

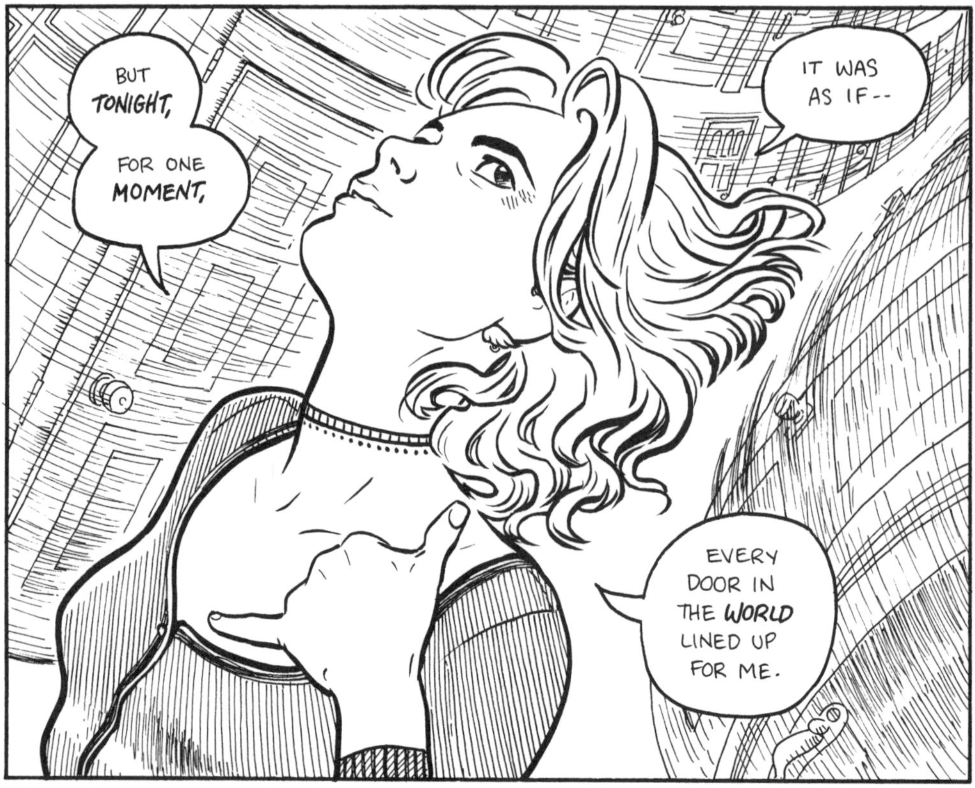
BUT TONIGHT,
FOR ONE MOMENT,
IT WAS AS IF--
EVERY DOOR IN THE WORLD LINED UP FOR ME.

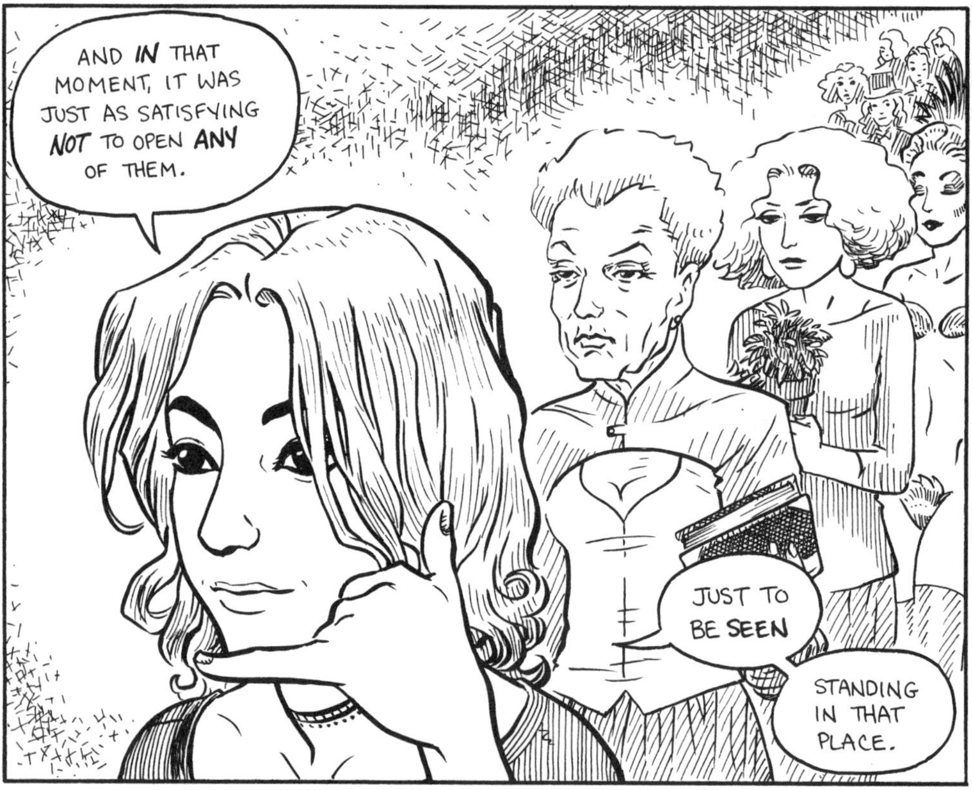
AND IN THAT MOMENT, IT WAS JUST AS SATISFYING NOT TO OPEN ANY OF THEM.
JUST TO BE SEEN
STANDING IN THAT PLACE.

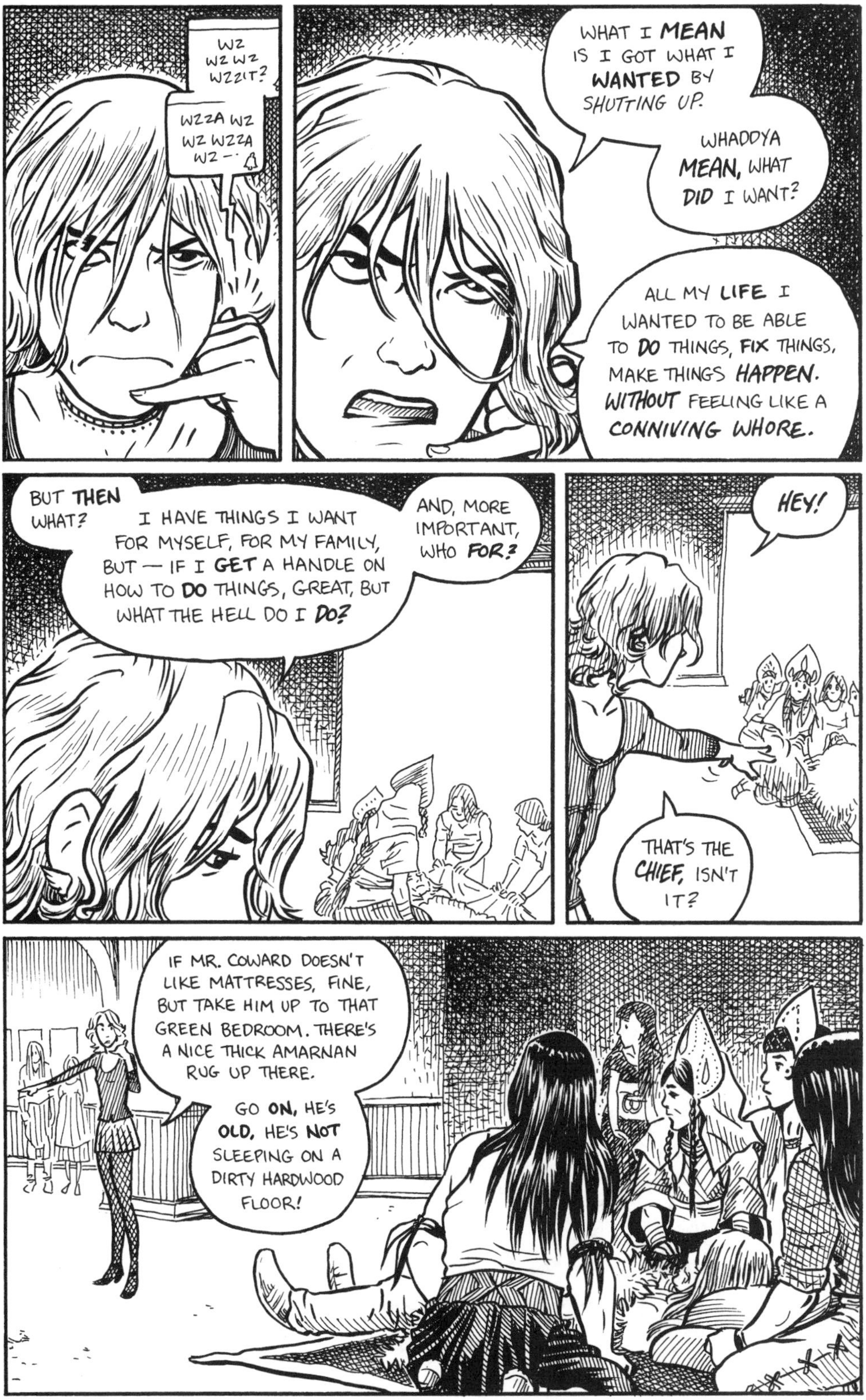
WZ WZ WZ WZZIT?
WZZA WZ WZ WZZA WZ--
WHAT I MEAN IS I GOT WHAT I WANTED BY SHUTTING UP.
WHADDYA MEAN, WHAT DID I WANT?
ALL MY LIFE I WANTED TO BE ABLE TO DO THINGS, FIX THINGS, MAKE THINGS HAPPEN. WITHOUT FEELING LIKE A CONNIVING WHORE.
BUT THEN WHAT? I HAVE THINGS I WANT FOR MYSELF, FOR MY FAMILY, BUT — IF I GET A HANDLE ON HOW TO DO THINGS, GREAT, BUT WHAT THE HELL DO I DO?
AND, MORE IMPORTANT, WHO FOR?
HEY!
THAT'S THE CHIEF, ISN'T IT?
IF MR. COWARD DOESN'T LIKE MATTRESSES, FINE, BUT TAKE HIM UP TO THAT GREEN BEDROOM. THERE'S A NICE THICK AMARNAN RUG UP THERE.
GO ON, HE'S OLD, HE'S NOT SLEEPING ON A DIRTY HARDWOOD FLOOR!

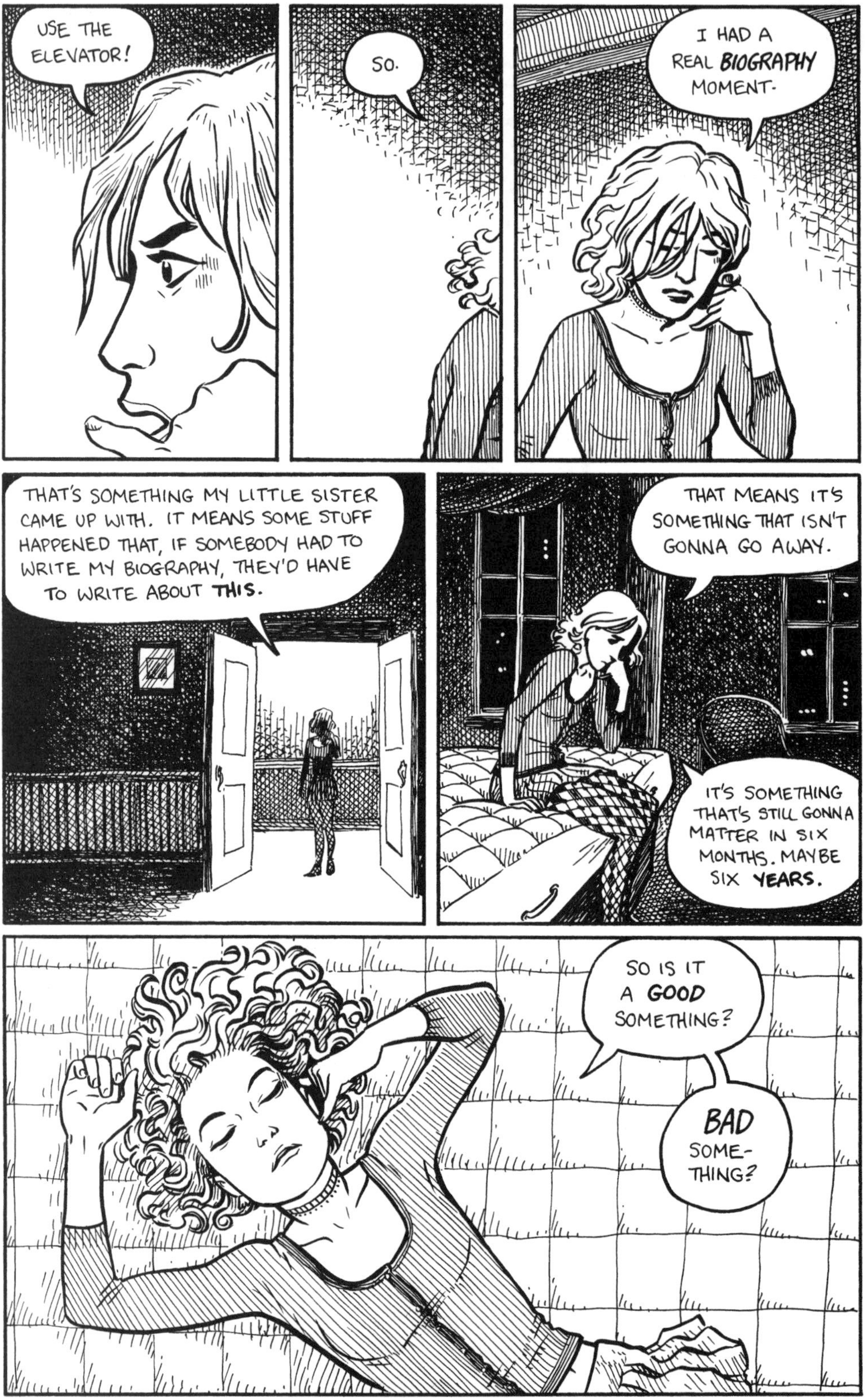
USE THE ELEVATOR!
SO.
I HAD A REAL BIOGRAPHY MOMENT.
THAT'S SOMETHING MY LITTLE SISTER CAME UP WITH. IT MEANS SOME STUFF HAPPENED THAT, IF SOMEBODY HAD TO WRITE MY BIOGRAPHY, THEY'D HAVE TO WRITE ABOUT THIS.
THAT MEANS IT'S SOMETHING THAT ISN'T GONNA GO AWAY.
IT'S SOMETHING THAT'S STILL GONNA MATTER IN SIX MONTHS. MAYBE SIX YEARS.
SO IS IT A GOOD SOMETHING?
BAD SOMETHING?

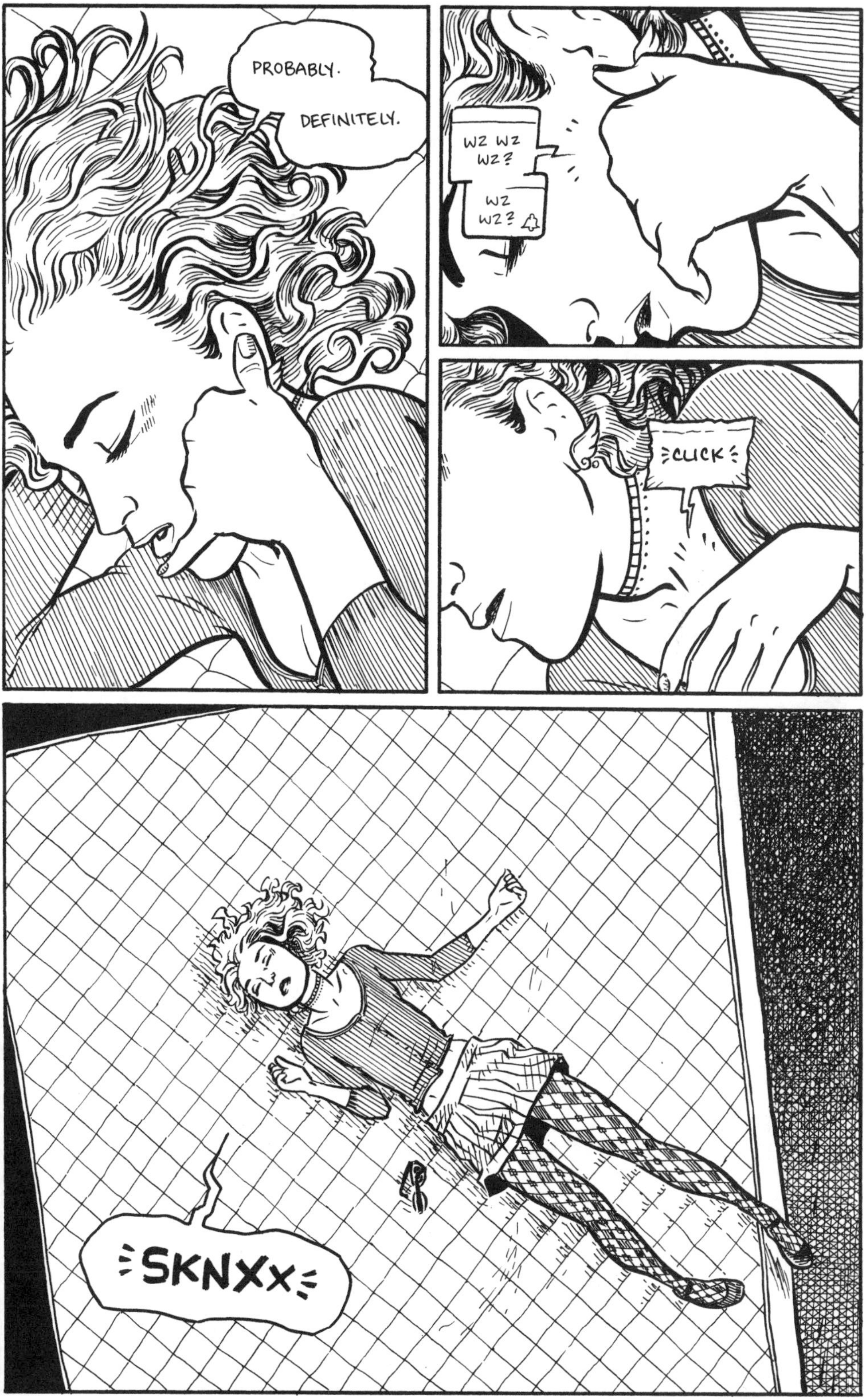
PROBABLY.
DEFINITELY.
WZ WZ WZ?
WZ WZ?
CLICK
SKNXx

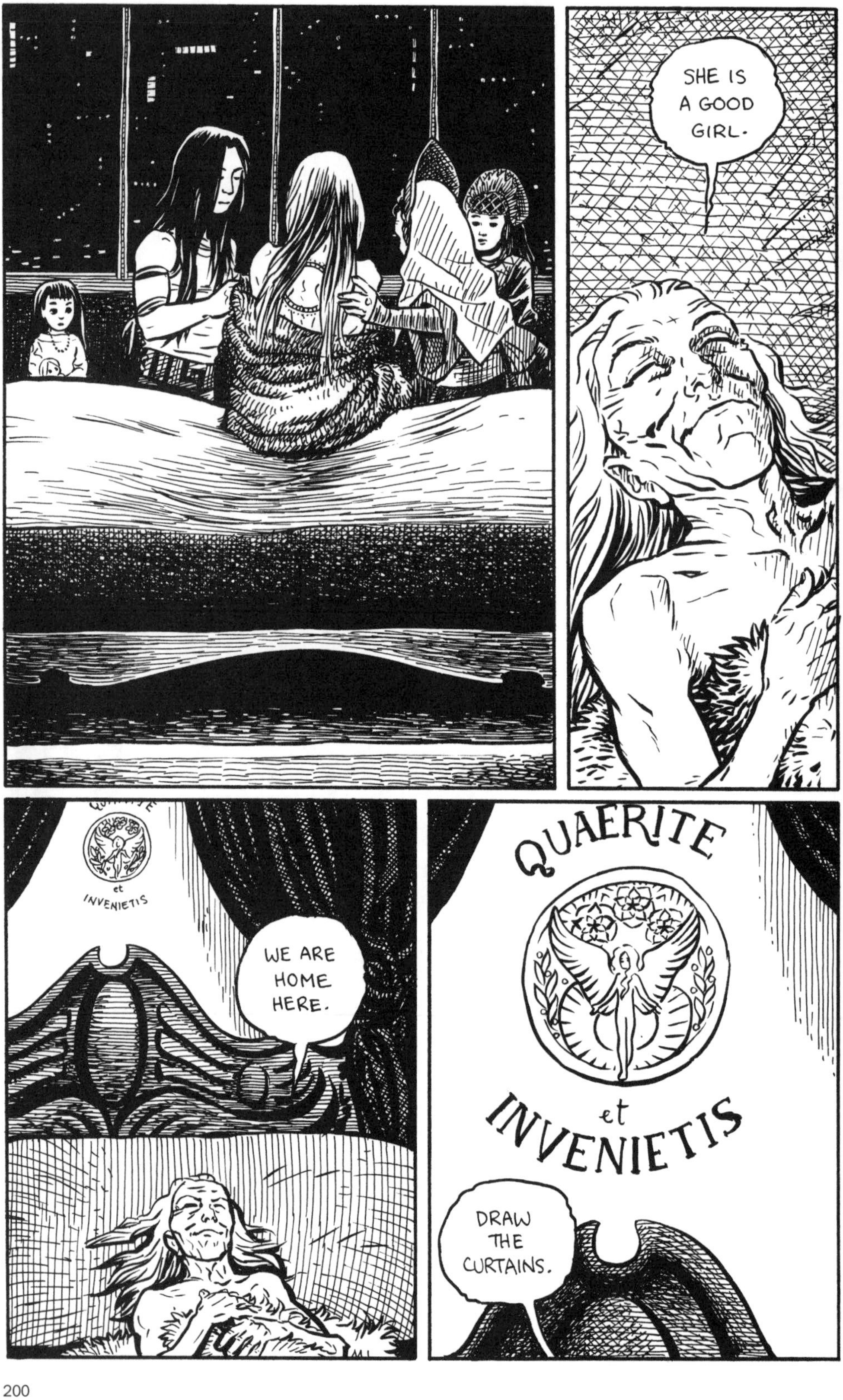
SHE IS A GOOD GIRL.
et
INVENIETIS
WE ARE HOME HERE.
QUAERITE
et
INVENIETIS
DRAW THE CURTAINS.

SEEK

and
ye SHALL FIND

COVER

This was an attempt at a "window" image, something simple and gnomic which would sum up the story as best I could in a single image. The focus of much gallery art is to exist on its own as a single image. Comics work in sequence, so selection of images for covers is often at odds with the type of art they are meant to represent. I try to do something that says, "If you stick with it long enough to figure out what this means, it'll be worth it."

At any rate, I liked the thematic contrast between the title, *Voice*, and the gesture, which says "silence." Bildungsromans in prose are often about boys becoming men. Get into visual media and there are a lot more girls becoming women. Finding one's voice = coming into power = maturity, yatata yatata yatata.

PAGE 7

There are five chapters in this book, and I hoped to suggest Rachel's progress with them. Here, she is one of many pawns, interchangeable, disposable, and anonymous.

PAGE 8

Pawns again: A large number of girls who look almost identical competing in a beauty pageant. They look even more alike than the typical run of pageant girls for a reason; familiar though beauty pageants are, their reasons for competing are a bit different. The stakes are higher. The parents of these girls are members of a large, powerful, multi-family clan called the Llaveracs. The proper pedigree alone does not guarantee full membership in the clan. Each young person who applies for full membership into his or her parents' clan (and there are many, many more than just the one these girls are trying to get into) must compete for entry according to his or her clan's standards. For instance, Lejeb clan kids have to pass rigorous mental math marathons. Medawar girls have to graduate medical school. Milos must present and defend their doctoral theses in history. Each clan follows what it values, and the Llaveracs are, among other things, drama queens. They wouldn't dream of holding an examination like this without turning it into a circus. So...beauty pageant, because they

have very strict notions as to what their members should look like.

PAGE 9

Gettin' in on the judges. Bit risque for your typical pageant, but the things Llaveracs consider to be in poor taste are best described as complicated.Best hope I never find time to depict Llaverac kiddie pageants, because they're just horrifying.

PAGE 10

My poor agent.

Uhm, yes, in much the same way that Tolkien's dwarves all look male at first glance, all Llaveracs look female. They are not hermaphrodites. The males just have curvy figures and feminine or gender-neutral names and cultivate a feminine appearance. They do have all the boy stuff, but they keep it all inside. Literally. They have a natural "tuck" kinda like a dolphin. Back to what few things Llaveracs think are inappropriate...calling attention to one's boy bits, should one have them, appalls them.

The judge who nearly lost an eye is the clan's own representative. The guy sitting to her left is there representing Medawar clan, who specialize in medicine and criminal justice, a down-to-earth, brown-bread kind of people who decry the fripperies that Llaveracs love but still can't stay too far away from them. Big rivalry.

PAGE 11

Girl in foreground is our protagonist, Rachel. Rachel's a girl. I'm pretty sure.

In the background: dad's got a boob window. And no, that she calls him "dad" doesn't automatically ensure that "he" is male. Llaveracs juggle pronouns and they don't care how many they drop.

PAGE 12

Rachel's unmaking herself. The exaggerations of female glamour are such, you can put them on a woman, a man, a child, a whatever, and some of the response will still elicit. It's amazing how artificial it is, and how it can still affect you in spite of your awareness of its artificiality. I will never get tired of picking it apart.

Rachel's friend Veronike, or Vero, is a Lejeb. They all have that funny two-toned hair naturally. Most clans' exams are televised, but few are as closely watched as the Llaveracs'.

PAGE 13
Little floaty screens. I don't have rocket boots in this world, or neon hula hoops, but I do have little Magic Computer Windows. People who have had computers surgically inserted into their brains can summon up little dynamic touchscreens out of thin air. Celebrities can wander the streets surrounded by haloes of tiny newspaper articles about them. Vero's just studying.

PAGE 14
This is Marcie, Rachel's youngest sister. Rachel, Marcie, and their middle sister Lynne are all daughters of Emma, who is a full-member Llaverac, and Brigham, a full-member Medawar. To say that the families frown upon mixed marriages would be saying too little. Rachel takes after her mother. Lynne and Marcie don't.

PAGE 15
Marcie is working as a page for the competition. Their grandfather is quite rich and powerful, heading a major movie studio. Grandmother, who is not seen in this book, is a comparatively mousy, tweedy creature. But still, these names and characteristics don't necessarily mean "grandaddy" is actually male, nor "grandmum" female. The Llaveracs like all the controversy, but are quick to slap the hands of people who speculate too tediously.

PAGE 16
Trudi's one of the pageant organizers, and more than a bit plump for her clan. So she's gone all Belle Epoch with it.

Can't remember for the life of me which clan the dude in the suit represents. Probably my notes on him are in *that* tottery stack of notes over there. On the bottom.

PAGE 17
Aha, there's Grandad. Maternal grandfather, or so says the paperwork, but really, this clan does love sexual anonymity. Married couples either go into hiding when a female begins showing signs of pregnancy, or they both affect maternity clothes (leopard-print, natch), or they avoid the whole thing by using surrogate mothers to actually carry their offspring to term. Stretch marks; what a dirty job!

PAGE 18
All the showgirls, buttering-up wherever they can. At right, Panel 2, the Llaverac clan judge is showing off another of a long line of his own illegitimate children. Lord Rod has a mission.

The major clans have a peerage system of earls and barons and knights and such. Many have royal heads of state. The way titles are passed down isn't always what one might expect.

PAGE 19
The Lejeb judge is Vero's uncle. Milo judge is Medina, who is the head of her clan. Maugeri isn't a major clan, since they aren't rich enough to grab a place at the table. Then there's Lord Rod, testing the waters.

PAGE 20
Trooping home. Rachel and Marcie live in Anvard, which is a huge multileveled city. Fancy elevators take pedestrians from level to level. The amount of daylight any given neighborhood gets depends on its proximity to the inner skin of the dome that protects the whole place from the elements. Some streets closer to the hub of the dome have light piped in from the outside if they can afford it, others make do with streetlights, others do without.

PAGE 21
Full membership in a clan is a necessity for white-collar livin'. If Rachel gets in, she will at least carry a knighthood, and she'll have enough pull to get her sisters into schools and jobs if they want.

"Dad" is Brigham Grosvenor, a Medawar man, who has been a little out of it for a very long time.

Any clan family member who doesn't win full membership is considered culled from the herd. Marcie doesn't look Llaverac enough to compete, and Lynne wouldn't do it to save Jesus from the Martians. Their family has always been on easy terms with a lot of non-clan people, spent a lot of time living outside the city. So Marcie hasn't thought much about her mixed parentage.

PAGE 23
The Ascians are not a clan. They are a tribal nomadic group recently taken up residence in greater numbers in Anvard. Everybody in Anvard is either in a clan, attached to a clan, or works for a clan. They run everything. A large number of people wash in and out of the city on a regular basis, living outside for varying lengths of time, but the Ascians live mostly outside. They are not affiliated with any clan. This is not the easy way to live.

PAGE 24
A night neighborhood is one that is never or almost never lit, even by streetlights. Sometimes the residents pool money to have the streets lit for special occasions. This one is lit only by wild-growing TV kudzu. There is no sky in Anvard, only roof.

Note that she isn't holding an actual cell phone. Rachel has a skull computer, and so her phone connection is activated by her making "phone hand" and concentrating. Yeah, pretend to talk on the phone for emphasis in a conversation, you will find yourself running down your minutes.

Rachel got off at the wrong stop to get away from the quarrelling Ascians. Never a good idea if you are a fictional character. Now is the right time for readers to start yelling "Hang up the phone! Don't go down there!" She's actually just headed for the next lift over, perfectly safe...

PAGE 25
Bye-bye, ring.

PAGE 26
And bye-bye, chapter one.

PAGE 27
Chapter two: from Pawn to Victim.

PAGE 29
Their sister Lynne has a number of little apartments all over town. Marcie knows where all of them are, and how to get in. Rachel only knows about two, and neither of them are the nice ones.

Lynne. Lynne, Lynne, Lynne. Lynne's mother was a female Llaverac who married a male Medawar. Dad thought it only right to let his wife take care of the kids and didn't even realize one of his daughters was a son until quite late in the game, as Lynne was born with the Llaverac boy bits. Brig just never got his head around the idea.

Information is currency in some circles of Anvard. Lynne is an info-trader, who peddles physical and digital files of any and everything. An infotrader is something between an investigative journalist, a pornographer, a spy, and whatever else he or she can think of to do to use the right piece of information at the right time. Lynne is, in short, everything Rachel is not.

PAGES 30–31
Rachel loves her sister, and really would do anything for her, but so would Lynne. Marcie knows which side of her bread is buttered. Marcie does like being with Rachel, just to be with a sister that she doesn't have to be appalled and occasionally afraid of, but she doesn't understand Rachel in the least. Lynne adopted Marcie when Marcie was born, and her relationship to Marcie is pretty much Lynne's only redeeming quality.

PAGE 32
That didn't take long.

Marcie is the star of a book earlier in the *Finder* series, called *Talisman*. Marcie's talisman is this book, which was in the stolen bag.

Beep boop. Even I'm not sure what equipment is in this sanctum of Lynne's.

PAGE 33

Grandad's house is always open to them, partly because it's so damned big Grandad might never know they're in there. Rich Anvardians pay for cubic footage.

PAGE 34

Write, Marcie, write. Marcie does insist on writing with a pen on an actual piece of paper.

PAGE 35

Back at the competition, next day. Loverlee costume, loverlee handler. Handlers are like personal trainers.

PAGE 36

Yes, the ring *does* matter.

PAGE 37

The Llaveracs are ruled by a queen (of course). The crown does not pass down by primogeniture. Think getting into the clan is weird? Wait till their Academy Awards get handed out.

A full clan member can marry someone of the proper heritage who isn't a full clan member. The full member then may pass down his or her ring to one of his or her offspring. If the kid gets in, then the ring belongs to that kid. That kid may choose to pass his or her ring to a full sibling, a half sibling, or a total stranger if he or she chooses. The recipient of the ring then has a chance to compete for membership in that clan. So the rings may be passed around quite a bit, but they are not owned communally by a family. The latest winner of membership is the owner, and is legally free to refuse any petition to pass it to someone else. Lots of titanic family rifts over things like this.

PAGE 39

Let's misbehaaaaave!

PAGE 40

There are a lot of freestanding buildings in Anvard, though everything's floor is something's ceiling. Many buildings retain the peaked roofs of architectural styles developed to keep off the weather. Why is that, given that most neighborhoods are not open to the inner skin of the dome, let alone the sky? There is still

weather in large enough spaces in Anvard. Water vapor still collects and drifts around and occasionally creates rain in some areas. Even in those areas that don't commonly experience that still have to deal with overhead things that leak. And the rich folks are always doing things like building snow machines. That's why, in spite of the streets being enclosed, there are still sewer drains, and the cars still have windshield wipers.

Medawars are all cops (inside the city) or soldiers (outside). The rank and medal markings on the cop's face are not tattoos, but attention-enhancing biofoils. No reason they shouldn't reflect rank and honor.

PAGE 41

John Grosvenor, Rachel's first cousin. Son of her father Brigham's brother Marcus.

He says he's marrying "a nice anesthesiologist"—all female Medawars are in medicine. They start medical training as kids. Med Scouts do the same things as Girl Scouts, but they stitch up their craft projects with surgical knots and their cookies all have rather unusual ingredients.

PAGE 42

Brigham had a ring, yes. He could have passed it on to someone else. In a way, he did: He stood at the highest point of a vista overlooking the lower city and threw it as hard as he could. Someone could have found it. He was pissed over being punished (reassigned to a very remote army post) for marrying outside of his clan. He thought of this as a gesture of defiance.

The Pax Lares is a large, overarching document that regulates twelve of what were then the most powerful clans, organizing their political relationships and attempting to place checks and balances on their power. The ring thing was meant to keep any one clan from becoming too numerous.

PAGE 43

I was originally going to have poor, messed-up Dad still living with his wife in her weird semi-organic tree apartment, but when I got around to inking the book, it seemed more likely that Emma had enough money to have him cared for somewhere else. He is almost never himself anymore.

PAGE 44

"Aunt Dess" is Odessa Irwin, Brigham's sister. She never made doctor, because no ring was available to her. She's a hell of a good nurse.

Yes, John just made a sort of reflexive pass at Rachel. Everybody's raised to think of Llaveracs as the sexiest, most glamorous things that ever walked. Having Rachel for a cousin is pretty missing-top-step for him: too close to remember his place all the time.

PAGE 45

Brigham is pretty vigorous for as out of it as he is.

PAGE 46

Female full-clan Medawars wear their hair in elaborate braids. For surgeons, this means wigs. Dess is not full clan, but she still puts her hair up. Hair hanging loose looks immature to her.

PAGE 47

There you go: fancy braids.

That still image of Jaeger is part of a film clip of him jumping Brigham's doctor. The other family photos are film clips as well. More on who Jaeger is later.

PAGE 48

This is Emma, maiden name Lockhart, mother of Rachel, Lynne, and Marcie, wife of Brigham, daughter of crazy grandad from the beauty pageant party. She is a full Llaverac clan member, and passed her ring on to Rachel. She isn't really the performing-arts type, preferring botany, gardening, landscape art. By trade, she is now a Rememberer, which is a topic for another book, but it means she's not around very much either. She also earns enough money doing it to live in this weird living elven-princess apartment where grass grows on the floor and the couches and chairs are alive and covered with moss and leaves and sometimes berries.

PAGE 49

Zing!

"Rodzina" or "Rodzhina" is Polish, and means "family." It isn't used as a personal name in Polish, as I understand it.

PAGE 50

The rank of Earl is closest to king (or ruling queen, as in this case). Even though the rings get passed around a lot, they do become orphaned from time to time. If the holder dies without officially passing his or her ring down, it reverts to the Crown. The Llaverac queen has entrusted one of her earls with the dispensation of whatever rings come back orphaned.

Zing!

Brigham fathered a child on his brother's wife with the brother's full knowledge and consent. There is a term for this kind of consent, which is a big fat open secret in the clans, and Rachel will encounter it in her turn, later in life. It happens between full clan members, and isn't always a great idea, but physical conformation to an imagined standard is very important to most clans. There is push and pull between the desire for the familiar and the unfamiliar, even among people whose variations are so subtle that they barely exist.

Brig and Emma had better reasons for wanting "insurance" than most. They wanted to break free of restrictive customs, they did love each other, but they were aware of how screwed any kids they had together would be. At least ONE kid had to gain full membership to give the others any chance.

PAGE 51

Here's Lynne again, in club drag. And the second of way, way too many bars and nightclubs, hoo boy. Why did I make this book so atmospheric? My hands hate me.

PAGE 52

I found this costume of Lynne's in a Japanese fashion magazine, so it was out of date for Japan before the camera's flashbulb cooled, but it suits her very well. Lynne has boobs, and enjoys kicking the shit out of people who stare at them when she shows them off.

Lord Rod's library: purely for the beauty of books. Most content is stored on computers, in memory palaces, online, etc., etc. Rod likes dead trees.

Live tree: All the trees in Anvard are in pots. Like Coconino County. Well, there is a ground level that has dirt, and there are trees growing in that dirt. People put little walls around them to make them look like they're in pots.

PAGE 53
Incunabula! One of the best words ever.

PAGE 54
Note that Lord Rod is wearing his own ring. Presently.

PAGE 55
You don't have boys with boobs and an endocrine balance that's very good for male fertility. Boy junk hangs loose for a reason. Male Llaveracs aren't terribly fertile. That's why Lord Rod has such a reputation as a rake. He must be working pretty hard, especially at his age, to make that many babies.

PAGE 56
Lynne is haloed by "snake eggs," little flying cameras with huge memory storage, in this case slaved to her mind. Whatever draws her attention—a sound behind her, a half-seen gesture, whatever—attracts the attention of one or more snake eggs. Lynne doesn't want to miss a thing.

At least Rachel knows she's got Lynne's full attention.

PAGE 57
The more Lynne acts like a bad-tempered drag queen, the more trouble you're in.

Lynne has been alienated from Rachel since Rachel hit puberty. Rachel was never a Med Scout; Lynne was. Lynne suspected Rachel wasn't of mixed parentage long before it ever occurred to Rachel, because it basically never occurred to Rachel.

PAGE 59
Phantom.

Phantom's name is Jaeger.

PAGE 60
Not literally a phantom. But Jaeger comes and goes, he is half Ascian, he was one of Brigham's non-clan soldiers. Complicated.

PAGE 61
Third step: From pawn to victim to sidekick.

PAGE 62
Another bar! Yay. Blue-collar non-clan place.

Those of you who are looking at the penciled version of this page on-line: the inked version is two panels, where the penciled one was only one. The pacing works better with that panel border across the middle: top of the panel serves as a scene-setter, bottom starts the action, such as it is.

PAGE 63
Brigham's family came back to the city without him. He lived apart from them for quite a while, partly in prison. More about that in *Finder: Sin-Eater.*

PAGE 64
I think she's talking to Vero again, but she's got a lot of friends. Rachel views the phone as a form of divination. Need to make a decision? Don't roll dice or check your horoscope, call up each and every one of your friends. Peer-o-mancy.

PAGE 65
The whole underwear-as-outerwear thing has always fascinated me. T-shirts, after all, used to be underwear, and now they're standard uniform. Rachel is wearing a bodyliner which does all manner of things. It generates her little floaty touchscreens, if nothing else. And wicks sweat.

That guy is from a Moebius drawing I just happened to spy when I needed an extra.

Page 66-67
Rachel is easily challenged. This doesn't change the primal nature of the confrontation.

PAGE 68
Boing.

PAGE 69
An Alexandrian solution.

PAGE 70
Mmm . . . yeah, I'm not getting into this one in this book. It's not crucial to the plot.

PAGE 71
First of several like-a-looks.

PAGE 72
Individual clans have clan-specific how-to-bring-up-baby books, based on the expected personality range and traits of a full-blood child of that clan. They have clan-specific fashion designers and shopping in which the available sizes are skewed towards what's average for that clan. Llaveracs tend to have narrow feet, so the shoes in the really high end malls are very pinchy to everyone else. Doctors sometimes specialize in particular clans, as they tend to have the same problems, not even getting into the issues of inbreeding. Medawars and Llaveracs both have brown eyes, so Jaeger's light-colored eyes were a source of endless amazement to Rachel as a child.

PAGE 73
These like-a-looks are from the Cole Porter number. Meowwwrrrr.

PAGE 74
So the guy they're looking for is the guy that just left Rachel, and Rachel really didn't pick up on it.

PAGE 75
In the photo with Jaeger (it's a physical piece of photo paper for once) are Jan and Tasha. They're based on Janis (from the Electric Mayhem Band) and Natasha (of Boris and), cartoon hotties of my youth; how I love them.

Oh, yeah. That black top Rachel is wearing is the top half of another bodyliner smartsuit.

PAGE 76
Pedro's is just a regular girlie bar most nights a week. Ped o's is the name it uses on Dude Night.

Jaeger worked as a bouncer on Dude Night at Ped o's on occasion, and he left his "calling card."

PAGE 77
Rachel's skull computer stores her phone numbers. So she doesn't even have to remember which button is whose on her speed dial.

PAGE 79
That TV kudzu gets everywhere. It is mechanical, but it does grow.

PAGE 80
Here's Brom. Brom is also in *Sin-Eater* and *Five Crazy Women.*

PAGE 81
You can have a messy desk and lose things even if none of it is on little slips of paper, and no memory is endless.

PAGE 82
Brom is a vampire cowboy. I will tell his whole story sometime.

PAGE 83
This guy does have a street name, but if I tell you now it won't be as funny.

PAGE 84
There's the gunshot wound, arriving at great speed. And the senior Med Scouts, clearing the waiting room.

PAGE 85
Yep, that's the only one she can remember. She'll find a pen eventually.

This is basically an alley with a few boards to separate it from the street. It also has a few rooms through the outside walls of the adjoining buildings. Anvardian buildings are a bit termite-moundy.

PAGE 86
This guy was originally designed to look like Joe from the kids' show *Blue's Clues*, played

by Donovan Patton. I thought making him cute as pie would be a pleasant tension between appearance and impact. He's a twinkie hit man. The weird goatee came later, after a lot of people got confused about how much like Jaeger he looked.

Fingers bend like this after they've healed from being broken. Repeatedly.

PAGE 87

This tells you a little of what Jaeger does for a living. He's not in the Army anymore.

Poor Rachel. She needs a pen.

PAGE 88

I like the old moon-on-the-privy-door thing. I like the idea that the men's room should have a sun on it, but historically this wasn't the case. The crescent shape wasn't even all that common, and it was just for ventilation.

PAGE 89

Rachel knows this symbol is associated with Jaeger, because he had it tattooed on his hands. Usually on his hands.

PAGE 90

Back when most people weren't literate, shop signs were just images. Criminal societies still retain this "we're meeting here tonight" signifier. Hang the snake on the lamp. The crown and the wings are always there. It's just poker night for most people.

PAGE 91

The fourth panel was originally intended to be a sort of Jaime Hernandez quote. In one of his weirder Izzy Ortiz stories, he depicted a bunch of creepy old ladies doing something awful to Isabel in a fever dream, and in one panel there were a bunch of severed tentacles on the floor by/around one old lady/witch/demon figure's sandalled feet. I wanted to do something similar here, where it'd be kind of creepy, but the tentacles are just from careless calamari preparation. But I'm not Jaime, so it didn't come off, so I changed it in the final version to a skinned whole deer carcass. Given Rachel's physique, and her cloven-hoof boots, it seemed creepier.

PAGE 92

Creepy old daddy bears. Don't mess.

These are the local patriarchs. They run the neighborhood. They're not actually all mobsters.

PAGE 94–95

In the inking process, I split page 94 into two, to make the painted ceiling more impressive, and to emphasize the transition from the warm, old-school kitchen to the sparkly suburban mall street.

PAGE 96

Another bar! Yay!

Fern bar. Nice place for nice girls. She ran away from the pubs for a while.

PAGE 97–98

Slow-speed chases can be very suspenseful. She runs out; he follows. She runs to the bus stop; can't make the bus come faster. He's going to catch her before she can get on. She runs; she can leap onto the bus through its rear door. Unfortunately that doesn't keep him from getting on too.

PAGE 99

I love drawing this idiotic Llaverac couple. Just because that one has mutton-chop sideburns doesn't mean he's the male. On the other hand, it doesn't mean he isn't. They could both be male. Or both female.

As a full member of her clan, Rachel would also have an exceptionally good chance at establishing a relationship with a banker, who would help her start her personal endeavors. Many clan people are landlords. Llaveracs do enjoy restoring old buildings or furniture or what have you, given how ludicrous the sums of money that building something new would take. They like making things pretty. It's part of their religious devotions, insofar as they have religion.

The Red Ripleys tattoo themselves with jigsaw puzzle pieces, according to their rank in their cell. It's a big, very organized gang.

The Sweathogs I used just because I love the name. Hogs don't sweat.

The Sweathogs and the Red Ripleys and all the rest are the street-level affiliations of non-clan people. They maintain their freedom by buying favors with powerful clan members. The bigger gangs spread themselves around, not wanting to be any one clan's personal army. The Ascians have no patron to protect them.

PAGE 101
They do work. They're just outrageously unfair.

PAGE 102
I draw too many empty streets in this city. At least this joint's got a crowd: opening night (free wine) for a suspense thriller starring a Llaverac. One thing's for sure about being a star in this city, if you have clan heritage, you probably won't have any trouble finding a body double, or a stunt double, or another actor to play your character old, or young, or dead. Roll 'em out!

There are traditional holiday plays that call for specifically typecast actors from the twelve major clans. The clan people have specific roles, like the Commedia Dell' Arte or pantomimes. Funnier still is when these plays are performed by children of all one clan, wearing iconic signifiers that represent the other clans. "Why do I have to be the Llaverac? I don't want to wear the boobs!"

PAGE 103
I love restroom signs. The regular glyphs that stand for "men pee in here" and "women pee in here" don't look like anybody I know.

PAGE 104
Llaveracs are always ready to share cosmetics and swap clothes. Not to do so would be Letting The Side Down. Refusing to share water at the wells, that sort of thing.

Yes, *thank* you, Donnie. I think I listened to every Coen brothers movie I own while I was working on this last rush to complete *Voice*. I can't listen to music or the radio while I work. The tracks are too short and make me itch. I like to listen to conversations when I'm work-

ing. The Coen brothers write the best dialogue. And their soundtracks are amazing. And yet I don't listen to their music soundtracks. Eh.

PAGE 105
Rachel's made a huge effort to change her look to more glitz-style Llaverac in hopes of confusing her stalker dude.

PAGE 106
See? She found a pen. Even with a skull computer, she still has to write things on her arm from time to time.

Little corner grocery with an upstairs room. Totally illegal. That's why there is no upstairs. Not for her, anyway.

Page 108
Ha ha, Rachel. You're a ho-bag.

Yes, honey, those are the same two guys who were fighting on the Schart Street lift. Incidentally, I picked the name Schart because of all the books I have in my studio illustrated by Trina Schart Hyman. Beautiful stuff.

PAGE 109
The thug from the corner grocery is clearly a Red Ripley, as is the woman who runs the place. The thug, Baldamar Martin, is also an indentured servant on the lam from his master. He entered into an indenture, or limited period of semi-slavery, in lieu of prison time. He's moonlighting as a bouncer unbeknownst to Lord Jaynes, who holds his indenture papers. Mr. Martin is deeply in trouble.

PAGE 110
If Rachel wasn't in full Llaverac drag, if it wasn't conformation competition time, if there was anything the cops meant to charge her with, she really wouldn't be able to stomp out of the precinct house just any old time. The other cops know she's only there because Kelley felt like harassing her.

PAGE 111
Enter Psykhe! She's the One Girl Llaverac encounter. Three at the beginning, with the three girls at the Crescent bar, looking for drugs. Two

on the bus, discussing real estate and local gang activity. And last one, here, in the form of Psykhe, who is following the conformation pageant closely and has in short order become a fervent Rachel fan.

PAGE 112

Every girl who wins full membership in Llaverac clan is knighted. All other titles revert to the Crown upon death—none are passed down to a child, but are awarded to newly-minted full members as available.

PAGE 113

That's the problem with competing. You can go in solidly wanting just to do well, willing to settle for less, ready to be satisfied that you did the best you could with what you had, and next thing you know you'll die if you don't WIN.

PAGE 114

Plague year. I haven't mentioned the local nasty diseases since *Sin-Eater*. I'll get around to them eventually.

PAGE 115

Yes, Rachel ran afoul of some Medawar Lester Molester back in the distant outpost. And, no, she shouldn't blame herself for his actions; she was a child. She's wrestling with where her responsibilities do begin. Adulthood isn't a transformation—one day you're not one, next day you are—but if initiative and accountability don't start on your eighteenth birthday, how far back do you go? This is an easy question to answer for some people, and a very hard one for Rachel.

PAGE 116

Paul Colbert (or Colvin or whatever I chose at the last minute) isn't a bad cop. He knows his neighborhoods, he knows the people in them.

PAGE 117

Da-daa . . . this is Jaeger's younger half-brother Roy, who was last seen as a small child way, way back in *Fight Scene*, which has become part of *Sin-Eater*. Roy gets to play knight in shining armor as far as Rachel's concerned, because she'll fall in love with anybody who solves her latest problem.

Rachel didn't end up on this doorstep accidentally. This is one of the addresses Brom gave her. Brom knows Roy because Brom knows Jaeger.

PAGES 118–119

Roy was deliberately designed to look like a cute teeny-bop version of his older brother. I think he'll do.

PAGE 121

Roy's mother was a blonde fluffy sort of girl who knew a way out of the company town when she saw one. Roy and Jaeger's father may have been half-Ascian.

PAGE 123

Lots of clan people are culls. It isn't the end of life. But if she doesn't win her membership, Rachel has to depend on her mother and grandparents for a lot of things. As a cull, she probably couldn't get a major bank loan. She can own property, but not a lot. She can go to college, but only if someone sponsors her. It's either go home and do what Mom and grandfolks want, or find a sponsor. Sponsors don't always expect to have sex with their protegees, but the protegee had better be mighty talented. Membership brings independence. This society really is a club.

Roy's not broke, but he can't afford the software that keeps the millions of pop-up ads out. He has the homemade stuff, but the wars between the advertisers and the consumers gallop on apace.

PAGE 124

Rachel actually feels bad that her family has never done anything for Roy. She was raised with noblesse oblige, in buckets.

PAGE 125

His full name is Royal Sudamer Ayers. So says a lot of paperwork. Most of Jaeger's paperwork, such as there is, says all different things.

PAGE 126

There are seasons in Anvard. The dome is not glass, but a very complex and only half broken structure which absorbs light, heat, and other radiant energy into its outer skin, filters some of it, and doles the rest out to its interior through its inner skin. It also breathes. It would do a lot of other things if it didn't have so many holes in it.

Yes, Roy stole that bench. He's quite the rags to . . . well, not riches, but fewer rags story.

Roy is extremely proud of this little house, because he owns it outright. He and Jaeger were brought up in a company town far, far away from any city, and these towns are worse than indentured servitude. Digging himself out of that place and learning to make a system work for him to the point that he's not broke and can make himself a place to live is a huge source of pride. More about what he actually does for a living in some other book.

PAGE 127
The joke about leaving a beer and a bowl of cat food on the porch is one we used to make about one of the several people Jaeger is based on.

PAGE 128
It's a hollow book because books are talismanic to Marcie.

PAGE 129
That used to be a Totoro. Marcie had it in *Sin-Eater*. Emma was in a male drag phase when she met and married Brigham. The bronze star is awarded for valor on the battlefield.

PAGE 130
Yes, Roy. No, Roy. Sometimes, Roy.

PAGE 133
He's not a bad boy.

PAGE 134
Rachel is not-so-secretly kinky for masculine-looking men. This hasn't helped her adjust to the idea of throwing in her lot with the Llaveracs.

PAGE 135
More fight! Fight! Fight!

PAGE 136
Oh, it's Brom. And the stalky guy. Hi guys.

Ta-daa! Stalky guy's street name is Snatch. Because his very dense black goatee has no shape, it grows right up to the margin of his lower lip. He also has a big red scar in a very suggestive spot on his chin. I decided to give this dreadful characteristic because early readers were confused about who Brom was beating up, whether it was Stalky Guy or actually Jaeger. So: horrible beard and awful nickname.

PAGE 138
Blinky.

PAGE 139
Ha ha. Condom exchange. Back to the plague some other time.

PAGES 140–141
There's probably too much stuff in this little abandoned grocery. When Ascians hold a big party like this, it's always a religious ritual. There will be loads of food and booze because that's what their gods like. But they use everything they have, all out. They probably wouldn't have all this stuff on the shelves unused. I wanted Rachel's drunken reverie to be very vivid.

That's Chief Coward, last seen in *King of the Cats*.

PAGE 142
Coward always smiles.

PAGE 143
She needs that.

PAGE 144
All hair, all the time.

PAGE 145
Fourth: femme fatale. Lots of people skip this stage. Whyyyyy?

PAGE 146
There are fewer notes for this book than for previous books because I did a better job of getting the good stuff into the story.

PAGE 147

This neighborhood used to have more money, and therefore more light. That tree was a whole lot healthier once upon a time.

PAGE 148

Lots of theaters, lots of playhouses.

PAGE 149–151

If this was Voodoo, this guy would be Legba. This is a priest dedicated to Olpapa, a doorway deity who is always the first god invoked. He opens the door to the spirit world. As far as the Ascians are concerned, this man is literally Olpapa in the flesh, because to be a priest or priestess means to allow yourself to be possessed by the god. All the paraphernalia belongs to the man, and are his personal effects, but the soot-mark across one eye is Olpapa's specific emblem: one eye open, one eye closed. This emblem can be expressed in any way that works: a pair of sunglasses with one lens popped out, a blindfold with a hole cut in it. None of the other spirits can come across until Olpapa does.

These guys with the white crosses painted on their faces are Marosse. Marosse is a death god. All of them are Marosse; he is not picky about who he possesses or how many at one time.

Ascian gods have recently discovered blocked hats. They are in transition, just as their devotees are.

These guys are all speaking for the gods, with the voices of the gods. Are they playing the role of the god, or literally channeling the god? The Ascian who does this would not understand the question. They study their gods, they gravitate to the gods that are the most like them. They are, in a way, the god's fan club. They make themselves suitable to the god's spirit. They hope the god will give them his word to speak into the world of men. This is the nature of their devotions.

PAGE 152

They all assume that there are gods native to this city that they haven't met, and the clans embody them.

PAGES 153–154

They are cutting themselves. Fie to you, black and white book.

PAGE 155

Probably why there are so many Marosse possessions.

PAGE 156

Coward has been trying to pick apart some of the peculiarities of his world all of his life. Now, in his old age, his life has led him here. Outside wasn't that much easier.

PAGE 158

She was supposed to give the bottle of booze to Olpapa. That's her cover charge.

PAGES 159–160

The reason you can do so much while blacked out is because your memory doesn't actually go kaput until you fall down go boom. THEN it rewinds and erases.

PAGE 162

Fragments.

PAGES 164–165

One early reader described this ridiculous dress as a wearable duvet. But look, she had a money dance.

PAGE 166

These Ascians have collected a lot of things over the years. Coward is and has been quite the curious cat, and he raises curious cats.

PAGE 167–168

By "his," they mean Jaeger's. He left it with them way back in King of the Cats.

Crazy steam car! Got it straight out of a Richard Scarry book. He rocked the rock house. Love the teapot.

PAGE 169

Can't remember what clever idea I had behind this last evolution-of-Rachel chapter head drawing. It was all structured-storytelling Alan Moore and shit too.

PAGE 170

Ah, little tyrants. They're just irritated, but their irritation changes the course of other people's lives.

But she would never have yelled at them like this yesterday.

PAGES 171–172

There's Marcie. Marcie loves to explore ins and outs, and so she knows all the servants' passages and hidey-holes in this building. There are more than a few.

PAGE 173

Lord Snotrag knows his rings.

PAGE 174

Back when Llewellyn Laverack was alive, the Pax Lares was not even a gleam in its framers' eyes, and lots of rings were made. Most of them do feature the Black Angel, which is a sculpture widely regarded as an icon of Anvard. Like Rodin's *Little Mermaid* in Copenhagen, or America's Statue of Liberty.

"Who the hell are you?" Awww.

Lord Rod does not like Rachel because he does not like her family.

PAGES 175–177

Aha.

It's an open secret in the clan. It would indeed be quite a scandal outside.

PAGE 178

Rachel has no proof, so Rod must be very vulnerable to scandal right now. Or he's just very intrigued.

PAGE 179

Crazy floor show part over; now for the drumrolls.

PAGE 180

Flounce, flounce, flounce. No dissertations for these girls.

PAGE 181

This costume of Rachel's is partly all the handlers could do with her bruising and the circles under her eyes. But mostly spite.

It sets her apart from the others, but she's supposed to be exemplifying an ideal. Even though this really kind of suits her, she's like Jezebel in a red dress while all the other girls are of one kind.

PAGE 182

So now she's back in high school, and all the other girls who sort of didn't like her now hate her.

PAGE 183

Tattoos are discouraged in clan hopefuls. Do whatever you like once you're in.

The Finder glyph is not a tattoo at this point, just Sharpie. The Ascians thought she needed it.

PAGE 184

Uh huh.

PAGE 185

I love the missing top step. YIKES

PAGE 186

On the original pencilled version of this page was a vague scribble and a note about how This Page Shows A Fancy Mansion But I Have Jury Duty.

PAGE 187

See, it *was* important for Rachel to get past the handlers.

PAGE 188

We're all so used to the words "prince" and "princess" that we don't think of what they mean. They come from the same root as "principal." Just means "first." Like she says. That's why the winner gets a crown.

Rachel wasn't the only one who came away with a title beyond knight. The winner is now a princess, the first runner-up became a countess, Rachel became a duchess, and one other girl became a viscountess.

PAGE 189

The present Llaverac queen is sort of a female Keith Richards.

There's a whole heap of other weird things too; a lot of the nobles have official birthdays entirely independent of their actual birth dates.

PAGE 190

Wish I'd had room to show her casually stepping over the rug as they roll it past the spot where she's standing, but I had to have room for the portrait gallery. The one in the middle is very loosely based on a portrait of Cornelia Vanderbilt.

PAGE 191

Rachel knows her mother lied to her about Lord Rod being her biological father. She doesn't know who her real father is, and doesn't want to get into it.

If she misses her period...yeah, quite a party with the Ascians. Too bad she doesn't remember much of it.

Another day, another stalker, ho hum.

PAGE 192

Llaveracs do look a lot alike. Good news for hopeful obsessives.

PAGE 193

When Ascians are on your side, they're on your side.

PAGE 194

And when they're on your side, what's yours is theirs. But at least she's got bodyguards. And they have a patron.

PAGE 195

Might be talking to Vero again.

PAGE 196

Influence is funny that way. Action and inaction: the outcome depends on the moment.

PAGE 198–199

I thought about having this mattress sink down under her weight, pinning her, and she'd just hang up and go to sleep, but decided against it.

PAGE 200

For his purposes, a very good girl.

"Ask, Seek, and Knock: the Matthews sisters! Everybody give them a big hand! Tip your waitresses!"

PAGE 201

Since the tone of these notes has turned into the tone used on director's commentaries, I'll conclude by saying thank you for reading, I hope you enjoyed it, and there will be more. Good night.

FINDER

CARLA SPEED McNEIL

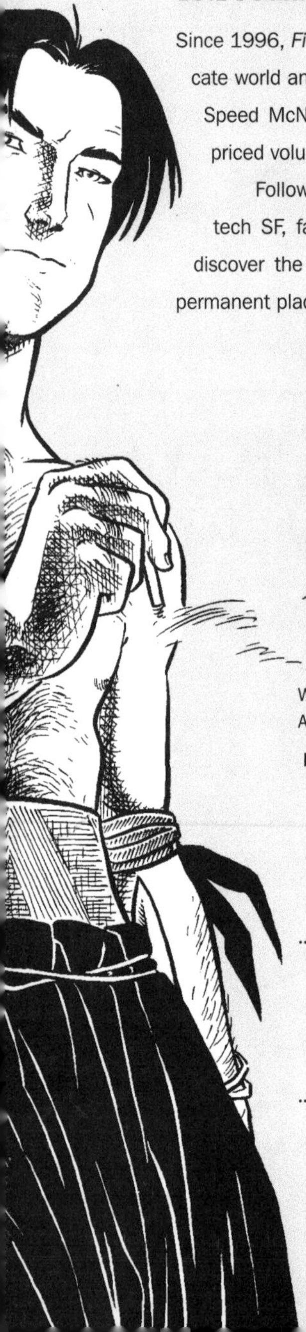

LOSE YOURSELF IN A WORLD BEYOND YOUR WILDEST DREAMS...

Since 1996, *Finder* has set the bar for science-fiction storytelling, with a lush, intricate world and compelling characters. Now, Dark Horse is proud to present Carla Speed McNeil's groundbreaking series in newly revised, expanded, affordably priced volumes!

Follow enigmatic hero Jaeger through a "glorious, catholic pileup of high-tech SF, fannish fantasy, and street-level culture clash" (*Village Voice*), and discover the lush world and compelling characters that have carved *Finder* a permanent place in the pantheon of independent comics.

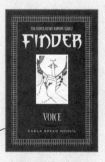

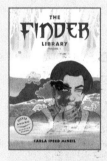

FINDER: VOICE
Winner of the 2009 Eisner Award for Best Webcomic.

ISBN 978-1-59582-651-0
$19.99

**THE FINDER LIBRARY
VOLUME 1**
Collecting the multiple Eisner Award-nominated story arcs "Sin Eater," "King of the Cats," and fan favorite "Talisman."

ISBN 978-1-59582-652-7
$24.99

To find a comics shop in your area, call **1-888-266-4226**
For more information or to order direct: On the web:
DarkHorse.com
E-mail: mailorder@darkhorse.com
Phone: 1-800-862-0052
Mon–Fri 9 AM to 5 PM Pacific Time